SOCIAL POLICY REVIEW 25

Analysis and debate in social policy, 2013

Edited by Gaby Ramia, Kevin Farnsworth and Zoë Irving

First published in Great Britain in 2013 by

Policy Press
University of Bristol
6th Floor, Howard House
Queen's Avenue
Clifton
Bristol BS8 1SD, UK
t: +44 (0)117 331 4054
f: +44 (0)117 331 4093
tpp-info@bristol.ac.uk
www.policypress.co.uk

North America office:
Policy Press
c/o The University of Chicago Press
1427 East 60th Street
Chicago, IL 60637, USA
t: +1 773 702 7700
f: +1 773-702-9756
sales@press.uchicago.edu
www.press.uchicago.edu

© Policy Press/Social Policy Association 2013

British Library Cataloguing in Publication Data
A catalogue record for this book is available from the British Library.

Library of Congress Cataloging-in-Publication Data
A catalog record for this book has been requested.

ISBN 978 1 44731 274 1 hardback
ISBN 978 1 44731 286 4 paperback SPA members' edition (not on general release)

Cover design by Policy Press
Front cover: photograph kindly supplied by www.alamy.com
Printed and bound in Great Britain by TJ International, Padstow.
Policy Press uses environmentally responsible print partners.

MIX
Paper from
responsible sources
FSC® C013056

Contents

Notes on contributors

Sigrid Betzelt is professor of sociology of work and organisations at the Berlin School of Economics and Law (University of Applied Science), Germany. Her research focuses on labour market and social policy reforms at the national level and from a comparative European perspective, especially with regard to their effects on social rights, gender and inequality. She has published on changes of work and employment structures from national and comparative perspectives.

Silke Bothfeld is professor of political science at the University for Applied Science Bremen, Germany, for comparative social policy and industrial relations. Her research interests include normative aspects of social policy, the work–welfare nexus, gender issues and theories of public policy. She has carried out research projects on activation policies, labour market policy, family and equal opportunity policies from a national and comparative perspective.

Sabrina (Hongxia) Chai is teaching fellow in the Department of Social Policy and Social Work, University of York, UK. She specialises in public policy, comparative social policy, governance and Chinese politics. She recently completed a book titled *Local governments in China* (with others, Edward Elgar Publishing, 2013).

Gary Craig is professor of community development and social justice at Durham University, UK. He is also emeritus professor of social justice and associate fellow of the Wilberforce Institute for the Study of Slavery and Emancipation at the University of Hull, UK, where he has led the team researching modern slavery. He has recently published *Social justice and public policy* (edited with others, Policy Press, 2008), *Community capacity building* (with others, OECD, 2010), has collated a reader, *Child slavery now* (Policy Press, 2010), and co-edited the book *Understanding 'race' and ethnicity* (Policy Press, 2012).

Kevin Farnsworth is senior lecturer in social policy at the University of Sheffield, UK. His research centres on political economy and welfare systems. His recent publications include *Social policy in challenging times*, edited with Zoë Irving (Policy Press, 2011) and *Social versus corporate welfare* (Palgrave, 2012).

Anders Freundt is a graduate student of political science at the University of Copenhagen, Denmark. He works as a research assistant at the Centre for Welfare State research, University of Southern Denmark where he is co-author of several working papers in comparative politics. Freundt has also been the translator of three papers (by Anne Skevik Grødem, Joakim Palme and Jon Erik Dølvik) for the Danish journal *Politik og Økonomi* (no 4, December, 2012).

Susan Harkness is reader in social policy at the University of Bath, UK. Her research focuses on women and the labour market with a particular interest in lone parents and low-income mothers, and the impact that welfare policy has on them. She has previously worked in the Department of Economics at the Universities of Bristol and Sussex, and at the Centre for Economic Performance, London School of Economics and Political Science.

Ben Hawkins is a research fellow teaching global health policy at the London School of Hygiene and Tropical Medicine. His current research focuses on the role of corporate actors and the use of scientific evidence in health policy making at the national and international level. His recent publications focus on the role of the alcohol industry in policy debates surrounding minimum-unit pricing of alcohol in the UK.

Elke Heins is lecturer in social policy at the University of Edinburgh, UK. Her research focuses on welfare reform from a comparative perspective, with a particular interest in labour market and employment policy as well as health policy. She has published on the concept of flexicurity, the Ghent system of unemployment insurance, and the reform of the UK primary care contract.

Dan Horsfall is lecturer in comparative social policy at the University of York, UK, where he has worked since 2010. Daniel currently holds a postdoctoral fellowship with the British Academy, investigating the impact of the financial crisis on how advanced welfare states should be classified. He has recently published on the theme of welfare state change (in *Policy Studies*).

Zoë Irving is senior lecturer in comparative social policy at the University of Sheffield, UK. Her current research interests are in the social policy of small island states and comparative analysis of social policy responses to economic crisis. She has previously published in the area of gender, work and employment and is co-editor with Kevin Farnsworth of *Social policy in challenging times* (Policy Press, 2011), and co-author with Michael Hill of the eighth edition of *Understanding social policy* (Blackwell Wiley, 2009).

Phyllis Jeroslow is a doctoral candidate in the School of Social Welfare at the University of California, Berkeley, where she researches comparative welfare state policies and child well-being. She currently teaches units relating to children and public policy in the Department of Child and Adolescent Development at San Francisco State University, USA, and is a training and curriculum specialist at the California Social Work Education Center, University of California, Berkeley.

Nam K. Jo is teaching fellow in the Department of Social Welfare in the SungKongHoe University, South Korea. He has been investigating the relation between culture and welfare and recently published his work in the *Journal of European Social Policy*.

Jon Kvist is professor in comparative social policy at the Centre for Welfare State Research, University of Denmark. He has 20 years' experience in undertaking European social policy analysis and in managing large research projects and networks at a Nordic and European level. He has published on comparative welfare state studies, comparative methodology and on international challenges, especially the relationship between the European Union and national policies.

Lynne Livsey is a social gerontologist and independent early career researcher specialising in social policy and ageing, with particular interest in social care and housing. She gained her MSc and PhD at the Institute of Gerontology, King's College London, and worked as a research assistant on the ESRC-funded project, 'Behind Closed Doors: Older Couples and the Management of Household Money' with Debora Price. She is currently researching housing solutions for older people in rural areas, and critical gerontological work on the financing of later life.

Julia S. O'Connor is professor of social policy and a member of the Institute for Research in Social Sciences at the University of Ulster, Northern Ireland. Her main area of research is welfare states in comparative perspective, focusing on countries belonging to the

Organisation for Economic Co-operation and Development and the European Union.

Maggie O'Neill is professor of criminology and principal of Ustinov College at Durham University. She is chair of the European Sociological Association's research network on Biographical Perspectives on European Societies and board member of the Human Dignity and Humiliation Studies Global Network. *Asylum, migration and community* was published by Policy Press in 2010 and *Transgressive imaginations: crime, deviance* and culture, co authored with Lizzie Seal, was published by Palgrave in 2012.

Debora Price Formerly a barrister, Debora is a senior lecturer in social policy at the Institute of Gerontology, King's College London, UK. Debora's research interests centre on pensions and pension systems, the sociology of money, social policy relating to finance over the lifecourse, financial services for an ageing population and the financial consequences of family formation and dissolution. Her research has generally focused on inequality, poverty and social exclusion, with particular regard to age, generation, gender and family structures.

Gaby Ramia is associate professor in the Graduate School of Government at The University of Sydney, Australia. His research interests include the relationship between industrial relations, social policy and social protection; contractualism, public administration and employment services; and cross-border education and international student welfare.

Anne Roemer-Mahler is a research fellow at the Centre for Global Health Policy at the University of Sussex, UK. She has published on the role of the pharmaceutical industry in the global politics of access to medicines and is currently researching collaborations between governments and pharmaceutical companies to strengthen health security.

Ilana Shpaizman is a PhD candidate in the Federmann School of Public Policy and Government at the Hebrew University in Jerusalem, Israel. Her research interests are in immigrant integration policy making, privatisation, gradual institutional changes and the ideational approach, with a special focus on the Israeli immigration and integration policy.

Adrian Sinfield is professor emeritus of social policy at the University of Edinburgh, UK, and has worked on social security, poverty, unemployment and the social division of welfare. He has been both chair and president of the Social Policy Association and received its first lifetime achievement award. Co-founder of the Unemployment Unit and chair for its first 10 years, he was vice-chair of the Child Poverty Action Group for eight years.

Carolyn Snell is lecturer in social policy at the University of York, UK, specialising in the links between social policy and the environment. Her current research focus is the relationship between fuel poverty and climate change policy. Before moving to York social policy, Carolyn was a researcher at the Stockholm Environment Institute.

Paul Spicker holds the Grampian Chair of Public Policy at the Robert Gordon University, Aberdeen, UK. His research includes studies of poverty, need, disadvantage and service delivery; he has worked as a consultant for a range of agencies in social welfare provision. In 2007 he was a special adviser to the House of Commons Work and Pensions Committee for their report on benefits simplification. His published work on social security includes *Poverty and social security* (Routledge, 1993) and *How social* security works (Policy Press, 2011).

Simon Grundt Straubinger is a graduate student of political science at the University of Southern Denmark. He continues to work there as a research assistant in the Centre of Welfare State Research where he has published, with colleagues, several working papers on microsimulation of public benefits in European countries. In addition, he has published in the Danish journal *Tidsskriftet Politik* about the reporting of public opinion polls.

Harriet Thomson is researcher and PhD candidate in the Department of Social Policy and Social Work at the University of York, UK. Her research explores fuel poverty across the European Union, with a particular focus on measurement and policy responses. She is founder of the EU Fuel Poverty Network (www.fuelpoverty.eu).

Introduction

Gaby Ramia

Social Policy Review is an annual publication of the Social Policy Association (SPA), a long-standing and respected British learned society. The SPA has continued to thrive in the last 12 months. One excellent indicator of its continued health and growth is an internationalisation agenda. In her welcome to delegates of the SPA Conference at the University of York in July 2012, the Head of the York Department of Social Policy and Social Work acknowledged the historical significance of the meeting. It was the first time that the SPA Conference was to be held jointly with the East Asian Social Policy Research Network (EASP), 'an organization of doctoral students and academics interested or involved in the analysis of East Asian social policies' (EASP, 2013). The conference was widely hailed among delegates from both associations as a major success. The EASP has been working more closely with British scholars in recent years, in particular, with members of the conference host department at York, and international and comparative social policy issues have featured increasingly in research. They are also conspicuous in this volume of *Social Policy Review*.

Another marker of the geographical expansion of the SPA is seen in the editorial team of the *Review*. For the first time, the lead editor is Australian, based at the University of Sydney. Also, the 'shadow editor', the unnamed fourth member of the editorial team who becomes an editor in the following volume, is a Dutch scholar based at the Erasmus University of Rotterdam.

Of course, internationalisation does not infer any lack of action on the UK home front. Indeed, as even a casual observer of UK social policy could attest, the opposite is the case. The scope and significance of policy activity within and by the current Coalition government is well worthy of scholarly attention, which it is given especially in Part One. Authors there deal exclusively with important contemporary UK social policy developments and debates. As is customary, Part Two of the volume contains chapters that originated as papers presented at the SPA Conference, in this case, the 2012 meeting. Consistent with the shared conference, these chapters combine East Asian and British perspectives and analyses. Finally, Part Three is a collection of works based around a particular contemporary social policy theme, again with both British and overseas contributors.

Part One

Contemporary debates and developments in the UK

Gaby Ramia

Part One deals with a wide span of welfare issues in the UK, with a focus on current and ongoing policy developments. These include: universal credit; fuel poverty; climate change policy; health policy, in particular, developments in relation to the National Health Service (NHS); the financing of later life and especially pensions; adult social care; housing equity; and 'the politics of old age'.

These issues are covered in four chapters. The authors explore policy interconnections and the politics behind policymaking as the British government responds in its own ways to widespread need, growing inequality and other social problems in the context of a financial crisis. Naturally, the effectiveness of the responses is placed under the microscope, for the most part, with major questions regarding the Conservative ideology that underpins the Cameron government's policy agenda.

In Chapter One, author Paul Spicker interrogates the government's introduction of Universal Credit, a controversial scheme designed to unify various means-tested benefits for people of working age. The scheme brings together six existing benefits: income-related Jobseeker's Allowance and Employment and Support Allowance, Working Tax Credit and Child Tax Credit, Housing Benefit, and Income Support. Spicker argues that analysts of Universal Credit must drill down to the detail of the scheme and the benefits that it covers. He sees defects in 'the concept and design' of the Universal Credit agenda, as there were in previous grand schemes in social policy history. He also sees potential for the benefit system to break down if it cannot prove to be practically viable. Governments, Spicker contends, cannot easily meet the multiple objectives that must typically be met in 'simple' and 'unified' benefit programmes.

Carolyn Snell and Harriet Thomson, authors of Chapter Two, discuss the Coalition government's attempt to reconcile two key dimensions of its energy policy: climate change and fuel poverty. Climate change relates to the '*use* of non-renewable forms of energy', and fuel poverty is 'often associated with the *underuse* or excessive cost of household energy' (p 23). As part of their analysis, Snell and Thomson discuss the Energy Act 2011 and its flagship policy, 'The Green Deal'. For reasons that are explained in the chapter, the authors argue that attempts to deal with climate change can have the undesirable effect of increasing fuel poverty. In their words, 'one policy outcome may damage the progress of the other' (p 41).

In Chapter Three, Elke Heins examines NHS reforms in relation to primary care and commissioning, principally through the government's Health and Social Care Act 2012. Taking effect in April 2013, the Act reorganises the way that NHS services are commissioned. At a time when marketised 'new public management' experiments are being questioned by many governments around the developed world, the UK government is establishing a regulated market in which 'any qualified provider' from either the public or private sectors can compete for the right to be an NHS provider. Heins argues that this development needs to be understood in its historical context, with past marketisation measures having achieved at best 'ambivalent' outcomes. In the case of the 2012 Act, given growing budgetary pressures, doctors are likely to outsource their new-found 'decision-making powers', given to them in the market context, to private providers where possible.

Finally, in Chapter Four, Debora Price and Lynne Livsey examine 'the politics of old age' in the contemporary UK setting. In particular, they analyse recent developments in the financing of later life, principally through changes in pensions and long-term care. Along the way, they also deal with associated challenges for older citizens, including the management of income, assets and savings in the context of competitive or quasi-competitive service regimes. These programmes, Price and Livsey argue, require older people to have made what can be conceived as the 'right' financial decisions 'for the whole of their adult lives'(p 67). In this way, individuals are constructed by government as 'malleable subjects' who can be 'nudged' into 'becom[ing] financially capable, fiscally competent, actuarially aware subjects' (p 67). The authors contend that new social inequalities can emerge through amended risk and reward mechanisms.

Reference
EASP (2013) East Asian Social Policy, www.welfareasia.org/about

ONE

Introducing Universal Credit

Paul Spicker

Introduction

Universal Credit is an ambitious reform intended to unify means-tested benefits for people of working age. The idea of simplifying and unifying benefits attracted strong support at the outset, but growing doubts about the practical viability and the detailed operation of the scheme have raised questions about what its impact will be. There is a risk in the short term that the system will crash, but in the longer term, defects in concept and design may prove just as important.

There are times when social policy analysts have little choice but to get down to the detail, and the discussion of social security needs that rather more than some other parts of the field. Broad-brush categories like 'dependency' or 'inequality' rapidly disintegrate when the circumstances that are being described run to millions of people in hugely varied circumstances. Fashionable categorisations like 'social risk management' (World Bank, 2001, 2012) or Esping-Andersen's (1990) 'worlds of welfare capitalism' do not help very much when they are exposed to an incoherent and inconsistent reality (see Mabbett and Bolderson, 1999; Castles, 2009). In the same way, and for the same reasons, policy initiatives that begin with a grand, overarching vision tend not to sit well with the complex circumstances that benefits have to deal with. Over the years, many writers have advocated broad-brush, universal schemes – among them, negative income tax (Friedman, 1962), schemes that combine tax and benefits (Dilnot et al, 1984), and basic income (Van Parijs, 1992). These schemes have important limitations. The first is that any benefit intended to make provision at similar costs to existing schemes can only make some people in need better off by making some other people in need worse off. The Conservative Tax Credit Scheme of the 1970s (Cmnd 5116, 1972) foundered because it did not protect the position of women; proposals for a unified disability benefit in Ireland

(Government of Ireland, 1996) failed to attract support because of lack of agreement between different constituencies; recent proposals for a Citizens Pension have hit the rock of reduced entitlements for higher earners (Reade, 2012).

The second is that benefits are complicated for good reasons. They are trying to meet multiple objectives, and to respond to a wide range of needs and commitments. The situations they are dealing with are complicated. Simplification is only possible if some objectives, some needs and some existing commitments are set aside – or if benefits are increased by so much that it does not matter. When governments promise schemes that will be simple, unified, coherent and able to deal with all our social ills, it is often a warning that we need to stand by with the fire wagons.

The Beveridge scheme (Cmnd 604, 1942) was supposed to be universal, unified and adequate. The first major challenges to the scheme came in the 1950s, as it became clear that a system of flat-rate contributions and benefits could not match the continental systems for adequacy (Labour Party, 1959). It also became clear that insurance left important gaps, and much of the attention in the 1960s focused on the development of National Assistance, the means-tested safety net, to become Supplementary Benefit (see Kincaid, 1973). In the 1970s, there were further developments: the establishment of several non-means-tested benefits for people with disabilities, and the creation of new means-tested benefits that supplemented the income of people in work. Since the 1980s, the emphasis on insurance-based benefits, apart from pensions, has been reducing. The complexity of the current system reflects, then, years of incremental development, the accretion of new roles and functions and the sheer range and diversity of the circumstances that the benefits system has to respond to.

Major reforms of the benefit system have been trumpeted on several previous occasions. The reform of pensions in the 1970s was 'the result of the biggest rethink of the welfare state since Beveridge' (*The Guardian*, 1985). The Fowler reviews in the 1980s were to be 'the most comprehensive review of the social security system since Beveridge' (Dean, 1984). Labour's welfare reform programme was to be 'the biggest welfare shake-up since Beveridge' (Heffer, 1998). And the current Secretary of State for Work and Pensions, Iain Duncan Smith, has of course presented his scheme for Universal Credit as 'the biggest change since Beveridge introduced the welfare system' (Porter and Riddell, 2010). In retrospect, however, many of the most important changes in the benefits system have taken place incrementally at other times –

among them, the development of benefits tested by need rather than means, Family Income Supplement, Child Benefit, the end of Sickness Benefit and the move to long-term incapacity benefits, the Housing Benefit system, the effective collapse of the National Insurance system for unemployment in the 1990s, and the introduction of Tax Credits.

The current programme of reform has three elements. One is an attempt to reduce costs: the measures undertaken to do that have included reducing protection against inflation, raising the pension age, reassessing capacity to work and introducing other restrictions on entitlement. Two thirds of the budget goes on people of pensionable age (DWP Statistics, 2012a); there is no way of reducing benefits by the levels the government has been talking about without hitting pensioners. Most of the measures are ephemeral, which means that discussing them in detail is not particularly appropriate for this volume. They fall short of the levels of economy that the government has been talking about, and that probably means that the Treasury will be back for more (Spicker, 2010).

The second element is conditionality. The government has ratcheted up sanctions against those who fail to work. At the time of writing, the government is proposing to increase the requirements for work search, to cut off benefits for unemployed people who fall ill and to impose sanctions for up to three years. Conditionality has been a recurring theme in benefits since at least the 16th century. The Welfare Reform Act 2012 retains the Tudor principle of progressively increasing the sanctions for persistent idlers, but by comparison with the Act of 1572, when the penalties for the idle poor included whipping, branding and effective enslavement, the threat of years of penury and debt recovery in 2012 seems almost modest.

The third element of the reforms, and the subject of this chapter, is the attempt to redesign benefits for people of working age. The centrepiece of the reforms is the proposal for Universal Credit, which aims to bring together six other benefits: income-related Jobseeker's Allowance and Employment and Support Allowance (ESA), Working Tax Credit and Child Tax Credit, Housing Benefit, and Income Support. Because many claimants receive some of these benefits simultaneously, the numbers claiming cannot simply be added together, but there are more than five million claims made for people out of work and four million claims for Tax Credits for people in work. The Department for Work and Pensions (DWP) estimates that there should be 8.3 million claims (DWP, 2012c).

Universal Credit

The aims of the Universal Credit system have been outlined in a series of documents. It begins with a report prepared by the Centre for Social Justice (CSJ, 2009), a think tank founded by Iain Duncan Smith, a former leader of the Conservative Party who has become the Secretary of State for Work and Pensions. In the period between losing the leadership and becoming a cabinet minister, Duncan Smith devoted attention to 'broken Britain' and the growth of an underclass, doomed to dependency in generation after generation. His preface to the CSJ report begins:

> As leader of the Conservative Party I frequently encountered significant social breakdown and dysfunctionality across the country. I met people trapped by dependency and left behind by society. This emerging underclass lives in communities consistently defined by five characteristics, which become the pathways to poverty: family breakdown; educational failure; drug and alcohol addiction; severe personal indebtedness; and economic dependency – caused by intergenerational worklessness. (CSJ, 2009, p 6)

Duncan Smith explains that he has three criticisms of the present system:

1. It creates a series of disincentives to work;
2. It imposes penalties on constructive behaviour apart from work (such as marriage and cohabitation, saving, and home ownership);
3. It is very complex – making it costly to administer and reinforcing dependency. (CSJ, 2009, p 6)

The Green Paper *21st century welfare* emphasises: affordability; rewarding work and personal responsibility; reduced worklessness; a simpler system; and reduced scope for error and fraud (Cm 7913, 2010). The White Paper explained that the objectives were to emphasise incentives, reduce complexity and limit welfare dependency (Cm 7957, 2010). The purpose of the Universal Credit scheme is, then: to discourage dependency, either by removing disincentives to work or by replacing them with positive incentives; to reward desired social behaviour; and to simplify the benefits system.

Dependency

The current debate on social security is driven by three key beliefs, that:

- the critical problems in benefit relate to 'out of work' benefits (Cabinet Office, 2010) (this is a relatively new category, which did not feature in the statistics before the present government took office; it pulls together a range of groups, including unemployed people, people who are sick and unable to work, carers, and lone parents);
- expenditure on welfare is growing because of increasing demands from people of working age (Cabinet Office, 2010); and
- the nature of provision leads to long-term dependency, generation after generation (CSJ, 2009).

The figures show a different story. Most of the money, by far, goes to people over working age. There has been some growth in expenditure, but it is mainly attributable to older people and the extension of tax credits to people in work, not to the growth of 'out of work' benefits (see DWP Statistics, 2012a). This remains true despite increasing unemployment because unemployment itself accounts directly for a very limited part of expenditure on benefits; if Jobseeker's Allowance accounts for only 3% of the DWP budget, then unemployment could go up by a million while altering the balance of expenditure only by a small fraction.

Long-term dependency is dominated by pensioners and people who are not expected to work. The DWP Longitudinal Survey shows that very few 'job-seekers' on income-related benefits have been in receipt of benefit for more than five years. The figure is 4,720 out of 1,328,910 – about one person in 280. Fully 1,050 have been on benefit for 10 years; that is less than one person in 1250. By contrast, people on incapacity benefits are relatively likely to remain on benefits long-term: 1.48 million, or 57%, have been on benefits for more than five years, 922,000 or 36% for more than 10 (DWP Statistics, 2011). (That includes about a quarter of a million people formerly in receipt of Severe Disablement Allowance, who are now bundled in with the Incapacity Benefit [IB] figures.) So, the impression of long-term dependency among people of working age is overwhelmingly attributable to people who it is not reasonable to expect to work. (That is not a subjective test: it is the basic criterion for entitlement to incapacity benefits contained in the Welfare Reform Act 2007.)

Most of the reforms that have taken place around ESA were set in motion before the Coalition government came to power, and separately from the introduction of Universal Credit. The key elements were as follows:

- The replacement of the insurance-based IB with the largely means-tested ESA. This has been done through a time limit on contributory entitlement – a principle already established for Jobseeker's Allowance;
- The process of reassessment, leading to the rejection of many claims on the basis that people were fit for work. To date, a large number of claims have been excluded because the claimant failed to repeat the process, and many who have gone through the process have been found fit for work. There have been many criticisms of the process itself, and the agency (Atos Healthcare) employed to conduct it; the Harrington Review describes the process as impersonal and mechanistic (Harrington, 2010). More than 80% appealed that process, but after that, the story is hazy: there has been a moderately high success rate of appeals heard, but many more appeals have not been not considered at all, seeming to disappear in the process.
- The introduction of work-oriented measures to prepare people to move into the labour market. Following the Gregg report, ESA claimants are divided into a support group, a minority who are not expecting to engage in work-related activity, and a return-to-work group, who are so expected (Gregg, 2008). Only a small proportion have been admitted to the 'support group', people who were recognised as not appropriately required to be prepared to work (DWP Statistics, 2012b).

In relation to job-seekers, the principal change directed at dependency has not been Universal Credit, but the introduction of the Work Programme, aimed at 'long-term' claimants. If long term means 'on benefit for several years', there are very few long-term unemployed people in Britain. The Freud Review, prepared for the Labour government, had suggested that all unemployed people should go through a programme of intensive support (Freud, 2007) – a fairly ill-thought-out proposal, when Freud himself acknowledged that the Jobcentre Plus regime saw nine out of ten unemployed people return to work in a year. The Review made little or no reference to existing knowledge about labour market policy, and showed no awareness of the possibility of 'deadweight' – paying for intervention for people whose situation will be resolved regardless

– or 'spillovers' – continuing to intervene after problems are resolved. David Freud was ennobled and became a minister in the Coalition government. Early returns on the outcomes of the Work Programme suggest that the intervention may lead to slower rates of engagement in the labour market than if the government did nothing (DWP Statistics, 2012c; Ross, 2012).

Behaviour

The next part of the programme of reform has been a focus on behaviour, principally understood as engagement with the labour market. 'At the heart of these solutions', Iain Duncan Smith writes, 'is recognition that the nature of the life you lead and the choices you make have a significant bearing on whether you live in poverty' (CSJ, 2009). This might seem to imply some emphasis on the promotion of family life, whether that is done by supporting families or penalising people for irregular lifestyles. It is difficult, however, to see anything in the programme of reform that would support such a view. Universal Credit will have compulsory joint claims; all claims made that relate to a couple should be made by both members of a couple, and both will be asked for a statement of consent and 'claimant commitment'. 'Couples' include not only established couples, but also people living together as man and wife, and people in same-sex relationships who are not civil partners but who 'are to be treated as living together as if they were civil partners if, and only if, they would be treated as living together as husband and wife were they of opposite sexes' (Welfare Reform Act 2012, s 39). When civil partnership was established, parliament took great pains to emphasise that civil partnerships could and should not be considered as analogous to the situation of man and wife. It is not clear, then, what the clause means – which suggests that it is probably about sex, but the legislators are too coy to say so.

Making a joint commitment as claimants constitutes a public acknowledgement of a relationship. Some people will not sign, because they do not think they have such a relationship, they do not want to make such an acknowledgement or wish to repudiate or terminate the relationship. The new scheme does not specify the circumstances where either one of a presumed couple denies that there is a relationship, when a relationship should be considered to have terminated or when it has formed. There is one interesting further decision, however, which may have been made about cohabitation, or 'living together as man and wife'. Bereavement Allowances, the national insurance provision for parents whose partner has died, have always had a cohabitation rule – some of the earliest case law on cohabitation came from it; widows who remarried or cohabited with a new partner were struck off the benefit. In a consultation, the government proposes to get rid of the rule altogether (DWP, 2012a). That makes sense – people who are making provision for children after their death do not usually opt for something that is conditional on whether their partner remarries – but it runs in the opposite direction to much else that is happening in the benefits system.

Incentives to work

Incentives feature in the plans in two main ways. The first part is rooted in the belief that benefits should always pay less than work, a principle that has dominated policy in Britain since the Poor Law. 'Less eligibility' was based in Ricardo's 'iron law of wages', the belief that the only way to protect the position of people in work was to be sure that they were not undercut by people out of it (Poynter, 1969). This implies that benefits are kept generally low – if this was about incentives, they should only be lower than a person's prospective wage. That principle is seen as an issue of fairness; the introduction of 'benefit caps', to ensure that no one on benefits gets more than the average for people in work, is part of the same idea. There is precious little evidence to link 'better-off calculations' with the rate of return to work; people are as likely to be concerned with prospects, security of income and compatibility with their circumstances.

The second part is concerned with the 'poverty trap', also referred to as the Marginal Rate of Deduction. Part is the attempt to even out the rate at which benefits are withdrawn as someone starts to earn through work. This, like less eligibility, is really a question of perceived fairness, rather than economic behaviour; again, there is very little evidence to show that people's decisions about working hours are directly affected by hourly rates of pay or taxation.

The intention is to ensure that people whose earnings increase will not lose more than 65% of extra income through having benefits withdrawn. The CSJ documents were originally thinking of 55% (CSJ, 2009), but that would have meant that people kept their benefits for longer, and it would have been costly. Because the assessment is being made only after tax and national insurance contributions, that leads to an effective Marginal Rate of Deduction of 76%. That is disappointingly steep – more than 30% greater than the top rate of income tax. Beyond that, there will still be interactions with support from other sources, particularly Council Tax benefits. Furthermore, owner-occupiers who move into work will lose all housing support: the DWP has said that this

> recognises the different characteristics and work incentives facing owner occupiers compared to other out of work claimants. Owner occupiers who claim income-related benefits will previously have obtained and sustained mortgages and, usually, they have done this while they are in full-time work. (DWP, 2012b, para 82)

The level of conditionality that is being introduced depends heavily on sanctions – penalties for failing to comply with directions, for failing to take up opportunities and for refusing work. It has been suggested that this will apply to people who work part time when they could commit themselves to work for more hours. Sanctions can last for up to three years, will be imposed on couples and where hardship payments are made, they are recoverable, which means that after the three years are up, the claimant may face years more of repayment.

There is also a new expectation, which is to engage in work search for 35 hours a week:

> A claimant is to be treated as not having complied with a work search requirement to take all reasonable action for the purpose of obtaining paid work in any week unless … the claimant takes action for the purpose of obtaining paid work for the claimant's expected hours of work per week minus any relevant deductions. (Drafts of Universal Credit Regulations 2012, s 86; Jobseeker's Allowance Regulations 2012, s 12)

An explanatory memorandum clarifies that 'we propose that claimants are expected to have spent up to 35 hours a week (or their agreed number of hours, if less) looking or preparing for work' (DWP, 2012b, para 238). This bears no relationship to the process of looking for or preparing for work. The test used to be that claimants took at least three steps in a week; that will not do. A person might send a hundred letters of enquiry in a week and still not meet the test; a person who has learned how to use Internet sources and where to look may be able to complete in an hour what at first took 15. It might have been reasonable to say that claimants cannot refuse to spend less than 35 hours in a week when opportunities present themselves, for example, by spending a day travelling to an employment agency; but this is not what the regulation actually says. It is different to say that 35 hours is the expectation, when very few claimants will be able consistently to generate 35 hours of job-seeking activity. It is a recipe for inconsistent administration. It invites claimants to lie.

Simplification

Universal Credit is not a negative income tax scheme, or a basic income, but it is being represented as a major simplification. Within the new benefits, each of the component elements – conditions related to job-seeking, incapacity, housing, work and so forth – continues to have its distinct mode of operation. Although a unified benefit might seem to offer some prospect of easier transitions between states, there will still be complications when unemployed people fall, workers become unemployed or sick people move to part-time work. Universal Credit is better described, then, as a portmanteau benefit; it has a common title, and some common conditions, but it is really a group of benefits under a shared masthead.

Portmanteau benefits have some limited advantages over multiple benefits: they are able to rely on common rules and procedures (though the same is true currently of many benefits with different names) and a common point of entry, which should in principle make it less likely that people will fail to claim. However, they are also intrinsically complex, and it is not at all clear that much is gained by having one benefit with six compartments rather than six benefits with one. There have been many examples of portmanteau benefits – the industrial injuries regime and the State Pension all have distinct component elements. The most important comparators, however, are the large-scale means-tested benefits, intended like Universal Credit to deal with millions of people in disparate circumstances.

The prime example was Supplementary Benefit, a basic means-tested benefit that was provided for pensioners, unemployed people, people with incapacities, lone parents and others, which also included housing support and discretionary payments in emergencies. In 1978, the Labour government introduced a controversial review of the benefit, which, by that time, had come to have nearly five million claimants. The report, *Social assistance*, argued that it was not possible, with so many people, to maintain the pretence that the benefit was responding to each person individually or that it was feasible to adjust sensitively and responsively to the needs of each person. The scheme had to be adapted to its 'mass role' (DHSS, 1978). The reforms were introduced in 1980 by the incoming Conservative government. (Eight years later, the same government reformed Supplementary Benefit again, renaming it Income Support.) Universal Credit declares the intention of doing exactly what previous governments had come to believe was impossible – responding to fluctuating circumstances with individualised, personalised assessment.

Another key portmanteau benefit was the 'unified' Housing Benefit. Rate Rebate had been introduced in 1967, Rent Rebate and Rent Allowance in two stages in 1972–73. Housing Benefit was based on a combination of these benefits, along with the support for rents previously managed as part of Supplementary Benefit. The responsibility was transferred to local authorities. The result was described, in its day, as 'the greatest administrative fiasco in the history of the welfare state' (*The Times*, cited in Walker, 1986, p 39). The local authorities were not prepared for the complexity of the scheme, or the sheer numbers involved.

Both Supplementary Benefit and Housing Benefit were dogged by the problems of trying to respond sensitively and equitably to complex circumstances. Can Universal Credit avoid the same fate? When the scheme was proposed, the government seemed confident that it would be possible to process claims in 'real time', relying on the miracle of modern technology to give an instant, accurate response. The programmes and equipment to do this had not been developed; subsequently, they pulled back from the idea, though they will be relying on the new pay-as-you-earn system, designed for taxing employees, developed for Her Majesty's Revenue and Customs (HMRC). Doubts have been expressed about whether this can work; HMRC has opted for an 'Interim Solution', which will separate information from payments, a recipe for delaying instructions to alter payments (Black, 2012). However, even if real-time systems were in place, they could not function as intended; the 'technological fix' was always an illusion. Universal Credit is set to depend on information not only about income, but also on the employment, health status, rent and household circumstances of both members of a couple. Both members of a couple are being asked to sign a claimant commitment, and things that happen to one person, including sanctions and deductions, will affect the entitlements of the other. A computer system, however good it is, can only go as fast as the information that goes into it. So, the design of the new scheme now depends on a different principle: that it is the responsibility of claimants to report their own circumstances, and everything overpaid, for any reason, has to be repaid. This principle was introduced for Tax Credits, and it has been the source of major problems. The Ombudsman comments:

There are many for whom the experience has been, and indeed remains, highly distressing. Whilst they may be only a relatively small proportion of the overall numbers claiming tax credits, they are a significant number, and the impact on the customers concerned, typically those on the very lowest incomes who are amongst the most vulnerable in society, is huge. (Parliamentary and Health Service Ombudsman, 2007, p 43)

Some people who have previously claimed have been forced to repay thousands of pounds, and many of those people have said that they cannot afford to claim again (Gerrard, 2008; see also Parliamentary and Health Service Ombudsman, 2007, pp 3–4).

Additionally, there are new features in the benefit. Probably the most important are the shift to online application, the end of girocheque payment and the move to monthly benefits. At the time of writing, the effects are difficult to predict. The current plan is that the benefit will be piloted in the six months from April 2013, and it will open to new claims from October – there has already been some slippage in the timetable, and there may yet be more. The plans for the pilot are limited: there will be about 1,500 cases per month for six months, based in one area of the country, making 9,000 in total, benefit calculations will not be done with the new computer system, and the government has also announced that local authorities will be invited to add their own pilots for advice work. If this was a structured sample indicating patterns in the population, 9,000 may seem adequate; however, when taking all comers in one location, in preparation for a scheme that is expected to deal with nearly 10 million claims, it is not very many. The pilot can be expected to pick up a reasonable range of the main circumstances, but it is not necessarily good enough for practical administration. The central problem is diversity. Previous attempts to identify segments of the 'customer market' in social security have failed, because there are simply too many variations (Bryson and Kasparova, 2003). The experience of Supplementary Benefit over the years was that rules had to be developed to deal with aberrant cases, and, over the years, that led to the progressive growth of increasingly detailed rules. Equally, the experience of previous partial implementation – for example, in Housing Benefit, Tax Credits or the implementation of the Community Charge – does not suggest that any problems identified will lead to revision of the timetable or the principles. If there are problems, the rules have been put in place to ensure that the responsibility falls on claimants rather than the administrators.

Aims and methods

The most basic test of any policy is how it relates to its aims. The aims reviewed at the outset of this chapter are fairly general, and some are hard to pin down. At a subordinate level, however, the DWP has identified some operational aims, which are easier to verify. Universal Credit is intended to:

- *Simplify the system.* The arcane rules governing worklessness, incapacity and housing liabilities all remain; there will be new complexities relating to new tests for availability for work.
- *Improve work incentives.* There will be some smoothing of Marginal Rates of Deduction, and an assertion of the value of benefits in work, but that is probably all that is intended under this heading. On the whole, it is striking how little has been done to integrate benefit systems with the realities of a casualised and precarious labour market.
- *Smooth transitions in and out of work.* Linking rules have generally meant that people should not have suffered, but there have been problems in the past; for example, although Housing Benefit is supposed to be maintained regardless of work status, some local authorities have continued, despite several legal cases to the contrary, to suspend Housing Benefit and insist on a new application on a change of employment status. In more general terms, complexities arise because of the growing importance of marginal labour and sub-employment, including zero-hour contracts (where people have to hold themselves available to be called on) and pseudo-'self-employment', where employers use nominal self-employed status to avoid the inconvenience of administration, tax and national insurance. Without a minimal degree of regulation, the complexities will remain.
- *Reduce in-work poverty.* The effect of increasing tapers has been to reduce the amount of benefit people get while in work.
- *Cut back on fraud and error.* Error appears from the figures to be a much larger source of problems than fraud. Three factors – earnings and employment, income from occupational and personal pensions, and living together – make up 44% of all the losses through fraud and error; others include rules about capital, household composition, housing costs and so on (DWP Statistics, 2012e, Table 6.1). All of these factors will continue to apply in the new system. The main method that has been taken to deal with this is to make claimants

personally responsible for repaying benefit – which does not reduce error, only the financial consequences to the Treasury of such error.

Probably the most evident concern, however, is about the immediate implementation of the scheme. Much of the process has been secretive, which makes it difficult to say with confidence how smoothly it is proceeding, but a trickle of reports suggest that it is in trouble. *Computer Weekly*, which has led the field with its incisive reporting, received a leaked Major Projects Authority report to the effect that 'Tight deadlines left the Department for Work and Pensions with little choice but to use "unproven" agile methods'; HMRC had also been told that it could not deliver its real-time information system by April 2013 (Ballard, 2011). There are 'too many moving parts in too many places' (Hall, 2012). Treasury officials and HMRC have warned the Chancellor that the system is liable to fail through overambitious targets, lack of preparation and unreasonable deadlines; the *Daily Telegraph* reported: 'Flagship reforms of the welfare system are in serious danger of arriving late and billions of pounds over budget, or even failing altogether' (Kirkup, 2011). The government has been pushed to deny that the scheme is a 'car crash in the making' (Hardman, 2012). A crash is avoidable; but it will need time, resources and a readiness to adapt to the mass role of the benefits. None of this has been forthcoming to date.

The means test

The central problem with Universal Credit is a failure of concept rather than administration. Universal Credit has been designed as a complex, multifaceted means-tested benefit intended to cover the circumstances of millions of people. Means tests have a dreadful reputation (see, eg, Van Oorschot, 1995), which is only partly deserved. The principal accusations made against means-testing are that it is complex, that people do not understand how the system works and that people fail to claim. Those are all true, but they are also true of benefits that are not means-tested, such as benefits for disability. However, there are issues that are distinctive to means-tested benefits. They include problems of equity, including:

- identifying the thresholds at which people will become entitled;
- how to treat different forms of capital, such as owner occupation, inheritance and possession of goods; and

- how to ensure equity of treatment between households with different compositions (the problems of equivalence and cohabitation).

They also include complicating elements that are part of the process of assessing means, for example:

- the treatment of unearned income, such as occupational pensions or regular income from families;
- managing the relationship to other benefits (which are, of course, a form of income);
- the treatment of non-dependants in the household;
- assessing the position of small businesses and self-employed people; and
- dealing with fluctuations in income (see Spicker, 2011).

The last two points are particularly important. Small businesses and independent workers – their numbers have grown because of unemployment and casualised labour markets – will have to make returns monthly instead of annually, generally within seven days of the end of each month. They will be assumed to earn at least the minimum wage. Even with that assumption, the general problem of dealing with fluctuations in income means that benefits may vary widely from month to month. The incomes of people in the lower reaches of the income distribution are often radically unstable – research for HMRC suggests that about a third have incomes that are 'erratic' or 'very erratic', potentially halving or doubling in the course of three months (Hills et al, 2006). Tax Credits depend critically on assessments around this unstable income. The Ombudsman has been particularly critical, questioning 'whether a financial support system which included a degree of inbuilt financial insecurity could properly meet the needs of very low income families and earners' (Parliamentary and Health Service Ombudsman, 2007, p 5). The central case of Universal Credit is that it is intended to yield a stable final income package, by varying the level of benefit exactly in line with fluctuating income – but it is relying on perfect information to do it.

The basic problems of means-testing necessarily apply to the proposals for Universal Credit. Beyond that, however, Universal Credit falls into a further class of means-tested benefits, intended not just to provide a basic income, but to supplement income and earnings – the model of Tax Credits and Housing Benefits. The principle works by setting an assessment level and then gradually reducing benefit entitlement as income increases – the 'taper'. This leads immediately to two problems. The first is that it is difficult to work out what people are entitled to and, no less important, what the level of income is at which they are no longer entitled. The second is the 'poverty trap', which the government has taken to calling the Marginal Rate of Deduction: the combined effect of taxation and the withdrawal of benefits. The principle of the taper is well-established in the UK benefits system; it has been in operation, in one form or another, since 1967, when it was first used for Rate Rebate (the equivalent of Council Tax Benefit). Then there was Family Income Supplement in 1971, the forerunner of Family Credit, and then Rent Rebate and Allowance, introduced in 1972 and 1973, respectively. These benefits were eventually translated into Housing Benefit (1982–83) and Tax Credits (after 1999).

Housing Benefit has never worked well, but it is maintained by governments because it is difficult to see how to get out of it. The benefit is complex: take-up for those in work and private rented housing is poor, and the design of the benefit means that people on higher incomes, with higher rents, may get more in benefit than people on lower incomes with lower rents. It is difficult to work out who is entitled, what they are entitled to and when they cease to be entitled. There have been huge administrative problems; some local authorities have developed and continued in practices that are contrary to law (such as the suspension of benefit for people who start work), and the regulations change with frightening rapidity. And yet, Housing Benefit effectively became the model for Tax Credits – with the same model of assessment minus taper, coupled with the removal of the operation from benefit authorities who might have known what they were doing. Tax Credits were predictably blighted with administrative problems, as people found that benefits had been wrongly calculated, phone lines were blocked and they were expected to repay miscalculated benefits. Despite the problems, HMRC estimates the figures for Child Tax Credit to be 81–85% by caseload and 91–94% by expenditure, and Working Tax Credit to be 62–66% by caseload and 82–86% by expenditure (HMRC, 2012). That compares to figures for income-based Jobseeker's Allowance that put take-up at 60–67% by caseload and 61–70% by expenditure (DWP Statistics, 2012d). The difference is, frankly, hard to believe. HMRC has acknowledged that there have been serious problems in the design and administration of the benefits. If take-up is affected by ignorance, complexity, bad experiences, stigma or barriers to access, the take-up of Tax Credits should be markedly lower.

Means-tested benefits are not, of course, the only benefits that are subject to problems. There are other aspects of the benefits system that are cumbersome, badly designed and problematic for claimants and administrators alike. They include, for example:

- benefits that people cannot work out that they are entitled to;
- the problem of repaying money that people did not know they should not receive;
- rules that tell people they must work at the same time as recognising that it is not reasonable to work (the current position for ESA);
- the medical reassessment of claimants;
- benefits that penalise claimants for circumstances outside their control;
- the cohabitation rule; and
- complex assessments that require people to report changes across multiple dimensions.

Universal Credit has the lot. It is as if someone has started with a list of everything in the benefits system that causes problems and designed the new benefit around it.

We have enough experience of badly designed benefits to have some idea of what is likely to happen in the long term. They cannot just be snuffed out, because too many people would be affected. The benefits have to adapt to the conditions where they are being applied, so they become complex. Where rules have not been thought through, old rules have to be recycled or carried forward to do the job – that is why there are still elements of the Unemployment Assistance Act 1934 in the present-day system. If they are too cumbersome to be administered, their constituent parts have to be managed separately, and they are ultimately likely to be broken away – this is what happened to Supplementary Benefit. Even if Universal Credit fails spectacularly, it will lumber on; but it may not look much like the initial vision.

References

Ballard, M. (2011) 'Universal Credit deadline forced DWP to use "unproven" agile development', *Computer Weekly*, 4 October.

Black, J. (2012) 'Written evidence to the House of Commons Work and Pensions Committee, HC 576 Progress towards the implementation of Universal Credit', www.publications.parliament.uk/pa/cm201213/cmselect/cmworpen/writev/576/m71.htm

Bryson, A. and Kasparova, D. (2003) 'Profiling benefit claimants in Britain: a feasibility study', Department for Work and Pensions Research Report 196.

Cabinet Office (2010) 'The state of the nation report: poverty, worklessness and welfare dependency in the UK', http://socialwelfare.bl.uk/subject-areas/government-issues/welfare-state/cabinetoffice/135897web-poverty-report.pdf

Castles, F. (2009) 'What welfare states do', *Journal of Social Policy* vol 38, no 1, pp 45–62.

CSJ (Centre for Social Justice) (2009) *Dynamic benefits: towards welfare that works*, London: CSJ.

Cm 7913 (2010a) *21st century welfare*, London: Department for Work and Pensions.

Cm 7957 (2010b) *Universal Credit: welfare that works*, London: Department for Work and Pensions.

Cmd 6404 (1942) *Social insurance and allied services*, London: HMSO.

Cmnd 5116 (1972) *Proposals for a tax credit system*, London: HMSO.

Dean, M. (1984) 'The diagnosis nobody wants to hear', *The Guardian*, 10 October.

DHSS (Department of Health and Social Security) (1978) *Social assistance*, London: DHSS.

Dilnot, A., Kay, J. and Morris, C. (1984) *The reform of social security*, Oxford: Clarendon Press/IFS.

DWP (2012a) *Bereavement benefits for the 21st Century*, London: DWP.

DWP (2012b) 'Explanatory memorandum for the Social Security Advisory Committee: Universal Credit Regulations 2012, para 82'.

DWP (2012c) 'Universal Credit: impact assessment', www.dwp.gov.uk/docs/universal-credit-wr2011-ia.pdf

DWP Statistics (2011) 'Work and Pensions Longitudinal Study', http://statistics.dwp.gov.uk/asd/asd1/adhoc_analysis/2011/oow_ben_duration.xls

DWP Statistics (2012a) 'Benefit expenditure tables', http://research.dwp.gov.uk/asd/asd4/medium_term.asp

DWP Statistics (2012b) 'Employment and Support Allowance: Work Capability Assessment', http://research.dwp.gov.uk/asd/workingage/index.php?page=esa_wca

DWP Statistics (2012c) 'Work Programme: cumulative figures job outcomes', http://statistics.dwp.gov.uk/asd/asd1/work_programme/Job_outcome_gross%20table_final.xls

DWP Statistics (2012d) Income related benefits estimates of takeup in 2009–10', http://statistics.dwp.gov.uk/asd/income_analysis/feb2012/tkup_full_report_0910.pdf

DWP Statistics (2012e) Fraud and error in the benefit system: 2011/2012 estimates', http://statistics.dwp.gov.uk/asd/asd2/fem/fem_1112.pdf

Esping-Andersen, G. (1990) *The three worlds of welfare capitalism*, Brighton: Polity.

Freud, D. (2007) *Reducing dependency, increasing opportunity*, London: Department for Work and Pensions.

Friedman, M. (1962) *Capitalism and freedom*, Chicago, IL: University of Chicago Press.

Gerrard, P. (2008) 'Tax Credits and Child Benefit', DWP Annual Forum, Glasgow, 20 November.

Government of Ireland (1996) *Report of the Commission on the Status of People with Disabilities*, Dublin: Stationery Office.

Gregg, P. (2008) *Realising potential*, London: Department for Work and Pensions.

Hall, K. (2012) 'How agile is Universal Credit?', *Computer Weekly*, 25 September.

Hardman, I. (2012) 'Iain Smith denies threat to Universal Credit', *Spectator*, 10 September.

Harrington, M. (2010) 'An independent review of the Work Capability Assessment', www.dwp.gov.uk/docs/wca-review-2010.pdf

Heffer, S. (1998) 'Only the family can save the welfare state as Labour prepares to tackle the dependency culture', *Daily Mail*, 24 March.

Hills, J., Smithies, R. and McKnight, A. (2006) *Tracking income*, London: LSE Centre for the Analysis of Social Exclusion.

HMRC (Her Majesty's Revenue and Customs) (2012) 'Child Benefit, Child Tax Credit and Working Tax Credit take-up rates', www.hmrc.gov.uk/statistics/fin-takeup-stats/cwtc-take-up.pdf

Kincaid, J. (1973) *Poverty and equality in Britain*, Harmondsworth: Penguin.

Kirkup, J. (2011) 'George Osborne is warned of disaster over welfare reforms', *The Telegraph*, 25 September, www.telegraph.co.uk/news/politics/labour/8788299/George-Osborne-is-warned-of-disaster-over-welfare-reforms.html

Labour Party (1959) *National superannuation*, London: Labour Party.

Mabbett, D. and Bolderson, H. (1999) 'Theories and methods in comparative social policy', in J. Clasen (ed) *Comparative social policy: concepts, theories and methods*, Oxford: Blackwell.

Parliamentary and Health Service Ombudsman (2007) 'Tax Credits – getting it wrong?', HC 1010.

Porter, A. and Riddell, M. (2010) 'Iain Duncan Smith: my welfare reforms are Beveridge for today, with a hint of Tebbit', *Daily Telegraph*, 6 November.

Poynter, J. (1969) *Society and pauperism*, London: Routledge and Kegan Paul.

Reade, S. (2012) 'How politics put paid to the Coalition's pensions reform', *i*, 22 September, p 49.

Ross, T. (2012) 'Iain Duncan Smith's Work Programme "worse than doing nothing"', *Daily Telegraph*, 27 November.

Spicker, P. (2010) 'Cutting social security', *Radical Statistics*, vol 103, pp 40–9.

Spicker, P. (2011) *How social security works*, Bristol: Policy Press.

The Guardian (1985) 'The pension they all approved', 2 May.

Van Oorschot, W. (1995) *Realising rights*, Aldershot: Avebury.

Van Parijs, P. (ed) (1992) *Arguing for basic income*, London: Verso.

Walker, R. (1986) 'Aspects of administration', in P. Kemp (ed) *The future of housing benefits*, Glasgow: Centre for Housing Research.

World Bank (2001) *Social protection sector strategy: from safety net to springboard*, New York, NY: World Bank.

World Bank (2012) 'Social protection (Article 28)', http://go.worldbank.org/R8ABRRLKX0

Reconciling fuel poverty and climate change policy under the Coalition government: Green Deal or no deal?

Carolyn Snell and Harriet Thomson

Introduction

There are two dimensions to energy policy: climate change is commonly associated with the *use* of non-renewable forms of energy and subsequent greenhouse gas emissions, whereas fuel poverty is often associated with the *underuse* or excessive cost of household energy. In the UK, there are legally binding targets in place to both reduce fuel poverty and address climate change.

This chapter considers recent policy changes relevant to climate change mitigation and the alleviation of fuel poverty. The chapter aims to assess the extent to which policy developed under the Coalition government furthers and balances climate change and fuel poverty goals, reflecting on the Energy Act 2011 and its flagship policy, the 'Green Deal'.[1] This chapter is organised as follows. First, energy is discussed as a policy problem, and the need to address fuel poverty and climate change policy objectives simultaneously is outlined. Second, fuel poverty and climate change policy between 2001 and 2010 is outlined. Policy changes under the Coalition government are then described, and the differences between the two administrations' approaches are highlighted, most notably, the shift away from public spending to financial provision through the private sector. Within this section, the broader policy context is also discussed, as many climate change policies have roots within EU-level legislation. Third, the likely impact of policy change is analysed, assessing whether fuel poverty and climate change policy aims are likely to be furthered. Fourth, the concluding discussion reflects on whether policy changes have effectively balanced fuel poverty and climate change objectives.

Energy as a policy problem

As described earlier, there are two elements to energy policy: fuel poverty and climate change. Discussions around fuel poverty originated in the 1970s, following global oil price shocks (Boardman, 1991). Energy-inefficient homes are considered to be the main cause of fuel poverty, in addition to fuel prices and low incomes (Boardman, 2012). Fuel poverty is currently defined as where a household 'needs to spend more than 10 per cent of its income on all fuel use and to heat its home to an adequate standard of warmth' (DTI, 2001, p 6), and it became a policy priority in the early 2000s.

There is a scientific consensus that human activities have an impact on the global climate (see, eg, UNFCCC, 2012), and it is recognised that climate change is associated with the 'combustion of coal, oil and natural gas that fuel 80 per cent of word energy use and through deforestation' (Schneider et al, 2010, p 1). Emission reduction targets have been set out at the international, European and national level, and in the UK, a reduction in greenhouse gas emissions of 80% by 2050 was set out in the Climate Change Act 2008.

At a superficial level, energy policies attempting to address these different goals can be viewed as in conflict with each other. Fuel poverty policy attempts to improve thermal comfort, and climate change mitigation often focuses on the reduction of energy use. Where fuel poverty is dealt with in isolation, it may impact negatively on climate change; subsidising energy bills may remove households from fuel poverty but may also lead to overall increases in energy use. On the other hand, climate change policies that do not consider the needs of the fuel-poor may have a disproportionate effect on them; increased taxation on non-renewable energy use is known to have the greatest financial impact on those in low-income groups (Johnson et al, 1990). Given this potential conflict in the aims and outcomes of energy policies, it is widely acknowledged (Huby, 1998; Cahill, 2002; Fitzpatrick, 2011; Hills, 2012; Ürge-Vorsatz and Herrero, 2012) that in order to reconcile and achieve the dual policy goals of reduced fuel poverty and climate change mitigation, their interaction must be recognised.

Fuel poverty and climate change policy

Policy development and delivery

The context that energy policy operates within is complex, with a large number of stakeholders operating across many sectors. Within the British public sector alone, policy is splintered across numerous governmental departments, public bodies and offices. While the majority of climate policy is delivered through the Department of Energy and Climate Change (DECC), energy efficiency is also delivered in part via housing regulations and policy through the Department for Communities and Local Government (DCLG), and some fuel poverty support mechanisms are provided through the benefits system. In addition to this, the industry is regulated by the Office of Gas and Electricity Markets (OFGEM), and a number of other public sector departments and organisations, such as NHS Trusts and local authorities (attempting to fulfil either social or environmental policies), are also involved in policy development and delivery.

Policy between 2001 and 2010

As noted earlier, concern regarding fuel poverty grew in the 2000s. Figure 2.1 gives an indication of fuel poverty levels from 1996 to 2010, with projections for 2011 and 2012. A strong V-shape can be observed in Figure 2.1, with the number of households in fuel poverty declining sharply until 2003, followed by a large increase. Hills (2012) attributes the V-shape to the sensitivity of the current fuel poverty definition to fuel prices, which started to rise very sharply from 2003.[2]

Figure 2.1: Fuel poverty in England, 1996–2010, projected to 2012

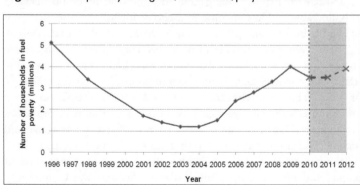

Source: DECC (2012g, p 78).

Given these trends, legal commitments were set out in the Warm Homes and Energy Conservation Act 2000 to eliminate fuel poverty by 2016, and the Fuel Poverty Strategy was developed:

> The Fuel Poverty Strategy has policies to target the three main factors that influence fuel poverty – household energy efficiency, fuel prices and household income, and we have put in place a strong package of programmes and measures to address these concerns. (Department of Trade and Industry, 2001)

By the end of the Labour administration in 2010, a number of fuel poverty measures were in place. These measures included: direct state support through winter fuel and cold weather payments made to vulnerable groups (using various eligibility criteria, in the case of the former, the criteria simply being age-based), and new regulations requiring energy companies to offer social tariffs and banning the disconnection of vulnerable customers during winter months (OFGEM, 2009). Running alongside fuel poverty policies were household-level energy efficiency schemes. The Labour government introduced a number of household energy efficiency/generation measures, most notably, the Feed in Tariff (FiT) and Carbon Emissions Reduction Target (CERT). Through FiT, households installing micro-generation measures such as solar panels were remunerated for generating energy and feeding it into the National Grid. Through CERT, energy companies were required to invest in and encourage domestic energy efficiency (DECC, 2012a). Households could access this regardless of whether they were a customer and initially the programme was synonymous with free energy-efficient light bulbs and highly subsidised loft insulation materials. Through CERT, households could access highly subsidised energy efficiency measures, with 40% of funding targeted at the 'priority group' made up of 'vulnerable and low-income households including those in receipt of eligible benefits and pensioners over the age of 70' (DECC, 2010a).

There were also a number of measures that addressed both climate change and fuel poverty simultaneously. First, Warm Front, the means-tested state-funded programme aiming to improve the energy efficiency of 'vulnerable' households, was created. Under the Warm Front programme, 'vulnerable' was defined in terms of a number of factors, including receipt of certain benefits, energy efficiency rating, age and income. Warm Front covered up to £3,500 of improvements in 2011 (Directgov, 2012a), and usually resulted in the fitting of energy-efficient boilers and loft or cavity wall insulation. Second, the Community

Energy Saving Programme (CESP) was introduced, funded through energy companies and targeting 4,500 areas identified as vulnerable to fuel poverty and likely to benefit from energy efficiency measures (DECC, 2012b).

Policy under the Coalition government

At the time of writing, the Conservative-led Coalition government remains committed to both policy goals, if only due to the legal commitments set out in the Warm Homes and Energy Conservation Act 2000 and the Climate Change Act 2008. The Coalition government has made numerous changes through the Energy Act (DECC, 2011a) and also as a result of cutbacks in other policy areas.

In terms of specific fuel poverty alleviation measures, winter fuel payments remain in place, although not without controversy. Critics argue that winter fuel payments were cut in 2011, although, in reality, the debate is more complex as payment levels relate to the extent to which payments are topped up and increased with inflation (see, eg, BBC, 2012). Equally, cold weather payments remain in place, as does the regulation of pricing, disconnection and the definition of vulnerable customers. In addition to this, the Warm Home Discount Scheme (WHDS) has been introduced and has replaced the requirement on energy companies to offer social tariffs. The scheme provides some customers with a rebate of £130 during the winter months. Groups such as pensioners on specific benefits are entitled to this and the rebate is supported through some information-sharing with the Department for Work and Pensions (DWP). Other groups may be entitled to the rebate, although this will be determined by the definition of vulnerable customers used by the energy company in question (Directgov, 2012b). It should be noted that information-sharing represents a significant policy change, and has arguably been influenced by the case of Mr and Mrs Bates who died following disconnection of their gas supply. At the time, the disconnection of Mr and Mrs Bates's gas supply could not be referred to social services as this would have breached the Data Protection Act (*The Telegraph*, 2003).

In addition to the WHDS, there are two other substantial changes. First, the introduction of the Green Deal, which provides loans at a commercial rate to encourage household energy efficiency improvements. Households are eligible for a loan if they meet the 'golden rule'; that is, any increase in costs associated with the loan is offset against reductions in energy costs due to improved efficiency. Loans and improvements are delivered through private companies, and the loan repayment is recovered through the energy bill. The debt remains with the property and must be declared at the point of sale. The Green Deal expands the energy sector and the range of private sector bodies involved within it. According to DECC (2010b, p 5), the Green Deal will 'revolutionise the energy efficiency of British properties', where 'businesses provide the capital ... getting their money back via the energy bill' (DECC, 2010b, p 2). Energy companies will have an overseeing role as Green Deal payments are made through energy bills. Beyond energy companies, organisations providing loans and those making/selling energy-efficient products will all have an expanded role within the Green Deal. The Green Deal was launched at the beginning of October 2012, with householders being able to take up energy efficiency audits and surveys; however, no work or loans will be approved before 2013 (DECC, 2012c).

The second change, and the most significant in terms of the reconciliation of fuel poverty and climate policy, is the withdrawal of Warm Front and CESP at the end of 2012, and the introduction of the Energy Company Obligation (ECO). ECO sits alongside the Green Deal, and supports customers who do not meet the 'golden rule' either because their homes are too energy-inefficient or underheated/impoverished. Households qualifying for ECO will see the shortfall that prevents them from achieving the golden rule being subsidised rather than through a loan. ECO removes state involvement in energy efficiency improvements for the disadvantaged and instead makes these available through cross-subsidisation of energy bills. ECO also supports those in 'hard-to-treat homes' – in most instances, those with solid wall properties but also those who are not on the mains gas network – which may mean that those close to the fuel poverty threshold are subsidising those who are not (for an analysis of the distribution of income deciles and hard-to-treat homes, see CSE, 2011).

The European context

Current UK compliance issues with the 2006 EU Directive on value added tax threaten to derail the Green Deal scheme. At present, energy-saving materials are taxed at a VAT rate of 5%, but in order to comply with European legislation, this rate needs to be increased to 20%, something that the government is set to challenge at the time of writing. This VAT increase would affect insulation, draught-proofing material, central heating system controls, hot water system controls and a range of micro-generation technologies. As highlighted by Croft (2012), the

European Commission's stance on this issue seems at odds with its energy efficiency targets.

Beyond complications with tax compliance, policy at the UK level is also shaped by EU targets and directives. First is the Renewables Obligation (RO), which was introduced in 2002 and committed the UK to generating '15% of our energy from renewable sources by 2020' (DECC, 2012d) as part of European climate change targets. Second is the third phase of the EU Emissions Trading System (ETS), a carbon 'cap and trade' scheme that begins in 2013 and aims to lower EU carbon emissions (for more details, see EC, 2012). Both the RO and EU ETS have an impact on electricity bills (gas is treated differently), and the estimated costs on the average bill are highlighted later. Third, and following on from the Renewable Heat Payment (RHP), which provides partial grants to incentivise households to install renewable heat technology, a Renewable Heat Incentive (RHI) for domestic households is due to be launched in 2013 alongside the Green Deal, which will pay a domestic tariff for heat generation. Originally, the RHI was to be funded by energy companies through a Renewable Heat Levy; however, the Coalition government announced in 2010 that the Treasury would be funding the scheme (Ares, 2012).

The rationale for concurrently launching the Green Deal and RHI is to 'allow for a more whole-house approach to heat production and energy saving' (Energy Saving Trust, no date), and for the RHI and FiT to complement Green Deal finance (DECC, 2011b, p 12). Given the substantial cost of micro-generation technology, the golden rule is unlikely to be met; however, DECC have stated that Green Deal providers may have the option to use Green Deal finance (DECC, 2011b, p 12), but they are not intending to create a specific mechanism for combining the finance streams. Offsetting Green Deal repayments with a financial incentive such as the RHI or FiT could potentially enable lower-income households to access prohibitively expensive renewable technology by removing capital barriers. It is likely that the upfront cost of micro-generation technology was the main reason why 'the more affluent, larger housing groups were the major beneficiaries of domestic (householder) grants' (Gardiner et al, 2011, p 7) under the Low Carbon Building Programme, which, like the RHP, provided partial grants towards the cost of installing micro-generation technology.

A fourth policy that has been introduced as a result of European legislation is the roll-out of 'smart' gas and electricity meters to all domestic households and small businesses in Great Britain from 2014 to 2019. The motivation behind smart meters is to reduce energy consumption by making energy use 'visible'. DECC is overseeing the national roll-out, with energy suppliers bearing the financial burden of the project as well as responsibility for replacing the meters. There has been some concern expressed about how energy suppliers will recover their costs, particularly as there are few regulations:

> suppliers will be required not to levy a one-off or upfront charge on their domestic customers for the smart metering equipment, including in-home displays.... Beyond this, no additional constraints will be imposed on suppliers as to how they recover their costs. (National Audit Office, 2011, p 35)

The estimated costs to consumers for the smart meter roll-out are varied. Evidence submitted to the House of Commons Committee of Public Accounts (2011, Ev 25) estimates the lifetime cost of smart meters to be £350 per consumer, a figure that is 'likely to rise rather than fall as the full cost of technology and systems are known'. However, the National Audit Office (2011, p 35) estimate that smart meters will deliver a net annual saving of £23 for the average dual fuel customer by 2020, although this figure depends on multiple factors, including the final cost of delivering a smart meter roll-out, whether households are able to reduce their gas and electricity consumption, and whether they can switch to cheaper tariffs as a result of having a smart meter (National Audit Office, 2011, p 35). The quality of feedback provided by smart meters will be a key determinant of initial household ability to reduce energy consumption, while longer-term, additional incentives may be required. As Darby (2006, p 4) states, 'a new type of behaviour formed over a three-month period or longer seems likely to persist – but continued feedback is needed to help maintain the change'.

The impact of policy change on fuel poverty and climate change goals

Fuel poverty reduction

Table 2.1 demonstrates the average impact of the various schemes discussed earlier on energy bills. The cost to suppliers of achieving CERT (from April 2008 to December 2012) is estimated to total £5.5 billion (DECC, 2012a). An overall cost for CESP is harder to establish, although most estimates for the lifetime of the scheme (DECC, 2012b) are £350 million. Clearly, there are limitations to these calculations, especially given that costs of schemes may have benefits (eg CERT should lead to a reduction in bills where measures such as insulation have been taken up).

Table 2.1: Breakdown of average household gas, electricity and energy bills in 2011

	Gas	Electricity	Overall
Wholesale energy cost	£339 (51%)	£261 (43%)	£600 (48%)
Transmission, distribution and metering	£125 (19%)	£113 (19%)	£238 (19%)
Other supplier costs and margin	£137 (21%)	£136 (23%)	£273 (22%)
Energy and climate change policies, of which:	£28 (4%)	£61 (10%)	£89 (7%)
Carbon Emissions Reduction Target Extension		£17 (3%)	£38 (3%)
EU Emissions Trading Scheme	N/A	£20 (3%)	£20 (2%)
Renewables Obligation	N/A	£17 (3%)	£17 (1%)
Warm Home Discount	£6 (1%)	£5 (1%)	£10 (1%)
Community Energy Savings Programme	£2 (0%)	£1 (0%)	£3 (0%)
Feed in Tariffs	N/A	£1 (0%)	£1 (0%)
Better billing	£0 (0%)	£0 (0%)	£0 (0%)
VAT	(5%) £31	(5%) £29	(5%) £60
Total	£660	£600	£1,260

Source: DECC (2011c)

Predicting the impact of policy change on energy bills is difficult, and estimates vary significantly. For example, for the ECO, the predicted cost to the energy bill payer varies. The Association for the Conservation of Energy (2011) suggests an average increase of £80, DECC suggest £60, and the Climate Change Committee (2011, p 26) suggest £40–60 per year. As with CERT and CESP, the proposed cost of ECO will be funded through energy bills. The key difference between ECO and CERT/CESP is the eligibility criteria. CERT varied to some extent by area, for example, in Yorkshire, loft and cavity wall insulation was provided free through the Yorkshire Energy Partnership, which was supported by a number of local authorities in the area. CERT also relied heavily on consumer action; motivated individuals could find cheap or free measures online and could also purchase subsidised products such as insulation materials in DIY shops. On the other hand, eligibility for ECO will be assessed through strict criteria relating to the likelihood of being in fuel poverty or living in a 'hard-to-treat home'. The Green Deal will effectively take free or cheap measures away from those who are not defined as being in either of these two groups, but these households will have to both meet the costs of energy efficiency improvements that they choose to make through the Green Deal loan system *and* pay for the cost of ECO through energy bills.

On 11 June 2012, the government published its response to the Green Deal/ECO consultation, finalised a number of settings and clarified eligibility criteria. The 'hard-to-treat' homes aspect of ECO has been divided into two elements, Carbon Savings and Carbon Savings Communities (see Table 2.2). It is projected that only £540 million of the £1.3 billion annual cost of ECO will be used to help fuel-poor households, although this figure is well above the 'indicative 75:25 split as set out in the consultation' (DECC, 2012e, p 29) favouring carbon savings. DECC's (2012f, p 7) impact assessment of the same date suggests that the allocation of funding will 'result in delivery of around 47% of the insulation measures supported through ECO to low income and vulnerable households'.

There are a number of criticisms that have been levied at these proposals. First, it is argued by many that financing ECO through the bill payer rather than the tax payer is regressive (see Boardman, 2012), since this will hit the poorest bill payers the hardest, and that unlike the taxation system, energy costs remain the same regardless of income. For example, the Hills (2012, p 109) fuel poverty review argues that 'Since energy expenditure makes up a large proportion of overall spending for lower-income households, this increase in energy costs represents a relatively regressive means of funding a policy'. This view is echoed by Energy UK (the trade association for the energy industry) and National Energy Action (a fuel poverty charity), who argue that 'It therefore seems perverse that, in order to address rising levels of fuel-poverty and carbon emissions, the very households struggling to achieve affordable warmth are required to make a disproportionate contribution to the solution' (Stockton and Campbell, 2011, p 16).

Second, the proportion of the ECO budget put aside for disadvantaged households has been criticised (Hills, 2012; Tovar, 2012). The Hills review models the effects of paying for ECO through increased bills on different income quintiles and finds that:

a more equitable distribution of the costs and benefits of ECO would mean those in the lowest three income decile groups breaking even on average ... our best estimate is that to remove the regressive effect more than half of the spending under ECO would need to be targeted towards the fuel poor. (Hills, 2012, p 114)

Table 2.2: Finalised ECO components and criteria

ECO component	£ million	Criteria
Affordable Warmth	350	Qualifying benefits will include: Child Tax Credit with a household income under £15,860, income-related Employment and Support Allowance, income-based Jobseeker's Allowance, Income Support, State Pension Credit, Working Tax Credit with a household income under £15,860. All benefit criteria have various qualifying components. Eligible households will be those in private tenures only.
Carbon Savings obligation	760	Energy suppliers will be able to deliver both solid wall insulation and non-standard cavity wall insulation under the ECO Carbon Saving obligation. Insulation for non-standard cavity walls is less likely to be funded entirely by Green Deal finance but can deliver socially cost-effective carbon savings. Supporting insulation for non-standard cavity walls will provide greater certainty for the cavity wall insulation industry during the transition from the existing CERT and CESP schemes to the Green Deal and ECO.
Carbon Saving obligation: Communities	190	This new element is designed to target insulation measures in low-income communities defined using the bottom 15% of Lower Super Output Areas from the Index of Multiple Deprivation, or equivalent indexes in Scotland and Wales. Suppliers will be required to deliver 15% of their overall Carbon Saving Communities obligation to rural, low-income households in settlements with a population size under 10,000. To qualify for this assistance, a rural household should be in receipt of a qualifying benefit or tax credit under the ECO Affordable Warmth eligibility criteria. A wider range of measures will be eligible under the Carbon Saving Communities obligation, including cavity wall, loft and solid wall insulation. We expect that loft and cavity wall insulation will be the most frequently delivered measures.

Source: Adapted from DECC (2012e, pp 29–30)

In addition to all bill payers funding energy efficiency measures targeted at the fuel-poor (as they did through CESP previously), the idea that all bill payers should support improvements to 'hard-to-treat homes' is considered by some to be regressive (Boardman, 2012), with the potential of pushing some households into fuel poverty (Tovar, 2012). However, the final impact assessment conducted by DECC (2012f) suggests that regressivity has largely been addressed. DECC (2012f, p 72) argues that 'despite the potential for costs being recouped through bills to be regressive, the average impact across income groups is broadly proportionate as a percentage of average income in each income decile group'.

As described earlier, there will be other support in place, namely, the mandatory WHDS, which replaces support currently required of the big six energy companies. While there is a 'core group' (see Table 2.3), some of the eligibility criteria are at the discretion of the energy companies. It may well be that these criteria favour the elderly the most, but, while an important group, they are not the only group that suffers from fuel poverty.

Table 2.3: The core group – Warm Home Discount Scheme for low-income pensioners

Year	Eligibility	Annual discount	No of consumers helped
2011/12	Households in receipt of guarantee element of Pension Credit	£120	600,000
2012/13	Households in receipt of guarantee element of Pension Credit and over 80 and in receipt of savings element of Pension Credit	£130	TBC
2013/14	Households in receipt of guarantee element of Pension Credit and over 75 and in receipt of savings element of Pension Credit	£135	TBC
2014/15	All households in receipt of guarantee and savings element of Pension Credit	£140	TBC

Source: Consumer Focus (2010)

Consumer Focus finds that during the transition from social tariffs to the WHDS, some customers may no longer be eligible for support. This is likely to be down to a number of reasons other than a change in household circumstances:

- The qualifying criteria for a supplier's voluntary social tariff is different for the qualifying criteria (still to be finalised) for the Broader Group.
- The 'cap' on those customers eligible for the Broader Group is less than the existing number of customers on a supplier's voluntary social tariff. (Consumer Focus, 2010, pp 2–3).

They also find that the WHDS may be less than support offered through the social tariff.

Ultimately, the impact of the policy changes described earlier on fuel poverty will be determined by the Green Deal/ECO settings and delivery (Guertler, 2012; Tovar, 2012), and also changes in the energy market that are beyond the government's control. Clearly, the households most likely to gain from these measures are those eligible for support, as Boardman (2012, p 145) suggests, 'the extent to which the fuel poor will suffer from these ever-increasing costs is entirely dependent on whether they are a beneficiary or not of the programmes'. The regressive nature of the financing system means that, as identified by Hills (2012), the worst hit will be those on the lowest incomes who are ineligible for measures or support (or who do not take them up).

The way in which the broader groups are defined for the WHDS will also determine the impact on fuel poverty, as some customers will no longer qualify for this form of support. Given the current focus on those of pensionable age for the core group, it may well be those of working age who are most affected. Equally, as Walker and Day (2012) argue, targeting in this way can be over-simplistic, and may exclude those who need support the most. They highlight the current campaign being run by Macmillan Cancer Support that is attempting to get those terminally ill with cancer recognised under the WHDS. Indeed, the effects of the Green Deal/ECO must be viewed in the context of charges and support measures as a whole; a household that is not eligible for ECO and is negatively affected by the transition from social tariffs to WHDS will be hit the hardest.

Climate change mitigation

Having considered the impact of policy change on fuel poverty, this section now considers whether the Green Deal can have a positive contribution to climate change targets. DECC (2012f) identifies three possible risk areas: market failure, consumer appetite and predicted costs. First, while the Green Deal will attempt to correct a number of market failures associated with improved household energy efficiency, for example, that households do not have access to capital to make energy efficiency improvements, or sufficient information regarding energy efficiency, 'it is not currently possible to quantify the extent to which these failures will be addressed' (DECC, 2012f, p 54). In other words, how successful the Green Deal will be in addressing these is uncertain. Second, assumptions within DECC's models about 'consumer appetite for measures' are also highlighted as a concern, with levels of take-up being uncertain: 'There is a risk that households do not make energy efficiency decisions in the same way as assumed. There is also a risk that households could react disproportionately to any adverse publicity' (DECC, 2012f, p 54). Third, DECC highlights 'costs and the performance of measures', commenting on the difficulties of using predictive models given the variability and unpredictability of energy markets (DECC, 2012f, p 54). As such, the benefits of the Green Deal in terms of greenhouse gas emission reductions are likely to vary on a number of technical settings and social factors. Essentially, the number of households taking up Green Deals (ie quantity) and the effectiveness and longevity of work carried out (ie quality) will determine the overall environmental effect. Some of the key criticisms that have been raised during the consultation period of the Energy Act are discussed in the following.

It is likely that the extent of possible efficiency improvements will be restricted by the household meeting the 'golden rule' (which, in itself, will be influenced by the interest rate of the Green Deal and the price of the work). If the cost of the work or interest rate is prohibitively high, or the energy savings low, then it is likely that cheaper, shorter-term improvements will be undertaken rather than those that support long-term changes to the energy mix (see Kelly et al, 2012, p 6876). Indeed, every 1% increase in finance costs necessitates a 7% reduction in fuel bills by energy efficiency measures in order to meet the golden rule (Keepmoat, 2012). Even within DECC, it is acknowledged that households taking up a Green Deal loan may end up worse off, and that whether a household will *actually* (rather than theoretically) meet the golden rule will be hard to predict (DECC, 2012f). This is partly due to the building performance and certification tools used.

In order to calculate if an energy efficiency measure is cost-effective and meets the golden rule, an assessment of the energy performance of a property will be undertaken using a Reduced Data Standard Assessment Procedure (RdSAP). As the name suggests, the RdSAP has reduced data requirements compared with the Standard Assessment Procedure (SAP), which is used for calculating the performance of new buildings, in order to reduce the time required for carrying out building performance assessments on existing dwellings, and to ensure that it can be used by someone with limited knowledge of building energy analysis (Kelly et al, 2012, p 6875). The RdSAP makes certain assumptions concerning standard occupancy, lighting patterns and heating patterns, aspects that are likely to have the largest impact on whether the golden rule is met.

Previous work has found that these standard assumptions are insensitive to cultural differences in the use of rooms, leading to incorrect assumptions of energy consumption (Todd and Steele, 2006), and, as Kelly et al (2012, p 6875) further state: 'there is a trade-off between model simplicity, accuracy and comparability with other dwellings that may lead to confusion and produce grossly inaccurate estimates about a particular building's energy consumption and overall energy performance'. A further criticism levied at the Green Deal process is that RdSAP assumes all homes constructed after 1983 have cavity wall insulation (Kelly et al, 2012) , which means that the owners and residents of the 2.3 million cavity-walled homes constructed after 1983 with clear cavities and no insulation may be given incorrect Green Deal advice (Lainé, 2012).

There is a body of evidence suggesting that the Green Deal methodology is insufficiently robust, and in relation to the use of SAP and RdSAP for meeting climate change and fuel poverty policy objectives, Kelly et al (2012, p 6876) argue:

> SAP and RdSAP confound cost-effectiveness, energy efficiency, environmental performance and GHG [greenhouse gas] emissions adding unnecessary complexity and confusion to the SAP calculation procedure. As a result it is not clear which of the many national policy aims – reducing fuel poverty, increasing energy efficiency, decreasing overall energy use, or reducing carbon emissions – is being captured by the various performance measures.

Consumer Focus comment that 'Misselling has remained an issue in the energy supply market despite 10 years of regulation, and it is vulnerable consumers who are most at risk' (Consumer Focus, 2011, p 7). Warm Front, discussed earlier, has not been without criticism, although the majority of this is anecdotal rather than academic. Various news reports highlight problematic aspects of Warm Front, including: poor service (*The Guardian*, 2011), additional charges and poor targeting (*The Telegraph*, 2009), inflated prices (BBC, 2008), long waits (BBC, 2010), and unclear complaints procedures (*The Mirror*, 2008). As Consumer Focus (2011, p 7) point out, it will be essential that the:

> Green Deal must be delivered in such a way as to minimise household mistrust, especially when dealing with vulnerable households. The quality assurance scheme for installers and advisors for Green Deal needs to include provision for vulnerable people to ensure they feel safe.

Arguably, the branding of the Green Deal will be essential; while Warm Front was marketed as a governmental initiative (and still received the criticisms described earlier), the reliance on the private sector for Green Deal/ECO delivery *could* lead to even lower levels of customer trust. Indeed, Charles Yates, associate director of professional services network Grant Thornton, stressed the importance of trust and branding in *The Guardian* on the day of the launch of the Green Deal. He commented that:

> The Marks and Spencers of this world could be very powerful advocates, these are very trusted brands. It would be a very positive sign to see a big advertising campaign – this is not just the green deal, it is the M&S green deal. (*The Guardian*, 2012)

However, he went on to describe the reticence of large retailers (such as B&Q, John Lewis and Tesco) to sign up, suggesting that 'If they thought [the scheme] was robust enough to get involved, it would be a big vote of confidence – the fact that they are not shows we are still not there yet' (*The Guardian*, 2012).

The quantity of households taking up the Green Deal is also difficult to predict. There have been some studies that consider the possible Green Deal interest rates that demonstrate little support for the current proposed rate of around 7%. Furthermore, as identified by Stockton and Campbell (2011, p 10), many households are debt-averse, particularly as they are 'already struggling to afford essential goods and services'. The addition of interest to the Green Deal charge may also be problematic for some religious groups that are prohibited by their faith from handling interest payments (DECC, 2011a, p 149). Green Deal providers have the flexibility to develop repayment structures that do not incorporate interest payments, although this could increase costs, costs that could be spread beyond the target household (DECC, 2011a), and this would also depend on the willingness of Green Deal providers to create such a repayment structure.

There are questions around the types of household that might take up a Green Deal and, closely related, how the Green Deal will be marketed. Presumably, as households do not see any financial benefits, and it is possible with some measures that the debt may outlive the home improvement, it will be difficult to sell this as an energy efficiency measure (at least on the grounds of cost). On the other hand, where the improvement has a long lifespan, and meets the golden rule, it could be sold on the basis of 'future cost savings'. Equally, the Green Deal could be promoted as a financial mechanism supporting general home improvements or on environmental grounds. If the Green Deal is sold on environmental grounds, it could be argued that those who would be interested could probably save up and just buy the improvements outright, thus saving money immediately, and in the long run (no interest to pay). Given the issues of implementation raised earlier, there are concerns that the Green Deal will fail to achieve a high take-up rate. Indeed, DECC are projecting a relatively modest uptake of Green Deal measures, which declines rapidly over time (see Figure 2.2).

Figure 2.2: Take-up of Green Deal measures

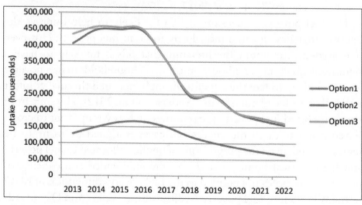

Source: DECC (2011a, p 210)

Based on the DECC forecast, the Climate Change Committee (2011, p 121) are estimating a carbon gap of at least three MtCO2 compared to the uptake levels required in order to meet carbon budgets. The Association for the Conservation of Energy (2012, p 2) is highly critical regarding the potential of the Green Deal and ECO, arguing that it is incompatible with the UK's carbon reduction targets and energy security objectives. In addition to this, it should be noted that the Green Deal does not support decarbonisation, that is, a shift to alternative energy sources. This is supported by the FiT, RO and RHP; however, these measures are currently small in scale.

Concluding discussion

The Green Deal supports 'free' household energy efficiency improvements, and the 'hard-to-treat' dimension of ECO promotes the uptake of energy efficiency measures that might be prohibitively expensive otherwise. In terms of environmental outcomes, both the Green Deal and ECO are likely to have a positive environmental impact (for an assessment of this, see Kelly et al, 2012, p 6876), although the extent of this will depend on many of the factors discussed earlier. However, while the hard-to-treat homes element of ECO will undoubtedly encourage energy efficiency, there is a ceiling to these energy savings. Indeed, it must be noted that the FiT and RO are predicted to cost the bill payer far less than ECO but have a longer-term impact in terms of their contribution to decarbonisation, diversification of the energy supply and the use of renewable energy (Kelly et al, 2012, p 6876).

The fuel poverty dimension of ECO is likely to help improve the energy efficiency of those most likely to be in fuel poverty. However, it is argued throughout the literature that this is unlikely to have a significant effect on greenhouse emissions as households in fuel poverty are more likely to feel the benefits through increased thermal comfort rather than reduced energy use (Anderson et al, 2012). The shift from state-supported fuel poverty programmes such as Warm Front to cross-subsidisation through the energy bill payer is argued by many to be regressive, and given the proportions of funding allocated to fuel poverty and 'hard-to-treat homes', could have the unintended consequence of pushing households not entitled to the fuel poverty dimension of ECO or the WHDS into fuel poverty. Additionally, as Walker and Day (2012) argue, it removes state responsibility from identifying and addressing fuel poverty, placing it in the hands of the private sector, where cost efficiency is a higher priority and accountability may be reduced. Whether this approach can effectively support the fuel-poor is questionable, as it may be tempting for suppliers to target 'easy wins', for example, providing support to those in receipt of particular benefits.

Also, removing subsidised support from households that could currently claim under CERT is likely to have negative environmental consequences. As described earlier, it is less likely for a household to take a loan for energy efficiency measures if there are few perceivable benefits, and those who are concerned and committed to the environment are probably likely to have taken up these measures already. Equally, households that are debt averse are unlikely to take up a Green Deal. Even households that are entitled to the fuel poverty dimension of ECO will need to be convinced – without the government 'branding' associated with Warm Front, there may be a degree of mistrust and a lack of understanding about the nature of ECO.

The premise of this chapter was that the dual policy goals of fuel poverty alleviation and climate change mitigation need to be addressed concurrently, and where they are not, one policy outcome may damage the progress of the other. This chapter set out to consider whether policy developed under the Coalition government balances and furthers climate and fuel poverty concerns sufficiently. While it is evident that Coalition policy does consider and, to some extent, attempts to address social and environmental objectives simultaneously, there are clear limitations to this approach. The provision of ECO in addition to the Green Deal indicates an attempt to support the fuel-poor; however, whether this will reach and support those in most need is questionable. Additionally, whether the Green Deal will have a significant impact on emission reduction targets is also debatable, given problems associated with measurement, take-up and impact. In summary, without addressing the issues outlined in this chapter, policy outcomes may be limited in terms of their impact on both fuel poverty and climate change.

Notes

[1] It should be noted at this point that this chapter focuses on *household-*level climate change policies and their interaction with fuel poverty policy, rather than climate change policy more broadly.

[2] The responsiveness of the current definition to fuel prices, which can often mask improvements in poverty and energy efficiency standards (see Hills, 2012), is one of the reasons the UK definition of fuel poverty has been under review by Professor John Hills.

References

Anderson, W., White, V. and Finney, A. (2012) 'Coping with low incomes and cold homes', *Energy Policy*, vol 49, pp 40–52.

Ares, E. (2012) 'Renewable Heat Incentive', House of Commons Library, Standard Note SN06328.

Association for the Conservation of Energy (2011) 'Costs of the ECO: the impact on low income households', Report for Eaga Charitable Trust.

Association for the Conservation of Energy (2012) 'Dead CERT: framing a sustainable transition to the Green Deal and the Energy Company Obligation', ACE.

BBC (British Broadcasting Corporation) (2008) 'Heating grants – do you recommend them?', www.bbc.co.uk/blogs/theoneshow/consumer/2008/11/20/heating-grants-have-they-cost.html

BBC (2010) 'MPs to probe Warm Front energy scheme complaints', http://news.bbc.co.uk/1/hi/business/8486495.stm

BBC (2012) 'DUP blasts government over cuts to winter fuel payments', live parliamentary feed, http://news.bbc.co.uk/democracylive/hi/house_of_commons/newsid_9644000/9644663.stm

Boardman, B. (1991) *Fuel poverty: from cold homes to affordable warmth*, London: Belhaven Press.

Boardman, B. (2012) Fuel poverty synthesis: lessons learnt, actions needed. *Energy Policy*, vol 49, pp 143–8.

Cahill, M. (2002) *The environment and social policy*, The Gildredge Social Policy Series. London: Routledge.

Climate Change Committee (2011) 'Household energy bills –impacts of meeting carbon budgets', http://downloads.theccc.org.uk.s3.amazonaws.com/Household%20Energy%20Bills/CCC_Energy%20Note%20Bill_bookmarked_1.pdf

Consumer Focus (2010) 'Energy suppliers broader group schemes', www.consumerfocus.org.uk/files/2010/01/Energy-suppliers-broader-group-schemes.pdf

Consumer Focus (2011) 'Access for all', www.consumerfocus.org.uk/files/2011/11/Access-for-all.pdf

Croft, D. (2012) *VAT on 'energy-saving materials' in a nutshell*, London: Association for the Conservation of Energy.

CSE (Centre for Sustainable Energy) (2011) 'Analysis of hard to treat housing in England: Internal Research Paper 2011', www.cse.org.uk/downloads/file/analysis_of_hard-to-treat_housing_in_england.pdf

Darby, S. (2006) *The effectiveness of feedback on energy consumption: a review for DEFRA of the literature on metering, billing and direct displays*, Oxford: Environmental Change Institute.

DECC (Department of Energy and Climate Change) (2010a) 'Insulation for the nation – 3.5 million more homes to be lagged', press release 30 June, www.decc.gov.uk/en/content/cms/news/pn10_075/pn10_075.aspx

DECC (2010b) 'The Green Deal: a summary of the Government's proposals', www.decc.gov.uk/assets/decc/legislation/energybill/1010-green-deal-summary-proposals.pdf

DECC (2011a) 'Energy Act 2011', www.decc.gov.uk/en/content/cms/legislation/energy_act2011/energy_act2011.aspx

DECC (2011b) 'What measures does the Green Deal cover?', www.decc.gov.uk/assets/decc/what%20we%20do/supporting%20consumers/green_deal/1734-what-measures-does-the-green-deal-cover.pdf

DECC (2011c) 'Estimated impacts of our policies on energy prices', www.decc.gov.uk/assets/decc/11/about-us/economics-social-research/3593-estimated-impacts-of-our-policies-on-energy-prices.pdf

DECC (2012a) 'Carbon Emissions Reduction Target (CERT)', http://webarchive.nationalarchives.gov.uk/20121217150421/www.decc.gov.uk/en/content/cms/funding/funding_ops/cert/cert.aspx

DECC (2012b) 'Community Energy Savings Programme (CESP)', http://webarchive.nationalarchives.gov.uk/20121217150421/www.decc.gov.uk/en/content/cms/funding/funding_ops/cesp/cesp.aspx

DECC (2012c) 'Green Deal – green light', http://webarchive.nationalarchives.gov.uk/20121217150421/www.decc.gov.uk/en/content/cms/news/grndl_grnlit/grndl_grnlit.aspx

DECC (2012d) 'The Renewables Obligation (RO)', www.decc.gov.uk/en/content/cms/meeting_energy/renewable_ener/renew_obs/renew_obs.aspx

DECC (2012e) 'The Green Deal and Energy Company Obligation: government response to the November 2011 consultation', www.cibse.org/content/Technical_Resources/Consultations/143_green%20deal%20govt%20response%20doc.pdf

DECC (2012f) 'Final stage impact assessment for the Green Deal and Energy Company Obligation', www.gov.uk/government/uploads/system/uploads/attachment_data/file/42984/5533-final-stage-impact-assessment-for-the-green-deal-a.pdf

DECC (2012g) 'Annual report on fuel poverty statistics', www.gov.uk/government/uploads/system/uploads/attachment_data/file/66016/5270-annual-report-fuel-poverty-stats-2012.pdf

Department of Trade and Industry (2001) *UK fuel poverty strategy*, London: HMSO, www.decc.gov.uk/en/content/cms/funding/fuel_poverty/strategy/strategy.aspx

Directgov (2012a) 'Heating and insulation improvements from the Warm Front scheme', www.direct.gov.uk/en/Environmentandgreenerliving/Energyandwatersaving/Energygrants/DG_10018661

Directgov (2012b) 'Benefits in retirement', www.direct.gov.uk/en/Pensionsandretirementplanning/Benefits/BenefitsInRetirement/DG_185940

EC (European Commission) (2012) 'European Union exchange and trading scheme', http://ec.europa.eu/clima/policies/ets/index_en.htm

Energy Saving Trust (no date) 'Renewable Heat Incentive', www.energysavingtrust.org.uk/Professional-resources/Funding-and-finance/Renewable-Heat-Incentive

Fitzpatrick, T. (ed) (2011) *Understanding the environment and social policy*, Bristol: Policy Press.

Gardiner, M., White, H., Munzinger, M. and Ray, W. (2011) *Low carbon building programme 2006–2011: final report*. London: Department of Energy and Climate Change.

Guertler, P. (2012) 'Can the Green Deal be fair too? Exploring new possibilities for alleviating fuel poverty', *Energy Policy*, vol 49, pp 91–7.

Hills, J. (2012) *Getting the measure of fuel poverty: final report of the Fuel Poverty Review*, London: Centre for Analysis of Social Exclusion.

House of Commons Committee of Public Accounts (2011) *Preparations for the roll-out of smart meters*, London: HMSO.

Huby, M. (1998) *Social policy and the environment*, Buckingham: Open University Press.

Johnson, P., McKay, S. and Smith, S. (1990) *The distributional implications of environmental taxes, IFS Commentary No. 23*, London: The Institute for Fiscal Studies.

Keepmoat (2012) 'Sustainable homes, parity projects', www.parityprojects.com/uploads/5/4/8/6/5486259/the_green_deal_-_a_summary_guide_to_the_big_decisions_for_rps_and_las.pdf

Kelly, S., Crawford-Brown, D. and Pollitt, M.G. (2012) 'Building performance evaluation and certification in the UK: is SAP fit for purpose?', *Renewable and Sustainable Energy Reviews*, vol 16, pp 6861–78.

Lainé, L. (2012) *Filling the gaps – accuracy of Green Deal advice for cavity-walled homes*, London: Consumer Focus.

National Audit Office (2011) 'Preparations for the roll-out of smart meters', www.nao.org.uk/publications/1012/smart_meters.aspx

OFGEM (2009) 'Review of vulnerable customer disconnections', www.ofgem.gov.uk/Sustainability/SocAction/Publications/Documents1/Review%20of%20vulnerable%20customer%20disconnections%20report.pdf

Schneider, S.H., Rosencranz, A., Mastrandrea, M.D. and Kuntz-Duriseti, K. (eds) (2010) *Climate change science and policy*, Washington, DC: Island Press.

Stockton, H. and Campbell, R. (2011) *Time to reconsider UK energy and fuel poverty policies?*, York: Joseph Rowntree Foundation.

The Guardian (2011) 'Warm front heating scheme', www.guardian.co.uk/money/2011/jan/15/warm-front-heating-scheme

The Guardian (2012) 'Government's Green Deal spurned by retailers', www.guardian.co.uk/environment/2012/oct/01/green-deal-spurned-retailers

The Mirror (2008) 'Complaints hidden in £800 million Warm Front scheme', http://blogs.mirror.co.uk/investigations/2008/11/complaints-hidden-in-800-milli.html

The Telegraph (2003) 'Elderly couple died after gas was cut off', www.telegraph.co.uk/news/uknews/1450104/Elderly-couple-died-after-gas-was-cut-off.html

The Telegraph (2009) 'Millions of pensioners left in the cold by Warm Front scheme', www.telegraph.co.uk/news/uknews/4449339/Millions-of-pensioners-left-in-the-cold-by-Warm-Front-scheme.html

Todd, S. and Steele, A. (2006) 'Modelling a culturally sensitive approach to fuel poverty', *Structural Survey*, vol 24, no 4, pp 300-10.

Tovar, M.A. (2012) 'The structure of energy efficiency investment in the UK households and its average monetary and environmental savings', *Energy Policy*, vol 50, pp 723–35.

UNFCCC (United Nations Framework Convention on Climate Change) (2012) 'Background on the UNFCCC: the international response to climate change', http://unfccc.int/essential_background/items/6031.php

Ürge-Vorsatz, D. and Herrero, S. (2012) 'Building synergies between climate change mitigation and energy poverty alleviation', *Energy Policy*, vol 49, pp 83–90.

Walker, G. and Day, R. (2012) 'Fuel poverty as injustice: integrating distribution, recognition and procedure in the struggle for affordable warmth', *Energy Policy*, vol 49, pp 69–75.

THREE

Doctors in the driving seat? Reforms in NHS primary care and commissioning

Elke Heins

Introduction

After a protracted parliamentary process, on 27 March 2012, the Health and Social Care Bill of the Coalition government gained Royal Assent to finally become the Health and Social Care Act 2012. This latest National Health Service (NHS) reform taking full effect in April 2013 introduces a radical reorganisation of the way NHS services will be commissioned and establishes a regulated market in which 'any qualified provider' from the public or private sector can compete for the provision of NHS services. While the NHS continues to be publicly financed and free at the point of use, the Act entails an accelerated move to a fully functioning market for health care in England. Notably, it claims to put General Practitioners (GPs) 'in the driving seat of the NHS' (*GP Online*, 22 July 2010) by transferring the responsibility for most NHS commissioning to them.

This chapter discusses the main changes to the organisation of health care commissioning and delivery in England as a result of the Health and Social Care Act 2012. The latest reform has to be understood, however, in the context of past market reforms in primary care, that is, services provided by GPs, dentists, pharmacists and optometrists that usually form the first point of contact for patients. Specifically, the changing role and type of GPs will be examined.

Attempts to transfer more decision-making power about service provision to GPs have been made repeatedly through past primary care reforms, yet the outcomes were ambivalent. The experience with GP fundholding in the 1990s has shown that not all GPs were enthusiastic about gaining greater managerial influence (Surender and Fitzpatrick, 1999) and efforts to support 'entrepreneurial' GPs to set up as social enterprises since the mid-2000s in fact strengthened large-scale commercial providers of health care (Heins et al, 2009). Given that the transfer of commissioning decisions is taking place in a time of heightened budget pressures, it is likely that GPs will take up the opportunity to outsource their new decision-making powers to the private sector.

First, the rationale behind a general trend towards marketisation of the UK NHS is briefly reviewed and the concerns related to such trends are highlighted. Second, policies to introduce a competitive market in UK primary care are presented. Third, hypotheses around market behaviour in health are set out and the evidence from the emerging primary care market is discussed. Fourth, the most important changes to health care commissioning and the new role of GPs in this as stipulated by the Health and Social Care Act are outlined. Finally, the chapter assesses the potential consequences of the Act for the NHS and its patients and makes comparisons to developments in other welfare sectors.

The rationale for National Health Service marketisation

Since the inception of the NHS in 1948, the provision of primary health care was exclusively in the hands of GPs. While the clinical autonomy of health professionals remained, nationally uniform terms and conditions were stipulated by the Department of Health. Although GPs stayed technically outside the NHS, choosing to be independent contractors to the Department of Health, rather than salaried public sector staff, in essence, they were part of the NHS, exercising a monopoly over primary care services (Pollock et al, 2007). They enjoyed eligibility for NHS pensions and other benefits and were officially included in NHS workforce counts. Practices have been run either single-handedly or, increasingly, in partnership with other GPs in a team consisting of locums, nurses, receptionists and other ancillary staff, offering a wide range of primary care services to a large population registered with their 'family doctor'. However, a number of reforms over the last three decades have significantly altered this model of a publicly provided integrated primary care service.

Since the late 1970s, slower economic growth and thus increasing scarcity of resources for the welfare state, together with escalating health care costs due to population ageing and a rise in non-communicable diseases, triggered intensified discussions on the economic consequences of the welfare state (Korpi, 1985). Debates about the future affordability of public health care in the light of this mounting reform pressure led to calls for a more efficient NHS. Although acknowledging a number of potential 'market failures', economic theory assumes that competitive welfare markets increase efficiency and consumer welfare when replacing public sector monopoly provision (Bartlett and Le Grand, 1993; Le Grand et al, 2008; Barr, 2012).

At about the same time, New Public Management (NPM) ideas became popular. In a nutshell, NPM seeks to apply private sector principles and management styles to the public sector. NPM comprises a fragmentation or 'unbundling' of public sector units and services, the introduction of explicit performance standards and measurement, parsimonious resource use (ie cost savings), and greater competition through the introduction of market principles and bringing in new providers, including from the private sector (Hood, 1991). Ideas of marketisation in the UK public sector, including the NHS, were also promoted by trends towards welfare 'consumerism' and 'choice' as a way to increase health service responsiveness (Farnsworth, 2006; Greener, 2008).

Regarding the NHS, the aim was to introduce 'a patient-led service' to improve quality and value for money (Hewitt, 2007). Hewitt (2007), then Secretary of State for Health, praised the entrepreneurial spirit arising from competition and the potential to generate 'the quality and efficiency that the public are looking for'. 'Entrepreneurial' GPs were seen as the future of primary care provision in the UK. The concept of welfare entrepreneurs is but one example of how the new welfare state is intended to be more innovative, dynamic, business-like, market-friendly and responsive to its service users than the old 'paternalistic' welfare state (Jenson, 2011). Central features of the new 'entrepreneurial' welfare state were the use of competition as a means to improve service quality and the empowerment of service users by turning them from passive 'welfare clients' into active 'welfare consumers'. It is assumed not only that the private sector is more responsive to consumer wishes and more efficient in delivering corresponding services, but also that service users see themselves as customers who want choice (Shaw, 2009).

Concerns about a National Health Service market and suggestions to mitigate them

There are, however, widespread concerns about patient care, costs, accountability and fragmentation of services when commercial providers are allowed to compete as providers of public services (Pollock and Price, 2006; Salisbury, 2008). Two particular risks of introducing profit-oriented providers into health care are cream-skimming, that is, providers trying to select only the low-risk/high-profit patients for treatment, and quality-shirking. The vast literature on this topic also reminds us that certain conditions need to be met for markets to work, and that these are difficult to meet in relation to public goods such as health care (Greener, 2008; LeGrand et al, 2008; Crouch, 2011; Barr, 2012).

While GPs could set up their business as they wished, both the New Labour and the current Coalition governments have been supporting entrepreneurship in the form of third sector organisations that sit between the public and private sector to counteract some of the mentioned concerns. The third sector includes voluntary or charitable organisations but also so-called social enterprises, that is, a diverse range of ventures operating as self-sustaining, profit-making businesses but using their profits for a social purpose rather than for private reward. While these are seen as innovators just as other entrepreneurs, in welfare markets, these have the added advantage of instilling trust in their business conduct due to their defining non-distribution constraint and 'social mission' (Hansmann, 1980). Trust is pivotal in markets, such as health care, that are characterised by huge information asymmetries between providers and consumers, that is, under conditions where there is the possibility that profit-oriented firms would decrease quality or demand inflated prices in order to increase manager salaries or dividends for shareholders (Toepfler and Anheier, 2010).

NHS primary care marketisation since the 1990s

In relation to the NHS, the application of NPM principles meant the introduction of contracts to incentivise particular medical services and the creation of an internal market. As a consequence, a number of services were outsourced (initially limited, however, to the provision of auxiliary services such as catering and cleaning). In relation to primary care, it was the NHS and Community Care Act 1990 that first introduced a range of market mechanisms. Most importantly, it created the system of GP fundholding, in which GPs, who signed up voluntarily for the system, purchased services for their patients from hospitals who had to compete for the GPs' custom.

Although the incoming New Labour government in 1997 initially abolished the internal market and GP fundholding, the purchaser–provider split remained as newly created local arms of the Department of Health called Primary Care Trusts (PCTs) commissioned health care from NHS providers. Based on NPM principles, New Labour focused on improving facilities and quality of care by setting national standards, offering pay incentives through the achievement of various target indicators, extending the private sector's role in the NHS and creating a new GP contract (DH, 2000).

The contractual changes encouraging the entry of new providers

The General Medical Services (GMS) contract introduced in 2004 distinguishes between four types of services: essential, additional, out-of-hours and enhanced services (the latter comprising services that were formerly provided in hospitals, eg, diagnostic tests) (DH, 2008b; National Archives, 2004). The new GMS contract thus offers flexibility in the range of services provided by comprising a limited core service that can be topped up with locally negotiated additional elements. These additional services constituted an entry point into primary care for new providers (Pollock and Price, 2006). In addition, many GPs chose to opt out of evening and weekend provision under the terms of the new contract (by 2012, only 10% of practices retained their out-of-hours responsibilities; see NHSCB, 2012b, p 27) and thus created a particular niche for new market entrants accredited by the Department of Health to deliver these services.

The breaking up the GPs' primary care monopoly by new providers has been enabled not only by the fragmentation of the standard GMS contract, but also by the introduction of three alternative contract forms known as Personal Medical Services (PMS), Primary Care Trust Medical Services (PCTMS) and Alternative Provider Medical Services (APMS). PMS contracts had already been launched in 1998 to allow a more tailored, local specification of services for specific populations, for example, homeless patients. Currently, around 44% of primary medical services are provided through PMS contracts (NHSCB, 2012b, p 26). PCTMS enabled PCTs to employ GPs directly on a salary. APMS permits GP services to be delivered by a wider range of agencies, including not only GPs, but also the commercial sector and third sector organisations such as so-called 'social enterprises', as long as they meet the provider conditions set by the Department of Health (DH, 2009).

APMS contracts allowed PCTs substantial freedom in the development of contracts and service specifications. This flexibility and the easing of market entry for providers outside the NHS were intended to provide patients with greater choice, convenience and improved access, and more responsive services to particular groups. In particular, the provision for poorly served populations ('under-doctored areas') was to be improved. Finally, it was designed to relieve pressure on hospitals by moving services from hospitals 'into the community' (DH, 2009).

APMS contracts received a significant boost in May 2008 with the launch of the 'Equitable Access to Primary Medical Care' (EAPMC) programme. The aim was to introduce at least 100 new surgeries in the 25% of PCTs with the poorest provision as well as one GP-led health centre ('polyclinic') in each PCT. APMS was the recommended contracting route for EAPMC procurements (DH, 2008a).

Significant extra investment was made available for new providers of primary care to enable competition and provider diversity. A Third Sector Commissioning Task Force was established in 2005 (Third Sector Commissioning Task Force, 2006). In addition, a number of Department of Health programmes offered funding for social enterprises in order to achieve 'a level playing field' for these organisations in the face of competition from the established NHS providers and much larger and commercially more experienced for-profit providers (DH, 2006, pp 175–6). The Conservative–Liberal Coalition government has been continuing to provide capital for social enterprises with the aim 'to create the largest social enterprise sector in the world' (DH, 2010a, p 5).

Hypotheses around market behaviour in primary care and early evidence

While there was a clear intent of subsequent governments to strengthen the third sector and 'entrepreneurial GPs', the literature on emergent markets identifies a number of obstacles for new and relatively small provider organisations. It postulates that incumbents could 'fight off competitors by either undercutting their prices, using various tools to resist competitors' entry into the market, or coopting competitors by copying them or buying them out' (Fligstein and Dauter, 2007, p 18). Firms exploiting 'first-mover advantages' are likely to come from nearby markets. Particularly at the beginning of market-opening processes, there would be a high rate of failure as firms have many resource dependencies that make survival difficult. Yet, companies could use their social relationships with larger corporate entities or governments to build coalitions that can produce a stable market and state regulation can influence the outcomes of emergent markets (Fligstein, 1996).

Larger firms will use their size, access to governments and other resources to hold challengers at bay and sustain their advantage in a given market over time (Fligstein, 1996; Fligstein and Dauter, 2007). There are some serious doubts as to how realistic it is for smaller organisations, such as from the third sector or local GPs, to achieve success when contracts are awarded on the basis of competitive tendering. Putting together a bid capable of winning requires substantial financial, legal and operational expertise, as well as time, and implementation often incurs a high risk of initial loss-making (Reynolds and McKee, 2012).

Early research evidence on the use of APMS contracts and the entry of new primary care providers was contradictory. Some surveys suggested a low take-up by PCTs of APMS contracts but found that more than two thirds of contracts were won by 'entrepreneurial' GPs (Walsh et al, 2007; Middlemiss, 2008). However, a survey in 2008 found that although half of the bids for APMS tenders came from GPs, 91% of contracts were awarded to private firms (Iacobucci, 2008). This contradiction was due to the emergence of hybrid provider organisations, led by GPs or other health care professionals, but operating as private limited companies (Ellins et al, 2008; Heins et al, 2009). Depending on the classification of such GP-led commercial undertakings, the message was ambiguous: either GPs seem to be doing relatively well in the new market or they are facing the threat of being sidelined by commercial companies.

A clear assessment of how successful entrepreneurial GPs are has, to date, been difficult because contract award data are not collected centrally by the Department of Health. Often, the figures rely on ad hoc surveys by health care practitioner journals without any specified methodology, rendering the reliability and robustness of the data doubtful. In the absence of routine data about the providers of APMS contracts, Heins et al (2009) as well as the NHS Support Federation (2010) surveyed all English PCTs under the Freedom of Information Act. Heins et al (2009) found that more than half of the 71 APMS contracts on which information could be obtained – in fact, the disclosure of data was an emerging issue of concern – went to commercial providers and GPs often only won contracts when they competed among themselves or had no competitors at all. Notably, the APMS contract share of third sector organisations was minimal at under 10% (Heins et al, 2009, Table 3). The exception was out-of-hours care, where non-profit organisations often emerged out of pre-existing GP cooperatives covering defined local areas and could exploit there status as incumbents.

The NHS Support Federation yielded very similar results. This more recent study, moreover, indicates a substantial increase in private sector provision since the previous comprehensive analysis. It found that there were 227 GP surgeries run by 23 different commercial primary care providers in 2010. It also confirmed the often-misleading status of some companies classified as 'GP-led'. Many of the commercial companies are managed by GPs, but have a profit-making intent and a traditional corporate management structure unlike traditional NHS practices. They found 18 companies started by locally operating GPs that turned to considerable nationwide business expansion (NHS Support Federation, 2010, p 1).

One company that arose from a GP cooperative background is Harmoni, which subsequently, backed by private equity investors, became the largest independent sector provider of out-of-hours care in the UK with a patient population of 8 million by 2011. The portfolio of Harmoni extended from out-of-hours services to GP-led health centres (introduced under the EAPMC initiative) and prison health care services (Laing & Buisson, 2012). While this is considered a typical portfolio for the new players in the English primary care market, the second largest for-profit provider of primary care, The Practice Plc, with estimated revenues of £45 million in 2011, is exceptional in that its activities not only include eight EAPMC health centres on the basis of APMS contracts, but also 60 general practices on national GMS and PMS contracts (Laing & Buisson, 2012, p 23).

The Practice Plc is expanding through buying up practices from competitors, for example, Chilvers & McCrea, one of the early market leaders in independent sector primary care provision, and UnitedHealth, a large health care multinational who withdrew from primary care provision after a few years. Two providers, namely, Harmoni and Virgin Care (belonging to the venture capital conglomerate Virgin Group Ltd), are expanding their market share by offering local GPs the expertise of their vast companies through joint ventures or franchising opportunities. This represents an example of the above-mentioned strategy of co-opting competitors.

In line with the previously stated hypotheses about emergent markets (Fligstein, 1996; Fligstein and Dauter, 2007), competitors to existing GPs came from nearby markets, either primary care markets outside the UK or from neighbouring sectors within the UK, for example, social or long-term care, which have already had experience of marketisation.

Larger companies and first-movers could exploit some advantages and grew their primary care businesses relatively quickly. The fact that the formally GP-led company The Practice Plc has become the market leader, and has even taken over surgeries from the health care giant UnitedHealth, which withdrew from primary care provision altogether (Dowler, 2011), is an interesting development in this respect.

However, what seems to be at first sight a notable success of a home-grown British business over a huge multinational is an ambivalent development for several reasons. First, UnitedHealth officially withdrew from primary care provision to focus on commissioning support (Dowler, 2011); hence, the decision has to be understood as a strategic move in order to avoid any likely conflicts of interest as being both a commissioner and provider of primary care services. The company signed a contract with the Department of Health in 2010 to advise PCTs on commissioning ahead of the White Paper that proposed moving commissioning responsibility to GPs. In October 2010, UnitedHealth was involved in launching the first guide for GP commissioning in reaction to the White Paper (NAPC, 2010). Arguably, the control over the spending function of the NHS is more promising for a big company with excellent connections to the Department of Health and offers much more control over the whole NHS than simply running GP practices.

Moreover, as previously hypothesised, the first tenders of UnitedHealth in the mid-2000s were won by considerably underbidding the price of other competitors. In other words, these early practices were functioning as loss-leaders in order to gain early market dominance, which had to be balanced out by other more profitable activities of the company. With only six practices running after five years though, the primary care experiment seemed to be a costly failure. The general expert view is that primary care businesses require a large, multi-contract operation that can offer the necessary administrative and managerial infrastructure and economies of scale to thrive in the new market (Ireland, 2011).

Despite the amount of tenders won by the commercial sector after the roll-out of the EAPMC programme in 2008/09, only around 2% of primary care practices were in the hands of commercial companies (Laing & Buisson, 2012). Market analysts Laing & Buisson (2012, p 23) thus came to the conclusion that NHS-funded primary medical care remains very largely a 'closed shop of locally based independent practices'. However, this is likely to change soon due to the reforms introduced by the Coalition government that allow 'any qualified provider' to bid for all GP services.

The Health and Social Care Act 2012

The latest NHS reforms were first outlined in a White Paper in July 2010 (DH, 2010a) and became law in March 2012 (Health and Social Care Act 2012). Given the immense public concern around the proposed measures, the passage of the Bill was anything but straightforward (Pollock et al, 2012; Ruane, 2012). The Act was widely perceived as the most radical reform of the NHS since its inception and even led to the founding of a new political party (National Health Action Party [NHA]) in November 2012 by a group of health professionals campaigning strongly against the Act.[1]

The Health and Social Care Act fundamentally reorganises the way care is commissioned within the NHS. Among the most controversial changes is the abolition of all 151 PCTs in England and their replacement with 211 independent statutory bodies called Clinical Commissioning Groups (CCGs). In the run-up to the Health and Social Care Act, each GP practice in England had to join one of the CCGs who, from April 2013 on, are responsible for the commissioning of hospital care, mental health services and community services.[2] CCGs have to be approved and are overseen by the independent NHS Commissioning Board (NHSCB) established in 2011 and taking on full functions in April 2013. This 'arm's length body' allocates resources and provides commissioning guidance to CCGs, reviews the performances of individual practices, and holds them to account (NHSCB, 2012b, p 19), but CCGs are 'directly responsible for commissioning services they consider appropriate to meet reasonable local needs' and they 'will have the freedom to pursue innovative approaches to delivering care' to improve outcomes for patients (DH, 2012a).

The rationale behind the reform is to 'put GPs in the driving seat' as they are seen as best placed to understand the needs of their patients and local communities. Andrew Lansley, then Health Secretary, who oversaw the implementation of the Health and Social Care Act, emphasised the benefits that local decision-making and clinical leadership would bring:

> The Health and Social Care Act will deliver more power to clinicians, it will put patients at the heart of the NHS, and it will reduce the costs of bureaucracy. We now have an opportunity to secure clinical leadership to deliver improving quality and outcomes. (DH, 2012b)

This means that GPs will be in control of up to £65 billion of the £95 billion NHSCB's budget to design health services for their local area. In order to avoid obvious conflicts of interest, primary care services (GP, dentists, specialist services) will be commissioned by the NHSCB itself, which has the powers to make contractual arrangements 'with any willing provider' (later rephrased to 'any qualified provider') of primary care that meets NHS standards and prices (DH, 2010c). Providers will be licensed by Monitor, the regulator of all NHS services in England. In other words, competitive tendering with the requirement to abide by UK and EU competition law will not be the exceptional alternative, as under APMS contracts, but will become the norm, thus significantly increasing the potential for commercial sector provision.

Competition is assumed to reach new heights as patients will be able to choose their GP regardless of location under the principle of 'money following the patient' (DH, 2010a). Importantly, while patients now have the freedom to choose a GP outside their local area, CCGs, in turn, do not have to secure all health services for everyone living in a defined geographical area, as was the duty of PCTs. This implies the potential exclusion of people from free NHS services except emergency care (Pollock et al, 2012).

Implications of the Act for commissioning and primary care provision

The Department of Health (DH, 2010b) expects GP practices to do most commissioning themselves, but highlights that they will be free to contract this out to independent sector providers. Crucially, the reforms take place against the backdrop of the current financial climate. While the Department of Health has had its overall budget protected from cuts and is thus in a favourable position compared to other government departments, the English NHS, which takes up the vast bulk of the health budget, has been required to save up to £20 billion by 2014/15 to help it cope with increasing pressures from population ageing, lifestyle-related diseases and rising drugs prices (DH, 2010a). Hence, GPs have to take on responsibility for rationing.

There is considerable scepticism as to the readiness of GPs to take on these managerial functions (Mays, 2011, p 201). As the experience with GP fundholding in the 1990s revealed, most GPs did not have a strong interest in the management side of running a practice and were rather worried about the administrative burden this entailed (Surender and Fitzpatrick, 1999). Research has highlighted that contracting skills are still underdeveloped in the NHS (Petsoulas et al, 2011) and a survey of GPs in 2010 found that most were not confident about their commissioning skills (Ireland, 2010). Hence, GP commissioners will need external support in this new role (Naylor and Goodwin, 2010). UnitedHealth is already taking advantage of this business opportunity (UnitedHealth UK, 2012).

The NHSCB acknowledges that doctors should focus on their strengths as clinicians and may need support for the non-clinical elements of commissioning. It explicitly mentions the independent sector as a potential supplier of commissioning support (NHSCB, 2012a, pp 3–4). In addition, outgoing PCTs have been asked to manage the transition to the new structures and the ex-NHS commissioners have been encouraged to set up their own social enterprises to provide commissioning services to the NHS under a 'Right to Provide' scheme (Provider Development Directorate and Social Enterprise Unit, 2011). Lansley announced in March 2011 that the government will make an extra £10 million available through the Social Enterprise Investment Fund to support NHS staff wishing to set up social enterprises (DH, 2011). The reform thus relies on the outsourcing of commissioning from the public sector to ex-public sector workers who are asked to take on responsibilities and risks that formerly lay with statutory bodies. If these social enterprises fail, the strategy ultimately relies on the availability of commercial providers to fill any gaps in the commissioning role now given to GPs.

Only around 2% of English GP practices are currently run by the independent sector but the landscape is very likely to change towards increased marketisation and privatisation due to the passing of the Health and Social Care Act. As evidence from abroad demonstrates, growth in private providers is often only incremental after the initial legislation to allow for private competition, yet can lead to a transformation of a system like the NHS in the longer term (Blomqvist, 2004). A health market analysis estimated in autumn 2012 that a £20 billion opportunity for private companies is opening up (Catalyst Corporate Finance, 2012). With the handover of commissioning responsibilities to GP consortia and the extension of competition through the 'any qualified provider' approach, the NHS might over time turn into a 'financing-only mechanism that will contract for care with providers while remaining indifferent to their ownership' (Greer and Rauscher, 2011, p 811).

Greater private sector involvement in the future is also more likely as many practices that were run directly by now-abolished PCTs are being re-tendered, with private firms dominating the award of initial contracts

(*Pulse*, 24 August 2011). Given the high set-up costs of tendering for NHS contracts and the non-clinical expertise required to compile viable bids, it is not surprising that it is mainly large-scale companies that are dominating the market at the expense of smaller third sector organisations or independent GP groups.

Private oligopolies could be replacing the public monopoly of the NHS: third sector and social enterprises, heavily affected by government cuts despite the ambitions to promote them, stand little chance when tendering against companies with a wide expertise in drafting tenders and a growing track record of public-service contracts (Reynolds and McKee, 2012; Williams, 2012). The rate of outsourcing of public sector services is at its highest since the 1980s (Plimmer and Warrell, 2012). This implies the risk that a small number of companies gain a large share of the market and can thus negotiate contracts in their favour (Williams, 2012).

The distinction between GP-led and commercial providers is becoming increasingly blurred. Some nominally 'GP-led' primary care companies have expanded so much through mergers and takeovers that they have more in common with large health care corporations than small GP-led companies. They also display other firm behaviour typical of larger corporations. For example, they divert into other health care activities, take over practices or sell their business to other companies if the opportunity is there. Most spectacular so far, Harmoni, the biggest out-of-hours provider in England, which originated as a local GP cooperative, was bought in November 2012 by the private company Care UK for £48 million. Harmoni had just won 12 contracts to run the new '111' non-urgent health assistance phone line, beating off competition from NHS Direct, the current state-backed provider (Ramesh, 2012).

They also employ other doctors, and, importantly, often less-qualified and thus cheaper health care staff, on salaries[3] and close practices when these are not profitable enough (Lawrence, 2012). This trend is accompanied by increasing tensions within the profession between the self-employed and the growing number of salaried GPs. While practice-owning GPs are independent providers to the NHS, they usually have a long-term commitment to their practice and the area they work in. GPs working on salary will not have such commitments or, even if they have, carry the risk of being made redundant if the business is not going well. This has significant implications for the continuity of care, particularly for patients with long-standing diseases.

While salaried employment might be attractive for those doctors who do not want to take on the managerial responsibility of a partner in a practice and prefer the flexibility their status entails, there are some disadvantages connected with their position. Whether the contractor they work for has NHS Health Service Body status or not has important implications for staff terms and conditions as only contracts with companies with NHS status can offer NHS pensions and other nationally regulated benefits (Lind, 2013).

Many of the new 'innovative' firms are actively advertising services that are not covered by the NHS, such as vaccinations for patients not members of specifically defined high-risk groups or individual health checks. The break-up of the GP contract and the related question of how to define essential versus non-essential services bears the risk that, in the future, more treatments will be considered 'extras' only available for a fee.

Finally, conflicts of interest between GPs as both providers of services and commissioners are likely to increase in the context of moving more and more treatments from hospital into primary care (Mays, 2011, p 202).

Conclusions

The year 2012/13 has been a year of transition for the NHS towards more marketisation. The reasoning behind the introduction of a market in primary care was to improve access to services in poorly served areas, grant patient choice and achieve more efficient and innovative provision, resulting from competition and incentive-setting. A verdict on whether efficiency has been increased or quality has been changed (either for the better, as predicted by neoclassical economic theory, or for the worse, as feared by critics) is not possible due to the novelty of these policy changes. However, the experience with the APMS contracting route has shown that it was the commercial sector that picked up a large share of the emerging market, although the expectation is that it will mainly be 'entrepreneurial' GPs who will revitalise the NHS.

It is increasingly difficult to classify some nominally GP-led companies as such as they are behaving very similarly to large commercial health care companies. This is not surprising given that when the market rules, an organisation better adapts to these rules in order to secure market survival. There is an indication that primary care, which used to be solely organised as small surgeries run either single-handedly or by a few partners, is turning into big business. While the market share of independent sector providers within the whole of NHS primary care is still small, the latest NHS reforms of the Coalition government make it likely that this is going to increase significantly soon, be it through service provision or commissioning. The implications include the ousting of public and third sector organisations with consequences for public accountability and transparency.

Another area that deserves careful attention in the future is the development of private primary care outside the NHS. It is likely that private practice will be on the rise if the NHS is starved of cash and services deteriorate to an extent that large parts of the population feel that the service they are getting is not good enough anymore. For instance, private GP clinics advertise their services with the promise of offering instant and longer-lasting appointments than in the NHS (eg www.doctorsdirect.co.uk). If many wealthier parts of society are indeed opting out of public primary care, then this service would actually follow a path that has been taken by many other welfare sectors before, such as education, housing or dentistry, leading away from a publicly funded universal welfare service. In the light of the ongoing marketisation, the NHS risks becoming little more than a logo.

Notes

[1.] The NHA aims to field candidates in up to 50 constituencies against MPs who backed the controversial health bill, including high-profile politicians such as David Cameron and Andrew Lansley.

[2.] Every CCG must have a governing body with decision-making powers. This must include at least two lay members – one with a lead role in championing patient and public involvement and the other with a lead role in overseeing key elements of governance. The governing body must also include at least one registered nurse and one doctor from secondary care, although in order for there to be no conflict of interest, these individuals must not be employed by a local provider. Governing bodies' meetings will be public.

[3.] By September 2011, the number of salaried GPs in England who are employed by another GP, an independent sector company or the NHS directly has increased to 8,858 (21%). This represents an average annual increase of 25.8% since 2001 (see: https://catalogue.ic.nhs.uk/publications/workforce/numbers/nhs-staf-2001-2011-gene-prac/nhs-staf-2001-2011-gene-prac-work-rep.pdf).

References

Barr, N. (2012) *The economics of the welfare state* (5th edn), Oxford: Oxford University Press.

Bartlett, W. and Le Grand, J. (1993) 'The theory of quasi-markets', in J. Le Grand and W. Bartlett (eds) *Quasi-markets and social policy*, Basingstoke: Macmillan Press, pp 13–34.

Blomqvist, P. (2004) 'The choice revolution: privatization of Swedish welfare services in the 1990s', *Social Policy & Administration*, vol 38, no 2, pp 139–55.

Catalyst Corporate Finance (2012) 'Healthcare services sector M&A update', www.catalystcf.co.uk/uploads/Catalyst_Healthcare_2012.pdf

Crouch, C. (2011) *The strange non-death of neoliberalism*, Cambridge: Polity.

DH (Department of Health) (2000) *The NHS Plan: a plan for investment, a plan for reform*, London: HMSO.

DH (2006) *Our health, our care, our say: a new direction for community services*, Cm 6737, London: HMSO.

DH (2008a) 'Equitable Access to Primary Medical Care services (EAPMC): procurement at PCTs. Version 1 (1 February 2008)', www.dh.gov.uk/en/Procurementandproposals/Procurement/ProcurementatPCTs/index.htm

DH (2008b) 'Standard General Medical Services contract', www.dh.gov.uk/en/Healthcare/Primarycare/Primarycarecontracting/GMS/DH_4125638

DH (2009) 'Alternative Provider Medical Services (APMS) guidance', http://webarchive.nationalarchives.gov.uk/+/www.dh.gov.uk/en/Healthcare/Primarycare/Primarycarecontracting/APMS/DH_4125918

DH (2010a) *Equity and excellence: liberating the NHS*, Cm7881, London: Department of Health.

DH (2010b) 'Liberating the NHS: commissioning for patients', www.dh.gov.uk/en/Consultations/Liveconsultations/DH_117587

DH (2010c) 'Principles and rules for cooperation and competition', www.dh.gov.uk/prod_consum_dh/groups/dh_digitalassets/@dh/@en/@ps/documents/digitalasset/dh_118220.pdf

DH (2011) 'Social Enterprise Fund', http://webarchive.nationalarchives.gov.uk/+/www.dh.gov.uk/en/Managingyourorganisation/Socialenterprise/SocialEnterpriseInvestmentFund/index.htm

DH (2012a) 'Factsheet B1', www.dh.gov.uk/healthandsocialcarebill

DH (2012b) 'Health and Social Care Bill gains Royal Assent', www.dh.gov.uk/health/2012/03/royalassent/

Dowler, C. (2011) 'UnitedHealth pulls out of UK primary care provision', *Health Services Journal*, 20 April.

Ellins, J., Ham, C. and Parker, H. (2008) 'Choice and competition in primary care: much ado about nothing?', HSMC policy paper 2, University of Birmingham.

Farnsworth, K. (2006) 'Capital to the rescue? New Labour's business solutions to old welfare problems', *Critical Social Policy*, vol 26, no 4, pp 817–42.

Fligstein, N. (1996) 'Markets as politics: a political-cultural approach to market institutions', *American Sociological Review*, vol 61, no 4, pp 656–73.

Fligstein, N. and Dauter, L. (2007) 'The sociology of markets', *Annual Review of Sociology*, vol 33, no 6, pp 1–24.

GPonline (2010) 'Editorial: Reform puts GPs in the driving seat of the NHS', *GPonline*, 22 July.

Greener, I. (2008) 'Markets in the public sector: when do they work, and what do we do when they don't?', *Policy & Politics*, vol 36, no 1, pp 93–108.

Greer, S. and Rauscher, S. (2011) 'When does market-making make markets? EU health services policy at work in the United Kingdom and Germany', *Journal of Common Market Studies*, vol 49, no 4, pp 797–822.

Hansmann, H.B. (1980) 'The role of nonprofit enterprise', *Yale Law Journal*, vol 89, no 5, pp 835–901.

Heins, E., Pollock, A.M. and Price, D. (2009) 'The commercialization of GP services: a survey of APMS contracts and new GP ownership', *British Journal of General Practice*, vol 59, no 567, pp 750–3.

Hewitt, P. (2007) 'Commissioning new providers. Speech by Rt Hon Patricia Hewitt MP, Secretary of State for Health, 20 February 2007', www.dh.gov.uk/en/News/Speeches/DH_074569

Hood, C. (1991) 'A public management for all seasons?', *Public Administration*, vol 69, no 1, pp 3–19.

Iacobucci, G. (2008) 'Exclusive: PCTs favouring firms over GPs on APMS tenders', *Pulse*, 29 January.

Ireland, T. (2010) 'Private firms eye changing NHS', *GPonline*, 5 August.

Ireland, T. (2011) 'Stunted growth', *Health Investor*, vol 8, no 4, pp 27–8.

Jenson, J. (2011) 'Redesigning citizenship regimes after neoliberalism. Moving towards social investment', in N. Morel, B. Palier and J. Palms (eds) *Towards a social investment welfare state? Ideas, policies and challenges*, Bristol: Policy Press, pp 61–87.

Korpi, W. (1985) 'Economic growth and the welfare state: leaky bucket or irrigation system?', *European Sociological Review*, vol 1, no 2, pp 97–118.

Laing & Buisson (2012) *The role of private equity in UK health & care services*, London: Laing & Buisson Ltd.

Lawrence, F. (2012) 'When privatisation of GP practices goes wrong', *The Guardian*, 19 December.

LeGrand, J., Propper, C. and Smith, S. (2008) *The economics of social problems* (4th edn), Houndmills, Basingstoke: Palgrave Macmillan.

Lind, S. (2013) 'Ex-NHS staff able to access NHS pension scheme, DH confirms', *Pulse*, 26 February 2013.

Mays, N. (2011) 'The English NHS as a market: challenges for the Coalition government', in C. Holden, M. Kilkey and G. Ramia (eds) *Social policy review 23: analysis and debate in social policy, 2011*, Bristol: Policy Press, pp 185–205.

Middlemiss, P. (2008) 'GPs win 70% of APMS contracts', *GPonline*, 23 January.

NAPC (National Association of Primary Care) (2010) 'National Association of Primary Care (NAPC) and UnitedHealth UK launch first how-to guide for GP consortia', press release, NAPC, London.

National Archives (2004) 'National Health Service (General Medical Services Contracts) regulations 2004', www.opsi.gov.uk/si/si2004/20040291.htm

Naylor, C. and Goodwin, N. (2010) *Building high-quality commissioning. What role can external organisations play?*, London: The King's Fund.

NHSCB (NHS Commissioning Board) (2012a) 'Developing commissioning support. Towards service excellence', http://data.parliament.uk/DepositedPapers/Files/DEP2012-0954/PQ111107.pdf

NHSCB (2012b) 'Securing excellence in commissioning primary care', www.commissioningboard.nhs.uk/files/2012/06/ex-comm-pc.pdf

NHS Support Federation (2010) *NHS unlimited? Who runs our GP services*, Brighton: NHS Support Federation.

Petsoulas, C., Allen, P., Hughes, D., Vincent-Jones, P. and Roberts, D. (2011) 'The use of standard contracts in the English National Health Service: a case study analysis', *Social Science & Medicine*, vol 73, no 2, pp 185–92.

Plimmer, G. and Warrell, H. (2012) 'Biggest wave of UK outsourcing since '80s', *Financial Times*, 16 July.

Pollock, A.M. and Price, D. (2006) 'Privatising primary care', *British Journal of General Practice*, vol 56, no 529, pp 565–6.

Pollock, A.M., Price, D., Viebrock, E., Miller, E. and Watt, G. (2007) 'The market in primary care', *British Medical Journal*, vol 335, no 7618, pp 475–7.

Pollock, A.M., Price, D., Roderick, P., Treuherz, T., McCoy, D., McKee, M. and Reynolds, L. (2012) 'How the Health and Social Care Bill 2011 would end entitlement to comprehensive health care in England', *The Lancet*, vol 379, no 9814, pp 387–9.

Provider Development Directorate and Social Enterprise Unit (2011) *Making quality your business: a guide to the right to provide*, London: Department of Health.

Pulse (2011) 'Private firms snap up PCT-run GP practices', *Pulse*, 24 August.

Ramesh, R. (2012) 'Healthcare sell-off makes GPs millions', *The Guardian*, 9 November.

Reynolds, L. and McKee, M. (2012) '"Any qualified provider" in NHS reforms: but who will qualify?', *The Lancet*, vol 379, no 9821, pp 1083–4.

Ruane, S. (2012) 'Division and opposition: the Health and Social Care Bill 2011', in M. Kilkey, G. Ramia and K. Farnsworth (eds) *Social policy review 24: analysis and debate in social policy, 2012*, Bristol: Policy Press, pp 97–114.

Salisbury, C. (2008) 'The involvement of private companies in NHS general practice', *British Medical Journal*, vol 336, no 7641, pp 400-1

Shaw, E. (2009) 'The consumer and New Labour: the consumer as king?', in R. Simmons, M. Powell and I. Greener (eds) *The consumer in public services: choice, values and difference*, Bristol: Policy Press, pp 19–38.

Surender, R. and Fitzpatrick, R. (1999) 'Will doctors manage? Lessons from GP fundholding', *Policy & Politics*, vol 27, no 4, pp 491–502.

Third Sector Commissioning Task Force (2006) *No excuses. Embrace partnership now. Step towards change! Report of the Third Sector Commissioning Task Force*, London: Department of Health.

Toepfler, S. and Anheier, H.K. (2010) 'Economic theories of nonprofit sector, economic', in H.K. Anheier and S. Toepler (eds) *International encyclopedia of civil society*, New York, NY: Springer.

UnitedHealth UK (2012) 'Partnership programme', http:// unitedhealthukpartners.co.uk

Walsh, N., Maybin, J. and Lewis, R. (2007) 'So where are the alternative providers in primary care?', *British Journal of Healthcare Management*, vol 13, no 2, pp 43–6.

Williams, Z. (2012) *The shadow state*, London: Social Enterprise UK.

FOUR

Financing later life: pensions, care, housing equity and the new politics of old age

Debora Price and Lynne Livsey

In this chapter we review recent developments in the financing of later life in two key areas: pensions and long-term care. In each policy arena, we observe the dominant hegemony that late life welfare should be provided mainly by the individual from wealth accumulated over the life course, after prudent financial management of income, assets and savings, and by the purchase of financial products and welfare services in competitive or quasi-competitive markets. For this conception of late life welfare to have any policy coherence, citizens must be sufficiently 'financially capable' to make what with hindsight, will have been the 'right' financial decisions for the whole of their adult lives. In the imagination of policy makers, individuals are therefore constructed as malleable subjects who can be 'nudged' and educated to become financially capable, fiscally competent, actuarially aware subjects throughout their lives, despite little empirical evidence that this is so. As a result, a highly individualised system of risk and rewards emerges with the potential to exacerbate social inequalities in later life (Taylor-Gooby, 2012).

The provision of financial information and financial literacy education therefore become essential ingredients of modern governance and governing, and 'Big State' and universal welfare policies are sidelined. One consequence of this is that when policies fail government blames citizens for any difficult financial predicament in which they might find themselves in later life, rather than, for example, demand side problems in labour markets, housing inequalities, social structures, failing markets, exogenous financial factors, or other social inequalities. This 'increasing role of financial motives, financial markets, financial actors and financial institutions in the operation of domestic and international economies' has been termed the 'financialisation' of daily life (Epstein, 2006 quoted in Finlayson, 2009: 401). In pensions and long-term care, the financial services industry is assuming a central role in the welfare reform agenda. This is at a time when financial markets are highly volatile, bank interest rates are close to zero, regulatory confidence in the financial services sector is low and rational actors might legitimately question whether increased privatisation offers a reliable route to fiscal security in retirement.

The chapter begins by examining recent developments in UK pensions policy, before considering parallel developments in the financing of social care in old age. After reviewing the role that housing owned by older people is expected to play in the new politics of later-life finance, we conclude with a discussion of the perceived benefits and risks underpinning these policy reform agendas and the implications for individual welfare in retirement.

Pensions policy

The last few years have been very active for pension reform in the UK. Both Labour and, since 2010, the Conservative-Liberal Democrat Coalition governments have been implementing proposals made by the Pension Commission (2005), which obtained cross-party and stakeholder consensus (Price, 2008). The transition to the new system began in 2010, with one of the major planks of the reform: automatic enrolment into employer pension schemes, rolling out in 2012. The Coalition has also radically reformed public sector pension schemes and proposes new reforms to the state pension. A fourth development, the Retail Distribution Review, has been implemented in financial services with implications for pension provision. Finally, the government has presented a new White Paper (DWP, 2012) aiming to stimulate the private pension sector to exceed the minimum pensions prescribed by law. These reforms will be set out in turn.

Auto-enrolment and the new employer pensions

The pension reforms that have been put in place were designed to halt the forecasted spread of pensioner poverty. The current UK pension (which will be further reformed for future cohorts of pensioners by the new single tier state pension discussed below) is based on: (i) an improved near universal basic state pension, albeit still substantially below the poverty line (£107.45 per week in 2012), (ii) a state second pension that is linked to work histories but that if accrued in full should take people approximately to around the government's minimum income standard, with (iii) adequacy above that level provided by voluntary employer pensions and other private pension investment. Leisering (2012) has called this the 'socialisation' of private pensions, since the government expects private sector pensions to perform basic social welfare functions of providing income adequacy in late life.

Auto-enrolment pensions will be provided by enrolling employees into an employer scheme that meets minimum standards, or, failing that, into a private sector trust-based scheme that has been set up by the government, the National Employment Savings Trust or NEST (NEST, 2013). The contract to administer NEST, worth £1 billion over 10 years, was awarded in 2010 to Tata Consultancy Services[1]. NEST will invest conservatively in diverse funds run by the financial services industry, with defaults for members who do not exercise investment choices. Minimum and maximum contributions from the employer and the employee are prescribed by law, and will be phased in. Employees earning more than £8,605[2] per annum must be enrolled. By 1 October 2018 contributions will be 8% of band earnings (between £5,564 and £42,475 for 2012/13), with 4% from the employee, 3% from the employer and 1% from tax relief. Auto-enrolment is, however, completely voluntary. Members can opt out at any time, but will be re-enrolled every three years, relying heavily on the principles of 'nudge' economics and inertia. In October 2012 the largest employers began the process with the transition phased over 6 years to 1 October 2018. (NEST, 2013).

Pension provision is generally in the form of Direct Benefit (DB) schemes, which pay out a predetermined amount each year in retirement according to some contribution and accrual formula, or Direct Contribution (DC) Schemes where money is accumulated and invested for a period until retirement, when the accumulated fund must be re-invested usually into the purchase of an annuity for life from an insurance provider according to prevailing rates. NEST and most of its alternatives outside the public sector are DC schemes. Consequently, investment performance, charges, and governance of the schemes in terms of how the market works, how the money is managed, how well investments perform, how charges are set, information provided and advice given, become key to the pensions that people accrue. The exclusion of low earners, limits on contributions and inability to transfer funds into the low charging NEST all pose restrictions that favour less efficient, more expensive financial services industry providers and restrict the proper functioning of this new market (HC, 2012)[3].

The Pensions Regulator plays a key role in this multi-billion pound industry – an estimated 9 - 10 billion pounds per annum from 5 - 11 million investors is forecast to divert to pension saving via the financial services sector or NEST (van deVen, 2012).Yet confidence in regulation in the financial services sector is low, and it is unclear how regulation in this new pensions industry will work.There appears to be no convincing theory of competition behind the new structure, since the purchasers of pensions (employers) are not the beneficiaries (employees), and the employer has no financial interest in what kind of pension is delivered ultimately by the scheme to employees, who will often be long gone from their employment. There is thus no convergence of interest in outcome between employer and employee, nor are employees part of the procurement process. They cannot (even theoretically) act as consumer regulators of this market since they have no choice to exit to another provider without almost certainly losing their employer's contribution.

Warnings abound. The National Association of Pension Funds found that for the first time in 2012, lack of trust in finance overtook affordability concerns as the main reason people gave for planning to opt out of auto-enrolment. FairPensions (2012) suggests that employees are vulnerable to conflicts of interests and lack of oversight from intermediaries in the investment chain. The Pensions Institute (2012) warns of high risks that employees will be enrolled into legacy schemes with very high charges and poor returns due to employer ignorance or indifference and market failures.They suggest that ultimate funds accrued could be worth as little as half of the value of an equivalent member in funds with lower charges, suggesting that "the whole auto-enrolment project will eventually lay itself open to accusations of pension mis-selling on a huge scale" (Pensions Institute, 2012: 9).The National Audit Office warned that the Pensions Regulator has inadequate processes in place to measure performance (NAO, 2012). The new Pensions Regulator Chair has indicated that he proposes to tackle the problem of 'dodgy' pension schemes (PP, 2012) although how and with what resources is questionable.The regulator faces the (possibly unachievable) challenge of measuring performance over the time scales and range of factors affecting pension outcomes over a working life.

The reforms have created a complex environment of private pensions, which the vast majority of the public are ill-equipped to manage.Advice will be non-existent for most people, whether in the accumulation stages of their pensions, on opt-out, or the purchase of an annuity. Pension pots for most people will be too small to attract any interest from financial advisers, and also small enough such that the risks associated with poor investment returns are very high (Emmerson and Wakefield, 2009).

Public sector pension reform

The Labour government had already reduced public sector pensions by raising pension age, and changing accrual rates and lump sum benefits. Subsequent projections showed that public liabilities for public sector pensions were expected to fall by 2050, and as a proportion of GDP to remain steady in the shorter term (IPSPC, 2011). However, the Coalition Government instigated further public sector pension decreases by changing annual pension increases from uprating with the Retail Price Index to using a much lower inflation measure that arguably does not reflect inflation experienced by citizens, the Consumer Price Index. This seemingly benign move dramatically reduced the value of public sector pensions since the compound impact over a lifetime is substantial (PPI, 2012b). This was followed by the establishment of the Independent Public Services Pension Commission led by Lord Hutton. Following the Hutton report recommendations (IPSPC, 2011), the government has proposed substantive additional changes in the 2012 Public Service Pensions Bill, including extending retirement age further, changing from final salary to career average pensions, and increasing employee contributions. It is estimated that the proposed reforms will result in a fall in the average value of benefits in the public sector from 23 per cent to 15 per cent of salary[4] (PPI, 2012b).

Despite an initial flurry of political activity by unions and professionals, the Labour Party did not oppose the Bill and neither will the majority of unions. The legislation is expected to pass uneventfully. In an era of substantial concern about future pensioner poverty, we are thus witnessing the significant erosion of the pension rights of more than 5 million public sector workers, without substantive protest or opposition.

The proposed new state pension

Despite initial opposition from the Prime Minister and the Treasury, the Pensions Minister, Steve Webb, a Liberal Democrat MP and free marketeer, has succeeded in introducing long awaited reforms creating a flat rate near universal state pension, thus eradicating perverse incentives in the system that discourage private pension saving through the threat of means testing. A substantial White Paper and Draft Bill were published in January 2013, with confirmation of this reform in the March 2013

Budget (DWP, 2013; HM Treasury 2013). The two parts of the state pension (one flat rate and one earnings-related) will be combined into a single-tier pension set at just above the government's minimum income standard for pensioners, £144 per week at current values, to be brought into effect only for those retiring after April 2016. The ability to opt-out of the State Second Pension under a scheme known as 'contracting out' will close, and National Insurance contributions for all employees formerly opted out will rise.

While those in receipt of pensions prior to the implementation of this proposal will continue to receive their pensions under the current system, these reforms will significantly reduce the risk of means testing for future cohorts of pensioners.

The reforms are intended to be cost neutral. Early analysis of the proposal by the respected Institute of Fiscal Studies (2013) suggests that 'the main effect will be to reduce [state] pensions for the vast majority of people', and that the distributional effects are very complex due to changed eligibility and contribution rates and the abolition of derived pension rights for widows and divorcees[5].

Although these reforms reflect universal ideals, it is important to note that without a guaranteed income base that eradicates the moral hazards of means testing, auto-enrolment, the flagship policy of voluntary private pension saving, cannot work. Thus this reform while granting a near-universal social right, is also essential to the expansion of private sector pensions.

The Retail Distribution Review (RDR)

Meanwhile, the RDR is a key part of the Financial Services Authority's consumer protection strategy (FSA, 2012b), aiming to make the retail investment market more transparent, efficient, and attractive to consumers. From January 2013 all regulated independent financial advisers must declare their charges, levy a fee for services, and may no longer take commission from products. The reforms have important implications for pensions in the new complex markets.

Employers making only the minimum contributions into an auto-enrolled pension scheme may no longer deduct the charges for the advice or services that they receive from the pension pot. For those paying above the minimum, they may deduct the fee but will have to show this on the member's account. Members and unions may be unhappy at these now transparent charges[6]. It is widely predicted that many employers, especially SMEs, will stop taking advice and shop on the internet or from salespeople for compliant schemes without much scrutiny. Alternatively, they will use NEST, which relies heavily on conservative default funds that will be sub-optimal for many people (HC, 2012).

The sector is expected to contract as it is perceived that once customers realise how much they are paying for independent financial advice, they will stop using it, with advice increasingly concentrated at the wealthiest end of the market. Privately[7], concern is being expressed at the growth of a new type of commission sale: a 'non-advice' sale, where the customer 'requests' a particular product and no 'advice' is given. This has potentially created perverse incentives for customers to be sold bad, unsuitable products outside any advice framework. Other attempts to undermine the new regulations in ways that are detrimental for consumers have already come to the attention of the FSA (2012a). The advice gap created means that those of modest means will be poorer still and will be without assistance with financial planning before, on or after retirement.

Re-invigorating workplace pensions

Thus despite all the reforms, the problems of future pensioner poverty and inadequate pension incomes remain. In November 2012, the government published a White Paper (DWP, 2012) suggesting the creation of new "Defined Ambition" pensions implicitly recognising the poor value for money, poor governance and lack of transparency – market failures – that have plagued the industry. The paper seeks financial services industry innovation to provide market based solutions to chronic problems of underfunding in pensions, particularly to share investment and longevity risks between employers and employees on a voluntary basis.

Pension reform

Declines in pension scheme participation have not been the "fault" of employees, but of well documented institutional and policy changes, the erosion of trust as a result of the poor ethical record of the private pensions industry, as well as volatile investment risks and other macro-economic factors, that steadily eroded both state and employer schemes over several decades (PPI, 2012a, Blake, 2000, Ring, 2002).

While the expansion of employer pensions to cover all employees via auto-enrolment is a major private welfare initiative with the potential to improve living standards in retirement, this is in the context of consistent and continuing erosion of other state, public sector and private pension rights. There is an absence of any convincing evidence that the mechanisms employed here to raise household saving – financial incentives, auto-enrolment and financial education – will have lasting effects (Crossley et al., 2012). The pension framework created by government now relies on individuals changing into voluntary, informed, successful savers, as if there were few structural and societal barriers, or exogenous factors, that might prevent this.

The persistent failure of policies that institutionalise competition and the private sector, and depend heavily on financial capability for their regulation, is consistently exposed in empirical research. A recent Department for Work and Pensions Report (MacLeod et al., 2012) found four in ten people with a private pension have no idea what their income will be in retirement, 60 per cent do not feel they know enough to decide how to save for retirement, and more than half of women do not know their state pension age. The Institute of Fiscal Studies (Crawford and Tetlow, 2012) reported that a third of those approaching retirement were unable even to estimate how much income they will receive from their private pension; 40 per cent approaching retirement have given no thought to how to finance retirement and 70 per cent of those purchasing annuities on retirement from non-employer DC funds do not shop around for the best rates. Twenty per cent have no private resources of any kind (including property) for retirement (MacLeod et al., 2012). A recent survey of 250 pension industry experts, with its moral overtones of failed citizen consumers, concluded:

> The general level of financial education is considered to be woefully inadequate. Respondents want to see governments taking a much harder-hitting approach to raising awareness among consumers of all ages, about the importance of taking responsibility for their future. They would also like to see national campaigns, not just to encourage auto-enrolment, but more fundamentally, to encourage people to prepare adequately for their life in retirement. (Aberdeen, 2012: 4)

At the lower end of the income distribution people are most at risk from bad employer pension provision (particularly among private sector smaller and micro-employers), volatile or poor investment returns, interest rate fluctuations, choices that turn out with hindsight to have been poor, and an advice deficit. Almost all of these factors are beyond their control. Their wages are also most likely to be depressed by the new regime, imposing a double penalty if low earners opt out of auto-enrolment (van de Ven, 2012). It remains unclear whether participating in the new pension framework will benefit those who risk means testing in old age or have substantial debt (Price, 2007, 2008, Emmerson and Wakefield, 2009). The ability of the new regulator to protect employees from being enrolled in plans that ultimately turn out to have been poor vehicles for their pension investment is questionable (NAO, 2012). Many low to middle earners will lose out from the levelling down of pension provision to minimum standards, since average contributions by those employers who make them are approximately double those that will be required by auto-enrolment (van de Ven, 2012). Advice will increasingly be hard for ordinary people to access. Public sector employees, many low paid, have had their pension benefits slashed. The state second pension will be abolished, and most people worse off under the proposed reformed system. The social divisions in pension provision have always been profound and for some are being exacerbated by new developments.

Social care in later life

Population ageing is linked to growing demands for long-term care, with older people accounting for around fifty per cent of total government spending on adult social care (Charlesworth and Thorlby, 2012). The challenge of meeting the growing cost of care in later life has dominated policy discussions since the 1990s in a system widely acknowledged as 'failing'. The 1997 Labour Government began a shift from a 'one-size-fits-all' system towards a more personalised consumerist model (Newman et al., 2008, HM Government, 2007, HM Government, 2009b). However, after thirteen years of discussion, Labour failed to implement a new funding settlement for social care in later life (Dickson, 2009).

The Coalition Government in 2010 inherited an under-funded and failing care system with a much criticised 'post-code-lottery' of geographically variable eligibility criteria and charging policies. The current complex funding system for adult social care relies on a means-test administered by local authorities who determine eligibility thresholds and charging policies, taking household assets and income into account. Those with assets below £14,250 are not expected to use their *assets* to pay for care, but may be expected to contribute from income (HM Government, 2012). Those with assets between £14,250 and £23,250 will pay something 'beyond their income'. Those with assets over £23,250 are currently liable for up to the full cost of any care organised by the state. Others, so-called 'self-funders' who don't approach local authorities for an assessment must fund their care costs in full. Housing assets are ignored in local authority means tests for domiciliary care, but included for residential care (Dilnot, 2011).

With their primary focus on deficit reduction, the Coalition dismissed Labour's proposals for free personal care as unaffordable. They established their own independent Commission on Funding of Care and Support chaired by economist, Andrew Dilnot. One of the Commission's key tasks was addressing the growing problems of unlimited care costs and 'asset depletion', with around 40,000 older people each year forced to sell their homes to fund long-term care[8].

In the Coalition Government's 'new' vision for adult social care (DH, 2010) local authorities retain their lead role as 'market-shapers', out-sourcing in-house services and ensuring a diverse market of care provision for individual consumers. However, Labour's complex system of performance targets is unravelled with the Coalition preferring individuals to have a prominent role in regulating care markets through the power of consumer 'choice, voice, and exit' to reward 'good providers' and sideline poor quality operators[9]. After The Law Commission (2011) recommended a simplified legislative framework, in July 2011 the Dilnot Commission (2011) published their much anticipated report.

Dilnot: Fairer Care Funding

The Dilnot report (2011) described the existing funding system as 'not fit for purpose' (p3). However, a fully state-funded system was ruled out. The report proposed a 'new model of shared responsibility' (p21) between the individual and the state, with an emphasis on forward planning by individuals:

> We need a new system so that, instead of being fearful about the financial consequences of needing care, people can plan and prepare for the future (p2) … We want people to start planning earlier because this will allow them to exercise far greater control than if they develop a significant care and support need or face distressing and critical circumstances (p61)

The Dilnot Commission proposed a cap on individual liabilities of between £25,000 and £50,000, with a figure of £35,000 recommended as 'appropriate and fair' (p5). They further proposed increasing the capital eligibility threshold for state-funded support from £23,250 to

£100,000, effectively exempting modest housing assets from the means test. Finally, they suggested, in addition to care costs, people should contribute between £7,000 and £10,000 a year to their living costs in residential care. The estimated costs of their reforms were £2.2 billion in 2015/16 rising to £3.6 billion by 2025/26[10].

Familiar policy prescriptions followed in relation to education, information and innovation that necessarily accompany a model of the self-caring, self-financing individual. Echoing pension debates, the Dilnot Commission identified the lack of financial capability in the public, and looked to the financial services industry to come up with solutions. The Commission's proposals entrenched the political view that the 'pay-back' for policy interventions that encourage the spread of affluence and home-ownership during the working life-course is that citizens should be willing to use their assets to meet income shortfalls and care related costs in later life.

Housing assets and social care in old age

Current generations of retirees are wealthier than their predecessors with levels of home-ownership amongst older people at their highest level in history (HM Government, 2009a). Under these conditions, housing wealth has emerged as a legitimate target for policy interventions that seek to forge a sense of shared responsibility between the individual and the state for funding long term care and ensuring financial security in later life. There is political consensus that housing wealth can and should be used to pay for long-term care[11]. The policy questions centre on how much people should pay and the best mechanisms for drawing housing equity into the care funding pot (Dilnot, 2011, Humphries et al., 2010, HM Government, 2010, HM Government, 2012).

After Dilnot

In July 2011, the Government published a draft Care and Support Bill for consultation , together with a White Paper, 'Caring for our future - reforming care and support' (DH, 2012). The White Paper proposes a national eligibility threshold from April 2015, and emphasises personalised services, user choice and control, early intervention, and integrated working between health and social care. A universal 'deferred' payment scheme will be introduced in April 2015 allowing anyone entering residential care to delay payment for their care until after they (or their spouse) dies. However, deferred payments must be 'cost-neutral' to government and loans against housing equity will carry interest and charges. Local authorities will have a statutory duty to develop and maintain diverse care markets, individuals acquire a new legal right to personal budgets and carers are offered better support.

In a separate progress report on funding (HM Government, 2012), the Government indicated support for the Dilnot funding proposals in principle but did not commit to adopting their suggested threshold figures. Government action was deferred until 2013 while they considered the 'affordability issues' and other 'trade-offs'. This included further consultation with the care sector and financial services industry, reflecting the expanded role that private insurance and personal savings are expected to play in any future funding settlement for adult social care, with the Government stating:

> We will continue to work with stakeholders to consider what the most appropriate level for a cap would be - balancing financial protection for care users, the cost of reform and creating a space for financial services. (HM Government, 2012:23)

From a Government perspective, the financial services industry is clearly entrenched as a partner in the social care reform agenda. Notably, the financial services industry advocated a higher cap than Dilnot of £50,000 because of the perceived incentive needed to stimulate demand for insurance and equity release products and make their involvement commercially worthwhile (HM Government, 2012:29).

The Coalition Government's funding reform

On 11th February 2013, the Government announced their heavily trailed plans to overhaul the funding system for adult social care. Adopting the principles of the Dilnot Commission but presenting higher threshold figures, Jeremy Hunt, Secretary of State for Health, outlined three key changes, with threshold figures modified again in the March 2013 Budget (Hunt, 2013; HM Treasury, 2013).

They key changes are as follows. First, with effect from April 2016, a cap on personal liabilities for care funding of £72,000 will be introduced for anyone of pension age[12]. Second, the upper limit of the means-tested threshold for qualifying for some state funded support with residential care fees will be raised from £23,250 to £118,000. However, it is likely that anyone with assets between £17,500 and £118,000 will probably have to pay some costs on a tapered system for residential care. It seems that housing assets will remain exempt from the means test for domiciliary care, but means tested thresholds for domiciliary care remain unchanged with an upper limit of £23,250. Finally, the Government recommended that individuals requiring residential care should contribute around £12,000 per annum towards 'hotel and accommodation costs' in addition to care costs. Progress towards the £72,000 cap will be monitored by local authorities, and will begin as soon as individuals are formally assessed as having an 'eligible care and support need'[13] (DH, 2013; HM Treasury 2013).

The cost of these reforms is estimated at £1 billion, and will be funded from two sources. The first will be savings arising from the recently announced pensions reforms – the abolition of the state second pension and related increases in National Insurance Contributions from April 2016. The second is the freezing of the inheritance tax threshold at the current level of £325,000 (individuals) and £650,000 (couples) for the next 3 years.

The Government has high hopes that these reforms will be fair and offer 'certainty and peace of mind' to people planning for future care costs in retirement (Hunt, 2013), even though a sum of £72,000 will appear catastrophically high to the vast majority of older people (Price et al., 2013). Public willingness to insure against care costs is assumed, with Jeremy Hunt stating:

> The intention is not that people should have to pay up to [£75,000[14]] for their care costs, but that by creating the certainty that this is the maximum they will have to pay, they can then make provision through insurance or pensions products so that they are covered up to the value of the cap, thereby reducing the risk of selling their home or losing an inheritance that they have worked hard to pass on to their family. (Hunt, Hansard 11 Feb 2013: Column 593)

The Government assumes that, as with other risks of life such as motoring, home and travel insurance, and boiler repairs, pre-paid insurance will buy 'peace of mind' (DH, 2013). However, these other insurances are relatively inexpensive, some are compulsory, and in these markets the 'hard to insure' are persistently let down by the industry. There are many other issues around control of premium costs and assessment of risks, especially for those with long term conditions. Lloyd (2013) has questioned whether the insurance industry is equipped or willing to provide suitable pre-funded policies. Meanwhile, only a small minority of pensioners hold savings and investments of more than £40,000[15], and with a period of austerity forecast, it is not clear how people can be expected to save more in the future (ONS, 2012). Furthermore, Price et al (2013) have demonstrated powerful psycho-social barriers to discussing and planning for care. Families may choose to 'take the risk' of not needing expensive care and face the problem when it arises.

Social care reform and later life

Under the current system, individuals either have such low income and so few assets that they rely on a residualised state care service, or they face a host of financial decisions, from initial savings and asset accumulation to funding home adaptations and selecting and employing domiciliary care staff to engaging with the financial services industry on savings, investment and equity release choices. All this in the absence of well-functioning markets in savings, care provision or insurance, with a dearth of information and advice, and as pension studies have demonstrated, without the capacity to make optimal financial decisions. In the care sphere, they will also now be expected to calculate and act on their actuarial risk of requiring social care – an impossible task for individuals since 25% will spend virtually nothing on social care in a life time, and half will spend between £20 and £50,000. Only 16% will spend more than £75,000 on long-term care (DH, 2013:6). Even if pre-funded insurance products emerge, few will be able to afford the high cost of premiums out of income or savings, if indeed they are insurable. There is no guarantee that personal saving or pension provision will make up the shortfall, meaning that the less wealthy will still be selling their homes to meet care costs (even if the sale is deferred until after they die) and facing large bills for domiciliary care.

There is likely to be increasing polarisation between those who can navigate their way through the complex financial maze with the aid of their own human and social capital and well paid financial advisors, and those who cannot. The latter will spend far more than they should on needs and services, depleting modest assets and incomes. Others will be excluded from the market and instead must rely on an increasingly residualised and poorly functioning state service.

While the Government's proposals are clearly more progressive than the current system and provide some element of pooled risk, those of low and modest means will still be contributing a far greater proportion of their lifetime accumulated wealth than the wealthy to the care system. The element of risk pooling is limited with three quarters of people spending less than £50,000 on lifetime care in any event and a quarter nothing at all. However, as other commentators have warned, while providing some protection to the assets of pensioners owning modestly priced homes, the reform proposals do not address the need to inject a much higher level of public spending into the struggling adult social care system (Humphries, 2013, Lloyd, 2013, ADASS, 2013).

Discussion

Post-War governments facilitated a mass expansion in home ownership through successive policy initiatives (Lowe, 2011). Amongst other functions, these policies reflected political expectations that individuals will accumulate assets and wealth throughout their working life-course and then spend these down in retirement. The state role is thereby reinforced as that of 'enabler', involving institutional and regulatory functions, and not 'universal provider'. The creation of responsible 'actuarial subjects' who assess their own lifetime risks and calculate their finances accordingly over their life course was a government endeavour begun under Thatcher, promoted by the Labour government from 1997 (Clarke, 2005), and continued apace under the Coalition government since 2010.

It is important in this context to note that whether individuals end up with housing equity or pensions is now mostly a geographical accident of where and when they purchased their home, who they worked for and for how long, and what interest rates prevail at key points in their lives such as the day they retire. It has relatively little to do with 'financial capability' or fiscal prudence exercised over their lifetimes. Indeed, many of those who have saved all their lives, having tried to conform to government expectations and behave as prudent financial planners are effectively 'abandoned' saver citizens (Clarke, 2005). They now endure falling interest rates, poor returns on savings and investments, pension scheme failures, terrible annuity rates and capital losses in financial markets, all factors outside their control. Returns on pension investments and savings intended for long term care will be affected by fund growth and average earnings growth, charges, investment returns, and interest rates at and after the point of retirement, none of which is related to individual consumer behaviour.

It is clear that the private sector is firmly established as a key player in the new world of welfare in later life. The government seeks to ensure that any state funded settlement provides sufficient incentive to the financial services industry to develop new products before they commit to policy action. We clearly see this in pensions and now in adult social care, with its related sphere of housing wealth and equity release.

But to what extent is it reasonable for people to trust the financial services industry to design optimal solutions? Regulation has been unsuccessful to date, and markets do not function efficiently, with mis-selling, poor advice, high management fees and overpriced products in the case of pensions, annuities and equity release; or, in case of long-term care insurance, no workable solution has developed despite the growth in the older population. It is easy to imagine people paying large sums into voluntary care insurance schemes to find they cannot access the money when they require support, for example to fund large or small equipment purchases, home adaptations, pay for low-level domestic support with cooking, shopping or cleaning, or to make up income shortfalls in retirement. The risks and calculations in all of these policy spheres are so complex and the profit margins so unpredictable that there is more evidence of product failure than success. In this, citizens are now reliant on government in its capacity as provider of residual state welfare and as regulator of two very complex industries for their future welfare.

There is clearly potential for substantial improvement in old age welfare in both the new pension and care systems. Auto-enrolment may assist many people to a more adequate level of retirement income, but the possible unintended consequences, such as reducing the income of others by 'levelling down', and the exclusion of the low waged in the private sector from supplementing what might become increasingly residualised state pensions, will need to be carefully assessed. Improvements to the state pension will be very welcome, but most people will be worse off under the new system, and the future downward pressure on a state pension that may increasingly be characterised as a benefit rather than a right of social value will also need monitoring. The Government's care reform proposals introduce an element of universalism to the care system that does not currently exist, but this is fairly limited in scope to protecting (to some extent) those with low to moderate housing assets and those with the most extreme care needs. Moreover, increased financialisation of care with competitive care markets and the much greater role for the financial services industry in savings and insurance introduces new unproven elements that may prove socially divisive.

We are therefore witnessing financialisation in three major policy areas for the provision of late life welfare: pensions, social care and housing, with the possibility of increasing privatisation of the National Health Service too. Yet research shows that the public do not have and are not likely to acquire the degree of financial acumen needed to make these new structures work in an optimal way. For late life financial well-being, citizens become increasingly reliant on government in its role as regulator of markets, firms and individuals, in an arena where regulation has hitherto failed to instil confidence. New forms of inequality are likely to emerge as differences in social, human and financial capital lead to marked differentials in the navigation of finances throughout the life course into late old age.

Acknowledgements

We are very grateful to the Economic and Social Research Council for funding this research as part of the project '*Behind Closed Doors: Older Couples and the Management of Household Money*', Research Grant RES-061–25-0090.

Notes

[1] Widely reported in the pension press after an announcement by the Pensions Minister, Steve Webb, e.g. www.creativebenefits.co.uk/news/nest-s-future-under-review/2466/

[2] This is linked to the basic tax threshold currently rising faster than inflation: £9,940 from April 2013.

[3] Although this may be complicated by EU rules on state aid (HC, 2012: 13)

[4] Compared with 10 per cent in private sector DC schemes, but leaving private sector DB schemes now with the highest benefits of all

[5] Contributions must now be made for 35 years rather than 30, derived rights are abolished, increases in state pension ages are brought forward, contracting out of the state pension is abolished with commensurate increases in National Insurance contributions and there are complex transitional arrangements.

[6] Possibly around £350 per employee

[7] Private communications with the author

[8] Currently, approximately 385,000 people are in residential care of whom two thirds are state supported, 1.1million receive care at home with 80 per cent state supported (DH, 2012).

[9] Although, again, the underlying theory of competition is unclear, given the frailty, disability, cognitive impairment, lack of financial literacy and advanced age of many of the proposed consumers

[10] At 2010/11 prices

[11] Although there may be resistance from the public (Price et al., 2013)

[12] A separate (and at the time of writing, unspecified) cap for adults aged 18-64 will be introduced as part of these reforms.

[13] The proposed national eligibility criteria were not available at time of writing

[14] The cap was originally to be £75,000

[15] For example, only 25% of over 85s have more than £30,000 in cash, savings and investments; and only 25% of those aged 65 – 69 have more than £41,000 (ONS, 2012).

References

Aberdeen 2012. *250 expert voices: the future of UK pensions. Pensions Intelligence research report, October 2012*, London, Aberdeen Asset Management.

ADASS 2013. Dilnot Provides Foundation for Wider Social Care Reform. Association of Directors of Adult Social Services, www.adass.org.uk/index.php?option=com_content&view=article&id=905&Itemid=489 (accessed 12-2-13).

Blake, D. 2000. Two decades of pension reform in the UK - what are the implications for occupational pension schemes? *Employee Relations*, 22, 223-245.

Charlesworth, A. and Thorlby, R. 2012. Reforming social care – options for funding. London: The Nuffield Trust.

Clarke, J. 2005. New Labour's citizens: activated, empowered, responsibilized, abandoned? *Critical Social Policy*, 25, 447-463.

Crawford, R. and Tetlow, G. 2012. *Expectations and experiences of retirement in defined contribution pensions: a study of older people in England*. IFS Report no. 73, London, Institute for Fiscal Studies.

Crossley, T., Emmerson, C. and Leicester, A. 2012. *Raising household saving*, London, The British Academy.

DH (Department of Health) 2013. Policy statement on care and support funding reform and legislative requirements, London: Department of Health, www.dh.gov.uk/health/files/2013/02/Policy-statement-on-funding-reform.pdf [accessed 11 February 2013].

DH 2010. *A vision for adult social care – capable communities and active citizens*, London, Department of Health.

DH 2012. *Caring for our future – reforming care and support. Cm 8378* London, Department of Health.

DIckson, N. 2009. Social care – time for political consensus, www.kingsfund.org.uk/blog/2009/07/social-care-time-political-consensus.

Dilnot 2011. *Fairer care funding. The report of the Commission on Funding of Care and Support*. London, Department of Health

DWP (Department for Work and Pensions) 2012. *Reinvigorating workplace pensions*, London, Department for Work and Pensions.

DWP 2013. *The single-tier pension:A simple foundation for saving.* Cm 8528, London, Department for Work and Pensions.

Emmerson, C. and Wakefield, M. 2009. *Amounts and accounts: Reforming private pension enrolment. IFS Commentary C110,* London, Institute for Fiscal Studies.

Epstein, G. A. 2006. Introduction: financialization and the World Economy, in: Epstein, G.A. (ed.) *Financialization and the World Economy.* Cheltenham: Edward Elgar.

FairPensions 2012. *Whose duty? Ensuring effective stewardship in contract-based pensions,* London, FairPensions.

Finlayson, A. 2009. Financialisation, financial literacy and asset-based welfare. *The British Journal of Politics & International Relations,* 11, 400-21.

FSA (Financial Services Authority) 2012a. *Commission ban* [Online]. www.fsa.gov.uk: Financial Services Authority, www.fsa.gov.uk/about/what/rdr/firms/adviser-charging/commission-ban [accessed 4 December 2012].

FSA. 2012b. *Retail Distribution Review* [Online]. www.fsa.gov.uk: Financial Services Authority, www.fsa.gov.uk/about/what/rdr [accessed 4 December 2012].

HC 2012. *Automatic enrolment in workplace pensions and the National Employment Savings Trust: Government response to the Committee's Eighth Report of Session 2010–2012. Second Special Report of Session 2012–13. HC 154,* London, House of Commons Work and Pensions Committee.

HM Government 2007. *Putting people first – a shared vision and commitment to the transformation of adult social care,* London, Her Majesty's Government.

HM Government 2009a. *Building a society for all ages.* Cm 7655. London: Department of Work and Pensions.

HM Government 2009b. *Shaping the future of care together.* Cm 7673. London: The Stationery Office.

HM Government 2010. *Building the national care service,* Cm 754, London: HM Stationery Office.

HM Government 2012. *Caring for our future – progress report on funding reform.* Cm 8381. London: The Stationery Office.

HM Treasury 2013. *Budget 2013. HC 1033.* London: HM Treasury.

Humphries, R. 2013. Reforming social care funding – a step in the right direction?, www.kingsfund.org.uk/blog/2013/02/reforming-social-care-funding-step-right-direction (accessed 12 February 2013).

Humphries, R., Forder, J. and Fernandez, J.-L. 2010. *Securing good care for more people.* London: The King's Fund.

Hunt, J. 2013. Social care funding. *Hansard*. 11 February, cols 592–608, www.publications.parliament.uk/pa/cm201213/cmhansrd/cm130211/debtext/130211-0002.htm#13021116000001 (accessed 12 February 2013).

IFS. 2013. *Welcome simplification of state pensions but younger generations lose* [Online]. London: Institute of Fiscal Studies, www.ifs.org.uk/publications/6547 [accessed 14 February 2013].

IPSPC 2011. *Independent Public Service Pensions Commission: Final report*, London, Independent Public Service Pensions Commission.

Law Commission 2011. *Adult Social Care*, London, The Stationery Office.

Leisering, L. 2012. Pension privatization in a welfare state environment: socializing private pensions in Germany and the United Kingdom. *Journal of Comparative Social Welfare*, 28, 139-151.

Lloyd, J. 2013. *Care funding – read the small print*, Public Finance, http://opinion.publicfinance.co.uk/2013/02/care-funding-the-cap-still-doesnt-fit/ [accessed 13 February 2013].

Lowe, S. 2011. *The housing debate*, Bristol, Policy Press.

Macleod, P., Fitzpatrick, A., Hamlyn, B., Jones, A., Kinver, A. and Page, L. 2012. *Attitudes to pensions: The 2012 survey*, London, Department for Work and Pensions.

NAO (National Audit Office) 2012. *Regulating defined contribution pension schemes: The Pensions Regulator. Report by the Comptroller and Auditor General. HC 466, Session 2012-13*, London, National Audit Office.

NEST. 2013. *National Employment Savings Trust* [Online]. London: National Employment Savings Trust, www.nestpensions.org.uk/ [accessed 1 January 2013].

Newman, J., Glendinning, C. and Hughes, M. 2008. Beyond modernisation? Social care and the transformation of welfare governance. *Journal of Social Policy*, 37, 531-57.

ONS 2012. *Wealth in Great Britain. Analysis of the Wealth and Assets Survey 2008/10*, London, Office for National Statistics.

Pensions Commission 2005. *A new pension settlement for the 21st century: The second report of the Pensions Commission*. London: The Stationery Office.

Pensions Institute 2012. *Caveat venditor*, London, Cass Business School.

PP (Professional Pensions) 2012. *TPR outlaws auto-enrolment into small DC and legacy schemes*, London: Professional Pensions, www.professionalpensions.com/professional-pensions/news/2229521/tpr-outlaws-autoenrolment-into-small-dc-and-legacy-schemes [accessed 4 December 2012].

PPI 2012a. *The changing landscape of pension schemes in the private sector in the UK*, London, Pensions Policy Institute.

PPI 2012b. *The implications of the coalition government's reforms for members of the public service pension schemes*, London, Pensions Policy Institute.

Price, D. 2007. Closing the gender gap in retirement income: what difference will recent UK pension reforms make? *Journal of Social Policy*, 36, 561–583.

Price, D. 2008. Towards a new pension settlement? Recent pension reform in the UK, in Maltby, T., Kennett, P. and Rummery, K. (eds.) *Social Policy Review 20. Analysis and debate in social policy, 2008*. Bristol: Policy Press.

Price, D., Bisdee, D., Daly, T., Livsey, L. and Higgs, P. 2013. Financial planning for social care in later life: the 'shadow' of fourth age dependency. *Ageing & Society*, Firstview article, 1–23, doi/10.1017/S0144686X12001018

Ring, P. 2002. The implications of the 'New Insurance Contract' for UK pension provision: rights, responsibilities and risks. *Critical Social Policy*, 22, 551–571.

Taylor-Gooby, P. 2012. Public policy futures: A Left trilemma? *Critical Social Policy*. Online first article, doi/10.1177/0261018312458044

Van de Ven, J. 2012. Implications of the National Employment Savings Trust for vulnerable sectors of the UK Labour market: a reduced-form statistical evaluation. *National Institute Economic Review*, 219, R77–R89.

Part Two

Contributions from the Social Policy Association/East Asian Social Policy Research Network Conference of 2012

Kevin Farnsworth

This section of *Social Policy Review* reproduces several papers from the joint SPA/EASP Conference held in York in July 2012. As usual, there were many great papers to choose from. All the papers that were selected for this section in some way speak to the core concerns of social policy, but also push at the boundaries of the subject. They each make insightful contributions to the welfare debate and, in line with the themes and breadth of the conference itself, represent a diversity of topics and national case studies. In addition to these papers from the York conference, we also reproduce in this section Ilana Shpaizman's paper, winner of the Best Postgraduate Paper at Lincoln in 2011. Collectively, these six papers draw together policy case studies from the UK, US, China, Japan, South Korea and Israel.

Gary Craig and Maggie O'Neill's topical chapter on British national and local policies on 'race' argues that due in part to deliberate strategies to water down equality legislation, and partly due to the unintended consequences of 'race' policy, especially at the local level, 'race' policy has operated to sweep racism under the carpet or, worse, served to reinforce and institutionalise racism. They illustrate, through case studies of three English regions, how central and local government policies have 'invisibilised' race and racism. This, according to the authors, has led to the development of an institutionalised indifference to racial disadvantage, undermining the social welfare of minority ethnic groups in the UK.

Ben Hawkins and Anne Roemer-Mahler argue that it is important not only to consider the impact of business activities on health, but also to foster a deeper and more considered approach to the question of how business interests influence the shape of public health policies and strategies. They argue that the concept of interconnectedness can advance insights into corporate political power and corporate political strategy by utilising literature drawn from political science and management studies. They illustrate that, for their chosen case studies – the alcohol and pharmaceutical industries – four dimensions of interconnectedness are of particular relevance: interconnectedness between markets, industries, levels of governance and branches of government.

Exploring the relationship between markets and social policy from a different angle, Dan Horsfall and Sabrina Chai examine the merits of applying the idea of the 'competition state' to China. They consider whether this typology fits the case of China and while they locate valuable observations that might illuminate and help to make sense of the relationship between macroeconomic and social policy, they also find that various factors – for example, the rural–urban divide, provincial versus state policies and the continuing development of 'welfare' in China, including the growing share of expenditure devoted to social policies – make China a complex case. This is exacerbated by gaps in the literature and gaps in the data. Their conclusion is that the future direction of social policy in China remains unclear, paving the way for more research on these crucial questions in the future.

One of the questions raised by the competition state thesis is what the consequences are for citizens of governments who are shifting social policies closer towards the needs of employers and the wider economy. Phyllis Jeroslow's chapter deals with related questions in examining the impact of in-work tax credits on poverty in the US. Jeroslow focuses specifically on the Earned Income Tax Credit (EITC) in the US, but many of the lessons she highlights could apply anywhere. She illustrates the failings of the EITC as an anti-poverty strategy, indicating that, as a policy, its benefits are just as valuable to employers as they are to the poor. Indeed, the EITC appears just as likely to lock the poor into low-wage jobs and long-term poverty as it is to alleviate poverty, a fact brought home to the reader by Jeroslow's reminder of the 35-year pedigree of such policies in the US.

Nam K. Jo's chapter shifts the focus away from the economy towards the question of how important culture is in policymaking. More specifically, she brings a fresh pair of eyes to the familiar debate concerning the impact of Confucianism in the South Korean and Japanese welfare states. Jo helps to unpack the meaning of Confucianism and its potential impact on social policy. She also explores the related issues of religion and culture. She then ambitiously sets out to measure the impact of Confucianism on policy. She concludes that Confucianism is important, but argues that its impact is subtler than others have maintained.

The last chapter in this section is Ilana Shpaizman's prize-winning paper on Israeli immigration and integration policies between 2004 and 2010. Her paper reveals the incoherence and contradictions that exist within immigration and integration policy, pulled in different directions by devolved market solutions on the one hand, and more centralised government control on the other. The chapter helps to shed light on these contradictions by exploring a range of institutional barriers and conduits to change, suggesting that economic growth and competition for skilled labour has led to malleable, if contradictory, policy outcomes.

FIVE

It's time to move on from 'race'? The official 'invisibilisation' of minority ethnic disadvantage

Gary Craig and Maggie O'Neill

The national policy context

This chapter demonstrates how, over the past 10 years in particular, official policy of both central and local government has resulted deliberately, and at times possibly unintentionally, in the growing 'invisibilisation' of the dimension of 'race'. Issues regarding the growing disadvantage of many ethnic minorities are thus becoming obscured in public debate.

The McPherson Inquiry into the Stephen Lawrence murder[1] marked an apparent watershed in official responses to racism, especially policing responses to racially motivated crimes. Despite legislation (including the Race Relations Amendment Act [RRAA] 2000) and policy guidance, the socially constructed criminalisation of black and minority ethnic (BME) communities continues. Minority groups are disproportionately represented within the prison population but under-represented in staff roles across the criminal justice system (Ministry of Justice, 2010; Sveinsson, 2012) and 'problems, limitations and contradictions' (Rowe, 2012, p 184) occur in ethnic monitoring.

Cantle's (2001) report following the 'race riots' of 1995 and 2001[2] introduced a focus on 'community cohesion strategies' in multi-ethnic communities, which were substantially emphasised following the 2001 US and 2007 London terrorist attacks. Subsequent research documents a clear shift away from discourses of multiculturalism and diversity towards a concern with issues of security and 'Islamophobia'. Meanwhile, everyday issues facing minority groups, including racism and racially shaped disadvantage, are fading from public and policy debate.

The wider socio-political context to these issues includes the racialisation of immigration and increasingly restrictive asylum policy, framed within the language of border controls and securitisation, with mainstream media promoting an 'outsider configuration' (Elias and Scotson, 1994). Migration debates do not generally link the local with the global; however, forced migration is 'not the result of a string of unconnected emergencies, but an integral part of North–South relations' (Castles, 2003, p 9). When political parties 'limit debate to peripheral issues on immigration, then the space for questioning' is, critically, greatly reduced (Pickering, 2005, p 5).

There is a greater need now to understand the reality and the experiences of racism while acknowledging that race is a socially constructed concept, and that racialisation connects with other socially constructed discourses in the processes of 'othering'. These material and intra-personal experiences include stigma, exclusion, disadvantage and humiliation.

Craig (2007; also Craig et al, 2012a) has argued that the stance of the British state has never fundamentally addressed the racism inherent in both immigration and domestic welfare policies and that the welfare of Britain's minority groups – measured by outcomes in every welfare sector – has largely been disregarded by the British state. Despite some liberal initiatives to improve the lot of Britain's minority groups, racism inherent in policy and practice persists (in relation to more recent migrants and refugees, see also O'Neill, 2010; Hynes, 2011). That experience is worsening under the present Coalition regime; reviews of the third sector (Craig, 2011) and of the impact of policy drives towards the so-called 'Big Society' (Abbas and Lachman, 2012; Lachman, 2012) show how expenditure cuts disproportionately disadvantage BME populations. This outcome contradicts government rhetoric (OCS, 2010), whose apparent commitment to greater support for the third sector makes little mention of the BME sub-sector.

Seemingly 'race'-neutral wider policies are also having a disproportionate effect on minorit groups. Although 60% of black and Asian people have no savings,[3] the Coalition government quickly moved to cut two schemes – the Child Trust Fund and the Savings Gateway – which might have been of particular help to them. The impact of the benefits cap is resulting in many London families being forced to face relocation to other cities, characterised by some as 'social cleansing' but appearing on occasion more appropriately to be described as ethnic cleansing. One landlord (*The Guardian*, 28 April 2012) was required to evict 40 families, all of whom were non-white British. These families were offered accommodation in Stoke-on-Trent, a stronghold of anti-minority fascist groups. This tendency for apparently even-handed policies to have a disproportionate effect on minority groups is apparent in multiple exclusion homelessness (Dwyer et al, 2011), where most of those found homeless were refused asylum-seekers and other minority groups, a consequence again of discriminatory and racist immigration policies.

Structural racism and discrimination has been widely manifest. Shortly before the merger of disparate equality organisations into the Equality and Human Rights Commission (EHRC), the incoming chair indicated that virtually every government department was open to prosecution for failing to observe the terms of the RRAA, prosecutions that have not materialised. Since Lawrence's death, around 100 racialised murders have occurred, and the disproportionate use of Section 60 'stop and search' powers by police continues to target black and Asian young people. Black people are up to 26 times and Asian people more than six times more likely to be stopped/searched than white people (EHRC, 2012). The 'Prevent' agenda, launched by the government in 2007 with funding to certain local authorities with significant Muslim populations to 'prevent violent extremism' (LGA, 2008), which was widely criticised for labelling all Muslims as potential terrorists, has also led to Asian people being stopped 42 times as often as white people under the Terrorism Act 2000.[4]

It is evident that the UK, within all areas of welfare, has far to go before the problem of racism has truly been confronted. The response, however, of major political parties has been to become even more indifferent. John Denham, New Labour Communities Secretary, on leaving office in 2010, argued – despite acknowledging the fact of racial inequality – that 'it's time to move on from "race"', suggesting that 'race' was no longer a priority when considering issues of inequality and that the policy focus should be on questions of poverty. This ignores wide-ranging evidence demonstrating the close association – often because of racism – between being in poverty and being a member of particular minority groups (Platt, 2007).

It might be expected that the ethnic dimension of all national policy should be prominent. Nevertheless, the Coalition government took the opportunity offered by Denham to further deny the salience of 'race'. Prime Minister Cameron announced (outrageously, in a speech about terrorism; *The Guardian*, 6 February 2011, p 1) that 'multiculturalism is dead', underscoring Home Secretary May's pronouncement that 'equality [had become] a dirty word' (speech at Coin Street, 17 November 2010). Her focus on 'fairness', a vaguer, less legally enforceable term, means that racial injustice will now be much more difficult to identify and correct, effectively 'invisibilising' the dimension of 'race'. A further example of this downgrading of the 'race' agenda is demonstrated by the loss of funding for regional BME networks, established barely 10 years ago by the Home Office Active Communities Unit. The EHRC – criticised by BME groups for downgrading its own attention to 'race' – has been stripped of its responsibilities for promoting social cohesion, and has lost the two commissioners responsible for promoting 'race' issues. The Government Equalities Office, maintaining oversight of equalities work *within* government, has had its budget reduced from £76 million in 2011 to £47 million in 2014, with race equality marginalised.

May has removed the requirement (introduced previously as part of the Equality Act) that public bodies take account of inequalities caused by socio-economic disadvantage (the Public Sector Equality Duty, which was disproportionately experienced by BME communities) when policymaking. Some local authorities are now dismantling equalities structures, weakening funding claims by BME voluntary sector organisations (BMEVCS). The Office for Civil Society undermined historic gains made by the BMEVCS by withdrawing funding in 2011 from all strategic national and regional 'race'-related partners, a decision described by the Chair of Voice4Change as 'a monumental blow to the BMEVCS and the disadvantaged communities they serve'.[5] Other major organisations serving more recent migrants lost all or most of their funding, and the budgets of mainstream organisations with specialist services for minority groups, such as many Citizens' Advice Bureaux (CABs), have been cut very substantially (with bureaux closures in many areas). Given the fragility of the BME sector, we might expect that a government committed to fairness would protect organisations serving them. The evidence suggests otherwise. By early 2012, the EHRC's budget had dwindled to less than that of one of its three constituent bodies, and a further seven local Race Equality Councils then closed as a result of cuts in EHRC and local authority funding. Most recently (at the time of writing), Prime Minister Cameron has announced that equality impact assessments (EIAs) are to be scrapped (see: www.number10. gov.uk/news/speech-to-cbi accessed 08.12.2012)[6] and rumours are circulating in Whitehall that parliamentary space is being cleared in order to further weaken the Equality Act (Private communication, 7 December 2012).

The government's present community cohesion policy blames the 'failure' of multiculturalism on the unwillingness of minority groups to 'integrate'. At the same time, the political Right has seized on politicians' indifference to claim that minority groups have unfair treatment, which generates disadvantage among the white working class. Characteristically, a strategic government policy document, tasked to address racial inequalities (DCLG, 2012), fails to mention the issue of individual or institutional racism at all. The de-racialisation of local policy characteristic of community cohesion rhetoric and practice contributes strongly – as our case studies show – to the significant invisibilisation of 'race' and ethnicity when councils determine targets for resource distribution. Worley (2005, p 487) argues that increased use of the word 'community' allows practitioners and policy actors to avoid naming which communities they are referring to by also de-racialising language, 'even though reference points are clear'. Community cohesion, however, inserts the 'feel-good factor' of community (Bauman, 2001) into discussions of issues and places otherwise marked by difference and disadvantage. Community cohesion became the central motif in national and local government policies responding to ethnic diversity and conflict, although it appears increasingly in disarray (Thomas, 2007; Pilkington, 2008; Robinson, 2009).

Mainstream media contributions to debates on 'race' now focus almost entirely on the 'problem' of immigration, reflecting the view that immigration (excepting that of some highly skilled migrants) is damaging to the economy, to specific groups of workers and to society more generally; the actual economic impact of immigration is in reality quite positive (Luchino et al, 2012). However, changes to the overseas domestic worker visa enable unscrupulous employers to exploit this vulnerable group of migrants even further and accounts now record the terrible conditions in which some migrants are now working.[7]

There is little doubt that racism continues to affect the lives and opportunities of minority groups disproportionately and that, in some areas, racism is worsening (see note 10). The Coalition government is creating a policy framework where it is increasingly legitimate to ignore the disadvantage faced by minority groups *because* of their ethnicity, both explicitly and implicitly downplaying the question of racial justice. This thus remains a pressing arena for political and policy action (Craig et al, 2012a; Vickers et al, 2012) but research has struggled to both keep pace with the social and political contexts to these debates (Bowling and Phillips, 2002; Singh Bhui, 2009; O'Neill, 2010; Rowe, 2012) and contribute to their resolution.

Given its dependence on government funding, this shift in focus will clearly impact on local government's own policy priorities. We now briefly describe three studies that demonstrate in different ways how the 'invisibilisation' of minority ethnic groups and the issues they face locally occurs in practice. Each represents work in progress.

York

The York study, funded by the Joseph Rowntree Foundation (JRF) (Craig et al, 2009), explores the implications of relatively rapid increases in the minority ethnic population in what was long regarded as a largely white Anglo-Saxon city. At a time of rapid socio-economic change, use of a limited range of largely outdated data (eg the 2001 census[8]) severely compromised effective policymaking and service-targeting on specific population groups. The study used a mixture of methods, including secondary data analysis, interviews with individuals and BME organisations, examination of the employment records of public and private organisations, and observation of informal, ethnically based networks.

Previously, the minority population was assumed to be around 5–6%. The study demonstrated that the non-white British population in York in 2009 was over 11%, with more than 80 different ethnic groups and languages represented locally. This figure was greeted with incredulity in some quarters. However, in 2010, the Office of National Statistics (ONS) estimated the city's minority population as about 11.6% of York's population (ignoring several hundred undocumented migrants also thought to be living locally). This growth in York's minority population was due to natural growth among the small settled BME population, an unrecorded refugee population 'leaking' from nearby dispersal areas, significant numbers of migrant workers living in the city but working, predominantly, in surrounding rural areas, substantial growth in the two universities' student populations, and the arrival of undocumented workers.

Analysis of local employment data from, and interviews with, representatives of public organisations demonstrated that none were observing all of the key requirements of the RRAA; for example, employing appropriate numbers of minority groups (most had 3% or less), using effective ethnic monitoring schemes or operating comprehensive race equality training schemes. Some organisations acknowledged that they had not worked on their equality policies for 'years'; others still used highly inappropriate, subjective categories of ethnicity, with data on ethnicity generally incomplete. Most private sector organisations in the city refused to cooperate with the research (the private sector is outside the terms of the RRAA), which is a serious issue as most ethnic minority groups locally were probably employed in the private sector.

Following publication, the JRF offered to act as a broker in setting up a round table discussion with major statutory and voluntary sector bodies, including the city council, to examine its findings and move the process of policy change forward. In the intervening three years since, no such round table has happened: the council initially responded by arguing that its ability to do much would be limited by the impending rounds of public expenditure cuts with which it was about to grapple. However, the austerity measures mean that statutory and voluntary agencies alike are having to do more for less. Given this, the position of minority groups needed to be protected given that they would face disproportionate disadvantage.

In 2011, under changed political control (to Labour), the city council announced the establishment of a Fairness Commission. In its first report (CYC, 2011), however, there was virtually no serious discussion of the issue of ethnicity. Vulnerable groups are mentioned several times in relation to the targeting of resources but minority groups were not identified as potentially among the most vulnerable.[9] Two York-based organisations central to local discussion on minority ethnic groups, one a generalised race equality body (which had recently lost EHRC funding) and the other supporting Travellers and Gypsies, a large, very marginalised local minority, have each struggled to attract adequate support (Neale et al, 2009). Appallingly, a representative of the newly formed GP Commissioning Group, addressing a voluntary sector conference late in 2011 on the question of health service reforms, admitted that no thought had been given during their planning process to ways in which minority groups' access to health services was impaired.

Within what is still largely a rural police area (North Yorkshire and York), the number of 'race' hate incidents has been steadily increasing, recent data showing a 9% annual increase in such incidents, a trend contrasting with that in many urban police forces.[10] Where police undertake ineffective 'race' hate reporting, and rural BME populations – as in North Yorkshire – are very remote or scattered, under-reporting will be highly significant – as a local consultation demonstrated (RAJINY, 2010).[11] A study of the first two cohorts entering the York Hull Medical School found that one quarter of all BME students had witnessed or experienced racist abuse or assault over the previous two years (Craig and McNamee, 2005).[12]

The flavour of local popular discourse on 'race' is best illustrated by public and statutory responses to a letter to the local newspaper arguing that the small local mosque should be given permission to improve its facilities. This letter provoked 19 pages of responses on the web; most of them could only be characterised as racist rants. The police argued that an extension to the mosque should be opposed since, as a faith-based building, it would be bound to attract hostility (an argument not applied to the Minster, York's world heritage tourist attraction). The council opposed the extension on the grounds that it would generate increased noisy traffic flows (this on a site adjacent to an industrial estate largely populated by builders' merchants) and because of a risk of flooding (next to the site of an official Gypsy/Traveller site, flooded fairly frequently, from which Travellers had frequently but unsuccessfully asked to be relocated).

The North East region

The second study[13] is a regional study of 'race', crime and justice issues facing the BME population in the North East region, carried out by a consortium of universities, and part-funded by the Ministry of Justice. The region, like North Yorkshire, has historically had a relatively small minority population. Again, it appeared from a policy review that the dimension of ethnicity has not, to date, been reflected in policymaking, a perception confirmed by the study's outcomes.

In the period 2001–2009, the North East region's population increased by 44,000 (1.7%). However, the white British population decreased from 96.3% in the same period to 92.5%. All minority groups have increased their presence but the most notable rise has been among the black African group, a 330% increase to 12,600, largely because of the growth in refugees, particularly in Newcastle upon Tyne and Middlesbrough, the two formally designated regional refugee dispersal areas. The non-white British population in these two cities had reached 16% and 12%, respectively, by 2009.

The 'white other' population increased from 0.9% to 1.8%: this is a catch-all category, certainly including both some of the East and Central European migrant workers operating largely in rural parts of the region, and refugees categorised as 'white other'. The regional overall BME (non-white) population was 5.3% in 2009, about one third of the level within the UK overall, although the regional rate of growth – as with many rural areas – is considerably greater than in the UK as a whole. Within the region, there are now about 147,000 non-white people, substantially more than widely anticipated.[14] Responses to the report's findings and to somewhat sensationalised press coverage were largely hostile or in denial of the issue of racism. The report led to the publication of a separate study detailing the impact of rural racism on isolated minority women (RACJ, 2012).

The main study involved qualitative interviews both with BME-led organisations, with more generalist community organisations and with key actors, secondary analysis of ONS and police data, literature and policy reviews, and two substantial consultations, one with BME groups and policy actors together, and the other with refugee-focused organisations. The key issue identified by BME people was overwhelmingly their continuing experience of racism, at individual and institutional levels, within both public and private sectors, with particular concern and a lack of trust relating to aspects of the criminal justice system. A later workshop brought key actors together to develop an action programme.

Analysis of police data on race hate crimes in the three police forces in the region highlighted that harassment, criminal damage, common assault and actual bodily harm were the most common racist crimes, taking place predominantly in public spaces by young people aged 11–25 years old. One police force did not, however, collect data relating to the gender or age of victims; another apparently did not document the ethnicity of offenders in 95% of cases. The (long-familiar) range of issues identified by BME respondents to the study included the following (these give a graphic picture of how racism works at a local level):

- racist bullying in schools;
- racist graffiti on housing;
- exacerbated difficulties in accessing work and training, and underemployment when accessing work (not recognising qualifications/experience);
- lack of help from business support organisations when setting up small enterprises;
- inadequate/missing interpretation and translation facilities when accessing services;
- poor levels of provision for women-only services, for example, health and recreation;
- inadequate provision for or understanding of minority elders' needs;
- generally hostile media treatment;
- a weakening of cultural identity;
- poor recruitment practices among public and private bodies; and
- discriminatory lending/mortgage practices among banks/building societies. (Craig et al, 2012b)

The research confirmed findings that racism and hostile behaviours impact on well-being, sense of selfhood, self-identity and belonging, and migrants' (particularly forced migrants') complex struggles to manage and sustain dual identities (O'Neill, 2010). Research participants stressed the need to promote better understanding among public sector services of different cultures, given rapidly increasing diversity in the North East, and for support to help them navigate and negotiate the system. Well-being, respect and recognition connected in the narratives of participants with calls for cultural citizenship, understood (following Pakulski, 1997) as the right to: presence and visibility (not marginalisation); dignity and lifestyle maintenance (not assimilation to the dominant culture); and dignifying representation. BME community members highlighted the importance of community groups, with leaders described as bridges to services, networks, support and information. Responses to racism and feelings of being unwelcome included movement and mobility, either within the region or to other regions with larger, more established, BME communities and where support, housing and employment opportunities were available.

Although many respondents had experienced improvements recently, they argued that there was little local evidence of effective anti-racist action being led by statutory organisations. Newcastle City Council had also established a Fairness Commission in 2011. Their first report to the council's Policy Cabinet early that year was, like its York counterpart, effectively colour-blind. None of the report's figures or tables identified the ethnic origin of those living in poverty. Although it had been commonplace for local authorities in the region to disregard the issue of ethnicity, often claiming that minority ethnic groups were few in number, this was never a justifiable argument and was certainly not now. The research team argued that all agencies in the region clearly needed to review their equality and diversity policies and address racial discrimination, and that the three police forces needed to develop consistent and comparable data collection of racially motivated crimes – the criminal justice system, in effect, being the last resort for promoting race equality for some people. One potential follow-up is to track cases of racism from reporting to prosecution/sentencing or attrition to better understand the experiences of racism and the practices of different elements of the regional criminal justice system.

The 'Northern city'

The third study describes research undertaken in a large city,[15] involving interviews and group discussions with policy actors, professionals and local activists. Here, sensitivities about 'race' and local community cohesion policy were so acute that the council only agreed to collaborate if researchers did not identify it. Notwithstanding obtaining this assurance, the council eventually refused to allow employees to participate (including in an anonymised survey) other than through a few interviews with senior staff. This study drew particular attention to some of the consequences of the shifts in government policy, noted earlier, away from explicit 'race' relations policy towards community cohesion policy – exploring how it was now displacing multiculturalism – which had underpinned government policies since the 1980s (Kundnani, 2002).

Some (Joppke, 2004; McGhee, 2008) have suggested that the promotion of social integration and public adherence to British shared values results in a drift away from, rather than an abandonment of, multiculturalism: a de-emphasising of respect for diversity in favour of emphasising shared values. The language of community cohesion promotes this drift, but, in doing so, obscures the dimension of 'race'.

The Local Government Association guidance (LGA, 2002, p 6) issued to local authorities defines a 'cohesive community' as one where:

> there is a common vision and sense of belonging for all communities; the diversity of people's different backgrounds and circumstances are appreciated and positively valued; those from different backgrounds have similar life opportunities; strong and positive relationships are being developed between people from different backgrounds in the workplace, in schools and within neighbourhoods.

While community cohesion is promoted, declining support for multicultural policies is increasingly explicit; community cohesion's language is both implicitly and explicitly based in a critique of multicultural policies. It has become dominant as a policy term used in the terrain vacated by multiculturalism, yet is accompanied by a rise in other equally amorphous terms, including 'equalities', 'diversity' and 'community involvement', all distancing from explicit engagement with a 'race' framework. The incorporation of community cohesion into strategies and guidelines in local councils, schools and the third sector has been coupled with a new framework to incorporate the six equality 'strands' (gender, 'race', disability, sexuality, faith and age), with 'equality' mainstreamed in local authorities (IDEA, 2009). Another significant influence in the case described here was the emerging 'Prevent' agenda, discussed earlier. Perceptions of difference were driven here by a general problematisation of Muslims, contrasting with an apparent downplaying of difference promoted through the community cohesion and equalities agendas.

This study focused on Somali and Yemeni (largely Muslim) populations living in one district. The research was designed to question approaches to multiculturalism; however, that the word 'multiculturalism' had become unfamiliar locally quickly became apparent. Hence, the research broadened away from terminology to look at cultural difference. This incorporated: support for BME groups; relationships and partnerships between the council and BME groups; integration and belonging; faith and 'race'; and the policies, activities and strategies associated with these topics. Certain terms were repeatedly utilised (and confusingly interchanged): activities relating to cultural differences were seen primarily as part of the community cohesion and equalities agendas. Inclusion, community involvement and 'Prevent' emerged as key concepts and strategies linked to cultural relations or diversity.

Local attitudes suggested a mix of pride and fear: pride that the city had not been subject to other towns' 'race relations problems'; fear of exposure in relation to managing cultural difference or cultural relations, particularly among council representatives. The latter demonstrated research fatigue; they had contributed to numerous community cohesion consultations and investigations while facing unprecedented funding cuts, frustrations exacerbated by demands for increased attention to 'community cohesion'. Meanwhile, cultural relations work was perceived to be increasingly undervalued.

The key response from community and council representatives to questions about multiculturalism suggested that it was no longer used as stated policy or practice. Not only was multiculturalism considered as a policy barely stated, it was either taken to be irrelevant or an area of work absorbed into (chiefly) community cohesion. This negation of the language of 'race', and nervousness about explicit reference to racialised language, echoes precisely that found by Worley (2005).

Four threats from the local rise of community cohesion were discernible for BME organisations: the breadth of the council's community cohesion agenda and 'equalising' of 'race'; the covert problematising of BME populations (in the absence of similar attention to 'white' groups); an insidious drift away from support for 'single group' funding; and the backdrop of severely reduced voluntary sector funding. In parallel with a community cohesion action plan being implemented, the equalities agenda was being mainstreamed. This added to the sense of a jumble of issues that lacked clear priorities. The equalities office had been disbanded, yet the equalities agenda incorporated community cohesion. Moving to a 'multi-strand' equalities approach appeared to have similar influences as the rise of community cohesion – diverse issues were being highlighted, none was prioritised. Indeed, the 'equalising' of 'race' as 'just' another equality issue was an explicit goal.

Within and outside the council, it was recognised that it had not complied with existing goals for minority ethnic representation in its workforce; BME employees were said by council and other respondents to be concentrated in lower-salary positions, indicating failures in recruitment, retention and promotion. Despite such well-recognised shortcomings in existing approaches to improving equity, the 'equalising' and mainstreaming of 'race' and ethnicity and the abandonment of an explicit engagement with 'race' frameworks was regarded by council representatives as more 'fair'. Notwithstanding this, and the negation of racialised language, community cohesion attention was directed to only certain types of community: reference points were indeed obscured, yet clear. Cohesion work seemed not to happen in either poor or affluent white areas, perceived by minority group respondents as insular and unfriendly. Among community representatives, this reinforced a stigmatising sense that certain, 'different', 'ethnic' people were troublesome, needing cohesion more than others. Ironically, 'race' no longer became a dimension of policy helping to target welfare resources on disadvantaged communities, but a means for increased surveillance on them.

Multiple threats were perceived by BME third sector organisations from the promotion of community cohesion despite evidence of some effort being exerted by both council and the voluntary sector to mould national agendas to local circumstances and needs. A prominent example was of the incorporation of the 'preventing violent extremism' programme into the community cohesion framework, in an attempt to ensure that wider relationships took precedence over counter-terrorism initiatives. This council received funding under the 'Prevent' programme from 2008. Learning from other areas, who reported that initial rounds of 'Prevent' funding had been detrimental to relationships between Muslim communities, the police and local authority, this council adopted a more careful approach. Despite this, a council officer described how wider perceptions could shape this work: "no matter what you say, people have legitimate grievances around the way that Muslims have been stigmatised". Hence, local policies to promote diversity, equality or integration were challenged by countervailing tendencies in other, contradictory national policies. This was best expressed by a Yemeni worker:

"so we have community cohesion on one side, but the other hand says there is no funding for ESOL [English for Speakers of Other Languages]. At the local level says we respect specialist services, but on the other hand you should work with other groups."

Multiculturalism – as the mainstream government 'race relations' policy approach over the past 20 years – has been substantially modified in this city, and across the UK, in more recent times, although it has not been abandoned altogether.[16] New policies undermining support for single identity groups certainly served to help rationalise difficult decisions to cut funds. Nevertheless, equalising 'race' and ethnicity as just one difference among others is clearly a deliberate goal of the community cohesion and equalities agendas (supported by an emphasis on the vague notion of 'fairness'). Represented by council representatives as universal and 'fair', this equalising seemed to community representatives to result in reductions in funding and a sense that their role was ignored; it ignored the disadvantage in many dimensions of welfare suffered by minority groups (Craig et al, 2012a). While the drawing together of all equality strands into the single focus of the EHRC and legislation under the Equality Act arguably challenged the view that discrimination is a minority group concern by making universal human rights the issue (Pilkington, 2008), it was also an effective tool here for de-prioritising support for local organisations and initiatives concerned with racial equality and recognition of difference. Thus, there are serious practical and political conflicts between community cohesion coupled with mainstreamed equalities and the advancement of socio-economic opportunities, social solidarity and respect for difference.

Although there has been no change in pre-existing legislation to tackle discrimination and promote diversity, other, newly introduced legislation serves to undermine possibilities for creating equality and multicultural respect. The emergence of 'Prevent' and the rise of anti-immigrant feeling, illustrated in events such as the election of a British National Party Member of the European Parliament, results in a dual, apparently contradictory process. The de-emphasis of 'race' or ethnicity in community cohesion and equalities policies aimed at managing difference has emerged at the same time as heightened security concerns, hostile media representations and xenophobia feed a reification of 'different', 'Other', identifiable and racialised groups, in particular, Muslims. This contradiction helps to explain anxiety on the part of council representatives in taking part in this research or for engaging in any discussion about racism and ethnic difference, tendencies repeated both in government policy (DCLG, 2012) and in other cities. Indeed, research in Oldham, Peterborough (Burnett, 2012) and Barking and Dagenham (Jones, 2011) shows how the language of community cohesion provides opportunities to avoid confronting these difficult questions, and, in particular, issues of 'race' and racial justice.

Conclusion

The conclusion from these vignettes is that poor as the responses of public authorities have historically been to race equality legislation at a time when the national policy and political context was benign, in the present national political context, there is now little political incentive for local statutory organisations – whether police, local government or health bodies – to take the issue of 'race' seriously at all. Indeed, government pronouncements positively discourage this and the funding context adds further weight to the tendency to ignore the needs of marginal minority groups. This then has an impact on funding for the voluntary sector. Local evidence remains more uneven at present but there is a perceptible tendency for agencies increasingly to dismiss the dimension of 'race' as not significant in the day-to-day work of those bodies, even though the 2011 census demonstrates that the minority ethnic population in the UK is probably around 16% on average (and substantially more than that in many areas). A campaign led by the Afiya Trust (www.afiya-trust.org) surveyed local authority adult social services departments, finding that more than 20% did not collect data on the funding allocated to BME voluntary and community organisations, or now conduct EIAs of their work.

Local authorities now appear willing – in part, of course, as they would argue, driven by the direction of funding streams – to regard policymaking as fair when it explicitly disregards the specific needs of disadvantaged minority populations. This is a depressing conclusion, not least because it is reminiscent of the 1990s when, faced with continuing hostility from Conservative governments, councils retreated from equal opportunities policies, failing to confront the issue of racial disadvantage and racism (Solomos and Back, 1995, cited in Rattansi, 2011, p 92).

The language of 'race', racial justice and racism, once part of everyday policy discourse in many areas, is now being obscured by a much more generalised discussion of issues such as cohesion, fairness and even equality. That this can now happen without any explicit reference to racism and the need for a socially just approach to policymaking for minority ethnic groups demonstrates how far UK public policy discourse has drifted from notions of social justice,[17] racial justice and real fairness (Craig et al, 2008). Under the cover of this indifference to racial disadvantage from the government and, increasingly, local governance bodies, the social welfare of most of the UK's minority ethnic groups is steadily deteriorating.

Notes

[1.] Lawrence, a black teenager, was murdered by a group of white men. The subsequent formal inquiry resulted in wide-ranging legislation placing a duty on public bodies to promote racial equality. Two of the gang were only convicted 15 years after Lawrence's death.

[2.] In both years, disturbances (characterised by some as 'race riots') took place in areas of some northern cities characterised by high minority populations and levels of disadvantage. Minority groups argued that they stemmed from continued discrimination, and were provoked by far-right groups. The government used the disturbances as an excuse for abandoning multiculturalist policies.

[3.] This compares with the UK average of 25% (see *The Guardian*, 30 January 2010).

[4.] See: www.homeoffice.gov.uk/counter-terrorism/review-of-prevent-strategy

[5.] See: www.voice4change-england-co.uk/content/bme-organisations-lose-seat-at-top-policy-making-table. In June, the Office for Civil Society (OCS) told Voice4Change that it could act as an advisor on a time-limited basis, giving it a grant merely to carry out one specific piece of consultation.

[6.] EIAs are actually not a legal requirement.

[7.] See, for example, the programme of work funded by the Joseph Rowntree Foundation (JRF) on forced labour, www.jrf.org.uk/work/workarea/forced-labour

[8.] By the time this chapter is published, the results of the 2011 census will be available. It remains to be seen whether it will be used to highlight the conditions of minority groups or generate a moral panic about immigration.

[9.] Press coverage in late 2012 suggests that the new city council has acknowledged that hate crime is becoming a serious issue and the Fairness Commission's second report identified some issues facing minority groups.

[10.] Home Office, 'Racist incidents by police force area, 2008/9–2010/11', www.statistics.gov.uk/hub/crime-justice/police/police-activity.

[11.] The data for 2011/12 showed a slight drop in the numbers of incidents recorded but a senior police officer volunteered in a meeting with activists in late 2012 that they significantly understated the problem.

[12.] And, perhaps unexpectedly, that there was no significant difference between the experience of students based in Hull and those based in York.

[13.] Others involved in the study were Carol Devanney (Durham University), Georgios Antonopoulos and Louise Wattis (Teesside University) and Bankole Cole and Paul Biddle (Northumbria University).

[14.] These categories are those used in the 2001 census. Codes used by police for recording data sometimes differ from these in terms of broad categories; for example, IC6 refers to Arabs and, presumably, 'Arab-looking people'.

[15.] This research was undertaken by Dr Hannah Lewis of the University of Leeds and Gary Craig as part of a three-country study (UK, Canada and Australia) examining the way in which multiculturalism was playing out at a local level, particularly in relation to Arab Muslims. This section of the chapter owes much to Hannah's work.

[16.] We acknowledge that multiculturalism has been widely criticised as a policy stance from an anti-racist perspective: the point here is that even its weak focus on difference and diversity is lost in a community cohesion approach.

[17.] The government claims that it is committed to social justice, but this commitment seems hollow when the present Secretary of State for Work and Pensions, who created the Centre for Social Justice, is currently cutting disability benefits for hundreds of thousands of people.

References

Abbas, M.-S. and Lachman, R. (eds) (2012) *The Big Society: the big divide?*, Oxford: Oxfam.

Bauman, Z. (2001) *Community: seeking safety in an insecure world*, Cambridge: Polity Press.

Bowling, B. and Philips, C. (2002) *Racism, crime and justice*, Harlow: Longman.

Burnett, J. (2012) *The new geographies of racism: Peterborough*, London: Institute of Race Relations.

Castles, S. (2003) 'Towards a sociology of forced migration and social transformation', *Sociology*, vol 37, no 1, pp 13–34.

Craig, G. (2007) 'Cunning, unprincipled, loathsome: the racist tail wags the welfare dog', *Journal of Social Policy*, October, vol 36, no 4, pp 605-23.

Craig, G. (2011) 'Forward to the past? Does the BME third sector have a future?', *Voluntary Sector Review*, vol 2, no 3, pp 367-89.

Craig, G. and McNamee, S. (2005) *Survey of medical students at the HullYork Medical School*, Hull: University of Hull.

Craig, G., Burchardt, T. and Gordon, D. (eds) (2008) *Social justice and public policy*, Bristol: Policy Press.

Craig, G., Adamson, S., Ali, N. and Demsash, F. (2009) *Mapping rapidly changing ethnic minority populations*, York: Joseph Rowntree Foundation.

Craig, G., Atkin, K., Chattoo, S. and Flynn, R. (eds) (2012a) *Understanding 'race' and ethnicity*, Bristol: Policy Press.

Craig, G., O'Neill, M., Cole, B., Antonopoulos, G., Devanney, C. and Admason, S. (2012b) *'Race' crime and justice in the North East region*, Durham: RCJ Research Group.

CYC (City of York Council) (2011) *Fairness Commission, first report*, York: City of York Council.

DCLG (Department for Communities and Local Government) (2012) *Creating the conditions for integration*, London: Department for Communities and Local Government.

Dwyer, P., Bowpitt, G., Sundin, E. and Weinstein, M. (2011) *The support priorities of multiply excluded homeless people and their compatibility with support agency agendas*, Salford: University of Salford.

EHRC (Equalities and Human Rights Commission) (2012) *Review of stop and search powers*, London: Equalities and Human Rights Commission.

Elias, N. and Scotson, J.L. (1994) *The established and the outsiders: a sociological enquiry into community problems*, London: Sage.

Hynes, P. (2011) *The dispersal and exclusion of asylum seekers*, Bristol: Policy Press.

IDEA (Improvement and Development Agency) (2009) *Key principles. Equality framework for local government*, London: Improvement and Development Agency.

Jones, H. (2011) 'Negotiating community cohesion policy', in C. Alexander and M. James (eds) *New directions, new voices: emerging research on race and ethnicity*, London: Runnymede, pp 12–14.

Joppke, C. (2004) 'The retreat of multiculturalism in the liberal state: theory and policy', *The British Journal of Sociology*, vol 55, pp 237–57.

Kundnani, A. (2002) 'The death of multiculturalism', *Race and Class*, vol 43, no 4, pp 67–72.

Lachman, R., with Malik, F. (2012) *West Yorkshire public sector cuts: the impact on the BME voluntary and community sector*, Bradford: JUST West Yorkshire.

LGA (Local Government Association) (2002) *Guidance on community cohesion*, London: Local Government Association.

Luchino, P., Rosazza-Bondibene, C. and Portes, J. (2012) *Examining the relationship between immigration and unemployment using National Insurance number registration data*, London: National Institute for Social and Economic Research.

McGhee, D. (2008) *The end of multiculturalism? Terrorism, integration and human rights*, Maidenhead: Open University Press.

Ministry of Justice (2010) *Statistics on race and the criminal justice system – a Ministry of Justice publication under section 95 of the Criminal Justice Act 1991*, London: HMSO.

Neale, M., Craig, G. and Wilkinson, M. (2009) 'Marginalised and excluded:York's Traveller community', www.travellerstrustyork.org.uk

OCS (Office for Civil Society) (2010) *Supporting a stronger civil society*, London: Office for Civil Society.

O'Neill, M. (2010) *Asylum, migration and community*, Bristol: Policy Press.

Pakulski, J. (1997) 'Cultural citizenship', *Citizenship Studies*, vol 1, no 1, pp 73–86.

Pickering, S. (2005) *Refugees and state crime*, Sydney: The Federation Press.

Pilkington, A. (2008) 'From institutional racism to community cohesion: the changing nature of racial discourse in Britain', *Sociological Research Online*, vol 13, no 3, p 6.

Platt, L. (2007) *Ethnicity and poverty*, York: Joseph Rowntree Foundation.

RACJ ('Race', Crime and Justice Research Group) (2012) *A place called Townsville: rural racism in a North East context*, Durham: 'Race', Crime and Justice Research Group.

RAJINY (Racial Justice in North Yorkshire) (2010) *Report of a consultation with black and minority ethnic groups in North Yorkshire*, Easingwold: Racial Justice in North Yorkshire.

Rattansi, A. (2011) *Multiculturalism: a very short introduction*, Oxford: Oxford University Press.

Robinson, D. (2009) 'Community cohesion and the politics of communitarianism', in J. Flint and D. Robinson (eds) *Community cohesion in crisis? New dimensions of diversity and difference*, Bristol: Policy Press, pp 15–34.

Rowe, M. (2012) *Race and crime*, Key Approaches in Criminology Series, London: Sage Publications.

Singh Bhui, H. (ed) (2009) *Race and criminal justice*, London: Sage.

Solomos, J. and Back, L. (1995) *Race, politics and social change*, London: Routledge.

Sveinsson, K.P. (ed) (2012) *Criminal justice vs. racial justice: minority ethnic over-representation in the criminal justice system*, London: Runnymede Trust.

Thomas, P. (2007) 'Moving on from "anti-racism"? Understandings of "community cohesion" held by youth workers', *Journal of Social Policy*, vol 36, no 3, pp 435–55.

Vickers, T., Craig, G. and Atkin, K. (2012) 'Addressing ethnicity in social care research', *Social Policy and Administration*.

Worley, C. (2005) '"It's not about race. It's about the community": New Labour and "community cohesion"', *Critical Social Policy*, vol 25, no 4, pp 483–96.

SIX

Corporations as political actors: new perspectives for health policy research

Ben Hawkins and Anne Roemer-Mahler

Introduction

In the field of health policy, corporations are important actors implicated in the production of ill health through environmental degradation and the promotion of unhealthy lifestyles and consumptions patterns. Equally, they make important contributions to tackling disease and ill health through the development of new medicines and technologies employed in the diagnosis and treatment of a range of conditions. They provide vital support structures to health care systems through the provision of front-line and ancillary services and the administration of health insurance systems. However, the importance of corporations for health policy is a result not simply of their core business activities, but also their ability to influence the political environment in which they operate.

The role of corporations as political actors is well recognised today (Matten and Crane, 2005; Newell and Levy, 2006; Scherer and Palazzo, 2011). This chapter builds on the existing literature about corporate political influence, which focuses on the structural and agency components of political power (Hacker and Pierson, 2002; Farnsworth, 2004; Farnsworth and Holden, 2006). It combines the insights drawn from this field with those from the discipline of management studies, which focuses on the internal developments of corporations' political strategies to give a more complete account of the role of corporations as policy actors. In addition, the chapter develops the concept of interconnectedness as part of our analytical framework for examining the role of corporations in health policy. The existing literature demonstrates that companies plan and conduct their political activities across countries and at different levels of governance, including at the local, national and multilateral levels (Sell, 2003; Holden and Lee, 2009). It shows that companies have targeted different branches of government to pursue their political interests, including parliament, civil service and the judiciary (Holden and Lee, 2009; Hawkins and Holden, 2012). Finally, companies from different industries sometimes collaborate, either explicitly by forming cross-industry alliances (Sell, 2003) or implicitly through learning from one another (Bond et al, 2010).

The concept of interconnectedness can advance insights into corporate political power and corporate political strategy derived from political science and management studies by highlighting how key features of globalisation are affecting corporate political activities. We distinguish four dimensions of interconnectedness that appear particularly relevant in shaping corporate political activity – interconnectedness between industries, markets, levels of governance and branches of government – and use these categories to examine the political strategies of the alcohol and pharmaceutical industries.

Corporate political power and strategy

Political scientists are interested primarily in the process of policymaking and the state. From this perspective, business is considered as a factor shaping policymaking. Some scholars emphasise the power of business as an interest group (Mizruchi, 1992; Greenwood and Jacek, 2000). Underlying this approach is a pluralist conception of the policy process characterised by open competition for policy influence between interest groups. Other scholars argue that business occupies a 'privileged position' in this competition (Lindblom, 1977) because it controls key economic resources (Strange, 1996; Greidner, 1997).

Hacker and Pierson (2002) argue that corporate political influence must be analysed in terms of both 'structural' and 'instrumental' power. Farnsworth (2004) offers a similar analysis, framed in terms of 'structure' and 'agency' power. Structural power results not from what corporate actors do in terms of lobbying or influencing activities, but from the particular position they occupy within the structure of the economy. Structural power is principally a consequence of businesses' ability to make free investment decisions that impact on levels of economic output and employment (Farnsworth and Holden, 2006, p 475). Governments may therefore be minded to pursue policies that support business interests. Yet, the structural power of business varies across institutional settings and over time. For instance, Hacker and Pierson

(2002) argue that decentralised federal systems augment structural power, and several scholars have noted that globalisation increases the structural power of businesses because it facilitates their ability to relocate investment (Stopford and Strange, 1991; Farnsworth and Holden, 2006). Where structural factors are inadequate to achieve a favourable policy environment, businesses must rely on agency to attempt to achieve the policy outcomes they favour. In order to account for corporate political influence we therefore need to analyse both the structural position of business groups in specific institutional settings and the activities they undertake to shape policy.

Much of the literature on corporate political influence treats the firm as a black box. Companies are usually conceived of as unitary, rational actors, whose political interests and activities can be directly and objectively derived from their economic interests. Yet, there are studies illustrating that the political interests and strategies of companies can vary considerably even within the same industry and with regard to the same policy issue (Levy and Newell, 2000; Levy and Kolk, 2002). The 'business conflict school' (Skidmore, 1995, p 247) has pointed out that conflicting interests *within* the business community can be an important factor shaping political processes and policy outcomes (Falkner, 2008; Roemer-Mahler, 2012).

In order to explain the variation in interests and strategies, we need to open the black box of the firm and examine how political interests are formed within companies, and which factors shape the development of specific political strategies. These questions have been addressed more fully by scholars from management studies. The Corporate Political Activity literature examines how the resources and capabilities of the firm, the institutional environment within which a firm operates (the regulatory environment and the organisation of the industry) and its corporate culture affect the formation and effectiveness of political strategies that the firm pursues (Getz, 1997; Hillman et al, 2004; Lawton et al, 2012). Corporate behaviour has to be explained by processes of decision-making, risk assessment and perceptions of economic interests that take place both inside the firm and in exchange with outside actors, and which are shaped by institutional structures that constrain activity and preference formation (Rehbein and Schuler, 1999; Levy and Newell, 2000; Brown et al, 2010). Of particular relevance for this chapter is research on the impact of the external institutional environment (such as the political system) on corporate political activity (Doremus et al, 1998; Hansen and Mitchell, 2001; Tian et al, 2009).

Another key question is when, and under what circumstances, companies will coordinate their political activities and engage in collective action. The literature has identified several factors that help business overcome the problem of collective action, including: economies of scale and industry concentration (Lehne, 1993); mediating mechanisms and social/economic ties between firms (Mizruchi, 1992); and leadership (Sell, 2003).

Interconnectedness, policymaking and political activity

In this chapter, we combine the structure and agency approach to studying corporate political power with the insights into the internal workings of the firm derived from management studies. In addition, we have identified a number of themes in the current literature on corporate actors in health policy. We conceptualise these themes in terms of *interconnectedness*. Specifically, we identify four dimensions of interconnectedness that are relevant for the study of companies as political actors: interconnectedness between *industries, markets, levels of governance* and *branches of governments*.

The first dimension of interconnectedness that we identify is that between different industries. It focuses on the extent to which corporations collaborate across industries and learn from the political strategies employed by other companies. Sell (2003) examines an interesting example of a cross-industry alliance of companies to promote stronger international standards of intellectual property (IP) protection. Dorfman et al (2012) examine the similarities that exist between the Corporate Social Responsibility (CSR) activities of tobacco and carbonated beverage companies.

The increasing interconnectedness between markets is manifest in the growing number of companies that operate transnationally. Yet, existing research on the political role of corporations focuses mainly on companies based in Europe and the US. The growing importance of markets in low- and middle-income countries means that we must examine more closely corporate political activities in these markets, in terms of both factors shaping those strategies and how they affect policy. Similarly, we must examine the way in which strategies pursued in one market may affect business interests in others (Blumentritt and Nigh, 2002; Wan and Hillman, 2006).

The third dimension of interconnectedness is that between different levels of governance. There is now a multiplicity of international organisations with an overt competence in health policy (eg the EU and the World Health Organization [WHO]) or whose decisions have ramifications for health policy even though their primary mandate is not health-related (eg the World Trade Organization [WTO], World Bank and International Monetary Fund [IMF]). In addition, governance at sub-state level affects health policy in many countries, for example, in federal systems and in the UK, in which health policy is a devolved competence. The literature on multilevel governance is now well established (Marks et al, 1996; Marks and Hooghe, 2003). In addition, research exists on how companies shape policy at various levels of governance (Sell, 2003; Holden et al, 2010; Roemer-Mahler, 2012). The concept of interconnectedness focuses our attention on how companies pursue political strategies across multiple layers of governance and the challenges this poses to effective health policy.

The final dimension of interconnectedness is that between different branches of government and agencies of the state, including executive, legislature, judiciary and semi-autonomous government agencies. There is a small body of literature demonstrating that companies coordinate their lobbying activities across various branches of government. Brook (2005) shows that US steel companies employed lobbying strategies that encompassed all branches of government. Similarly, Vanden Bergh and Holburn (2007) found that US accounting firms target their resources at the key governance actor on a given issue.

The pharmaceutical industry

The literature on the political role of pharmaceutical companies has focused on three policy areas: the protection of IP rights, the marketing of and authorisation for new drugs and pricing policies. Most studies investigating the power of pharmaceutical companies to shape public policies focus on their role as an interest group and their instrumental or agency power. The policy issue that has attracted most attention is IP regulation. In particular, scholars have examined the lobbying campaign of pharmaceutical companies from Europe and the US to establish internationally binding standards for IP protection (Weissman, 1996; Drahos and Braithwaite, 2001/02; Sell, 2003; T'Hoen, 2009). Pharmaceutical companies engaged in the development of new drugs command significant instrumental power, notably, monetary resources, the ability to organise collectively at both national and global levels, and expertise on IP (Liu, 1994; Drahos, 1995; Sell, 2003).

However, these companies' policy influence is the result of both agency and structural power. They are in a structurally privileged position, notably, as major exporters (Sell, 2003) and drivers of innovation (Lofgren and de Boer, 2004).

Interconnectedness between industries

Much of the literature on the power of pharmaceutical companies to shape IP regulation emphasises the importance of the companies' ability to mobilise a cross-industry coalition for the strengthening of international IP standards (Liu, 1994; Drahos, 1995; Sell, 2003). Indeed, collective action capability has been recognised as an important resource of political power for business more widely (Mizruchi, 1992). The concept of interconnectedness helps explain why pharmaceutical companies were able to mobilise cross-industry collective action.

The policy issue in question affected a wide range of industries in a similar and quite significant way. The protection of patents and copyrights had become a key pillar on which the business model for US and European companies in the pharmaceutical, chemical, computer and recording industries rested. Moreover, companies from all these industries were gearing up for expansion into the fast-growing Asian markets in the 1970s and 1980s when they discovered that their ability to gain market share in these countries was hampered by weak IP enforcement. The interconnectedness between different industries created by the issue of IP protection was, therefore, a key feature enabling cross-industry collective action. As Sell (2003) has pointed out, a group of CEOs translated this coalition of interests into a successful political campaign for IP protection at the global level.

Interconnectedness between markets

The interconnectedness between markets helps us understand why pharmaceutical companies have become strongly involved in IP policy debates in many countries across the globe since the 1970s and 1980s. In the 1970s and 1980s, US pharmaceutical companies developing new medicines came under increasingly competitive pressure from producers of generic drugs as a result of change in IP legislation in the US. The US Drug Price Competition and Patent Term Restoration Act of 1984 (usually referred to as the Hatch–Waxman Act), facilitated the entry of generic drugs into the US market. At the same time, new opportunities began to arise in the fast-growing markets of Asia and

Latin America (IMS, 2010). US pharmaceutical companies recognised, however, that a key obstacle to their further growth in these markets was limited protection of IP rights in these countries (Santoro, 1995). Weak IP enforcement enabled local pharmaceutical companies to reproduce medicines that had been developed by US and European firms (Kumar, 2002; Chaudhuri, 2005). The increasing interconnectedness of markets and the emergence of new competitors in Asia have been the key driving forces for US and European pharmaceutical companies to lobby for stronger IP protection across the globe (Sell, 2003; Roemer-Mahler, 2012).

Interconnectedness between levels of governance

The concept of interconnectedness helps us understand not only why pharmaceutical companies became increasingly involved in IP policymaking in many countries, but also why they chose a particular strategy. The interconnectedness between different industries affected by weak IP enforcement in emerging markets facilitated the creation of a cross-industry alliance. Similarly, the increasing interconnectedness between levels of governance provided an important determinant for the companies to target multilateral and bilateral trade agreements.

Sell (2003) points out that US pharmaceutical companies initially tried to strengthen IP protection in emerging markets by lobbying the US government to exert pressure on foreign governments. When, however, the Uruguay round of trade negotiations that led to the creation of the WTO began in 1986, the companies realised that this would be a more effective platform to address the issue. In particular, the companies realised that the dispute-resolution mechanism, which was to ensure the enforcement of WTO treaties in national policies, would be a powerful tool to force national governments to implement stronger IP protection. Hence, when the companies realised the increasing interconnectedness of governance levels in the area of international trade, they focused their efforts to have IP included in this emerging regime (Sell, 2003).

Interconnectedness between branches of the state

Finally, the concept of interconnectedness highlights that corporations pursue their political interests by targeting different branches of the state. This is well documented in the case of IP protection in India. When the Indian government introduced patent protection for pharmaceutical products in the wake of the WTO Agreement on Trade-Related Aspects of Intellectual Property Rights (TRIPS) it made use of a provision that allows governments some leeway in defining patentable subject matter (Article 27). In particular, the government introduced a section in the national Patents (Amendment) Act 2005 that prohibits patents on variants of existing chemical compounds that do not show enhanced efficacy. US pharmaceutical companies question whether this limitation is in line with international IP policies and have addressed the Indian government both directly through business associations like the US–India Business Council (USIBC, 2009) and indirectly through the US Trade Representative (PhRMA, 2010). In addition, individual companies have pursued a change of law through Indian courts.

In 2006, the Indian Patent Office (IPO) rejected the application of Novartis for a patent on a new, crystalline form of its cancer drug Glivec. Novartis appealed against the decision and has taken the issue all the way up to the Indian Supreme Court (the hearing is scheduled for the end of 2012). It is expected that the Supreme Court will also consider the validity of Indian patent law in light of international agreements on IP standards that India has entered into (Sampat et al, 2012).

The alcohol industry

Recent debates in UK alcohol policy offer important insights into the political strategy of the alcohol industry globally. Transnational alcohol corporations (TACs) enjoy considerable structural power as a result of the tax revenues they provide and the voters they employ, many of whom also enjoy the product they sell. In Scotland, particularly, whisky is a key component of national exports. However, structural factors have been unable to ward off increasing regulation of the alcohol market. In 2008, the Scottish Government announced its intention to introduce a minimum unit price for alcohol. This met with widespread opposition from many industry actors whose carefully orchestrated campaign against the measures led to their removal from the Alcohol Etc (Scotland) Bill (Holden and Hawkins, 2012). Following the 2011 Scottish elections, a new bill on minimum unit pricing (MUP) was introduced, which became law in May 2012. Subsequently, the UK government included a commitment to MUP in its alcohol strategy for England (HM Government, 2012) and launched a consultation on the policy in November 2012. TACs employed a range of strategies in an attempt to resist MUP in Scotland, including political lobbying of decision-makers, influencing public debates on policy and perceptions of alcohol, and efforts to undermine the scientific evidence base on which policy depends (Holden and Hawkins, 2012). While these proved successful the first time around, they were unable to head off the second attempt to introduce MUP. Having failed to stop MUP entering onto the statute books, alcohol industry actors have sought to challenge the legality of MUP under EU trade and competition law.

Interconnectedness between industries

Important similarities exist between the alcohol and tobacco industries in terms of the challenges they face and the means though which they engage in the policy process. Like the tobacco industry, the producer arm of the alcohol industry has become increasingly global in nature and is dominated by a small number of transnational corporations that have consolidated their position in markets across the world (Jernigan, 2009). Like transnational tobacco corporations (TTCs), TACs have faced increasing restrictions on how they can sell and market their product, through regulation of advertising and the times, places and price at which alcohol can be sold.

Despite this, important differences exist between TACs and TTCs. Alcohol control issues remain lower down the health agenda than tobacco. At the global level, there is no equivalent of the WHO Framework Convention on Tobacco Control (FCTC) to create an imperative for action to tackle alcohol-related harm. Unlike TTCs, TACs are seen as legitimate stakeholders in the policy process. They engage in co-regulatory regimes and CSR activities to a far greater extent than is possible for TTCs, delivering policy outcomes for government that increase their political relevance and influence (Hawkins and Holden, 2012).

Alcohol industry actors have employed a similar range of political strategies as TTCs in their attempts to stave off measures that run counter to their interests (Hawkins and Holden, 2012). Studies that have examined internal tobacco industry documents suggest that this is not coincidence but results from a transfer of knowledge between industries (Bond et al, 2010). However, this research is limited to a small number of cases in which co-ownership across industries (eg between Phillip Morris and the Miller Brewing Company) has led to ties between organisations. Further research is needed to establish whether cross-industry knowledge transfers may have been facilitated by the use of the same lobbying and public relations agencies or law firms by actors in each sector.

Interconnectedness between markets

Increasingly stringent regulation in its traditional markets has led TACs to focus increasingly on the development of new markets in populous and increasingly affluent emerging markets. This has profound implications for the political strategies employed by TACs. Holden and Hawkins (2012) found that the opposition of alcohol industry actors to MUP in Scotland was dictated to a large extent by their commercial interests in emerging markets. Since the majority of the whisky produced in Scotland is exported, the domestic arena constitutes a very small market for whisky producers. The commercial impact of MUP would have been relatively modest for global corporations. However, the policy was of huge symbolic importance for TACs' lobbying strategy elsewhere. It is far harder to make the case for self-regulation in markets such as China and India when the distillers' home government is taking such interventionist measures.

The focus on emerging market strategy went hand in hand with a more general fear that the introduction of MUP in Scotland may lead to the introduction of similar policies in other markets. The success of the policy would also remove one of the key industry arguments deployed against MUP: that it is untested and so there is no evidence to support its effectiveness (Hawkins and Holden, forthcoming).

Interconnectedness between levels of governance

The structure of the MUP debate in Scotland reflects the policy landscape of devolution in the UK. Health policy is a devolved competence under the remit of the Scottish government and the Scottish Parliament. The decision of the Scottish government to introduce MUP (as opposed to pursuing tax-based measures) also reflected the fact that taxation is a retained competence, decided at Westminster. Similarly, the institutional landscape of the devolved administration dictated the political strategy adopted by alcohol industry actors opposed to MUP. Initially, lobbying efforts focused on officials and ministers in the Scottish National Party (SNP) government, as they had done under previous administrations. When it became apparent that this would prove unsuccessful with the current incumbents, industry actors began to engage opposition Members of the Scottish Parliament (MSPs) who would be able to block the passage of the minority government's legislation through parliament.

Multilevel governance arrangements open up the possibility to corporations to shift the arena of decision-making to one in which the most favourable outcome is possible (Levy and Egan, 1998). Attempts at arena-shifting were evident in the debates on MUP (Holden and Hawkins, 2012). Industry actors opposed to MUP initially argued against any type of price-based intervention. As it became apparent that the government was determined to legislate on price, some producers and retailers began to argue that the appropriate mechanism for this was through taxation rather than MUP, arguing that a uniform policy was needed for all parts of the UK. These arguments, though, can be seen as an attempt to shift the forum of decision-making to Westminster, where it was felt that a Conservative-led government would not be willing to intervene in the alcohol market in such a way (Holden and Hawkins, 2012). Similar attempts at arena-shifting are evident in the ongoing legal challenge to MUP under EU competition law.

Interconnectedness between branches of the state

Arguments about the legality of MUP under EU competition law speak to another important dimension of interconnectedness: between the executive, legislature and judiciary. The lobbying strategy of TACs in Scotland first targeted officials and ministers before moving on to MSPs. When the majority SNP government were able to pass their legislation, attention turned to the courts in an attempt to block its implementation and have the law struck down.

Conclusions

In this chapter, we set out an analytical framework for examining corporate political power and strategy that draws on the insights from political science and management studies. In addition, we introduce the concept of interconnectedness to highlight how key features of globalisation are affecting the political role and activities of corporations.

We show that an interconnectedness of industries can be created when a policy affects a range of industries in a similar way. This interconnectedness between industries can then be an important determinant for collective action either through inter-industry coalitions or through inter-industry learning. In that way, interconnectedness between industries can help us to understand when one of the most important power resources (collective action) is available to business.

The concept of interconnectedness also contributes to our understanding of how the institutional environment shapes corporate political power and strategy. We show that in the cases of the pharmaceutical and the alcohol industries, the growing interconnectedness of governance has affected which governance institutions companies targeted (local, national or multilateral governance organisations). The case of the alcohol industry also shows that it can affect which issues companies emphasise (taxation rather than minimum prices). The case of the pharmaceutical industry highlights in particular that a high degree of interconnectedness between governance levels can be a valuable power resource for corporations. This is the case when companies succeed in capturing the highest level of governance with their political interests; something that happened when IP policy was integrated into the WTO.

To conclude, the concept of interconnectedness contributes to our understanding of the political role of corporations today because it highlights a range of structural features that have emerged through globalisation and that strongly affect the political strategies and power of corporations. Yet, the case studies examined in this chapter also emphasise the importance of agency in shaping how those structural features play out and the specific effects they have on the political activities of corporations in different industries and with regards to different policy debates.

References

Blumentritt, T.P. and Nigh, D. (2002) 'The integration of subsidiary political activities in multinational corporations', *Journal of International Business Studies*, vol 33, no 1, pp 57–77.

Bond, L., Daube, M. and Chikritzhs, T. (2010) 'Selling addictions: similarities in approaches between big tobacco and big booze', *Australasian Medical Journal*, vol 3, no 6, pp 325–32.

Brook, D.A. (2005) 'Meta-strategic lobbying: the 1998 Steel Imports Case', *Business & Politics*, vol 7, no 1, pp 1–24.

Brown, D., Roemer-Mahler, A. and Vetterlein, A. (2010) 'Theorising transnational corporations as social actors: an analysis of corporate motivations', *Business & Politics*, vol 12, no 1, pp 1-37.

Chaudhuri, S. (2005) *The WTO and India's pharmaceutical industry. Patent protection, TRIPS and developing countries*, New Delhi: Oxford University Press.

Doremus, P., Keller, W.W., Pauly, L.W. and Reich, S. (1998) *The myth of the global corporation*, Princeton, NJ: Princeton University Press.

Dorfman, L., Cheyne, A., Friedman, L.C., Wadud, A. and Gottlieb, M. (2012) 'Soda and tobacco industry corporate social responsibility campaigns: how do they compare?', *PLoS Medicine*, vol 9, no 6, pp 1–7.

Drahos, P. (1995) 'Global property rights in information: the story of TRIPs at the GATT', *Prometheus*, vol 13, no 1, pp 6–19.

Drahos, P. and Braithwaite, J. (2001/02) 'Intellectual property, corporate strategy, globalisation: TRIPS in context', *Wisconsin International Law Journal*, vol 20, no 2, pp 451–80.

Falkner, R. (2008) *Business power and conflict in international environmental politics*, Basingstoke: Palgrave Macmillan.

Farnsworth, K. (2004) *Corporate power and social policy in global context: British welfare under the influence?*, Bristol: Policy Press.

Farnsworth, K. and Holden, C. (2006) 'The business–social policy nexus: corporate power and corporate inputs into social policy', *Journal of Social Policy*, vol 35, no 3, pp 473–94.

Getz, K. (1997) 'Research in CPA: integration and assessment', *Business Society*, vol 36, no 1, pp 32–72.

Greenwood, J. and Jacek, H. (2000) *Organized business and the new global order*, Basingstoke: Macmillan.

Greidner, W. (1997) *One world ready or not: the manic logic of global capitalism*, New York, NY: Simon & Schuster.

Hacker, J.S. and Pierson, P. (2002) 'Business power and social policy: employers and the formation of the American welfare state', *Politics and Society*, vol 30, pp 277–325.

Hansen, W. L. and N. J. Mitchell (2001) 'Globalization of national capitalism: large firms, national strategies and political activities', *Business and Politics*, no 3, pp 5-19.

Hawkins, B. and Holden, C. (2012) '"Water dripping on stone"? Industry lobbying and UK alcohol policy', *Policy and Politics*, dx.doi.org/10.1332/030557312X655440.

Hawkins, B. and Holden, C. (forthcoming) 'Framing the alcohol policy debate: industry actors and the regulation of the UK beverage alcohol market', *Critical Policy Studies*.

Hillman, A., Keim, B. and Schuler, D. (2004) 'Corporate political activity: a review and research agenda', *Journal of Management*, vol 30, no 6, pp 837–57.

HM Government (2012) *The government's alcohol strategy*, London: HMSO.

Holden, C. and Hawkins, B. (2012) '"Whisky gloss": the alcohol industry, devolution and policy communities in Scotland', *Public Policy & Administration*, doi: 10.1177/0952076712452290.

Holden, C. and Lee, K. (2009) 'Corporate power and social policy: the political economy of the transnational tobacco companies', *Global Social Policy*, vol 9, no 3, pp 328–54.

Holden, C., Lee, K., Gilmore, A., Fooks, G. and Wanderer, N. (2010) 'Trade policy, health, and corporate influence: British American Tobacco and China's accession to the World Trade Organization', *International Journal of Health Services*, vol 40, no 3, pp 421–41.

IMS (2010) 'Pharmemerging shake-up. New imperatives in a redefined world', www.imshealth.com/imshealth/Global/Content/IMS%20 Institute/Documents/Pharmerging_Shakeup.pdf

Jernigan, D.H. (2009) 'The global alcohol industry: an overview', *Addiction*, vol 104 (Suppl 1), pp 6–12.

Kumar, N. (2002) 'Intellectual property rights, technology and economic development: experiences of Asian countries', Study Paper 1b, prepared for the UK Commission on Intellectual Property Rights, London.

Lawton, T., McGuire, S. and Rajwani, T. (2012) 'Corporate political activity: a literature review and research agenda', *International Journal of Management Reviews*, doi: 10.1111/j.1468-2370.2012.00337.x.

Lehne, R. (1993) *Industry and politics: the United States in comparative perspective*, Englewood Cliffs, NJ: Prentice Hall.

Levy, D. and Egan, D. (1998) 'Capital contests: national and transnational channels of corporate influence on the climate change negotiations', *Politics and Society*, vol 26, no 3, pp 337–61.

Levy, D.L. and Kolk, A. (2002) 'Strategic responses to global climate change: conflicting pressures on multinationals in the oil industry', *Business and Politics*, vol 4, no 3, pp 275-300.

Levy, D.L. and Newell, P. (2000) 'Oceans apart? Business response to global environmental issues in Europe and the United States', *Environment*, vol 42, no 9, pp 8-20.

Lindblom, C.E. (1977) *Politics and markets: the world's political-economic systems*, New York, NY: Basic Books.

Liu, P. (1994) 'U.S. industry's influence on intellectual property negotiations and special 301 action', *UCLA Pacific Basin Law Journal*, vol 13, no 1, pp 87–117.

Lofgren, H. and de Boer, R. (2004) 'Pharmaceuticals in Australia: developments in regulation and governance', *Social Science and Medicine*, vol 58, no 12, pp 2397–407.

Marks, G. and Hooghe, L. (2003) 'Unravelling the central state, but how? Types of multi-level governance', *American Political Science Review*, vol 97, no 2, pp 233–43.

Marks, G., Hooghe, L. and Blank, K. (1996) 'European integration from the 1980s: state-centric v. multi-level governance', *Journal of Common Market Studies*, vol 34, no 3, pp 341–78.

Matten, D. and Crane, A. (2005) 'Corporate citizenship: towards an extended theoretical conceptualization', *Academy of Management Review*, vol 30, pp 166–79.

Mizruchi, M. (1992) *The structure of corporate political action*, Cambridge, MA: Harvard University Press.

Newell, P. and Levy, D. (2006) 'Conceptualizing the corporation', in C. May (ed) *Global corporate power*, Boulder, CO: Lynn Rienner.

PhRMA (Pharmaceutical Research and Manufacturers of America) (2010) *Special 301 submission*, Washington, DC: Pharmaceutical Research and Manufacturers of America.

Rehbein, K. and Schuler, D. (1999) 'Testing the firm as a filter of corporate political activity', *Business & Society*, vol 38, no 2, pp 144–66.

Roemer-Mahler, A. (2012) 'Business conflict and global politics: the pharmaceutical industry and the global governance of intellectual property', *Review of International Political Economy*, doi: 10.1080/09692290.2011.645848.

Sampat, B.N., Shadlen, K.C. and Amin, T.M. (2012) 'Challenges to India's Pharmaceutical patent laws', *Science*, vol 337 (July), pp 414–15.

Santoro, M.A. (1995) *Pfizer: Global protection of intellectual property*, Harvard Business School Case Study 9-392-073, Cambridge, MA: Harvard Business School Publishing.

Scherer, A.G. and Palazzo, G. (2011) 'The new political role of business in a globalized world: a review of a new perspective on CSR and its implications for the firm, governance, and democracy', *Journal of Management Studies*, vol 48, no 4, pp 899–931.

Sell, S. (2003) *Private power, public law: the globalization of intellectual property rights*, Cambridge: Cambridge University Press.

Skidmore, D. (1995) 'Review: the business of international politics', *Mershon International Studies Review*, vol 39, no 2, pp 246–54.

Stopford, J. and Strange, S. (1991) *Rival states, rival firms: competition for world market shares*, Cambridge: Cambridge University Press.

Strange, S. (1996) *The retreat of the state: the diffusion of power in the world economy*, Cambridge: Cambridge University Press.

T'Hoen, E. (2009) *The global politics of pharmaceutical monopoly power. Drug patents, access, innovation and the application of the WTO Doha declaration on TRIPS and public health*, Diemen: AMB.

Tian, Z. and T. Hafsi and W. Wu (2009) 'Institutional determinism and political strategies: an empirical investigation', *Business&Society*, vol 48, no 3, pp 284-325.

USIBC (US–India Business Council) (2009) *The value of incremental pharmaceutical innovation: benefits for Indian patients and Indian businesses*, Washington, DC: US–India Business Council.

Vanden Bergh, R.G. and Holburn, G.L.F. (2007) 'Targeting corporate political strategy: theory and evidence from the U.S. accounting industry', *Business & Politics*, vol 9, no 2, pp 1-33.

Wan, W.P. and Hillman, A.J. (2006) 'One of these things is not like the others: what contributes to dissimilarity among MNE subsidiaries' political strategy?', *Management International Review*, vol 46, no 1, pp 85–107.

Weissman, R. (1996) 'A long, strange TRIPS: The pharmaceutical industry's drive to harmonize global intelletual property rules, and the remaining WTO legal alternatives available to third world countries', *University of Pennsylvania Journal of International Economic Law*, vol 17, no 4, pp 1069–125.

SEVEN

Square pegs and round holes: extending existing typologies fails to capture the complexities of Chinese social policy

Dan Horsfall and Sabrina Chai

Introduction

The last 30 years have been a time of profound change in China. The shift from a planned to a market economy has gathered pace, and from being considered an economically poor country just three decades ago, China now boasts the second-biggest economy in the world (IMF, 2011). This Chinese miracle of huge and rapid economic growth has brought China along with many other Asian nations into focus, with recent predictions suggesting that within the next 40 years, over half of global Gross Domestic Product (GDP) will be concentrated within the region (ADB, 2011). With attention focusing on China's stellar economic performance, many have sought to explain its economic success and understand the consequences that this is having, and is set to have, on social policies in the country (Wilding, 2008, p 18).

It is noted that China faces many key social policy dilemmas, which are thrown into even sharper relief given the attention China's economic performance has garnered. In particular, commentators have written extensively on the key question of the distribution of the benefits of growth beyond key cities/regions and beyond key elites (Guan, 2001, p 243; Kwon, 2005a, p 479; Redding and Witt, 2007, p 128; Zhang, 2009, p 227; OECD, 2010a, p 131; Yang et al, 2010, p 237). Similarly, there has been much commentary regarding the huge differential between both the resources apportioned to and the welfare outcomes experienced in rural and urban areas (Guan, 2001, p 245; OECD, 2010b, p 113; Yin, 2004; Zhang, 2009, p 230). Added to this are discussions around China's increasingly ageing and dependent population and the burden this is likely to place on the state (Zhang, 2009, p 227; ADB, 2011, p 20; OECD, 2011a, p 10; 2011b, pp 45, 51). It has been argued that this ageing of the Chinese population represents the key challenge for any programme of social welfare; the existence of large numbers of retirees is in fact a relatively recent phenomenon for a country with a historically young population (Kwon, 1997, p 475; Ramesh, 2004, p 324; Vodopivec and Hahn Tong, 2008, p 31; Glenn, 2009, p 38). All these issues are further complicated by the sheer size of the country, and by the fact that many of China's welfare structures are either embryonic or are in the process of being wholly reconstituted (Han, 2004, p 15; Goodman, 2009; Zhu, 2009, pp 20–1).

How China responds to these issues is of great interest to scholars across the social sciences. For comparative social scientists, how China apportions its resources in the coming years will undoubtedly add further fuel to the debate as to how China should be classified, or whether it truly does sit outside the Western-oriented typologies of welfare states. To date, the lack of robust comparative data has restricted the inclusion of China within comparative studies to a relatively small number of investigations. There have been some attempts, however, to place China within existing typologies and explain Chinese social policy as belonging to a wider world of welfare, though there is no consensus within this literature.

Existing classifications

Perhaps the most established and accepted classification of Chinese political economy sees it grouped with countries such as Japan, South Korea and Singapore as part of an East Asian model of developmental states (Holliday, 2000, p 706; Xia, 2000, p 2; Kwon, 2005a, p 483; 2005b, p 18; Redding and Witt, 2007, p 74; Kim, 2008, p 116; Glenn, 2009, p 37). While the aforementioned authors are keen to stress that there is much variation between developmental states in the region, common features include a strong state, which is extremely centralised and focuses most of its effort on economic growth. As such, financial resources are concentrated on economic development rather than 'wasted' on 'unproductive' welfare expenditures. The model, which was advanced to explain the perceived Japanese, Korean and Singaporean economic 'miracles', has been applied to the Chinese case from the early 1990s and it is clear that in many ways this is a natural extension of the model. China, like Japan and other East Asian developmental states, boasts a high economic growth rate, a Confucian cultural legacy and a one-party authoritarian system with which to guide development (Xia, 2000, p 2; Redding and Witt, 2007, p 86).

In many ways, the inclusion of China within the model of East Asian developmental states represents a neat fit. However, Xia (2000) is keen to highlight the fact that there are both cultural and 'ecological' factors that present obstacles to the Chinese developmental state. It is Xia's contention that the sheer size of China renders the traditional centralised approach to development problematic. Instead, in a clear divergence from other East Asian developmental states, China's developmentalism 'has a two-tiered structure in which the developmental role of the central state is nested within the context of central/local synergism' (Xia, 2000, p 3; see also Redding and Witt, 2007, p 132). Furthermore, Xia (2000, pp 210–11) notes that while the suppression of legislatures is a core feature of developmental states, China has in fact witnessed a reasonably large degree of legislative development. For these reasons, Xia has coined the phrase 'dual developmentalism' to describe the political economy of China. Whether one subscribes to this dual developmental categorisation or not, the core features are still identifiably developmental. The modifications Xia discusses, which were necessary to assimilate a country of China's size and with its communist legacy into the developmental model, do not present a fundamental divergence from the developmental approach of other East Asian nations. Rather, for those who advocate the developmental categorisation, the Chinese model should simply be thought of as an East Asian developmental state with Chinese characteristics (Xia, 2000, p 38; Huang, 2008, pp 276–81).

For some, however, the developmental state model tells only part of the story. Holliday accepts many of the key features of developmentalism, but insists that these are themselves features of a fourth world of welfare capitalism (Holliday, 2005, p 148). He notes that East Asian nations were almost entirely omitted from Esping-Andersen's (1990) *The three worlds of welfare capitalism*. The ostensible reason, Holliday contends, was that Esping-Andersen believed that the countries in his study needed to demonstrate that they not only were identifiably capitalist, but also had a welfare state that extended social rights (Esping-Andersen, 1997, p 180; Holliday, 2000, p 708; 2005, p 147). China's omission is perhaps not particularly noteworthy in itself, especially given the lack of available data at the time of Esping-Andersen's work; however, his criteria for inclusion is problematic for some authors. Holliday (2000, 2005) and Wilding (2008) both argue that this second criterion is unnecessarily restrictive and serves to obscure a distinctive fourth world of welfare capitalism, one in which social policies are largely subjugated to the needs of the economy. This branch of welfare capitalism is both productivist and developmental in principle, with a strong state pursuing the overriding policy objective of economic growth. From this central tenet of productivism flows only minimal social rights linked to productive activity, which in turn reinforces productive elements in society and shapes the state–family–market relationship towards growth (Holliday, 2000, pp 708, 715; Kwon, 2005a, p 479; Kim, 2008, p 111).

The notion that many East Asian countries inhabit a productive world of welfare is lent credence by the fact that Japan, Korea, Hong Kong, Singapore and Taiwan all have minimal social rights, have all actively pursued policies geared towards economic growth and have all, with perhaps the exception of Hong Kong, relied upon large-scale state intervention to support such growth (Kim, 2003, p 67; Kwon, 2005a, pp 478, 479; Kwon and Holiday, 2007, p 243; Redding and Witt, 2007, p 24; Wilding, 2008, p 22). For Holliday, these features, alongside geopolitical factors, outweigh the differences that exist in terms of both policy and administration within the East Asian nations (Holliday, 2000, p 714; 2005, p 158). As such, he argues, when framed in terms of a productivist approach, we can indeed talk about an East Asian model.

Holliday's categorisation of East Asian nations as belonging to a productive fourth world of welfare capitalism has found traction in the literature (see Goodin, 2001; Kim, 2003, 2008; Kwon, 2005a, 2005b; Wilding, 2008; Hudson and Kühner, 2009). However, as Hudson and Kühner point out, there are two key weaknesses within Holliday's work. First, Holliday's categorisation neglects the fact that productivist policies are not limited to East Asia. Indeed, as has been noted, many of Esping-Andersen's core liberal nations are said to have facilitated a shift from protective welfare policies towards more productive policies and, in many cases, blended the two approaches (Bonoli and Shinkawa, 2005, p 21; Kim, 2008, p 112; Hudson and Kühner, 2009, p 42). Second, Holliday's claims, while making qualitative sense, do not hold up under empirical investigation. Indeed, empirical explorations of the productive–protective mix within comparative social policy suggest that a truly productive world is better exemplified by traditionally liberal nations, such as the US and New Zealand, than East Asian nations (Hudson and Kühner, 2009, p 42; 2012, p 48). Furthermore, while there is clearly some productive intent within East Asian nations, it is not uniform. Hudson and Kühner's studies suggest that Korea has the strongest productive intent, yet in the Korean case, this is balanced by an equally strong set of protective policies. Malaysia and Singapore present weak productive behaviour, while China and Hong Kong blend weak productive and weak protective approaches, and Japan appears to follow a path that is not identifiable as either productive or protective (Hudson and Kühner, 2012, p 48). Ultimately, looking at empirical evidence and extending this not only to other East Asian countries such as China and Malaysia, but also to countries in Esping-Andersen's study (and beyond), it would appear that there is no distinct, East Asian productivist world of welfare capitalism (see also Kim, 2008; Wilding, 2008, p 23). More significantly for this chapter, China most definitely does not belong to such a model.

Holliday is quite right insofar as China's lack of a long legacy of welfare policy or distinguishable welfare state should not bar it from comparative studies of political economy. However, it may also be that a focus on the principles, institutions and tools of traditional welfare states may not be the most appropriate or illuminating. An alternative would be to consider the Chinese case from within the rubric of the competition state.

The Chinese competition state?

The competition state thesis emerged in the early 1990s as an analytical device to explain the changes brought about in the political economy of advanced welfare states by the rise of globalisation.[1] In short, it is argued that the confluence of globalisation, withering support for Keynesian economics in the wake of financial crises and a general withdrawal of support for welfare state structures and policies during the 1980s led to a moment of punctuated equilibrium in which the nature of political economy was radically changed (Cerny and Evans, 2003, p 19; 2004, p 52). Cerny and Evans, the key proponents of the competition state thesis, insist that the very principles of advanced welfare states were altered in accordance with the new economic realities created by the rise of the global economy and withering of territorially contained (and protected) markets (Cerny, 1997, p 259; 2008, p 25; 2010, p 17; Cerny and Evans, 2003, p 25; 2004, p 61; Evans, 2010, p 104). While this process had many effects, they argue that the most significant consequence was the embedding of a neo-liberal approach to social policy. Primarily, this meant the limitation of the state in the economic arena, and consequently precipitated a shift from government to governance, something Cerny and Evans insist has led to a gradual 'hollowing out' of the state (Cerny and Evans, 1999, p 26; 2004, p 59; Cerny, 2008, p 11). The fundamental goal of the state became to help create and maintain the conditions in which a market economy could thrive. Efficiency, competition and fiscal prudence became the key watchwords of the emerging paradigm (Cerny and Evans, 1999, pp 8, 17; 2003, p 23; Cerny, 2008, p 22).

Of course, an efficient economy has always been a coveted goal of governments. However, Cerny and Evans believe that where this had been in part a tool to ensure that citizens could be provided for, should such provision be needed, the goal of economic growth is now an end in itself. From this, all other policies flow, but only if they are deemed beneficial to the economy. The combination of an active pursuit of economic success and the shifts in governance have, Cerny and Evans believe, 'qualitatively disempowered the state and stripped it of legitimacy, to the point where the state can no longer perform its generic functions' (Cerny and Evans, 1999, pp 1–3), which they define as: stabilising the national polity; promoting the domestic economy in the public interest; promoting wider public interest; and social justice (Cerny and Evans, 1999, pp 1–2). Rather, the key focus of the state has become the controlling of inflation (Cerny and Evans, 1999, pp 10–11). One of the key criticisms of this and other hyperglobalist accounts of the effects of globalisation is that it is taken to signal the demise of the nation state. However, this is not what Cerny and Evans actually argue has happened. For Cerny and Evans, the state has been restructured to fulfil a different role. In particular, promoting competition or, perhaps more accurately, regulating to ensure competition, for Cerny and Evans, has become the new *raison d'*être of the state (Cerny and Evans, 1999, p 10; 2004, p 58; Cerny, 2008, p 24). In the arena of welfare, however, they are unequivocal, the welfare state is dead and 'the competition state is its successor, incorporating many of its features but reshaping them, sometimes quite drastically to fit a globalizing world' (Cerny and Evans, 2003, p 24).

Whether globalisation and the needs of the global economy have truly disempowered the state to such an extent that generous social programmes are no longer viable is a contentious issue and is one that is not the focus of this chapter. However, whether such a policy approach comes about by choice or coercion, Cerny and Evans insist we can now talk of competition states rather than welfare states. Table 7.1 presents a series of hypotheses pertaining to the competition state that Cerny and Evans suggest can be empirically investigated (Cerny and Evans, 1999, p 11). While they themselves have not undertaken such empirical investigation of many of these hypotheses, three studies (Horsfall, 2010, 2011, 2012) operationalised and explored Hypotheses 2–7 using data from the Organisation for Economic Co-operation and Development (OECD, 2010a, 2010b, 2010c, 2010d).

Cerny and Evans outline one 'ideal-type' of competition state, insisting that the UK and US fully conform and that other nations will eventually shift towards this model. They argue that competition states are marked by: low social expenditure; social assistance programmes that are not only minimal in terms of overall expenditure, but also ungenerous for those in receipt; low levels of employment protection; low levels of anti-competitive regulation; low levels of taxation; and a reliance on active labour market programmes (ALMPs) (Cerny and Evans, 1999, 2003). Furthermore, such competition states are likely to be highly decentralised, have witnessed the rise of New Public Management (NPM), be governed through a process of governance rather than government, and actively engage in policy transfer as part of a global economy (Cerny and Evans, 1999, 2003).

An empirical exploration of the hypotheses outlined in Table 7.1 that can be meaningfully measured, however, suggests that countries have not simply adopted a uniformly neo-liberal approach to the competition state. Measuring social expenditure, ALMP expenditure, employment protection legislation (EPL) (or market regulation) and corporate taxation suggests that although nearly all countries appear to

Table 7.1: Features of the competition state

1. New Public Management and the shift from government to governance
Hypothesis 1: *Competition states are leaders in the marketisation of public service production*
Hypothesis 2: *The shift from inefficient models of government to governance networks leads to a 'hollowing out' of the state*
2. Post-welfare contracting state
Hypothesis 3: *Social expenditure is lower in competition states than in more traditional welfare states*
Hypothesis 4: *Competition states make use of active labour market programmes (ALMPs) as an alternative to social assistance*
3. Government regulation of industry
Hypothesis 5: *Competition states are featured by low levels of product market regulation (PMR) and employment protection legislation (EPL)*
4. Taxation
Hypothesis 6: *Competition states have lower rates of taxation, especially in the arena of corporate taxation*
5. International policy transfer
Hypothesis 7: *Competition states actively engage in international policy transfer both as policy exporters and importers*

Source: Developed from Evans (2010) and Horsfall (2010)

have engaged with the competition state on some level, it is far from uniform. Rather, three different approaches to the competition state seem to emerge, as well as evidence that at least one country seems to act contrary to the competition state in all respects.

It is clear that there is some continuity between Cerny and Evans's competition state model and the developmental state, or the productivist models outlined by Holliday. In particular, in each model, economic growth is a primary goal, one to which social programmes are largely subordinated. Turning to China, there are many reasons why the competition state might be an interesting framework with which to consider the nature of political economy (Glenn, 2009, p 47). For instance, the form of governance detailed by Xia as being a source of discordance with the developmental state literature fits nicely with Cerny and Evans's view of a decentralised, more responsive and, ultimately, more efficient governance at the heart of the competition state (Cerny and Evans, 2004, p 59). Similarly, the focus of the competition state on limited welfare state structures and programmes, a balance between the rights of employers and employees that favours the former, low levels of taxation, and a generally pro-business environment makes qualitative sense when considered alongside China's economic boom (Cerny, 2008, p 15; 2010, p 18; see also Qian, 2002, p 3; Guan, 2005, p 238); indeed, so much so that Cerny himself is keen to suggest that China is a competition state (Cerny, 2008, p 15; 2010, p 18).

Table 7.2 has been constructed using data taken from the OECD (2010a, 2010b, 2010c, 2010d). To be located in the neo-liberal category, a country must exhibit low levels of social expenditure and must not demonstrate high levels of ALMP expenditure. If the country also exhibits low levels of corporate taxation or EPL, it is described as being a neo-liberal+ competition state. If a country exhibits both low levels of taxation and EPL, it is categorised as being strongly neo-liberal+. Similarly, if a country has high ALMP expenditure, but does not exhibit a low level of overall social expenditure, it is labelled as adopting an active approach to the competition state. As with the previous category, low levels of corporation taxation and/or EPL see a country labelled as being an active+, or strong+ active competition state. The third competition state form is one where welfare expenditure is not particularly low, nor are ALMPs particularly well funded, which runs contrary to the expectations of the competition state thesis. However, away from the traditional arena of the welfare state, countries are pursuing competition state principles in terms of low taxation and/or low levels of employment protection. Consequently, these countries have been categorised as having a welfare–competition state mix. As fuzzy set ideal-type methodology (see Ragin, 2000; Hudson and Kühner, 2012) affords the researcher a degree of flexibility, largely because it does not rely on mean averages to form the basis of its analysis, so including data on China is now possible.

Table 7.2: Countries grouped with regards to their approach to the competition state

Competition state types (2007)			
Broadly neo-liberal	Active	Welfare–competition state mix	Conservative welfare
Strong neo-liberal+ Slovak Republic, Australia , Ireland, Canada **Neo-liberal+** USA, Korea, **China (2008)**	Strong active+ Denmark, Switzerland **Active+** Norway, Sweden, Netherlands, Belgium, Austria	Strong pro-competitive UK, New Zealand **Pro-competitive** Portugal, Greece, Finland, Spain, Czech Republic, Japan, Poland, Italy, France	Rejection of competition state Germany

Source: Horsfall (2011, 2013)

These competition state types are produced through Boolean modelling of behaviours in the dimensions of social expenditure, ALMP expenditure per unemployed person, EPL and corporate taxation. Each type therefore represents different combinations of behaviours on each of the aforementioned dimensions.

While the methods used to produce Table 7.2 and the findings therein are not the key concern of this chapter (for further detail, see Horsfall, 2011, 2013), a few things are worth noting. As with other comparative investigations of empirical data, there appears no clear evidence of an East Asian model. In Table7.2, China is grouped closely with Korea, but also with the US and more loosely with Australia, Canada, Ireland and the Slovak Republic, while Japan is grouped separately. The fact that China appears to be categorised as a neo-liberal+ competition state is sure to raise a few eyebrows, but before that issue is explored, it is useful to explain what exactly has been measured to lead to such a categorisation. First, to be classified as following a broadly neo-liberal approach to the competition state, a country must demonstrate extremely low social expenditure levels as a proportion of GDP. In 2008, China had a social expenditure level of 6.5% as a proportion of GDP, close to that in Korea, and, as such, conforms on this most basic level to the expectations of a neo-liberal competition state (OECD, 2011b, p 75). To place this in context, the social expenditure levels in China and Korea, which stand at 6.5% and 7.6%, respectively, are much lower even than the US (16.1%) and the Slovak Republic (15.1%). A second requirement of countries in this categorisation is that they do not have particularly high expenditure on ALMPs, as high expenditure here is linked to more generous human investment schemes, rather than strict enforcement-based workfare schemes. Again, China can be considered as conforming to competition state expectations, with ALMP expenditure levels that are deemed negligible by the OECD (2011b, p 75).

As Table 7.2 suggests, the most recent data see China classified as a neo-liberal+ competition state. What this means is that China not only demonstrates low levels of social expenditure, but also conforms to competition state expectations in one other dimension. It is in the arena of corporation tax rather than EPL that China conforms to the expectations of the competition state. Had China also demonstrated competition state behaviour in the arena of EPL, China would be classified here as a strong neo-liberal+ competition state. However, while China has a corporation tax rate of somewhere between 10% and 25% depending on the type and size of corporation and thus can be seen as acting like a competition state in this regard (PWC, 2010, p 3), its EPL score is another matter. Calculated by the OECD in 2008 at 2.8, the Chinese EPL score indicates that on roughly half of all the OECD's indicators of employment protection, China scores relatively high (Venn, 2009, p 7; Eichhorst et al, 2010, p 15; OECD, 2010d). To place this in context, the US achieves a score of 0.9, the UK 1.1, Sweden 2.1, Germany 2.6 and France 2.8. The upshot being that in China, employees are afforded more protection than would be expected in a competition state.

It should also be noted that the methodology employed to produce Table 7.2 generally limits the number of variables that can be considered; however, other measurable indicators of the competition state such as the generosity of unemployment and pension benefits would see China categorised as a neo-liberal competition state (Guan, 2005, p 233; Eichhorst et al, 2010, p 25; OECD, 2010e, pp 137–8). Likewise, the OECD measures the general level of regulatory burden placed on industry and the markets to generate a product market regulation (PMR) score. Recent applications of the PMR measure to the Chinese case suggest that while the barriers to an open, competitive and business-friendly market have been scaled back in recent years (Redding and

Witt, 2007, p 86), the level of PMR is still far higher than we would expect to find in a competition state (OECD, 2010a, p 104). In particular, the links between state-owned enterprises (SOEs) and government agencies, the level of administrative burdens, the lack of private sector involvement in network sectors, and the barriers that still restrict foreign direct investment (FDI) remain problematic (OECD, 2010a, p 101; see also Gu, 2001; Qian, 2002, p 46).

So, what can be said of China as a competition state? By applying a methodology that has been developed very much with Western welfare states in mind, it can be argued that China should be considered as a neo-liberal competition state alongside the US and Korea. This *could* be said to reflect the fact that Korea and China are part of an East Asian model, one with shared histories and similar policy approaches. Moreover, the inclusion of the US in this group makes some qualitative sense given that the East Asian economic miracle was seen as a key inspiration of the American drive towards lower levels of state expenditure on social policies (Wilding, 2008, pp 19–20). However, while the categorisation of China alongside Korea immediately provokes interest given the perceived existence of an East Asian model of welfare, it is worth considering a couple of points. First, the model used to categorise China as a neo-liberal+ competition state only requires China to have low levels of taxation, low levels of social expenditure as a proportion of GDP and minimal expenditure on ALMPs. These are all features of the developmental and productivist state models that have been advanced previously, as well as, for that matter, most developing countries. Second, it may be the case that in many Western countries, these levels of expenditure and shifting policy priorities are the result of change over time, perhaps signalling a shift from a welfare state to a competition state. But in the Chinese case, this is simply the way things are, just as they have been throughout the 20th century (Guan, 2005, p 251; Wilding, 2008, p 20; Glenn, 2009, p 37). It may be that this reflects the fact that East Asian nations have had – until recently at least – relatively young populations as well as full employment. Some argue that this has limited the need for social policies such as pension or unemployment benefits (Kwon, 1997, p 475; Ramesh, 2004, p 324; Vodopivec and Hahn Tong, 2008, p 31; Glenn, 2009, p 38). The competition state thesis suggest that lower levels of expenditure reflect a declining legitimacy of the welfare state and inability of countries to maintain high levels of 'wasteful' welfare expenditure in the face of globalisation. As mentioned, even when discussing lower-spend nations such as the UK and US, this is a contentious assertion. In the Chinese case, however, it is possibly more problematic. Ultimately, while low levels of social expenditure and low levels of taxation in China point towards an ethos in which the economy is privileged, there is little evidence that this is a measure taken to integrate with a global financial market.

The real issue is that the competition state thesis is concerned with more than simply expenditure levels and tax rates. What is crucial is how the state contends with the global economy. Cerny and Evans developed their competition state thesis to reflect the fact that globalisation had rendered large-scale programmes of social welfare impractical, unviable and increasingly illegitimate (Cerny, 1997, p 259; 2008, p 10; Cerny and Evans, 2003, p 25). Moreover, the drive towards an efficient economy had led to the rise of NPM and a shift from government to governance, a process that ultimately disempowered states insofar as they were no longer able to privilege the needs of citizens over the needs of the economy (Cerny and Evans, 2003, p 19). Can it really be said that these processes and motivations have been or are being witnessed in the Chinese case? As Taylor notes, Chinese political economy 'is characterised by pervasive macroeconomic interventions, unclear lines of authority within an authoritarian party-state, close synergies between officials and business leaders, ambiguous property rights, and uneven enforcement of the rule of law' (Taylor, 2010, p 41). None of this, he argues, sits well within the rubric of the competition state as advanced by Cerny and Evans.

There is a wider issue also, which perhaps reflects a weakness in the competition state thesis. Hay has argued that the competition state simply represents a 'stylised' account of capitalism under Blair and Thatcher (Hay, 2004) and it is clear that there are similarities between core assertions of the competition state thesis and commentary surrounding the structural power of capital (see Gough and Farnsworth, 2000; Farnsworth, 2004). It is possible that the competition state thesis fits particularly well – at least in qualitative terms – with countries such as the US and UK, owing to the fact that the balance between capital and labour has historically favoured the former. Added to this, globalisation undoubtedly affords a greater degree of capital mobility, seen as a key source of the structural power of capital. In countries where policy elites have embraced the rhetoric of globalisation and where the historical balance between capital and labour favours the former, the competition state thesis is likely to resonate. In China, however, where the strength of the state, especially with regards to the freedoms of private enterprise, is particularly strong, the structural power of capital is undoubtedly mitigated. To that end, it is perhaps surprising that the competition state represents a neat fit for the Chinese case.

To further complicate matters, where many Western nations have adopted the rhetoric of the competition state without perhaps translating this into competition state behaviours (Horsfall, 2011, p 213), the Chinese state has made increasing social provision a target moving forward, as part of its two most recent five-year plans (APCO, 2010, pp 3–4; KPMG, 2011, p 3; OECD, 2011a, p 10). It is clear, then, that a snapshot of a limited range of macroeconomic indicators is not sufficient evidence to assert that China should be considered a competition state. What is required is a closer look at the issues of governance in the Chinese case and an exploration of how, if at all, China's state structure has changed alongside the period of globalisation that Cerny and Evans insist wrought huge changes within Western nations.

Here, we see very little evidence that the unstoppable tide of globalisation has wrought fundamental changes on the nature of Chinese bureaucracy. That is not to say that fragmented governance cannot be witnessed. Rather, 'hollowing out' in China has not led to a loss of state power; instead, governance has been used as an instrument of statecraft to re-establish the hegemony of the Communist Party of China (CPC) and its self-styled brand of state socialism. Chinese privatisation, in the sense of ownership transformation from the public sector to the private sector, is confined to small- and medium-sized SOEs (Cao et al, 1999; Kong, 2003, p 544; Liu et al, 2006). For the larger SOEs, it is more appropriate to characterise the reform as 'corporatisation' rather than privatisation, in that the 'new owners' are, in fact, state entities including holding companies and other SOEs (Koppell, 2007, p 264). Compared with the situation in Mao's era (1949–78), or in the 1980s, the state sector has indeed shrunk in the past three decades (Portyakov, 2004, p 374). However, the state sector continues to dominate, control and monopolise the 'commanding heights' of the national economy, which means the role of the Chinese state in key industries remains strong and calculated. The state enterprises today, in theory, have autonomy to run their businesses, but, in practice, the decisions of investment, appointment of major personnel and property purchase and handling are still in the hands of their supervising government departments.

Ultimately, during the last 30 years, the transition process in China has maintained political-ideological authoritarianism and state control of the whole economy. The party-state system remains intact and powerful, and state intervention remains extensive (Goodman, 2009). China's administrative reforms offer no strong evidence in favour of the 'hollowing out' hypothesis that lies at the heart of the competition state. Processes of 'hollowing out' have simply not undermined the power of the state. Rather, somewhat contradicting core expectations of the competition state, such changes to the nature of governance in China have become part of a strategy of statecraft for increasing the capacity of the state to steer.

Reflection: China, from competition state to welfare state or developmental state to Chinese welfare state?

The competition state thesis was advanced to make sense of the changes witnessed in the UK through the Thatcher and early Blair governments, suggesting an explanation based upon the ever-increasing power of globalisation to shape social policies. It is difficult to argue against the notion that the profound ideological changes witnessed during these governments occurred alongside a restructuring with regards to how the UK was governed. There was most definitely a change in the way that social policies are delivered, reflecting some separation of 'steering from rowing'. However, the competition state thesis advances the notion that it has been the unstoppable rise of globalisation and a technological shrinking of the world that has forced ideological change and shaped the nature of governance so as to render welfare states unviable. Moreover, despite concentrating on the UK and US cases, where many would argue that ideology most definitely came first, key advocates of the competition state thesis insist that as globalisation is a worldwide phenomenon, these new economic imperatives exert similar pressures on all nations. It was not simply the demise of the British welfare state that was predicted, but rather the death of welfare states.

Some have argued directly against the existence of a competition state even in the UK (see Hay, 2004), and many have advanced defences of the British welfare state (Hay and Rosamund, 2002; Castles, 2004; Ellison, 2006). Addressing this debate has not been the purpose of this piece. Rather, it has asked whether the principles of the competition state can be witnessed in the Chinese case. What it has demonstrated is that at a basic level, Chinese macro-level policies with regards to expenditure, labour market policies and taxation are similar to other countries that have been labelled 'neo-liberal competition states'. However, this does not do justice to the complexities of either the competition state thesis or the Chinese case. Indeed, on its own, the data used to categorise China tell us very little. Importantly, it does not tell us about the nature of governance in China, nor does it tell us anything about the structure of Chinese welfare. Even a cursory engagement with the literature details a process in China that runs contrary to the competition state thesis. Rather than shrinking, the Chinese welfare state is growing, not just in terms of expenditure as a proportion of GDP, but also as an ideological concept. The most recent five-year plan put social protection at the heart of policy, and the key instruments of a welfare state are taking shape. Even the rise of NPM and processes that can be considered as decentralisation and a move from government to governance have not occurred in the fashion detailed in the competition state thesis. Here, rather than a hollowing out of the state, what has been witnessed is a further diffusion of the state and the ability of the CPC to control provincial policy.

Dismissing the notion that the wider implications of the competition state can be witnessed within China, we are left to consider what the data on social expenditure, labour market policies, employment protection and taxation is actually telling us. While the developmental state and the competition state may appear similar in some respects – such as social expenditure – they describe very different trajectories. The direction of change is extremely important and while the competition state thesis was advanced to explain perceived welfare state retrenchment, China would appear to be expanding its welfare services. It is likely the case that the data presented in this piece simply capture a developmental state engaged in the formation of a welfare state. What that welfare state will look like is as yet unclear. Describing and perhaps labelling this maturing welfare state will require more than the analysis of macro-data. Similarly, simply extending theories attached to the 'Western' welfare states is unlikely to accurately capture the nature of the Chinese welfare state. It may be that a country as large and distinct as China, with such a unique historical legacy and political framework, will forever prove difficult to meaningfully categorise or typologise.

Note

[1.] For a full discussion of the competition state thesis, see Cerny (1997) Cerny and Evans (1999, 2003, 2004) and Hay (2004).

References

ADB (Asian Development Bank) (2011) *Asia 2050: realizing the Asian century*, Mandaluyong City: ADB.

APCO (2010) *China's 12th five-year plan: how it actually works and what's in store for the next five years*, Beijing: APCO Worldwide.

Bonoli, G. and Shinkawa, T. (2005) 'Population ageing and the logic of pension reform in Western Europe, East Asia and North America', in G. Bonoli and T. Shinkawa (eds) *Ageing and pension reform around the world: evidence from eleven countries*, London: Edward Elgar.

Cao, Y., Qian, Y. and Weingast, B.R. (1999) 'From federalism, Chinese-style to privatisation, Chinese-style', *Economics of Transition*, vol 7, no 1, pp 103–31.

Castles, F. (2004) *The future of the welfare state*, Oxford: Oxford University Press.

Cerny, P. (1997) 'Paradoxes of the competition state: the dynamics of political globalization', *Government and Opposition*, vol 32, no 2, pp 251–74.

Cerny, P. (2008) 'Embedding neoliberalism: the evolution of a hegemonic paradigm', *The Journal of International Trade and Diplomacy*, vol 2, no 1, pp 1–46.

Cerny, P. (2010) 'The competition state today: from raison d'Etat to raison du Monde', *Policy Studies*, vol 31, no 1, pp 5–22.

Cerny, P. and Evans, M. (1999) 'New Labour, globalization, and the competition state', CES Working Papers Series 70.

Cerny, P. and Evans, M. (2003) 'Globalization and social policy', in N. Ellison and C. Pierson (eds) *Developments in British social policy 2*, Basingstoke: Palgrave Macmillan Press.

Cerny, P. and Evans, M. (2004) 'Globalisation and public policy under New Labour', *Policy Studies*, vol 25, no 1, pp 51–65.

Eichhorst, W., Escudero, V., Marx, P. and Tobin, S. (2010) *The impact of the crisis on employment and the role of labour market institutions*, IZA Discussion Paper No 5320, November, Bonn: Forschungsinstitut zur Zukunft der Arbeit.

Ellison, N. (2006) *The transformation of the welfare state?*, Oxon: Routledge.

Esping-Andersen, G. (1990) *The three worlds of welfare capitalism*, Cambridge: Polity

Esping-Andersen, G. (1997) 'Hybrid or unique? The Japanese welfare state between Europe and America', *Journal of European Social Policy*, vol 7, no 3, pp 179–89.

Evans, M. (2010) 'Cameron's competition state', *Policy Studies*, vol 31, no 1, pp 95–116.

Farnsworth, K. (2004) *Corporate power and social policy in a global economy*, Bristol: Policy Press.

Glenn, J.G. (2009) 'Welfare spending in an era of globalization: the North–South divide', *International Relations*, vol 23, no 1, pp 27–50.

Goodin, R. (2001) 'Towards a post-productivist welfare regime', *British Journal of Political Science*, vol 31, no 1, pp 13–39.

Goodman, D. (2009) 'Sixty years of the People's Republic: local perspectives on the evolution of the state in China', *The Pacific Review*, vol 22, no 4, pp 429–45.

Gough, I. and Farnsworth, K. (2000) 'The enhanced structural power of capital: a review and assessment', in I. Gough (ed) *Global capital, human needs and social policies*, London: Palgrave.

Gu, E.X. (2001) 'Beyond the property rights approach: welfare policy and the reform of state owned enterprises in China', *Development and Change*, no 32, pp 129-50.

Guan, X. (2001) 'Globalization, inequality and social policy: China on the threshold of entry into the World Trade Organisation', *Social Policy and Administration*, vol 35, no 3, pp 242–57.

Guan, X. (2005) 'China's social policy: reform and development in the context of marketization and globalization', in H. Kwon (ed) *Transforming the developmental welfare state in East Asia*, Basingstoke: Palgrave Macmillan, pp 231–56.

Han, W. (2004) 'The evolution of income distribution disparities in China since the reform and opening-up', in Organisation for Economic Co-operation and Development (ed) *China in the global economy: income disparities in China – an OECD perspective*, Paris: OECD, pp 9–26.

Hay, C. (2004) 'Re-stating politics, re-politicising the state: neo-liberalism, economic imperatives and the rise of the competition state', *The Political Quarterly*, vol 75, no 1, pp 38–50.

Hay, C. and Rosamond, B. (2002) 'Globalisation, European integration and the discursive construction of economic imperatives', *Journal of European Public Policy*, vol 9, no 2, pp 147–67.

Holliday, I. (2000) 'Productivist welfare capitalism: social policy in East Asia', *Political Studies*, vol 48, pp 706–23.

Holliday, I. (2005) 'East Asian social policy in the wake of the financial crisis: farewell to productivism?', *Policy & Politics*, vol 33, no 1, pp 145-62.

Horsfall, D. (2010) 'From competition state to competition states?', *Policy Studies*, vol 31, no 1, pp 57–76

Horsfall, D. (2011) 'From competition state to competition states? An empirical exploration', PhD Thesis, University of York, UK, http://etheses.whiterose.ac.uk/1607/1/From_competition_state_to_competition_states__an_empirical_exploration_Horsfall_D_G.pdf

Horsfall, D. (2012) 'There and back again: convergence towards the competition state plan', *Policy Studies*, vol 34, no 1, pp 53-73.

Horsfall, D. (2013) 'A fuzzy set ideal-type approach to measuring the competition state', *Policy and Society*.

Huang, Y. (2008) *Capitalism with Chinese characteristics*, Cambridge: Cambridge University Press.

Hudson, J. and Kühner, S. (2009) 'Towards productive welfare? A comparative analysis of 23 OECD Countries', *Journal of European Social Policy*, vol 19, no 1, pp 34–46.

Hudson, J. and Kühner, S. (2012) 'Analyzing the productive and protective dimensions of welfare: looking beyond the OECD', *Social Policy & Administration*, no 46, pp 35–60.

IMF (International Monetary Fund) (2011) *World Economic Outlook database*, New York, NY: IMF.

Kim, Y.-H. (2003) 'Productive welfare: Korea's third way?', *International journal of Social Welfare*, vol 12, pp 61–7.

Kim, Y.-M. (2008) 'Beyond East Asian welfare productivism in South Korea', *Policy and Politics*, vol 36, no 1, pp 109–25.

Kong, Q. (2003) 'Quest for constitutional justification: privatisation with Chinese characteristics', *Journal of Contemporary China*, vol 12, no 36, pp 537–51.

Koppell, J.G.S. (2007) 'Political control for China's state-owned enterprises: lessons from America's experience with hybrid organisations', *Governance: An International Journal of Policy, Administration, and Institutions*, vol 20, no 2, pp 255–78.

KPMG (2011) *China's 12th five-year plan: an overview*, Beijing: KPMG China.

Kwon, H. (1997) 'Beyond European welfare regimes: comparative perspectives on East Asian welfare systems', *Journal of Social Policy*, vol 26, no 4, pp 467–84.

Kwon, H. (2005a) 'Transforming the developmental welfare state in East Asia', *Development and Change*, vol 36, no 3, pp 477–97.

Kwon, H. (2005b) 'An overview of the study: the developmental welfare state and policy reforms in East Asia', in H. Kwon (ed) *Transforming the developmental welfare state in East Asia*, Basingstoke: Palgrave Macmillan, pp 1–26.

Kwon, H. and Holliday, I. (2007) 'The Korean welfare state: a paradox of expansion in an era of globalisation and economic crisis', *International Journal of Social Welfare*, vol 16, pp 242-48.

Liu, G.S., Sun, P. and Woo, W.T. (2006) 'The political economy of Chinese-style privatisation: motives and constraints', *World Development*, vol 34, no 12, pp 2016–33.

OECD (2010a) *OECD economic surveys: China*, Paris: OECD.

OECD (2010b) *Tackling inequalities in Brazil, China, India and South Africa: the role of labour market and social policies*, Paris: OECD, http://dx.doi.org/10.1787/9789264088368-en

OECD (2010c) 'OECD social expenditure statistics (database)', doi: 10.1787/data-00166-en, http://stats.oecd.org/index.aspx?r_951879

OECD (2010d) *OECD indicators of employment protection. Database Version 2*, Paris: OECD.

OECD (2010e) *OECD employment outlook: moving beyond the jobs crisis*, Paris: OECD.

OECD (2011a) *China's emergence as a market economy: achievements and challenges*, Paris: OECD.

OECD (2011b) *Society at a glance. OECD social indicators*, Paris: OECD.

Portyakov, V. (2004) 'The economic reform conception in China: formation and evolution', *China Report*, vol 40, no 4, pp 357–77.

PWC (PricewaterhouseCoopers China) (2010) *The People's Republic of China: tax facts and figures – 2010*, Beijing: PricewaterhouseCoopers China.

Qian, Y. (2002) *How reform worked in China*, William Davidson Working Paper 473, California: Centre for Economic Policy Research.

Ragin, C. (2000) *Fuzzy-set social science*, Chicago: The University of Chicago Press.

Ramesh, M. (2004) 'Issues in globalisation and social welfare in Asia', *Social Policy and Society*, vol 3, no 3, pp 321–7.

Redding, G. and Witt, M.A. (2007) *The future of Chinese capitalism: choices and chances*, Oxford: OUP.

Taylor, M. (2010) 'Evolutions of the competition state in Latin America: power, contestation and neo-liberal populism', *Policy Studies*, vol 31, no 1, pp 39-56.

Venn, D. (2009) *Legislation, collective bargaining and enforcement: updating the OECD employment protection indicators*, OECD Social, Employment and Migration Working Papers, No 89, DOI: 10.1787/223334316804, Paris: OECD.

Vodopivec, M. and Hahn Tong, M. (2008) *China: improving unemployment insurance*, The World Bank Social Protection and Labour Working Paper No 0820, Washington, DC: World Bank.

Wilding, P. (2008) 'Is the East Asian welfare model still productive?', *Journal of Asian Public Policy*, vol 1, no 1, pp 18–31.

Xia, M. (2000) *The dual developmental state: development strategy and institutional arrangements for China's transition*, Aldershot: Ashgate.

Yang,Y.,Williamson,J.B. and Shen, C. (2010) 'Social security for China's rural aged: a proposal based on a universal non-contributory pension', *International Journal of Social Welfare*, vol 19, no 2, pp 236–45.

Yin, Y. (2004) 'Disparities between urban and rural areas and among different regions in China', in Organisation for Economic Co-operation and Development (ed) *China in the global economy: income disparities in China – an OECD perspective*, Paris: OECD, pp 49–64.

Zhang, H. (2009) 'China's social assistance: in need of closer coordination', *International Journal of Sociology and Social Policy*, vol 29, nos 5/6, pp 227–36.

Zhu, Y. (2009) 'A case study on social security coverage extension in China', ISSA Working Paper No 7, www.issa.int/aiss/content/download/91350/1830628/file/2-paper7-YZhu.pdf

EIGHT

The Earned Income Tax Credit as an anti-poverty programme: palliative or cure?

Phyllis Jeroslow

Introduction

The Earned Income Tax Credit (EITC), a federal rebate provision of the US tax code, is heralded as that nation's largest anti-poverty programme for low-income, working families (Berube, 2006; Holt, 2006). Notwithstanding more than 35 years of EITC implementation, poverty still plagues American families and children. While the EITC has been lauded for increasing labour force participation, particularly for lone mothers, and for lifting working families up to the federal poverty level (Greenstein, 2005; Acs and Toder, 2007), the short-term cash benefits of the EITC do not appear to support long-term economic gains for poor working families (Rainwater and Smeeding, 2003; Dowd and Horowitz, 2011). Additionally, the constraints of many low-wage jobs restrict the time and financial resources that parents can invest in promoting the development and success of their children (Dodson and Albelda, 2012). These limitations of the EITC as a 'making work pay' policy may have implications for workfare policies in other industrialised nations, such as the new Universal Credit in the UK.

The EITC is recognised as an integral part of the new 'workfare' state by incentivising work for parents with limited skills and education, but less well known is the EITC's prominent role as a wage supplement that reaches working households below and *above* the poverty line. The EITC's function to prop up low wages in response to international economic competition challenges conventional thinking about its explicit purpose as an anti-poverty programme. While the EITC provides much-needed income support to working families, income alone, as a subsidy for chronic low wages, is not enough to prevent many children of programme beneficiaries from experiencing deprivation that is likely to limit their life chances and adult earning potential (Heckman and Masterov, 2007), thereby reproducing poverty in the next generation (Sachs, 2011). Additionally, there is a growing consensus that poverty is not defined solely by income; it is more aptly described by a constellation of deprivation factors (Wilson, 1987). If poverty is to be surmounted in future generations, the federal anti-poverty agenda will need to blend income supports for parents with other forms of social assistance, and promote policies that build the human capital of their children.

The chapter begins with an overview of the EITC's functions, goals and target populations. The next section examines the poverty-reduction effects of the EITC relative to the US poverty threshold and explores reasons why US poverty rates for families and children have remained consistently high throughout the history of the EITC. The discussion then focuses on the labour activation effects of the EITC, including prospects for income mobility and intergenerational mobility. The chapter concludes with considerations for redirecting anti-poverty policy through strategies that serve the long-term interests of parents, children and the nation.

Earned Income Tax Credit functions, goals and recipients

The EITC is a means-tested, cash assistance programme for wage-earners administered through the Internal Revenue Service (IRS) as a redistributive transfer. For those who qualify, the EITC reduces tax liability based on annual family income (Hotz and Scholz, 2001; Holt, 2006). The amount of the cash transfer rises as the number of 'qualified' children in the household increases, with the category of 'three or more' children providing the maximum credit levels (Holt, 2006; US Department of the Treasury, 2012). The EITC is refundable; thus, if the amount of the credit exceeds the tax liability, the excess is refunded as a direct payment, and if the tax liability is zero, the entire amount is paid as a refund (US House of Representatives Committee on Ways and Means, 2004; Holt, 2006).

The history of the EITC reflects political debates about the intent and design of the safety net (Hotz and Scholz, 2001). Policy proposals that pre-dated the EITC in the late 1960s and early 1970s focused on eliminating poverty, but controversies about rights and responsibilities that occurred during this period ensured that any viable policy to alleviate poverty would also have to address cash welfare entitlements for non-working families, which by then had fallen into public disfavour (Ventry, 2000). As stated by the Senate Committee on Finance in 1975, the original purpose of the EITC was to provide 'an added bonus or incentive for low-income people to work' and an inducement for 'Families receiving Federal assistance to support themselves' (US Senate Committee on Finance, 1975). When first enacted in 1975, the government distributed a total of $1.25 billion in earned income credits to 6.2 million families who received an average credit of $201 (in nominal dollars; Beamer, 2005). By 2010, a greatly expanded EITC paid $59.5 billion to 26.8 million families (IRS, 2012).

The EITC is principally aimed at families with children, targeting lone mothers in particular, with only a modest credit implemented in 1993 for childless workers (Holt, 2006; Meyer, 2010). Using data from the Current Population Survey, Meyer (2010) estimates that nearly 50% of EITC dollars go to lone mothers and 7% to lone fathers, even though they together represent slightly over 10% of US households; 38% of EITC dollars are distributed to married couples with children, and only 5% reach child-free individuals (Meyer, 2010). Two-child families are the most common type of recipients (Holt, 2006). Viewed from another perspective, 60% of lone mothers and 50% of lone fathers receive the credit, compared to 20% of married couples (Hoffman and Seidman, 2003). Overall, approximately one in seven households (15%) nationwide qualify for the EITC (Hoffman and Seidman, 2003).

The median income of US families with children can be used as a comparator for the maximum benefits amounts afforded by the EITC while also illustrating the marked differences between the incomes of married couples and those of lone parents. In 2011, the median income for families with two or more children was $77,540 for married couples, $38,531 for lone fathers and $22,425 for lone mothers (US Census Bureau, 2012a). The maximum EITC credits for tax year 2011 were $3,094 for one child, $5,112 for two children and $5,751 for three or more children (US Department of the Treasury, 2012).

Poverty rates and the Earned Income Tax Credit

The EITC has received ongoing acclaim for its success in lifting people out of poverty (Holt, 2006; Meyer, 2010) and increasing the labour force participation of lone mothers (Acs and Toder, 2007). Recipients of the EITC boost their low earnings by as much as 45% (Meyer, 2010), with lone-parent families reaping the programme's greatest poverty-reduction impact (Simpson et al, 2010). According to the US Department of the Treasury (2012), about 3.3 million children in working families are lifted out of poverty each year. Greenstein (2005) has estimated that without the EITC, the child poverty rate would be 25% higher.

Despite these accomplishments, Hoffman and Seidman (2003) find that the EITC exerts only a modest reduction effect on overall poverty, since more than 60% of poor households are ineligible. Hoffman and Seidman (2003) calculate that the EITC reduced overall poverty rates by 0.2 to 0.4 percentage points in the 1980s, and by 1.0 to 1.5 percentage points in the 1990s. A further consideration is that the EITC is not exclusively targeted at families below the poverty threshold. Simpson et al (2010) estimate that EITC eligibility extends to 35% of households below the poverty line, 35% of households between 100% and 150% of the poverty line, and 25% of households between 150% and 200% of the poverty line.

Benefit levels are structured by phases that represent three ranges of annual income: 1) phase-in; 2) plateau phase; and 3) phase-out. In the phase-in range, the credit increases for each additional dollar earned up to a certain maximum level. At the maximum level, the amount of the credit reaches a plateau phase in which more income does not yield a larger tax credit. During the phase-out range, the tax credit gradually decreases to zero as income rises (Holt, 2006). The phases are related to the poverty line, such that the phase-in and plateau ranges correspond to earnings below the poverty line, while the phase-out range corresponds to earnings above the threshold (Urban Institute and Brookings Institution Tax Policy Center, 2012). Roughly 15% of recipients are in the phase-in range, 25% are in the plateau range and 60% are in the phase-out range (Ventry, 2000).

The claim that the EITC lifts families and children 'out of poverty' warrants further scrutiny. In contrast to the EU, the US uses a widely criticised, 'absolute' measure of poverty that has remained essentially unchanged since its origination in the 1960s, except for adjustments for inflation. The official US measure represents three times the food budget for nutritional needs during a temporary emergency, and does not reflect contemporary costs for transportation, housing and medical care (Pressman, 2011). A family is designated as 'poor' when its gross income, according to family size, falls below the poverty line (Pressman, 2011). For a family of two adults and two children, the US poverty threshold for 2011 is $22,811 and the poverty threshold for a lone parent with two children is $18,123 (US Census Bureau, 2012b). In comparison, European and other nations use a 'relative' measure to determine poverty thresholds typically based on 50% of a country's median income. Data for the late 2000s from the Organisation for Economic Co-operation and Development (OECD, 2012) indicate that the US has a higher poverty rate measured by 50% of median equivalised household income than found in other rich nations.

As an alternative to relative measures of income, some researchers in the UK calibrate poverty according to consumption needs for a predefined standard of living and then develop a budget based on the costs required to purchase identified necessities (Deeming, 2005). Several investigators of American poverty have simply doubled the absolute US poverty threshold to achieve a consumption-oriented measure known as the 'self-sufficiency standard' (Gershoff et al, 2003, p 83), although this method appears more arbitrary than the UK approaches. The self-sufficiency standard attempts to represent the real costs of living for a family's basic needs, independent of subsidies. Basic needs are conceived as housing, food, transportation, childcare, health care and miscellaneous items such as clothing, medicine and household items (Gershoff et al, 2003).

Since implementation of the EITC in 1975, the official US poverty rate for families with children has fluctuated from a low of 12.7% in 2000 to a high of 18.5% in 2011 and 1993 (see Table 8.1) (US Census Bureau, 2012c). Poverty rates for lone mothers during this period are consistently much higher (lowest 33%; highest 46.1%). For 2011, the poverty rate for lone mothers was 40.9%. Official US poverty rates do not take into account public assistance or received tax credits. Nevertheless, the overall trend reveals that poverty has persisted, and that poverty-alleviation strategies have not succeeded in significantly lowering poverty rates for families with children.

The rising incidence of child poverty has not adequately been addressed by US policies. Child poverty in the US increased by 50% in the last quarter of the 20th century (Rainwater and Smeeding, 2003), a time frame coincident with the enactment of the EITC in 1975 and its subsequent expansions. While industrialised nations during the 20th century achieved prodigious rates of economic growth and rising standards of living, a substantial proportion of American children lived 'in families so poor that [their] normal health and growth [were] at risk' (Duncan and Brooks-Gunn, 1997; Rainwater and Smeeding, 2003, p 132). Using the self-sufficiency standard for 2009, the National Center for Children in Poverty (NCCP) estimated that 42% of American children resided in low-income families, split between 21% designated as near-poor (between one and two times the poverty line) and 21%

Table 8.1: Poverty status of families by type of family, for all races with children under 18 years, for selected years

Year (author's comment)	All families			Female householder, no husband present		
	Total	Below poverty level		Total	Below poverty level	
		Number	%		Number	%
1975 (EITC begins)	31,377	4,172	13.3	5,119	2,252	44.0
1986 (EITC expands)	33,801	5,516	16.3	7,094	3,264	46.0
1990 (EITC expands)	34,503	5,676	16.4	7,707	3,426	44.5
1993 (EITC expands; highest poverty)	36,456	6,751	18.5	8,758	4,034	46.1
1996 (PRWORA begins)	37,204	6,131	16.5	8,957	3,755	41.9
2000 (lowest poverty)	38,190	4,866	12.7	8,813	2,906	33.0
2001 (EITC expands)	38,427	5,138	13.4	9,171	3,083	33.6
2009 (EITC expands)	38,820	6,630	17.1	9,872	3,800	38.5
2011 (latest data)	38,436	7,111	18.5	10,379	4,243	40.9

Notes: Numbers in thousands. Families as of March of the following year. PRWORA – Personal Responsibility and Work Opportunity Reconciliation Act.

Source: Adapted from US Census Bureau (2012c)

below the poverty line. In the same year, the number of children below the poverty line climbed to 15.3 million, and the number of children below twice the poverty line reached 31.3 million (NCCP, 2012). The experience of poverty can span a long period of childhood. Children who are born into poverty are more likely to remain poor than older children first entering poverty (Hoynes et al, 2006). For families who are able to leave poverty, there is a substantial rate of re-entry (Hoynes et al, 2006).

Child poverty varies by 'race', ethnicity and family structure. The poverty rate for white or Asian children raised in two-parent families is under 5%, while that of African-American and Latino children in one- and two-parent families ranges from 35% to 40%. Poverty rates soar close to 60% for approximately two thirds of African-American children who live in lone-parent households (Lindsey, 2009).

Hoynes et al (2006) examine why the overall poverty rate has been largely intractable, turning primarily to market forces and government anti-poverty policies for explanations. They conclude that government programmes have a greater effect on closing the poverty '*gap*' between income and the poverty threshold than on reducing the proportion below the poverty line. On the other hand, the authors find that labour market conditions, as defined by median wages, unemployment rates and inequality, provide the main evidence for persistent, high poverty rates (Hoynes et al, 2006).

Technological advances rendered obsolete many traditional low-skilled jobs and increased unemployment for American workers, while low-wage competition from abroad depressed wages for the low-skilled jobs that remained (Sachs, 2011). Such 'skill-biased technological change' (Yellen, 2006, p 3) was accompanied by the decline of trade unions, which weakened workers' bargaining power, especially for less-skilled men, and a fall in the real value of the minimum wage that particularly affected less-skilled women (Kahne and Mabel, 2010). In the 1980s, skill-biased technological change led to bifurcation of the American workforce by educational level, reflecting stark differences in real wages between college graduates and those with a high school education or less (Yellen, 2006; Sachs, 2011). Approximate median earnings in 2009 for college graduates were $48,000 compared to $27,000 for workers with a high school diploma (US Census Bureau, 2012d).

Inequality in the US rose more in the decades preceding the mid-2000s than in other advanced industrial nations, providing America with the dubious distinction of ranking near the top of the international scale on most measures of household income inequality (Yellen, 2006). Despite dramatic growth in US Gross Domestic Product (GDP) per capita, income gains accrued disproportionately to higher-income earners, thus widening inequality between those at the top and bottom of the income distribution (Yellen, 2006; Kahne and Mabel, 2010). Hoynes et al (2006) found that the steady increase in inequality was driven by declines in real wages for less-skilled workers earning below the median wage, and concluded that this devaluation provided the most cogent rationale for the upward trend in poverty rates. Yellen (2006) also linked America's elevated level of inequality to its high levels of overall and child poverty.

Another explanation for the persistence of poverty in the US cites inadequate federal policy responses to the dramatic rise in the percentage of lone-parent families. Between 1970 and 2000, the proportion of all families in the US headed by a lone parent, most often a mother, rose from 15% to more than 30% (Reich, 2000). Notwithstanding this conspicuous shift in family structure and the increased likelihood of poverty among lone-parent families headed by women, policy support for lone parents and their young children began to erode in the 1990s and has since remained a 'patchwork of means-tested plans' (Lindsey, 2009, p 103).

With the loss of manufacturing jobs in the US came the demise of the male breadwinner model. Concurrent with the growth of lone-parent families, many women entered the labour force in order to maintain their accustomed standard of living, including mothers of young children (Reich, 2000). As a result, public sentiment turned sharply against the federal programme 'Aid to Families with Dependent Children' (AFDC), known simply as 'welfare' in the American vernacular, which provided cash aid to poor, lone mothers without requiring work. In response to public discontent, and with bipartisan support from conservatives and liberals, President Clinton upheld his campaign pledge to 'end welfare as we know it' and enacted the Personal Responsibility and Work Opportunity Reconciliation Act of 1996 (PRWORA), a welfare-to-work programme. The EITC then assumed a major role as an incentive for reducing welfare entries and as a support for those in the transition from welfare to work (Grogger, 2004; Acs and Toder, 2007).

Labour activation, income mobility and intergenerational mobility

While the EITC is evaluated primarily for its effectiveness in leveraging labour force participation to alleviate poverty, one perspective that receives less attention concerns how the EITC serves the interests of capital in its capacity as a labour activation policy. Researchers studying similar programmes in European countries fill this gap by describing a 'new economic orthodoxy' (Dean and Mitchell, 2011, p 4) befitting a polarised labour market that exerts downward pressure on the lowest paid (Dean, 2012). The new doctrine preaches that competitive economies no longer need a reserve army of labour, and that it is preferable to maximise the labour supply even if wages are below subsistence (Jordan, 1998; Bonoli, 2005). Consequently, it becomes desirable and even necessary for governments to subsidise low-paying employers (Dean and Mitchell, 2011; Dean, 2012). In liberal welfare states, the cost of wage top-ups may fall disproportionately on better-paid taxpayers rather than on corporate coffers, even though employers are programme beneficiaries (Dean, 2012). The indirect, federal subsidy then constitutes a competitive advantage for employers who pay sub-subsistence wages (Grover, 2005). In turn, the EITC and derivative wage top-up programmes in the UK, including the former Working Tax Credit and the new Universal Credit, institutionalise low pay without solving the problem of in-work poverty (Grover, 2005).

In line with the analyses of Dean, Mitchell and Grover, as previously cited, evidence from other researchers suggests that the EITC has been more effective in its mission to increase the labour supply than in its goal to alleviate financial hardship for the poor (Grogger, 2004; Dowd and Horowitz, 2011). The success of the EITC in promoting work, particularly among low-skilled, less-educated lone mothers, is attributed to its incentive to 'make work pay' by providing more combined income through work and tax benefits than can be acquired through welfare payments and other public assistance (Ventry, 2000, p 10; Acs and Toder, 2007). Once employed, welfare-to-work mothers are typically launched into the phase-in or plateau phases of the EITC benefit structure (Meyer, 2010), where they join approximately 40% of recipients who are below the poverty line. Although the mothers remain poor, the gain in income may be several thousand dollars and thus effectively influences their decisions 'to work or not to work' (Acs and Toder, 2007, p 335; Meyer, 2010).

In a national study between 1986 and 2007, a period that encompassed several EITC expansions, lone mothers without a high school diploma accounted for the largest increase in workforce participation when compared by educational level with single, childless women (Meyer, 2010). Between 1993 and 1999, EITC expansions accounted for 10–16% of the marked decline in welfare participation rates (Grogger, 2004). Nevertheless, the success of labour activation through the combination of welfare reforms and EITC wage supplements did not translate into economic security for many who were off the welfare rolls. During the boom years of the American economy between 1992 and 2000, overall poverty rates for lone mothers fell dramatically (Blank, 2002), but the proportion of families with incomes below 50% of the federal poverty threshold increased (Zedlewski et al, 2002). Another study conducted in 1990 and 1996 found that low-income, lone mothers were less likely to rely on welfare, but no more likely than their pre-reform counterparts to have incomes that exceeded 150% of the poverty threshold (Acs et al, 2005). After the passage of PRWORA, exits from welfare increased and welfare entries decreased, but Acs and Loprest (2004) found that only 60% of welfare-leavers worked, and of this group, 85% still had incomes below twice the poverty threshold.

As demonstrated by the preceding studies of welfare reform, labour activation policies that seek to decrease poverty through employment may produce different consequences for the poor and near-poor. In this context, Meyer (2010) examined how the EITC differentially affects recipients at various points in the low- and moderate-income spectrum relative to the poverty threshold. Meyer (2010) found that the EITC sharply reduces the numbers of families at targeted levels of 50% and 200% of the poverty line, with strongest poverty-reduction effects at

75%. Presumably, the reductions for those at 75% of the poverty line boost families somewhat above the poverty threshold and serve as the basis for the claim of 'lifting' families out of poverty. In comparison, families at the 50% mark are likely to shrink the poverty gap between their earnings and the poverty line. Incomes that exceed 200% of the poverty threshold are generally considered moderate; thus, EITC refunds awarded at the 200% earnings point would elevate a household's status above the commonly accepted demarcation for low-income families. In contrast to the image of the EITC as a programme that primarily serves the poor, Hoffman and Seidman (2003) note that the 'near-poor' fare better than families below the poverty line. Households with incomes between 100% and 150% of the poverty threshold have the same probability of receiving EITC benefits as poor families, and better-off families qualify for a larger cash refund because their earnings are higher (Hoffman and Seidman, 2003).

Other researchers assess poverty by distinguishing 'episodic' poverty from 'persistent' (or chronic) poverty (Jantti, 2009, p 184). Dowd and Horowitz (2011) use a similar framework to differentiate the EITC's function as a temporary safety net from that of a long-term support for the years between 1989 and 2006, primarily for claimants with children. During this period, approximately 50% of taxpayers with children were EITC recipients, if only for a year or two (Dowd and Horowitz, 2011).

The average spell for EITC receipt is roughly three years, and spells are typically longer for young families headed by lone mothers and families with more children. Average spells are shortest for families with higher earnings who enter the EITC programme in the phase-out range (2.7 years), and longest for families who enter at the plateau phase (3.9 years) (Dowd and Horowitz, 2011). As noted earlier, former welfare recipients typically enter the EITC benefit structure in the phase-in range or in the plateau phase, where the spells last longer.

The EITC programme is characterised by 'churning', that is, the ongoing movement of families into and out of the parameters of EITC eligibility (Dowd and Horowitz, 2011). Almost one third of EITC recipients exit the programme each year; 20% of those who leave reclaim the EITC after one year, and a total of 44% reclaim eligibility over time (Dowd and Horowitz, 2011). For those who claim the EITC for short intervals due to a cutback in work hours or temporary joblessness (frequently due to the birth of a child), the EITC functions as a short-term safety net. But for those who receive EITC benefits for many years and who have multiple spells of cycling in and out of eligibility, the EITC serves as a long-term support for persistent poverty (Dowd and Horowitz, 2011).

One explanation for why EITC recipients in the plateau phase have longer eligibility spells is the lack of career ladders and skill development opportunities for most low-wage jobs (Dodson and Albelda, 2012). Lower skill levels are often associated with lower earning capacity (Yellen, 2006). Gershoff et al (2003, p 96) advise that 'work-first' approaches may be misguided if they are not accompanied by opportunities for skill development that could enable parents to obtain higher-paying jobs.

Work-first approaches may be misguided for additional reasons. Full-time work supplemented by an EITC refund does not guarantee freedom from material hardship (Gershoff et al, 2003; Pressman, 2011). Many jobs held by former welfare recipients provide wages below the poverty level and are considered 'low quality' (Dodson and Albelda, 2012, p 1). Low-wage jobs afford few, if any, employer-based benefits (eg health insurance, paid sick leave or paid vacation) and often require non-standard, inflexible schedules that can fluctuate at the employer's discretion from week to week, thereby precluding parents from attending to many of their children's needs (Dodson and Albelda, 2012).

Untoward consequences of low-wage jobs affect workers' children through multiple pathways. Economic deprivation in low-income families is associated with deficits in children's health, overall development and educational achievement (Duncan and Brooks-Gunn, 1997). Adolescents of low-income workers are more likely to drop out of school, assume the care of younger siblings and become parents while teenagers (Dodson and Albelda, 2012). Historically, American youth were able to use education as a springboard out of poverty, but opportunity structures for accessing education have changed (Lindsey, 2009). High levels of economic inequality have intensified the problem of child poverty by generating a wealth-based social stratification that begins early in a child's life and limits educational attainment (Sachs, 2011). Low-wage work is a contributing factor. Low-wage parents have a shortage of parental resources, in the form of time and money, which are considered necessary for promoting children's development (Gershoff et al, 2007). Parental investment is reflected in the purchase of books and toys, the provision of high-quality childcare, and time spent in enriching family activities, particularly those that affect cognitive development (Gershoff et al, 2007). Due to erratic job schedules and limited budgets, low-income parents are generally unable to obtain the high-quality childcare that affluent families can more easily access and afford. Families with low incomes pay an average of 22% of their household earnings for childcare in comparison to 6% for families with high incomes (Williams, 2010). In addition to the inability to finance high-quality childcare, many low-income parents cannot afford computer software or after-school programmes that build their children's academic and social skills. Nor can they afford time to invest in their children's schooling (Dodson and Albelda, 2012). For the school-age years, individual families and local communities in the US bear much of the fiscal responsibility for educational costs, resulting in a per-pupil spending gradient that mirrors economic inequality by sharply differentiating the resources available in affluent versus poor school districts. This differential is magnified for poor children, who frequently have greater learning needs, but who lack opportunities to learn from parents, especially lone parents, who have limited education (Sachs, 2011). For poor children who succeed in high school, the rising costs of education often pose yet another barrier to college attendance that keeps them trapped in poverty (Sachs, 2011).

International comparisons of correlations between the education levels of parents and children reveal that the US has the lowest social mobility of all OECD countries, thus shattering the image of America as a land of opportunity (Sachs, 2011). The 'startlingly strong correlation' between the income and educational attainment of American parents and that of their children demonstrates that children from poor households are likely to be poor as adults (Sachs, 2011, p 280). Contrary to the classic American myth, children's future prospects have become predicated by a 'caste system' more closely linked to the economic fortunes of their parents, and few options are available to children residing in low-income and poor neighbourhoods (Lindsey, 2009, p 162).

Parental investment in children's human capital is considered one of the key factors for the intergenerational transmission of labour market earnings (Mazumder, 2012). Higher family income is believed to reduce material hardships, lower parental stress and raise parental allocations of time and money to yield beneficial effects on children's cognitive, social and emotional competencies (Gershoff et al, 2007). In this respect, additional family income afforded by the EITC can be helpful for children. Even in families who receive the EITC, however, many children experience long-term effects of childhood deprivation across the life course. Some researchers conclude that income transfers such as the EITC are not sufficient to close gaps in child outcomes between low- and higher-income children (Berger et al, 2009). Sustained poverty rates, slim prospects for the economic mobility of low-wage workers and worrisome outcomes for their children demonstrate that the EITC is a palliative, not a cure. 'Life's a little easier with the EITC' proclaims the

IRS website. This platitude may indeed be true, but it does not signify a permanent solution for poverty either in the life course of a single family or across generations in the US population.

Conclusion: from palliative to cure

At present, the EITC together with other family-oriented federal policies have not provided an adequate response to the transformation of macroeconomic conditions, unprecedented inequality or the developmental needs of poor and low-income children, particularly for those living in lone-parent families. Deficits in the skills and education of American workers and dim prospects for building the human capital of their children threaten America's future prosperity (Sachs, 2011) and condemn many to a life marked by privation and unrealised potential. Unlike many other industrialised nations, social programmes in the US for parents with children under the age of six are aimed more at ensuring that mothers work than at improving the economic conditions of their children (Lindsey, 2009). The EITC preserves the status quo by enabling the subsistence of its recipients while supplying low-wage, flexible labour for employers, but it provides neither economic mobility nor a solution to intergenerational poverty.

The US has done the least of 30 OECD countries to move families out of poverty through government taxes and transfers (Yellen, 2006). The OECD publication 'Doing better for children' (2009, p 165) explains that 'the cheapest and easiest policy' for reducing child poverty is to shift children from slightly below to slightly above the poverty line – a central feature of the design of the EITC – but that such targets are ill-conceived and lead to inadequate policy responses. As shown by Dowd and Horowitz (2011), many people may exit poverty each year, but they remain close to the poverty line and face a substantial likelihood of re-entry (Jantti, 2009). The EITC functions more akin to what Sachs (2011, p 43) defines as 'an income transfer used for short-run consumption' rather than 'a government benefit that enables poor households to raise their long-term productivity'. In addition, linking the assistance of anti-poverty programmes to labour force participation risks neglecting children who have the greatest needs (Magnuson and Votruba-Drzal, 2009).

Employers may realise short-term gains from labour activation policies, but these may be at the expense of greater long-term productivity achieved through building the quantity and quality of a post-industrial workforce. Welfare-to-work programmes will not solve the shortage of young and skilled workers who, according to Heckman and Masterov (2007), have traditionally served as a major source of US economic growth. The US focus on employment as the primary road out of poverty has not succeeded. Jobs available to low-skilled individuals pay poorly and working conditions prohibit parents from investing time and money to support their children's development (Dodson and Albelda, 2012). In turn, failure to promote children's success limits their economic productivity as adults, affecting not only their personal lives, but also the productivity of the nation (Heckman and Masterov, 2007).

With one in five children growing up in poverty (Sachs, 2011), a comprehensive, national anti-poverty policy is long overdue – one that would, as Yellen (2006) suggests, enhance the long-run growth of productivity and likely raise the average standard of living over time. Child development advocates recommend a dual-generational strategy that invests in low-income children and provides supports to their parents. Such a coordinated approach would incorporate income subsidies such as the EITC within a web of interlaced family and child supports that extend far beyond cash transfers (Gershoff et al, 2003; Rainwater and Smeeding, 2003).

Heckman and Masterov (2007) prioritise investments in young children from disadvantaged environments, with the aim of reducing inequality associated with being born into a poor family. Early interventions, such as high-quality childcare and early education, can reverse some of the harm attributed to disadvantage while supplying a high economic return beneficial to the child, the child's offspring and society as a whole (Heckman and Masterov, 2007). Interventions for parents are also warranted to enable them to address their children's needs more effectively, which points both to the necessity for family supports in the community as well as to family-friendly workplaces in the low-wage sector. Community services could help parents provide the type of family environment, as described by Heckman and Masterov (2007), which fosters both the cognitive and non-cognitive skills necessary for children's success as students and workers. In the workplace, paid leave benefits and employee-driven flexibility in work schedules for low-wage employees would better allow parents to nurture their children (Dodson and Albelda, 2012).

The history of the EITC exemplifies American popular, but narrowly focused, sentiment that favours work incentives over welfare while ignoring attendant consequences in the larger contexts of life trajectories and economic productivity. The tenacious idea that poverty is the fault of the individual with little consideration for the vast structural, economic and technological transformations of recent decades constrains US policy to the point where the perpetuation of poverty not only harms individual families and limits the realisation of children's potential, but also fails to build a workforce consistent with the needs of the domestic and international economies. Americans now face the prospect of an increasingly bifurcated society comprised of families that are wealthy, educated and skilled, but who are isolated from families that are low-income, poorly educated and unskilled.

Over 60 years ago, Marshall (1950) explained how unequal outcomes produce inequalities in opportunity through stratification by education and occupation. Jantti (2009) finds that Americans' excessive valuation of equality of opportunity *over* equality of outcomes indicates that they fail to see the relationship between the two principles. It is now necessary for the American public and its legislators to connect the dots between inequality and poverty by providing the least economically fortunate with opportunities to succeed and contribute to a vibrant democratic society.

References

Acs, G. and Loprest, P. (2004) *Leaving welfare: employment and well-being of families that left welfare in the post-entitlement era*, Kalamazoo, MI: The W.E. Upjohn Institute for Employment Research.

Acs, G. and Toder, E. (2007) 'Should we subsidize work? Welfare reform, the Earned Income Tax Credit and optimal transfers', *International Tax and Public Finance*, vol 14, pp 327–43.

Acs, G., Phillips, K.R. and Nelson, S. (2005) 'The road not taken? Changes in welfare entry during the 1990s', *Social Science Quarterly*, vol 86 (SE), pp 1060–79.

Beamer, G. (2005) 'State tax credits and "making work pay" in post-welfare reform era', *Review of Policy Research*, vol 22, no 3, pp 385–95.

Berger, L.M., Paxson, C. and Waldfogel, J. (2009) 'Income and child development', *Children and Youth Services Review*, vol 31, pp 978–89.

Berube, A. (2006) *The new safety net: how the tax code helped low-income working families during the early 2000s*, Survey Series, Washington, DC: The Brookings Institution.

Blank, R. (2002) 'Evaluating welfare reform in the United States', *Journal of Economic Literature*, vol 40, December, pp 1105–66.

Bonoli, G. (2005) 'The politics of the new social policies: providing coverage against new social risks in mature welfare states', *Policy & Politics*, vol 33, no 3, pp 431–49.

Dean, H. (2012) 'Welcome relief or indecent subsidy? The implications of wage top-up schemes', *Policy & Politics*, vol 40, no 3, pp 305–21.

Dean, H. and Mitchell, G. (2011) *Wage top-ups and work incentives: the implications of the UK's Working Tax Credit scheme*, London: London School of Economics.

Deeming, C. (2005) 'Minimum income standards: how might budget standards be set for the UK?', *Journal of Social Policy*, vol 34, no 4, pp 619–36.

Dodson, L. and Albelda, R. (2012) *How youth are put at risk by parents' low-wage jobs*, Boston, MA: University of Massachusetts Center for Social Policy.

Dowd, T. and Horowitz, J.B. (2011) 'Income mobility and the Earned Income Tax Credit: short-term safety net or long-term income support', *Public Finance Review*, vol 39, no 5, pp 619–52.

Duncan, G.J. and Brooks-Gunn, J. (eds) (1997) *The consequences of growing up poor*, New York, NY: Russell Sage Foundation.

Gershoff, E.T., Aber, J.L. and Raver, C.C. (2003) 'Child poverty in the United States: an evidence-based conceptual framework for programs and policies', in F. Jacobs, D. Wertlieb and R.M. Lerner (eds) *Handbook of applied developmental science* (vol 2), Thousand Oaks, CA: Sage Publications, pp 81–136.

Gershoff, E.T., Aber, J.L., Raver, C.C. and Lennon, M.C. (2007) 'Income is not enough: incorporating material hardship into models of income associations with parenting and child development', *Child Development*, vol 78, no 1, pp 70–95.

Greenstein, R. (2005) *The Earned Income Tax Credit: boosting employment, aiding the working poor*, Washington, DC: Center on Budget and Policy Priorities.

Grogger, J. (2004) 'Welfare transitions in the 1990s: the economy, welfare policy, and the EITC', *Journal of Policy Analysis and Management*, vol 23, no 4, pp 671–95.

Grover, C. (2005) 'Living wages and the "making work pay" strategy', *Critical Social Policy*, vol 25, no 5, pp 5–27.

Heckman, J.J. and Masterov, D.V. (2007) *The productivity argument for investing in young children*, Working Paper 13016, Cambridge, MA: National Bureau of Economic Research.

Hoffman, S.D. and Seidman, L.S. (2003) *Helping working families: the Earned Income Tax Credit*, Kalamazoo, MI: Upjohn Institute for Employment Research.

Holt, S. (2006) *The Earned Income Tax Credit at age 30: what we know*, Research Brief, Metropolitan Policy Program, Washington, DC: The Brookings Institution.

Hotz, V.J. and Scholz, J.K. (2001) *The Earned Income Tax Credit*, Working Paper 8078, Cambridge, MA: National Bureau of Economic Research.

Hoynes, H.W., Page, M.E. and Stevens, A.H. (2006) 'Poverty in America: trends and explanations', *The Journal of Economic Perspectives*, vol 20, no 1, pp 47–68.

IRS (Internal Revenue Service) (2012) 'About EITC', www.eitc.irs. gov/central/abouteitc

Jantti, M. (2009) 'Mobility in the United States in comparative perspective', in M. Cancian and S. Danziger (eds) *Changing poverty, changing policies*, New York, NY: Russell Sage Foundation.

Jordan, B. (1998) *The new politics of welfare*, London: Sage.

Kahne, H. and Mabel, Z. (2010) 'Single mothers and other low earners: policy routes to adequate wages', *Poverty & Public Policy*, vol 2, no 3, article 7, DOI: 10.2202/1944-2858.1082, www.psocommons.org/ppp/vol2/iss3/art7

Lindsey, D. (2009) *Child poverty and inequality: securing a better future for America's children*, New York, NY: Oxford University Press.

Magnuson, K. and Votruba-Drzal, E. (2009) 'Enduring influences of childhood poverty', in M. Cancian and S. Danziger (eds) *Changing poverty, changing policies*, New York, NY: Russell Sage Foundation.

Marshall, T.H. (1950) *Citizenship and social class*, Sterling, VA: Pluto Press.

Mazumder, B. (2012) 'Is intergenerational economic mobility lower now than in the past?', Chicago Fed Letter, no 297 (April), The Federal Reserve Bank of Chicago.

Meyer, B.D. (2010) 'The effects of the Earned Income Tax Credit and recent reforms', *Tax Policy and the Economy*, vol 24, no 1, pp 153–80.

NCCP (National Center for Children in Poverty) (2012) http://nccp. org/publications/pdf/text_975.pdf

OECD (Organisation for Economic Co-operation and Development) (2009) 'Doing better for children', www.oecd-ilibrary.org/statistics

OECD (2012) 'Society at a glance, EQ2.1. Poverty has been rising', www.oecd-ilibrary.org/statistics

Pressman, S. (2011) 'How poor are America's poor?', *Challenge*, vol 54, no 2, pp 109–21.

Rainwater, L. and Smeeding, T.M. (2003) *Poor kids in a rich country: America's children in comparative perspective*, New York, NY: Russell Sage.

Reich, R. (2000) *The future of success*, New York, NY: Vintage Books.

Sachs, J.D. (2011) *The price of civilization: reawakening American virtue and prosperity*, New York, NY: Random House.

Simpson, N.B., Tiefenthaler, J. and Hyde, J. (2010) 'The impact of the Earned Income Tax Credit on economic well-being: a comparison across household types', *Population Research and Policy Review*, vol 29, pp 843–64.

Urban Institute and Brookings Institution Tax Policy Center (2012) 'Tax facts: historical EITC parameters', www.taxpolicycenter.org/taxfacts/displayafact.cfm?Docid=36

US Census Bureau (2012a) 'Current population survey annual social and economic supplement', www.census.gov/hhes/www/cpstables/032012/faminc/toc.htm

US Census Bureau (2012b) 'Poverty thresholds', www.census.gov/hhes/www/poverty/data/threshld/index.html

US Census Bureau (2012c) 'Historical poverty tables – families', www.census.gov/hhes/www/poverty/data/historical/families.html

US Census Bureau (2012d) 'Educational attainment in the United States: 2009', February, www.census.gov/prod/2012pubs/p20-566.pdf

US Department of the Treasury (2012) 'The Earned Income Tax Credit', www.eitc.irs.gov

US House of Representatives Committee on Ways and Means (2004) *2004 green book*, Washington, DC: Government Printing Office.

US Senate Committee on Finance (1975) 'Tax Reduction Act of 1975: report to accompany H.R. 2166', 17 March, Washington, DC.

Ventry, D.J. (2000) 'The collision of tax and welfare politics: the political history of the Earned Income Tax Credit, 1969–99', *National Tax Journal*, vol 53, no 4, pp 983–1006.

Williams, J. (2010) *Reshaping the work–family debate*, Cambridge, MA: Harvard University Press.

Wilson, W.J. (1987) *The truly disadvantaged: the inner city, the underclass, and public policy*, Chicago, IL: The University of Chicago Press.

Yellen, J. (2006) 'Economic inequality in the United States', Federal Reserve Bank of San Francisco (FRBSF) Economic Letter, no 2006-33-34, 1 December.

Zedlewski, S.R., Giannarelli, L., Morton, J. and Wheaton, L. (2002) *Extreme poverty rising, existing government programs could do more*, Assessing New Federalism, Series B, No B-045, Washington, DC: The Urban Institute.

NINE

Social policy and culture: the cases of Japan and South Korea

Nam K. Jo

Introduction

This chapter examines cultural explanations of the East Asian welfare state with the cases of Japan and South Korea. Two points are of concern as background to this investigation. First, the recent rising interest and development in cultural analysis of welfare within comparative social policy (eg Pfau-Effinger, 2004, 2005; Van Oorschot, 2007; Van Oorschot et al., 2008; Jo, 2011) suggest that the role of culture in welfare can be better understood with more empirical support when we see culture not as a broad and historical tradition that has shaped everything, but as a context at the same level with economic and political contexts for policymaking. Yet, there have been few non-Western cases analysed by this approach. Second, the cultural approach to 'East Asian welfare', if there is any, has seen little development over the last decade since 'the Confucian welfare state' thesis (eg Jones, 1990, 1993; Goodman and Peng, 1996). Certainly, the Confucian tradition cannot be overlooked (Esping-Andersen, 1997, p 181), but accepting it as a key driver of welfare state formation does not provide us with sufficient detail of which aspects of culture matter. This chapter is an attempt to take 'one step further' into the East Asian culture in relation to its welfare systems, with examples of Japan and South Korea, by empirically illuminating concrete features of cultural context of two countries in comparison with those of the Western welfare states.

Culture as a contextual factor for social policymaking

The idea of welfare is basically one of choice about what constitutes the 'good society' and how to achieve it, based on values and/or a consensus on 'who should get what and why' (Marshall, 1972, p 20; Titmuss, 1974, p 49; Rustin, 1999, p 257; Van Oorschot, 2000; Deacon, 2002, p 1; Van Oorschot et al, 2008, p 2). From this point of view, culture is key to an understanding of welfare and it is natural that researchers have devoted attention to cultural, ideological and religious traditions such as liberalism, hierarchism, socialism, Confucianism and Christianity as foundations of welfare (eg Jones, 1990, 1993; Van Kersbergen, 1995; Castles, 1998, pp 52–58; Lockhart, 2001; O'Connor and Robinson, 2008; Opielka, 2008; Stjernø, 2008; Van Kersbergen and Kremer, 2008; Manow and Van Kersbergen, 2009).

A difficulty of this approach, however, is that it does not facilitate empirical analyses of culture and its relationship with social policy (Van Oorschot et al, 2008, pp 9–10), while it informs us of the cultural foundations of welfare. As the conception of culture in this approach is broad and rather vague, the effects of culture often become historical and abstract and, as a result, the absolute and unequivocal role of culture tends to be lost (Jo, 2011, p 6). Thus, for example, critics have argued that the prominent cultural approach focuses on Confucianism as an explanation for East Asian welfare, but it is analytically not very fruitful (eg Holliday, 2000, p 706), for it is a 'catch-all' explanation akin to saying that 'in the West all the positions reflect an agenda informed by Judeo-Christian values' (Rieger and Leibfried, 2003, p 334, quoted in Ku and Jones Finer, 2007, p 125).

It was recently suggested that we need a perspective assuming a certain distance between culture and social structures and institutions, where culture and the social system are interrelated but not decisively determined by each other, in order to properly understand the relation between culture and social policy (Pfau-Effinger, 2005; Van Oorschot et al, 2008, pp 10–11). From this perspective, social policy is understood as the outcome of the interplay between culture and the social system mainly through social actors (the 'welfare culture approach'; see Pfau-Effinger, 2005), or, in other words, as the outcome of negotiation and compromises between ideas and interests made by political actors who 'act in economic, political and cultural context' (Van Oorschot, 2008, p 268). Here, the cultural context is assumed to be widely and deeply embedded cultural values, which are not static, but quite stable over time (Van Oorschot, 2006, p 24).

The term 'Confucian welfare state' is here argued to be oversimplistic. Although Confucianism, as the once-dominant political ideology and ethical framework, left its strong cultural footprints over the region, its influence is not the same everywhere, just as the influences of 19th-century liberalism or socialism are not uniform in Europe. Moreover, Confucianism is not a religion. There is no God, no religious institutions/ churches and no religious leaders – some Asians worship Confucius at a shrine, but it is very exceptional. Most Asians are accustomed to Confucian teachings and thoughts, but many of them have their 'religion' such as Buddhism, Catholicism and Islam (eg Buddhist Thailand, Catholic Philippines or Islamic Malaysia; see Croissant, 2004). In this, the term 'Confucian welfare state' is too simple and cannot represent all the East Asian countries, as 'Christian Democracy' cannot all the European countries. We need to look into Asian culture in more detail to better understand the relation between culture and welfare, which must vary from country to country in this region.

In an attempt to develop this approach into empirical analysis, I suggest that conceptualising and measuring the cultural dimension at an in-between level (between abstract cultural/ideological traditions and concrete but unstable perceptions/attitudes) would be able to more properly show popular and stable cultural values as the cultural context of society for policymaking (Jo, 2011). Following most studies on culture that see the value dimension as the most critical within various dimensions and sub-concepts of culture, and drawing on Haller's (2002) three different levels of values, 'societal values' fit the in-between-level cultural dimension, while 'universal values' (or basic human values; see, eg, Inglehart, 1977, 1990; Schwartz, 1992, 1999) and 'situational values' (or attitudes; see studies on welfare attitudes, eg, Blekesaune and Quadagno, 2003; Gelissen, 2008) approximate to the abstract-level cultural dimension and the concrete-level cultural dimension, respectively. A method to obtain examples of societal values out of opinion data can also be introduced, which produces underlying value dimensions comparable across countries, differing time points and levels (individual and country levels) and, in aggregated forms, stable over time (Jo, 2011). Societal values or the value characteristics of societies measured like this enable us to empirically compare cultural contexts between selected welfare societies and affirm a cultural impact on social policy (Jo, 2011).

A comparative examination of the cultural contexts of Japan and South Korea (with those of Western counterparts), drawing on this approach, is expected to be useful in that we can see and identify features of culture and cultural differences in more concrete terms rather than point out mere 'Confucianism'. It would help us to reason which aspects of culture may have been affecting which dimensions of welfare in this region instead of simply stating 'the Confucian tradition matters'.

Data and method

In exploring the cultural context of East Asian countries in relation to welfare, the chapter focuses on Japan and South Korea. Japan and South Korea (together with Taiwan, which is not included here because of a lack of data) are expected to represent *a* cluster of the East Asian welfare state. Researchers have observed that there can be two or three distinct subsets in this region: for example, social insurance-centred welfare states (Japan, South Korea, Taiwan and possibly China) and provident funds-centred welfare states (Singapore, Malaysia and Hong Kong) (eg Kwon, 2009, p S14); or facilitative (Hong Kong), developmental-universalist (Japan, South Korea, Taiwan) and developmental-particularist (Singapore) productive welfare capitalism (eg Holliday, 2000, p 707). Japan and South Korea appear to share more welfare features in common than with other East Asian countries. In addition, both countries have been world-leading economies for several decades and we would expect that not only social discourses on welfare, but also welfare politics, should be more 'mature' than other countries in the region. Finally, since investigating how stable extracted value dimensions are over time is critical in order to determine societal values (Jo, 2011), data across multiple time points are necessary. Both Japan and South Korea are the only East Asian countries that have continuously participated in the international survey programme on values (ie the World Values Survey) and have data available for the last three decades (at four intervals).

The World Values Survey data and the European Values Study data are analysed to extract examples of societal values not only available for Japan and South Korea, but also comparable across other societies. These international survey programmes are designed to enable researchers to expand object countries by integrating data from both surveys. From 1981 to 2009, the European Values Study was conducted four times (wave 1–4) while the World Values Survey proceeded until wave 5. However, data can be arranged into four time points as a whole. The findings discussed in this chapter follow Jo's (2011) method, which: groups variables based on correlations; extracts underlying factors at individual-level pooled data; iteratively compares and examines the factoring structure across time, country and level (individual and country levels) to identify and discard variables causing incomparability; and tests the stability of factors in aggregated (country-level) forms in terms of how strongly differences in those factors between societies have been maintained.

Thirty-four Organisation for Economic Co-operation and Development (OECD) member countries are selected. As more industrialised countries, they can give us a little more confidence about sample quality (Larsen, 2006, p 27). They share not only a comparable level of wealth, but also 'a common conception of social welfare' (Arts and Gelissen, 2002), and cover all countries of interest here – Japan, South Korea and the Western welfare state for the comparative reference. The pooled data set consists of 159,635 cases from 34 countries at four time points, which forms 116 societal-level cases (in terms of data for a country at a time point). After extraction, societal values (as features of cultural context) of two East Asian countries are compared with Western welfare states – for parsimony, more established welfare states are selected, which are commonly classified into four welfare regimes (see, eg, Esping-Andersen, 1990; Arts and Gelissen, 2002).

The societal values found in this analysis are not exhaustive. Methodologically, they are selected examples of societal values, the range of which is limited by which data are selected and analysed. Here, a long process of analysis produced six underlying dimensions (examples of societal values). All of them are comparable across time and place – they are found from data of any time point, any country and any country at any time point in the analysis. All of them are cross-level equivalent – they are found in analyses both at the individual and country levels. All of them are, to considerable extent, stable over time – the difference in them between countries has not seriously fluctuated (Hofstede, 2001) for three decades, showing that they are not static, but only gradually changeable (ie 'dynamically stable'; see Oyserman and Uskul, 2008, pp 149–50). They are Religiosity, Conservative Ethics, Political Activeness, Social Morality, Political Oriented-ness and Traditional Family Values (see Table 9.1).[1]

A different kind of familialistic welfare state?

With six societal values, the cultural context of Japan and South Korea could be sketched as of strong Traditional Family Values, weak Religiosity, strong Conservative Ethics, moderate Social Morality, moderate Political Oriented-ness and weak Political Activeness. While two countries do not show distinctiveness in Social Morality and Political Oriented-ness in comparison with the Western welfare states, their features of cultural context in terms of the other four societal values are interesting enough to invite our attention.

Table 9.1: Six societal values extracted from the European Values Study–World Values Survey data (1981–2009) for 34 OECD countries and items on which those are based

Societal values	Items
Religiosity	How important is God in your life (1–10) Religious person (0/1) How often attend religious services (1–7) Confidence in churches (1–4) Religious faith is an important child quality (0/1)
Conservative Ethics	Not justifiable: abortion (1–10) Not justifiable: divorce (1–10) Not justifiable: euthanasia (1–10) Not justifiable: homosexuality (1–10) Not justifiable: suicide (1–10)
Political Activeness	Political action: joining unofficial strikes (1–3) Political action: attending lawful/peaceful demonstration (1–3) Political action: occupying buildings or factories (1–3)
Social Morality	Not justifiable: cheating on taxes (1–10) Not justifiable: someone accepting a bribe (1–10) Not justifiable: claiming non-entitled government benefits (1–10)
Political Oriented-ness	Interest in politics (1–4) How often discuss political matters with friends (1–3)
Traditional Family Values	A woman has to have children to be fulfilled (0/1) Child needs a home with father and mother (0/1)

First of all, Japan and South Korea share strong Traditional Family Values (see Figure 9.1). This is not surprising – 'family' has been the most prominent concept in explaining East Asian welfare regardless of which approach scholars are taking (see, eg, Jones, 1993; Goodman and Peng, 1996; Holliday, 2000; Hort and Kuhnle, 2000; Croissant, 2004; Aspalter, 2006; Kwon, 2009; Kim and Choi, 2011). Here, however, it is noteworthy that the degree of Traditional Family Values in Japan and South Korea is not 'exceptionally high', although it is still the strongest (except Greece) within 22 societies. This observation supports Esping-Andersen (1997, p 186), who saw traditional familialism behind the similar emphasis on the traditional familial welfare function across Japan and Continental Europe despite the different background philosophical rationales of Confucianism and Catholicism. If strikingly stronger family-focused values do not exist in East Asian societies, from a cultural approach, why are East Asian families taking, or are forced to take, more welfare responsibilities (see, eg, Holliday and Wilding, 2003) with less governmental and non-governmental support than, for example, Continental European counterparts (eg, Kwon, 1997, pp 477–8)?

Figure 9.1: Strength (Z-score) of Traditional Family Values as the average level of three decades (1981–2009) across 22 countries

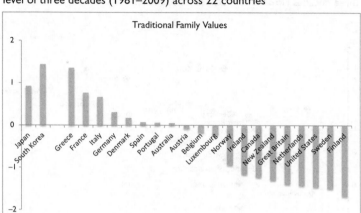

We may be able to seek further explanation from other aspects of the cultural context. As we see in Figure 9.2, Japanese and South Korean societies form deviant cases that are secular (weak Religiosity) but conservative (strong Conservative Ethics). In Catholic-oriented Western societies, stronger Conservative Ethics are found where stronger Religiosity exists, implying that those ethics are closely linked to Catholic teachings. However, relatively strong South Korean and Japanese Conservative Ethics accompanied with weak Religiosity is telling us that their conservative ethical views are not related to a religious faith. The relationship of Religiosity with welfare has not been argued consistently. While it was found that more religious European people tend to be more solidaristic with the needy (Van Oorschot, 2006), it was also reported in the analysis of 18 mature welfare states – most of them are European countries – that stronger Religiosity in society is correlated with stronger individual-blaming perceptions of poverty among the public (Jo, 2011). A possible interpretation of these findings is that people of a more religious society (ie a society of stronger Religiosity) can be 'individually' more ready to help the needy according to their religious teachings (eg through voluntary and charity organisations) but ultimately tend to emphasise the 'self-help' (for individual salvation) than 'collective' responsibility and programmatic approaches. Conservative Ethics are, in relation to welfare, possibly linked to applying stricter criteria of deservingness to the needy, since the public of stronger Conservative Ethics would have more stringent views about what are socially acceptable attitudes. Attitudes of the needy can affect how deserving the

Figure 9.2: Religiosity and Conservative Ethics as the average level of three decades (1981–2009) across 22 countries

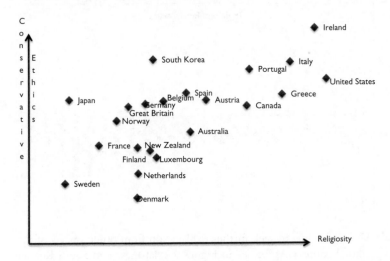

general public see the needy, and influence their answers to questions of deservingness criteria, such as 'Why are you needy?' and 'Are you one of us?' (Van Oorschot, 2000). In this, societies of stronger Conservative Ethics can be more conditional in providing institutionalised solidarity (ie state welfare).

Turning back to the two East Asian countries, both are relatively stricter in terms of Conservative Ethics but, unlike Western societies of stronger Conservative Ethics, not strongly religious. Here, we see a possible explanation of why in Japan and South Korea neither strong state welfare nor well-developed non-governmental supports outside the family by, for example, voluntary organisations are found. In these societies, individual (and voluntary) solidaristic activities have not been particularly encouraged by certain religious teachings (with weak Religiosity), while the public (of strong Conservative Ethics) have not had particularly generous views on collective responsibilities (ie state welfare) for the needy.

Elitist welfare or welfare without political bargaining

Another aspect of the cultural context of Japan and South Korea found here is that they share very low levels of Political Activeness (see Figure 9.3). If there is no particular reason for us to believe that the Japanese and South Koreans have enjoyed much more satisfactory politics than Western counterparts, the origin of this cultural feature should be sought from deeper cultural traditions. While it is a task beyond the scope of this section, linking this 'politically less active' culture to the Confucian tradition would be too simple, in that Confucianism cannot explain differences in levels of Political Activeness between Western welfare states, including the relatively less active Austrian and German cases.

Figure 9.3: Strength (Z-scores) of Political Activeness as the average level of three decades (1981–2009) across 22 countries

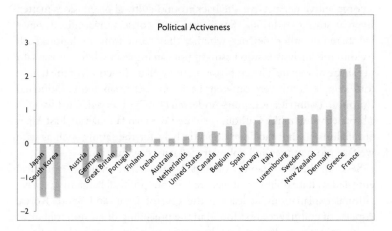

This 'political inactiveness' of the Japanese and South Koreans helps us to understand another main feature of East Asian welfare, that is, the overwhelming role of the state and the bureaucrats in welfare politics (see, eg, Lee and Ku, 2007). In these two countries, political and social agendas set by power elites (eg 'boosting national economy first') have rather easily mobilised the public, with few examples of fierce resistance, and the labour politics or class-struggle approach does not well work there (Goodman and Peng, 1996, p 210). Examples of organised political bargaining are not often found, and political bargaining by trade unions, which are weak, with small and further decreasing memberships, is still not legitimately/formally recognised.

Discussion

The preceding was an attempt to obtain a closer look at the linkage between culture and East Asian welfare through an empirical and comparative exploration of the cultural context of Japan and South Korea. It was found that the Japanese and South Korean cultural contexts are distinctive from those of Western welfare states on the basis of their strong Traditional Family Values and Conservative Ethics but weak Religiosity and Political Activeness. This finding may help us to deepen our understanding of East Asian welfare in two ways. First, from a comparative perspective, the background cultural origin does matter. Even if strong traditional familialism and conservative ethical views are shared by other societies, whether they come from a religious faith (within this analysis, Catholicism) or not can impact in different ways on the shape of welfare. The emphasis on the welfare functions of the family, for example, is not very different between East Asian and Continental European countries, as Esping-Andersen (1997) observed. Yet, if we take a broader view, unlike Catholic-oriented Western familialism, East Asian familialism has not facilitated outside help for the family, such as state welfare programmes and voluntary/charity organisations.

Second, the key features of East Asian welfare politics – political elite-led welfare politics and welfare without political bargaining – have cultural explanations, at least in the case of Japan and South Korea. Aspects of cultural context found in the preceding discussion told us, at least partly, why welfare politics have been much dominated by political elites who have often utilised social welfare programmes in times of political crisis (eg Ramesh, 2004, p 325) in these two East Asian welfare states. Given the quite stable cultural context, Japanese and South Korean welfare politics are unlikely to dramatically change in the near future.

Values and cultures such as Confucianism can often be found on the list of possible explanatory factors for the East Asian welfare model (eg Ku and Jones Finer, 2007, p 125) but rarely have they been accompanied by empirical data, and their explanations have remained abstract. Examinations of the cultural context are expected to facilitate more empirical and analytical approaches to the relation between culture and social policy, as we saw in this short chapter. The role of culture in welfare could be discussed as 'Which aspects of the cultural context matter in which aspects of East Asian welfare?', rather than as 'Confucianism matters in East Asian welfare'. This is related to the fact that the Confucianist account was not challenged but intentionally avoided in this study. The impact of the Confucian tradition cannot be the same across the region, and the Confucian welfare state thesis is oversimplistic, especially when we are equipped to investigate more concrete features of the cultural context of each East Asian welfare state in comparable terms. The second round of the cultural explanation of East Asian welfare has just started.

Note

[1.] Some of the terms used for the six examples of societal values may sound unconvincing, especially where based on two or three items. However, as noted earlier, several items were dropped in the analysis process in order to find 'comparable' factors, and in fact most of them were problematic only within one or two societal-level cases. That is, there were many discarded items that were closely related to the remaining items, and were considered while naming societal values. For example, after a repeated procedure of factor analysing and discarding some items, Traditional Family Values could be found from four items (in addition to two items in Table 9.1: 'Whether one must always love and respect their parents'; and 'Whether single mothers can be approved of') in most countries at most time points. Yet, two items were dropped again to further increase comparability of the underlying dimension. However, the interpretation of the factor was also informed from the finally discarded items.

Acknowledgements

I would like to thank Kevin Farnsworth for his helpful comments and suggestions. I also thank the participants at the 'Social Policy in an Unequal World' joint annual conference of the East Asian Social Policy Research Network (EASP) and the UK Social Policy Association (SPA) at the University of York in July 2012 for their feedback on an earlier version of this chapter. I acknowledge support from the research scheme for new faculty by SungKongHoe University.

References

Arts, W. and Gelissen, J. (2002) 'Three worlds of welfare capitalism or more? A state-of-the-art report', *Journal of European Social Policy*, vol 12, no 2, pp 137–58.

Aspalter, C. (2006) 'The East Asian welfare model', *International Journal of Social Welfare*, vol 15, pp 290–301.

Blekesaune, M. and Quadagno, J. (2003) 'Public attitudes toward welfare state policies: a comparative analysis of 24 nations', *European Sociological Review*, vol 19, no 5, pp 415–27.

Castles, F.G. (1998) *Comparative public policy: patterns of post-war transformation*, Cheltenham: Edward Elgar.

Croissant, A. (2004) 'Changing welfare regimes in East and Southeast Asia: crisis, change and challenge', *Social Policy & Administration*, vol 38, no 5, pp 504–24.

Deacon, A. (2002) *Perspectives on welfare: ideas, ideologies and policy debates*, Buckingham: Open University Press.

Esping-Andersen, G. (1990) *The three worlds of welfare capitalism*, Cambridge: Polity Press.

Esping-Andersen, G. (1997) 'Hybrid or unique? The Japanese welfare state between Europe and America', *Journal of European Social Policy*, vol 7, no 3, pp 179–89.

Gelissen, J. (2008) 'European scope-of-government beliefs: the impact of individual, regional and national characteristics', in W. van Oorschot, M. Opielka and B. Pfau-Effinger (eds) *Culture and welfare state: values and social policy in comparative perspective*, Cheltenham: Edward Elgar, pp 247–67.

Goodman, R. and Peng, I. (1996) 'The East Asian welfare states: peripatetic learning, adaptive change, and nation-building', in G. Esping-Andersen (ed) *Welfare states in transition*, London: Sage, pp 192–224.

Haller, M. (2002) 'Theory and method in the comparative study of values: critique and alternative to Inglehart', *European Sociological Review*, vol 18, no 2, pp 139–58.

Hofstede, G. (2001) *Culture's consequences: comparing values, behaviors, institutions, and organizations across nations* (2nd edn), California, CA: Sage.

Holliday, I. (2000) 'Productivist welfare capitalism: social policy in East Asia', *Political Studies*, vol 48, pp 706–23.

Holliday, I. and Wilding, P. (2003) 'Welfare capitalism in the tiger economies of East and Southeast Asia', in I. Holliday and P. Wilding (eds) *Welfare capitalism in East Asia: social policy in the tiger economies*, New York, NY: Palgrave Macmillan, pp 1–17.

Hort, S.O. and Kuhnle, S. (2000) 'The coming of East and South-East Asian welfare states', *Journal of European Social Policy*, vol 10, no 2, pp 162–84.

Inglehart, R. (1977) *The silent revolution: changing values and political styles among Western publics*, New Jersey, NJ: Princeton University Press.

Inglehart, R. (1990) *Culture shift in advanced industrial society*, New Jersey, NJ: Princeton University Press.

Jo, N.K. (2011) 'Between the cultural foundations of welfare and welfare attitudes: the possibility of an in-between level conception of culture for the cultural analysis of welfare', *Journal of European Social Policy*, vol 21, no 1, pp 5–19.

Jones, C. (1990) 'Hong Kong, Singapore, South Korea and Taiwan: Oikonomic welfare states', *Government and Opposition*, vol 25, no 4, pp 446–62.

Jones, C. (1993) 'The Pacific challenge: Confucian welfare states', in C. Jones (ed) *New perspectives on the welfare state in Europe*, London: Routledge, pp 198–217.

Kim, J.W. and Choi, Y.J. (2011) 'Does family still matter? Public and private transfers in emerging welfare state systems in a comparative perspective', *International Journal of Social Welfare*, vol 20, no 4, pp 353–66.

Ku, Y.-w. and Jones Finer, C. (2007) 'Developments in East Asian welfare studies', *Social Policy & Administration*, vol 41, no 2, pp 115–31.

Kwon, H.-j. (1997) 'Beyond European welfare regimes: comparative perspectives on East Asian welfare systems', *Journal of Social Policy*, vol 26, no 4, pp 467–84.

Kwon, H.-j. (2009) 'The reform of the developmental welfare state in East Asia', *International Journal of Social Welfare*, vol 18, pp S12–S21.

Larsen, C.A. (2006) *The institutional logic of welfare attitudes: how welfare regimes influence public support*, Aldershot: Ashgate.

Lee, Y.-J. and Ku, Y.-w. (2007) 'East Asian welfare regimes: testing the hypothesis of the developmental welfare state', *Social Policy & Administration*, vol 41, no 2, pp 197–212.

Lockhart, C. (2001) *Protecting the elderly: how culture shapes social policy*, Pennsylvania, PA: Pennsylvania State University Press.

Manow, P. and Van Kersbergen, K. (2009) 'Religion and the western welfare state – the theoretical context', in K. van Kersbergen and P. Manow (eds) *Religion, class coalitions, and welfare states*, Cambridge: Cambridge University Press, pp 1–38.

Marshall, T.H. (1972) 'Value problems of welfare-capitalism', *Journal of Social Policy*, vol 1, no 1, pp 15–32.

O'Connor, J.S. and Robinson, G. (2008) 'Liberalism, citizenship and the welfare state', in W. van Oorschot, M. Opielka and B. Pfau-Effinger (eds) *Culture and welfare state: values and social policy in comparative perspective*, Cheltenham: Edward Elgar, pp 29–49.

Opielka, M. (2008) 'Christian foundations of the welfare state: strong cultural values in comparative perspective', in W. van Oorschot, M. Opielka and B. Pfau-Effinger (eds) *Culture and welfare state: values and social policy in comparative perspective*, Cheltenham: Edward Elgar, pp 89–114.

Oyserman, D. and Uskul, A.K. (2008) 'Individualism and collectivism: societal-level processes with implications for individual-level and society-level outcomes', in F.J.R. van de Vijver, D.A. van Hemert and Y.H. Poortinga (eds) *Multilevel analysis of individuals and cultures*, London: Lawrence Erlbaum Associates, pp 145–73.

Pfau-Effinger, B. (2004) *Development of culture, welfare states and women's employment in Europe*, Aldershot: Ashgate.

Pfau-Effinger, B. (2005) 'Culture and welfare state policies: reflections on a complex interrelation', *Journal of Social Policy*, vol 34, no 1, pp 3–20.

Ramesh, M. (2004) 'Review article: issues in globalisation and social welfare in Asia', *Social Policy & Society*, vol 3, no 3, pp 321–7.

Rieger, E. and Leibfried, S. (2003) (citied in Ku and Jones Finer, 2007) *Limits to globalization: Welfare states and the World economy*, Cambridge: Polity Press.

Rustin, M. (1999) 'Missing dimensions in the culture of welfare', in P. Chamberlayne, A. Cooper, R. Freeman and M. Rustin (eds) *Welfare and culture in Europe: towards a new paradigm in social policy*, London: Jessica Kingsley, pp 255–74.

Schwartz, S.H. (1992) 'Universals in the content and structure of values: theoretical advances and empirical tests in 20 countries', *Advances in Experimental Social Psychology*, vol 25, pp 1–65.

Schwartz, S.H. (1999) 'A theory of cultural values and some implications for work', *Applied Psychology: An International Review*, vol 48, no 1, pp 23–47.

Stjernø, S. (2008) 'Social democratic values in the European welfare states', in W. van Oorschot, M. Opielka and B. Pfau-Effinger (eds) *Culture and welfare state: values and social policy in comparative perspective*, Cheltenham: Edward Elgar, pp 50–70.

Titmuss, R.M. (1974) *Social policy: an introduction*, London: Allen & Unwin.

Van Kersbergen, K. (1995) *Social capitalism: a study of Christian democracy and the welfare state*, London: Routledge.

Van Kersbergen, K. and Kremer, M. (2008) 'Conservatism and the welfare state: intervening to preserve', in W. van Oorschot, M. Opielka and B. Pfau-Effinger (eds) *Culture and welfare state: values and social policy in comparative perspective*, Cheltenham: Edward Elgar, pp 71–88.

Van Oorschot, W. (2000) 'Who should get what, and why? On deservingness criteria and the conditionality of solidarity among the public', *Policy & Politics*, vol 28, no 1, pp 33–48.

Van Oorschot, W. (2006) 'Making the difference in social Europe: deservingness perceptions among citizens of European welfare states', *Journal of European Social Policy*, vol 16, no 1, pp 23–42.

Van Oorschot, W. (2007) 'Culture and social policy: a developing field of study', *International Journal of Social Welfare*, vol 16, no 2, pp 129–39.

Van Oorschot, W. (2008) 'Popular deservingness perceptions and conditionality of solidarity in Europe', in W. van Oorschot, M. Opielka and B. Pfau-Effinger (eds) *Culture and welfare state: values and social policy in comparative perspective*, Cheltenham: Edward Elgar, pp 268–88.

Van Oorschot, W., Opielka, M. and Pfau-Effinger, B. (2008) 'The culture of the welfare state: historical and theoretical arguments', in W. van Oorschot, M. Opielka and B. Pfau-Effinger (eds) *Culture and welfare state: values and social policy in comparative perspective*, Cheltenham: Edward Elgar, pp 1–26.

Appendix: Data
European and World Values Surveys four-wave integrated data file, 1981–2004, v.20060423, 2006. File Producers: ASEP/JDS, Madrid, Spain and Tilburg University, Tilburg, the Netherlands. File Distributors: ASEP/JDS and GESIS, Cologne, Germany.

EVS (2010) European Values Study 2008, fourth wave, Integrated Dataset. GESIS Data Archive, Cologne, Germany, ZA4800 Data File Version 1.0.0 (2010-06-30) DOI:10.4232/1.10059.

World Values Survey 1981–2008 Official Aggregate v.20090901, 2009. World Values Survey Association (see: www.worldvaluessurvey.org). File Producer: ASEP/JDS, Madrid.

TEN

Load-shedding and reloading: changes in government responsibility – the case of Israeli immigration and integration policy 2004–10

Ilana Shpaizman

Introduction

The period 2004–10 was one of relative stability in Israeli immigration and integration policy. This is because there was no major change in the number of migrants coming to Israel or in their countries of origin, and there was no crisis in this sphere either. However, as this chapter demonstrates, by the end of 2010, one can discern that there has, in fact, been a major shift in immigration and integration policy orientation from a 'categorical universal' policy, where all the migrants receive the same assistance regardless of their economic status (Gal, 2008), to a selective policy, where more assistance is given to highly skilled migrants. Thus, it seems, Israel has entered the global 'race for talent' – the competition for highly skilled migrants (Shachar, 2006). A closer look reveals that Israeli immigration and integration policy has been simultaneously moving slowly along what seem to be two opposing paths. On the one hand, migrant integration services are being privatised, with the transfer of some government responsibilities for providing and producing services to the private sector. On the other hand, the government has increased its involvement in migrant integration policy by financing and regulating new services or by expanding old ones.

This chapter aims to explain this duality and to analyse the process of change using the framework of 'gradual transformative institutional change' (Streeck and Thelen, 2005), which enables scholars to analyse significant policy change during periods of stability. It also draws on the ideational approach in institutional analysis (see, eg, Béland, 2007), which helps to explain the mode and direction of change. The chapter focuses on the three subfields in Israeli immigration and integration policy that have undergone the most significant gradual transformative change and are central in the global 'race for talent' policy (Shachar, 2006): immigration encouragement, employment and returning emigrants.

The analysis presents three arguments. First, the incrementally evolving dual process has resulted in a transformative change: the shift of Israeli integration policy from universal to selective. Second, this transformative change has taken place through 'layering' – new arrangements that grow on top of pre-existing structures, intended to serve different purposes (Streeck and Thelen, 2005). Third, the dual process can be explained by the global ideas and policies of the 'race for talent'.

The Israeli case can be seen in this context as 'deviant' – 'a case that by reference of some general understanding of a topic demonstrates a surprising value' (Seawright and Gerring, 2008, p 302). Israel is an ethnic immigration country – the only criterion for migrant selection is ethnic origin (Joppke and Rosenhek, 2003); thus, the state cannot choose its migrants. Moreover, promoting Jewish immigration to Israel is perceived as one of the core values of the state of Israel (see, eg, Leshem and Shuval, 1998; Gal, 2008). Hence, one would expect it neither to have a high-skilled migrant policy, nor to participate in the global competition for skilled migrants. Finding evidence of such a policy may indicate the profound effect of global policies and ideas on local policy. Furthermore, it strengthens once again, the argument of Castles and Miller (2009) that this is the 'age of migration' not only because most people have personal experience of migration, but also because all countries, even ethnic migration ones, are being affected by global migration policies and the ideas behind them.

The chapter proceeds as follows: the first section introduces the analytical framework; the second elaborates on the methodology employed; and the third presents the empirical analysis of the policy changes and the ideas behind them in the three subfields. The final section discusses the chapter's implications and conclusions.

Analytical framework

Government responsibility

Government responsibility is a dynamic concept that moves along a continuum from none at all to full responsibility. It can be examined from three different perspectives. The first is the extent of government involvement as a provider of funds, regulator or producer of certain services or benefits: the more involved the government is, the greater its responsibility (Starr, 1989; Savas, 2000).[1] The second perspective is an elaboration of the first and refers to the division of labour/social responsibility between the private and the public sectors in different spheres (Clarke, 2004). The third perspective is the universality/selectivity of a given policy: the more universal the policy, the broader the government responsibility (Gilbert, 2002).

According to Gilbert (2002), in the last few decades, the state has moved from being a welfare state to being an 'enabling state' characterised by public support for private responsibility (individuals, the market and the voluntary organisations). In this 'enabling state', social policies are designed to enable people to work and become more self-reliant, and to expand the role of the market and the voluntary sector in providing social protection. Thus, government responsibility is being reduced. One of the justifications given for this process is 'load-shedding' – the belief that the government should be small since this will likely reduce demands on the state (Starr, 1989; Savas, 2000).

Because government responsibility is a dynamic concept, any changes usually evolve gradually (see, eg, Gilbert, 2002; Clarke, 2004). Consequently, in order to identify this process, one needs to use a gradual policy change framework.

Gradual transformative change

The current common perception of the policy process is one of punctuated equilibrium (True et al, 1999) – long periods of stability characterised by small and adaptive changes are interrupted by short periods of abrupt significant change in policy tools, programmes and goals. These abrupt policy changes are usually the result of an exogenous shock, such as a crisis or war, which shakes the system and moves it to a different place.

The main critique of the punctuated equilibrium approach is that it explains stability better than change. Because it focuses on stable institutions that prevent change, the only way change can be promoted is by unexpected exogenous shock. Consequently, this framework cannot explain endogenous factors of change and ignores gradual transformative changes that add up to major discontinuities. Thus, in order to understand change one should look not only at the process of change (incremental or abrupt), but also at the result of change (continuity or discontinuity) (Streeck and Thelen, 2005; Capano and Howlett, 2009). Streeck and Thelen (2005) call incremental change that results in discontinuity 'gradual transformative change', a change that leads to a significant shift from the status quo over time. This change, which unfolds without dramatic disruptions such as wars or revolutions, is usually a result of endogenous factors within the institutional framework that it transforms.

Streeck and Thelen (2005) identify five modes of gradual transformative change, the most common of which is layering (Van der Heijden, 2010). Layering happens when new institutions, mechanisms or practices grow on top of old mechanisms. It is constructed on the mechanism of differential growth, for example, the layering of a voluntary private pension system onto an existing public system. This mode of change usually emanates from a perception of policy failure. The new practices are first introduced at the margins of the system in order to complete or repair it, but gradually, because of differential growth, these practices extend and eventually, by default, crowd out or supplant the old system, which shrinks or stagnates. This introduction of a new layer in the margins without replacing the old system avoids objections from the major defenders of the status quo (Palier, 2005; Streeck and Thelen, 2005).

The gradual transformative framework helps describe how incremental changes can lead to a transformative change over time. However, it does not explain the direction of change, and its explanations of why a specific mode of change takes place are not satisfactory (Béland, 2007; Van Der Heijden, 2010). One way to narrow this gap is to examine the ideas behind the policy (Béland, 2007).

Ideas and the ideational approach

Ideas are organising principles, beliefs and assumptions that guide policymakers and help them shape their understanding of a certain policy (Berman, 1998; Jacobs, 2009; Mehta, 2011). An ideational approach in institutional analysis uses ideas to explain institutional outcomes. Studies on the role of ideas in policymaking have found that ideas provide cognitive and normative causal propositions that help to evaluate a situation, define the problem (the casual story behind the problem) and prevent other problem definitions. Moreover, ideas direct attention and act as road maps for decision-makers, helping them choose between the different alternatives under consideration (Jacobs, 2009; Mehta, 2011).

The 'race for talent' – ideas and policy

Various immigration scholars argue that there is a dualistic immigration policy in the Western world, in which there are relaxed entry and residence requirements for highly skilled migrants[2] and barriers and tough requirements for low-skilled migrants (Joppke, 2007; Castles and Miller, 2009). The aim of this dualistic policy is to decrease the number of low-skilled migrants and increase the number of highly skilled migrants. This is because many countries see skilled migration as a means of filling skilled labour shortages and improving their economic position in the world. As a result, immigration policy is no longer about passive gatekeeping, but an active policy aimed at recruiting highly skilled migrants (Iredale, 2001; Kuptsch and Pang, 2006; Shachar, 2006). Shachar (2006) calls this the 'race for talent'.

The 'race for talent' is realised by creating selective immigration programmes designed to attract highly skilled migrants. This process started in the US, Canada and Australia, and today it includes most of the EU states. There is constant competition between countries based on the assumption that each country is compelled to improve its offers of admission and settlement programmes in order to stay in the race. For example, most of the countries offer highly skilled migrants simplified application processes, tax exemptions and work permits for spouses and foreign students. Ultimately, the exchange package suggested is citizenship for talent. The whole approach of immigration policy for highly skilled migrants is market-oriented, since the prime objective is economic growth (Mahroum, 2005; Shachar, 2006).

The 'race for talent' also includes incentives proposed for emigrant professionals to return to their countries of origin. An example of these policies can be seen in South Korea, Taiwan and Ireland. The incentives to emigrants reflect an attitude change, since the emigrants are presently treated as long-lost children, and are seen as potential contributors to the national economy (Shachar, 2006).

The immigrant integration policy addressed in this chapter is direct immigrant policy: 'Special measures on behalf of immigrants' (Hammar, 1985, p 10). One of the major aims of immigrant integration policy in the Western world today for low- and highly skilled migrants is to make the migrant self-sufficient and as independent as possible from the state. Thus, each country wants to select migrants who can contribute as quickly as possible to the economy, without adding to the cost of social programmes and services (Arat-Koc, 1999; Hawthorne, 2005). As a result, the responsibility for integration is shifted from the state to the individual migrant and his/her community by privatising integration services. This tendency can be found in many countries with large-scale immigration such as Canada, Australia and the Netherlands (Arat-Koc, 1999; Hawthorne, 2005; Bruquetas-Callejo et al, 2007). Thus, the migrant's integration is seen through the perspective of economic instrumentalism: the more autonomous (non-state-dependent) the migrant, the more competitive the state will be in the global economy. It follows that the focus in integration policy is now on employment, in order to make full use of human capital in the global market (Joppke, 2007).

Along with the decrease in government responsibility for migrant integration, there are also opposite cases of an increase in government responsibility. For example, in Sweden, the government introduced new a integration programme in 2010, aimed at speeding the entrance of refugees and their families (mostly low-skilled migrants) into the labour market by providing additional funding, guidance and regulations to existing programmes (Wiesbrock, 2011). Another example is mandatory civic integration programmes introduced in various EU countries (Bruquetas-Callejo et al, 2007; Joppke, 2007).

Israel – immigration and immigrant integration policy

Israel is defined as an ethnic immigration state – it 'welcomes newcomers as immigrants ... only if they qualified ex ante as co-ethnics, that is, members of the state defining majority nation' (Joppke and Rosenhek, 2003, p 1). Israel's immigration policy is an 'open-door' policy to all Jewish migrants who want to settle in Israel in accordance with the Israeli 'Law of Return'. This policy was rooted in Zionist ideology, which viewed the state of Israel as an asylum for *all* the Jews around the world, and considered immigration as the main instrument for nation-building. Jewish immigration to Israel is a relatively settled issue and there is rarely any political or public debate on it (Leshem and Shuval, 1998). The organisation in charge of integration policy is the Ministry of Immigration and Absorption (MOIA). Despite the fact that Israel has non-ethnic migrants such as refugees, asylum seekers and temporary low-skilled labour migrants, all references to migrants in Israel in this chapter refer only to ethnic migrants. This is due to the fact that there is no direct immigrant integration policy for other migrant groups, and the immigration policy is mostly ad hoc (Avinery et al, 2009).

Gal (2008) calls Israeli integration policy 'categorical universalism' – all the people who are part of the category are entitled to get some benefits regardless of their economic status. Almost every migrant who comes to Israel is entitled to certain categorical universal assistance. The major universal assistance is the 'absorption basket', which contains 'in-cash' benefits intended to facilitate economic integration during the first year after arrival. The sum of the basket is a function only of family size (number of children), regardless of their place of origin or economic status (Gal, 2008). Along with the 'absorption basket', each migrant is entitled to other benefits such as tax exemptions in the first few years after arrival, educational assistance for the children, Hebrew lessons and vocational training programmes.[3] These benefits are also universal and the only criterion for eligibility is the number of years of residency in Israel.

This chapter analyses the policy changes in the Israeli immigration and integration policy in 2004–10. During this period, migration to Israel was more or less stable (about 20,000 migrants a year), with no significant change in the migrants' places of origin or occupations. The only significant change during this time was an increase in the number of returning emigrants: from 4,376 in 2005 to 11,100 in 2009 (MOIA, 2010a). Thus, this period provides an opportunity to analyse policy changes in a period of relative stability, using a gradual transformative change framework.

Methodology

Utilising a historical institutional analysis, this chapter focuses on the changes in immigration and integration policy of highly skilled migrants in Israel in 2004–10 and on the ideas behind these policy changes. More specifically, the chapter looks at the shifts in government responsibility for immigration and integration policy in three fields: immigration encouragement, employment and returning emigrants. The reasons for focusing on these fields are, first, that they have undergone significant gradual transformative changes and, second, as previously stated, that these fields are the core of highly skilled immigration and integration policies. Along with the policy change, the analysis will examine its underlying ideas. More specifically, it will focus on the 'race for talent' ideas, for example, immigration as an economic growth strategy, preference for highly skilled migrants, self-reliance among migrants, global competition and changing attitudes towards emigrants.

The analysis is based on available policy documents, consisting of two kinds: the first, direct policymaking documents on immigration and integration, such as government decisions, regulations and national budgets; and the second, documents describing MOIA policy, such as from the Committee for Immigration, Absorption and Diaspora Affairs (CIAD) in the parliament protocols and press releases. In addition, six in-depth elite interviews (Richards, 1996) were conducted by the author during 2010–11 with the major decision-makers in the fields in question: three General Directors of the MOIA from 2004 to 2010, two heads of departments in the MOIA and one personal consultant to the General Director.

Decrease in government responsibility is indicated by a decision to transfer the regulation, financing or production of integration or immigration services from the government to private organisations, or to the migrants themselves. An increase in government responsibility is indicated by its decision to operate in a new field (in the sphere of immigration and integration) or increase its involvement (financial and/or regulatory) in a field under the responsibility of the MOIA, evidenced by government decisions, officials' declarations in the parliament committee and national budget. A change will be considered as 'gradual transformative' when the shift in government responsibility takes place in a few stages during the examined period, the result of which is discontinuity of earlier policy objectives or policy tools. Ideas will be uncovered using qualitative content analysis of the in-depth interviews, statements by ministry officials to the CIAD, explanations for government decisions and press releases focusing on the reasoning behind the policy (Jacobs, 2009).

Empirical analysis

Immigration encouragement

Until 2002, the responsibility for immigration recruitment, or what is called in Hebrew 'immigration encouragement', was in the hands of the Jewish Agency for Israel (JAFI) (an international philanthropic organisation of the Jewish people). Although the JAFI is not a governmental organisation, in the field of immigration encouragement, it was considered by the government as a governmental agency.

In 2005, the government decided to give special financial support to private organisations that encourage immigration. One of the criteria for the governmental support was that the organisations receiving the support would provide additional financial assistance to the migrants they bring, to help them with financial difficulties caused by immigration. In 2010, the government decided to increase its support to the private organisations from US$1,000 (≈£620) per migrant to US$1,400 (≈£880), and the budget for this programme increased by NIS14 million (≈£2.3 million) (PMO, 2005, 2007, 2010b). In addition to the government support in 2007, JAFI transferred its responsibility for immigration encouragement in North America[4] to a private organisation by the name 'Nefesh Benefesh' (JAFI, 2007).

Alongside this reduction in responsibility, there was also a contrasting process of an increase in government responsibility. In 2004, mostly due to a decrease in the number of migrants (MOIA, 2010a), the MOIA decided to engage in immigration encouragement. At first, the involvement was modest and included activities for Jewish tourists coming for holidays, in order to persuade them immigrate to Israel (Interview 6, 2010). In 2005, Minister Tzipi Livni presented a four-year project of 'immigration encouragement'. In this project, in addition to the regular assistance each migrant receives upon arrival, those who come through special immigration encouragement programmes are entitled to additional Hebrew language hours, special assistance in employment, social and communal services, and a group counsellor who assists them during their first year in Israel. Consequently, this programme transfers more responsibility for the initial integration from the migrant to the government (MOIA, 2009a). In 2009, two changes were made to this programme. First, its target group was changed from migrants in Western countries in general, to professional migrants, such as doctors and engineers (professions of which there is a shortage in Israel). Second, the migrants also received a special adaptation grant in addition to the universal 'absorption basket' (PMO, 2009; MOIA, 2010b).

From 2004 on, the importance of immigration encouragement increased gradually, as can be seen in the ministry budget: in 2004, the immigration encouragement budget was NIS17.6 million (≈£3 million), less than 1% of the MOIA's total budget; in 2005, it rose to NIS72 million (≈£12 million); and in 2010, it reached NIS128 million (≈£42.6 million), more than 14% of the MOIA's total budget (MOF, 1997–2010).

All these changes in the field of immigration encouragement led to a shift from universal assistance to selective additional assistance to certain groups of migrants. This is a significant policy change since, up to then, special assistance had only been given to migrants from underdeveloped countries (such as Ethiopia), or migrants in distress (eg the disabled) (MOIA, 1992, 2010c), while highly skilled migrants received nothing more than the universal assistance.[5] The changes in this field evolved through layering: a marginal programme developed extensively and became the prime issue on the MOIA agenda.

Despite the high priority given to immigration encouragement by the MOIA, the parliament and specifically the CIAD has not conducted a *single* meeting regarding this issue. This corresponds to one of the characteristics of layering – lack of public debate since the changes do not threaten the existing structure (Palier, 2005).

What are the reasons behind these policy changes? It can be argued that since the number of migrants and their professional profile did not change significantly during this period, this change is embedded in the ideas of the 'race for talent', as Israel started to see itself as a competitor in the race. For example, in 2008, the Minister of Absorption stated that: 'The immigrants today are different; they have many more choices between the State of Israel and other countries. They are much pickier and we must adapt ourselves to the existing international competition' (Edri, 2008).

In addition, the logic behind these governmental decisions was, for the most part, market-oriented. Since 2006, the MOIA has proudly declared that it is not just a social, but also an economic, ministry, one that produces income for the state. More importantly, it gains more than it invests (Landver, 2009). Furthermore, the decision-makers argued that the government should support private organisations because they help bring migrants who can contribute to economic growth (Interview 5, 2010).

Employment

The MOIA provides various employment integration services, such as vocational training, personal consultation and employability skills. Until 2005, vocational training was provided by the MOIA for a period of seven years after arrival. This vocational training was perceived by the ministry as inefficient, since the migrants were obliged to wait for a minimum number of registrants in order to start a particular course of training, and the ministry was engaged in many complicated bureaucratic bidding procedures with various suppliers (Interview 3, 2010; Interview 5, 2010; Interview 6, 2010).

In 2005, the MOIA decided to privatise the vocational training, and introduced the 'Voucher Project'. In this project, each migrant receives a voucher worth NIS10,000 (≈£1,600), which allows him/her to enrol in any vocational training on the private market (Livni, 2005). Thus, the responsibility for finding appropriate vocational training was transferred from the government to the migrant. From 2005, the 'Voucher Project' became one of the major vocational training tools for migrants. This can be seen in the ministry budget: in 2005, the vouchers made up only 5% of the employment department's budget (NIS4 million; ≈£6,600); in 2008, this rose to 45% (NIS25 million; ≈£4.2 million); in 2010, after severe budget cuts throughout the ministry, it constituted 35% of the department's budget (NIS19 million; ≈£3.2 million) (MOF, 1997–2010).

In 2009, the MOIA decided to expand the entitlement period from seven to 10 years of residence, and to include not only migrants, but also returning emigrants, in the entitlement group. Thus, the number of potential beneficiaries increased. Nevertheless, the budget allocated for this project decreased from NIS26 million (≈£4.3 million) in 2006 to NIS10 million (≈£1.6 million) in 2010. As a result, the sum of the voucher decreased as well, from NIS10,000 (≈£1,600) to NIS7,000 (≈£1,160) for newly arrived migrants (up to five years of residence) and NIS5,000 (≈£833) for veteran migrants (more than five years of residence) (MOF, 1997–2010; MOIA, 2009b). Moreover, since 2004, the whole employment integration budget was decreased from NIS124 million (≈£20.6 million) in 2004 to NIS57 million (≈£9.5 million) in 2010, which significantly reduced the employment integration assistance (MOF, 1997–2010).

The decrease in government responsibility did not affect all migrants equally. In 2005–08, migrants who entered Israel through the special immigration encouragement programmes received not only the voucher, but also additional employment integration assistance of NIS2,000 (≈£333). In addition, the migrants who came through the special immigration encouragement programme in 2010 received a voucher of NIS8,000 (≈£1,300) instead of NIS7,000 (≈£1,160), in order to speed their entry into the labour market (MOIA, 2009b, 2010c).

In this field, one can identify gradual transformative changes in all three aspects of government responsibility. The government at first transferred the provision of services to the private sector, and then reduced its financing, thus transferring more responsibility from the public to the private sphere. In addition, the employment integration policy became less universal and more selective. These changes occurred through layering. The selective layer began marginally, as additional assistance given to a small group of migrants over and above the universal assistance. Over time, however, the additional assistance was extended while the universal services stagnated or were eroded. The 'Voucher Project' started as a small pilot on top of other employment programmes (such as employability skills and subsidised employment in the public sector), but by the end of the period, it had become one of the major vocational training tools.

The decision to allocate more resources to migrants from Western countries entering through the special programmes (mostly highly skilled) and to transfer more responsibility to the veteran migrants is puzzling, given the Israeli political system, where there is a significant migrants' political party (13–15 seats out of 120 in the parliament from 2004), whose voters are mostly veteran migrants. This puzzle becomes clearer when the ideas behind the policy are examined. First, the rationale behind the 'Voucher Project' as presented by the decision-makers before its implementation was to increase the migrants' freedom of choice and decrease their reliance on the government (Livni, 2005; Interview 3, 2010; Interview 6, 2010). Second, the prioritisation of highly skilled migrants was rationalised through economic reasoning, as can be seen in the explanation given by a former MOIA official:

> "I come to the treasury and I tell them: 'If I invest in these immigrants [migrants who come through the special programmes] it is a totally economic issue – if I invest in them I reduce the time period it takes them to move from taking from the state to giving to the state. Instead of being on welfare I make the migrant pay taxes as soon as possible.... These are the migrants that I want to invest in.'" (Interview 4, 2011)

Another reason for this prioritisation was the 'race for talent'. The decision-makers argued that there is a global competition for highly skilled migrants, and if Israel fails to integrate them properly into the labour market, they will leave for other Western countries (Interview 1, 2011; Interview 4, 2011).

Returning emigrants

Although the management of returning emigrants has always been under the responsibility of the MOIA, until recently, it was one of the less significant issues on its agenda. The budget allocated for this issue was on average only NIS2 million (≈£300,000) a year (MOF, 1997–2010). The only activity the Israeli government conducted in order to encourage the emigrants to return to Israel was running the 'Israeli Houses'– agencies at which former Israelis could get information regarding their rights as returning emigrants, and remain connected to Israel (Prigat, 2004).

This minor interest has changed significantly in the past eight years. In 2005, the plan to encourage former residents to return to Israel consisted of modest action, such as the expansion of the 'Israeli Houses' activities (Interview 6, 2010; Interview 1, 2011). In 2006, the issue of returning emigrants appeared for the first time on the ministry's agenda, as demonstrated in its budget explanations (MOF, 1997–2010). In 2007, the ministry decided to launch a serious campaign abroad, calling on emigrants to return, and also started to conduct employment fairs, mostly in the US, where the largest population of Israeli emigrants lives. In 2008, a special programme was launched, offering returning emigrants tax subsidies and other benefits (Halfon, 2007; Interview 5, 2010; Interview 2, 2011). The ministry's responsibility for this population increased further in 2010, when it decided to make the benefits received by the returning emigrants equal to those of the migrants. These benefits included tax exemptions on various products and educational assistance for children (Apartzev, 2010; PMO, 2010a; Interview 1, 2011). The increase in responsibility has been accompanied by an increase in finance. The total budget allocated for the return of former residents grew from NIS3 million in 2004 (≈£500,000) to NIS14 million in 2010 (≈£2.3 million) (MOF, 1997–2010).

The process of layering in this sphere is, to a large extent, similar to what occurred in the domain of immigration encouragement. The services started from the margins and now include most of the services and benefits given to migrants, along with tax exemptions and other financial incentives. All these changes occurred without directly reducing the entitlements and assistance given to migrants, but without increasing them either.

In this case, the policy change can be explained by a significant ideational change.[6] In 2004, when the government first started to talk about encouraging emigrants to return, the decision-makers believed that the government "must find the balance between a migrant who has never lived here and an Israeli citizen who never left" (Interview 6, 2010). When the first campaign for bringing back emigrants was about to start in 2007, the minister argued that the government should 'try to leave some gap between what a returning resident gets and what an migrant gets normally but still we can do more in order to encourage them to come back' (Boim, 2007). In 2010, when the rights of migrants and returning emigrants were almost equalised, the gap between the migrants and the emigrants was not mentioned (Landver, 2010). If the idea behind the policy is that migrants and returning emigrants are almost equal, then the policy change should contain *additional* benefits to the returning emigrants.

In addition, returning migrants were perceived in economic terms. An analysis of the ministry officials' statements suggests that the ministry had undertaken some kind of cost–benefit analysis that took into account the emigrants' contribution to the local economy. For example, in the government decision on returning emigrants, it was stated that because of the high employment potential of the returning emigrants, returns on the investment in them could be achieved through taxes within a year and a half on average (PMO, 2010a). A statement by the General Director offers another example: 'The MOIA is the only social Ministry that produces money for the State of Israel. 18,000 returning emigrants added two billion shekels to the GNP; According to our research, a returning emigrant creates about NIS100,000 in taxes' (Apartzev, 2010).

Discussion

Without any crisis or exogenous shock, immigration and integration policy in Israel has changed significantly in the last eight years, and has now been transformed through a process of layering, from a universal to a selective policy favouring the highly skilled migrant. The layering was executed through a dual process of decrease and increase in government responsibility. These two processes are embedded in the ideas and logic of the 'race for talent'.

In the field of employment, the MOIA privatised vocational training and decreased its financing of the employment integration services, transferring responsibility from the state to the migrants, who were expected to be self-reliant. At the same time, additional employment assistance was given to highly skilled migrants. The employment services, which used to be aimed at assisting all migrants living in Israel, are now aimed at assisting migrants with high human capital.

The transfer to a more highly skilled migrant policy and the entry into the 'race for talent' have also been realised in the increase of MOIA responsibility for engaging in new spheres of immigration encouragement and significantly expanding involvement in programmes to bring back emigrants. This expansion has been accompanied by privatisation of some of the immigration encouragement services, in addition to an increase in the funding and assistance given to highly skilled migrants who have come to Israel through government programmes. All these gradual changes have resulted in a transformation from a universal to a selective immigration and integration policy. In this policy, the migrant is perceived as an economic resource expected to contribute to state growth as soon as possible, and to rely as little as possible on the state.

Since these changes all happened gradually, it is hard to identify them and analyse their evolution and their significant result. The use of the concept of layering has helped understand the process of change, and has thus provided more empirical support for the argument that significant institutional change can be produced gradually within the institutional framework.

When these policy changes are examined through the prism of the 'race for talent' idea, the coexistence of increase and decrease in government responsibility is better understood. In a world where the migrant is perceived as an economic resource, it does not matter if the state assists him/her directly or through a private organisation. The only criterion is the efficiency of this assistance. Thus, if a private organisation can bring more migrants from North America than the government can, the responsibility will be transferred to the private organisation. In addition, when the aim is economic growth, the 'reloading' is consequently aimed at shedding the load of integration, which becomes lighter because the highly skilled migrants are expected to be more self-reliant. Thus, as opposed to European countries, where the process of transferring the responsibility for integration to the migrants is accompanied by an increase in government involvement in policies aimed at low-skilled migrants, in Israel, where you cannot persuade highly skilled migrants to come through the citizenship incentive, the only incentive the state has is the special assistance these migrants are given in various fields.

The ideational approach in this case helps us to understand not only the dual process, but also why this change has taken the form of layering. Since the ideas and policies of the 'race for talent' are aimed ultimately at reducing the number of low-skilled migrants and increasing the number of highly skilled migrants, and since Israel cannot choose its migrants and, thus, cannot change the immigration policy abruptly, the only way to increase the number of highly skilled migrants is by adding another layer to the existing policy and extending this layer gradually, without arousing objections. Consequently, it strengthens the argument that the ideational perspective can help us to understand the mode and direction of change (Béland, 2007).

Finding significant evidence of the effect of ideas of the 'race for talent' in Israel sheds some light on the profound influence of global ideas on policy and politics. If Israel, which perceives itself as a 'safe haven' for all the Jews in the world and sees immigration as an ideological mission of nation-building, is influenced by the ideas of the 'race for talent', this is truer of countries that do not see immigration as part of their ideological identity. It should be noted that some will say that, implicitly, Israel has always preferred highly skilled migrants. However, until now, its policies have never realised these preferences.

Conclusion

This chapter contributes not only to our understanding of current immigration and integration policy in Israel, but also to our knowledge about the influence of ideas on policy in times of relative stability and to our understanding of gradual institutional transformative change. This is not to say that ideas are the only explanation for this process, but only that an ideational approach helps us understand what at first glance seems to be a contradiction. In order to fine-tune the influence of ideas on policy in this sphere, further research is needed to examine the process of ideational change in Israeli immigration and integration policy before and after 2004. In addition, a closer inspection of rival explanations is also needed in order to clarify the role of ideas in the change mechanism, including explanations such as the role of different political actors, the influence of privatisation in other social policy spheres such as welfare policy on immigrant integration policy and organisational survival – the will of the MOIA to conserve its power in a period of decreasing immigration.

Notes

[1] As noted earlier, government responsibility is a dynamic concept. Thus, the government can decrease its responsibility as fund provider/ producer of services and, at the same time, increase its responsibility as regulator (Majone and Baake, 1996).

[2] Highly skilled migrants are usually defined as having a university degree or extensive experience in a given field (Mahroum, 2005; Shachar, 2006).

[3] For further elaboration, see: www.MOIA.gov.il

[4] North America has the largest Jewish community outside of Israel and therefore the largest source of potential Jewish migration to Israel (Sergio Della Pergola, 2010).

[5] This change is even more significant if we take into account the fact that

until 2002, migrants from Western countries, who were mostly highly skilled migrants, did not receive the full absorption basket (PMO, 2002). [6.] The ideational change is even more significant when we consider the fact that in the past, emigration from Israel was perceived by the public almost as treason (see, eg, Cohen, 2009).

References

Apartzev, D. (2010) 'Report of General Director to the Committee of Immigration, Absorption and Diaspora Affairs', www.knesset.gov.il/protocols/data

Arat-Koc, S. (1999) 'Neo-liberalism, state restructuring and immigration: changes in Canadian policies in the 1990s', *Journal of Canadian Studies*, vol 34, no 2, pp 31–56.

Avinery, S., Orgad, L. and Rubinshtain, A. (2009) *Dealing with the global migration: an outline for the Israeli immigration policy*, Jerusalem: Metzila Center, www.metzilah.org.il

Béland, D. (2007) 'Ideas and institutional change in social security: conversion, layering, and policy drift', *Social Science Quarterly*, vol 88, no 1, pp 20–38.

Berman, S. (1998) *The social democratic moment: ideas and politics in the making of interwar Europe*, Cambridge: Harvard University Press.

Boim, Z. (2007) 'Report of the Minister of Absorption, to the Committee for Immigration, Absorption and Diaspora Affairs', www.knesset.gov.il/protocols

Bruquetas-Callejo, M., Garces-Mascarenas, B., Penninx, R. and Sholten, P. (2007) 'Policy making related to immigration and integration: the Dutch case – a policy analysis', IMISCOE Working Papers, 15, www.imiscoe.org

Capano, G. and Howlett, M. (2009) 'Introduction: the determinants of policy change: advancing the debate', *Journal of Comparative Policy Analysis: Research and Practice*, 11(1), pp. 1–5.

Castles, S. and Miller, M. J. (2009) *The age of migration: International population movements in the modern world*, 3rd ed. NY, The Guilford Press.

Clarke, J. (2004) 'Dissolving the public realm? The logics and limits of neo-liberalism', *Journal of Social Policy*, 33(01), pp. 27–48.

Cohen, N. (2009) 'Come home, be professional: Ethno-nationalism and economic rationalism in Israel's return migration strategy', *Immigrants and Minorities*, 27(1), pp. 1–28.

Edri, Y. (2008) 'Report of the Minister of Absorption to the Committee for Immigration, Absorption and Diaspora Affairs', [online] Available from: www.knesset.gov.il/protocols

Gal, J. (2008) 'Immigration and the categorical welfare state in Israel', *Social Service Review*, vol 82, no 4, pp 639–61.

Gilbert, N. (2002) *Transformation of the welfare state: the silent surrender of public responsibility*, New York, NY: Oxford University Press.

Halfon, E. (2007) 'Report of the General Director of MOIA to the Committee for Immigration, Absorption and Diaspora affairs', www.knesset.gov.il/protocols/data

Hammar, T. (ed) (1985) *European immigration policy: a comparative study*, London and New York, NY: Cambridge University Press.

Hawthorne, L. (2005) '"Picking winners": the recent transformation of Australia's skilled migration policy', *International Migration Review*, vol 39, no 3, pp 663–96.

Iredale, R. (2001) 'The migration of professionals: theories and typologies', *International migration*, vol 39, no 5, pp 7–26.

Jacobs, A.M. (2009) 'How do ideas matter?', *Comparative Political Studies*, vol 42, no 2, pp 252–79.

JAFI (Jewish Agency for Israel) (2007) 'The agreement between the Jewish Agency for Israel and Nefesh Benefesh'.

Joppke, C. (2007) 'Beyond national models: civic integration policies for immigrants in Western Europe', *West European Politics*, vol 30, no 1, pp 1–22.

Joppke, C. and Rosenhek, Z. (2003) 'Contesting ethnic immigration: Germany and Israel compared', *European Journal of Sociology*, vol 43, no 3, pp 301–35.

Kuptsch, C. and Pang, E.F. (2006) *Competing for global talent*, Geneva: International Institute for Labour studies.

Landver, S. (2009) 'Report of the Minister of Absorption, to the Committee for Immigration, Absorption and Diaspora Affairs', www.knesset.gov.il/protocols

Landver, S. (2010) 'Report of the Minister of Absorption, to the Committee for Immigration, Absorption and Diaspora Affairs', www.knesset.gov.il/protocols

Leshem, E. and Shuval, J.T. (1998) *Immigration to Israel: sociological perspectives*, New Jersey, NJ: Israel Sociological Society.

Livni, T. (2005) 'Report of the Minister of Absorption, to the Committee for Immigration, Absorption and Diaspora Affairs', www.knesset.gov.il/protocols

Mahroum, S. (2005) 'The international policies of brain gain: a review', *Technology Analysis and Strategic Management*, vol 17, no 2, pp 219–30.

Majone, G. and Baake, P. (1996) *Regulating Europe*, London and New York, NY: Routledge.

Mehta, J. (2011) 'The varied roles of ideas in politics', in D. Béland and R. Cox (eds) *Ideas and politics in social science research*, New York, NY: Oxford University Press, pp 1–46.

Ministry of Finance (MOF) (1997–2010) 'MOIA budget proposal', www.mof.gov.il/BudgetSite/StateBudget/Pages/Fbudget.aspx

MOIA (Ministry of Immigrant Absorption) (1992) 'Special "absorption basket" for immigrants from Ethiopia', www.moia.gov.il/Hebrew/InformationAndAdvertising/Procedures

MOIA (2009a) 'Regulation no. 243: group immigration 2004–2009', www.moia.gov.il/Hebrew/InformationAndAdvertising/Procedures

MOIA (2009b) 'Regulation no. 258: "Voucher Project"', www.moia.gov.il/Hebrew/InformationAndAdvertising/Procedures

MOIA (2010a) 'Immigration data summary', www.moia.gov.il

MOIA (2010b) 'Regulation no. 305: immigration 2010', www.moia.gov.il/Hebrew/InformationAndAdvertising/Procedures

MOIA (2010c) 'Regulation no. 312: employment integration assistance for immigrants immigrating in the 2010 program', www.moia.gov.il/Hebrew/InformationAndAdvertising/Procedures

Palier, B. (2005) 'Ambiguous agreement cumulative change', in K. Thelen and W. Streeck (eds) *Beyond continuity: institutional change in advanced political economies*, New York, NY: Oxford University Press, pp 127–44.

Prime Minister Office (PMO) (2002) 'Immigration encouragement from Argentina, France and South Africa'.

PMO (2005) 'Government decision no. 4417: support for immigration encouragement programmes', www.pmo.gov.il/SECRETARY/GOVDECISIONS

PMO (2007) 'Government decision no. 2385: support for immigration encouragement programmes', www.pmo.gov.il/SECRETARY/GOVDECISIONS

PMO (2009) 'Government decision no. 4549: programmes for encouragement of immigration from the FSU for 2009', www.pmo.gov.il/SECRETARY/GOVDECISIONS

PMO (2010a) 'Government decision no. 1687: encouragement of returning residents', www.pmo.gov.il/SECRETARY/GOVDECISIONS

PMO (2010b) 'Government decision no. 2048: support for immigration encouragement programmes', www.pmo.gov.il/SECRETARY/GOVDECISIONS

Prigat, N. (2004) 'Report of the Director of the Department for Returning Residents, to the Committee for Immigration, Absorption and Diaspora Affairs', www.knesset.gov.il/protocols

Richards, D. (1996) 'Elite interviewing: approaches and pitfalls', *Politics*, vol 16, no 3, pp 199–204.

Savas, E.S. (2000) *Privatization and public–private partnerships*, New York, NY: Chatham House.

Seawright, J. and Gerring, J. (2008) 'Case selection techniques in case study research', *Political Research Quarterly*, vol 61, no 2, p 294.

Sergio Della Pergola (2010) *World Jewish population, 2010*, World Jewish Population Reports, Connecticut, CT: Mandell L. Berman Institute, www.jewishdatabank.org/Reports/World_Jewish_Population_2010.pdf

Shachar, A. (2006) 'The race for talent: highly skilled migrants and competitive immigration regimes', *New York University Law Review*, vol 81, pp 148–206.

Starr, P. (1989) 'The meaning of privatization', in S.B. Kamerman and A.J. Kahn (eds) *Privatization and the welfare state*, New Jersey, NJ: Princeton University Press, pp 15–48.

Streeck, W. and Thelen, K.A. (2005) *Beyond continuity: institutional change in advanced political economies*, New York, NY: Oxford University Press.

True, J.L., Jones, B.D. and Baumgartner, F.R. (1999) 'Punctuated-equilibrium theory: explaining stability and change in American policymaking', in P. Sabatier (ed) *Theories of the policy process*, Boulder, CO: Westview Press, pp 97–115.

Van Der Heijden, J. (2010) 'A short history of studying incremental institutional change: Does Explaining Institutional Change provide any new explanations?', *Regulation and Governance*, 4(2), pp. 230–243.

Wiesbrock, A. (2011) 'The integration of immigrants in Sweden: a model for the European Union?', *International Migration*, vol 49, no 4, pp 48–66.

Part Three

Themed section: work, employment and insecurity

Zoë Irving

In the post-financial-crisis world, one dimension of social policy that has been propelled to centre stage in advanced economies is employment and the lack of it. High unemployment and the rather limited and unsuccessful current attempts to deal with it serve as a reminder that *employment* policy, rather than social security conditionality, was central to 20th-century welfare settlements, whatever their variety. Since the heady days of post-war 'full employment', however, much has changed: the global (post-)industrial landscape, the gender division of paid work and, in the rich countries, the decline of collective responsibility for the maintenance of employment invested in the state, in favour of supply-focused individualisation. From the 1990s, welfare states embarked upon a range of reforms to relocate themselves in the changing global labour market, following strategies such as the promotion of 'life-long learning' to pioneer the sought-after 'knowledge economy', 'maximum participation' to ensure fiscal balance through 'making work pay', and 'activation' to prevent exclusion and reskill.

Despite all this intense policy activity, the crises and recessions since 2007 have altered the context in which these strategies operate. World unemployment currently stands at around 6%, but in the advanced economies, it is 8.7%.[1] While, in the past, phenomena such as 'under-employment' were associated with the global South, the EU now recognises this and a whole range of other 'supplementary forms' of unemployment in its statistical collections. Social policy practice and scholarship have a long-standing engagement with the problem of 'work' and its relationship to social security, but policy has an underwhelming record where reconciling the precarious and intermittent reality of post-industrial working life with the industrial social insurance principle is concerned. This failure of social policy to deal with the shift away from labour market security is all the more apparent in the current recession;

even Danish 'flexicurity', arguably the most developed post-industrial employment–social security model, has been unable to counteract the consequences of global economic interdependence.[2] Recognising that advanced economies are faced with a grave threat to social security, the chapters in Part Three provide a thought-provoking assessment of some key problematics in social and employment policy.

The section begins with Adrian Sinfield's exploration of 'what unemployment means'. In 1981, when Sinfield's book of this title was first published, the UK was in the early stages of a massive political and economic transformation. Three decades and two recessions later, as the chapter demonstrates, we see some differences but many similarities in the patterns and impact of unemployment. The current recession may be regarded as a problem of 'growth' rather than industrial restructuring, but, as Sinfield argues, the trend towards insecurity has its roots in the latter and the political project pursued during that formative period. Consequently, most of the social divisions of unemployment apparent in the 1980s endure today: divisions of ethnicity, regional impact, the cumulative effects of limited opportunities to acquire skills and the preponderance of low pay remain obvious. As the chapter concludes, the long-term effects on society of persistent and high unemployment are grave, all the more so when combined with a curtailment of social protection and a politics of division.

One of the differences between the unemployment in the recessions of the 1980s and now is that there was a much clearer distinction then between being 'in' and 'out' of work. Julia S. O'Connor's chapter is concerned with the space between these two points, occupied by the flexible and insecure forms of employment that have emerged in deindustrialising economies and become a component of the European growth strategy. Having explored the forms of precarious employment, and further dimensions to precarity, the chapter assesses the extent to which the existing regulation of non-standard employment at the EU level provides any security for those involved in precarious work. The conclusions are not encouraging for the protection of precarious workers and a clear association between precarity in employment and existing lack of power in the labour market is identified. Thus, women, young people and migrant workers are all disproportionately represented in the most precarious forms of employment, patterns of social division that are present in the concerns of all the chapters in this section.

While employment regulation is clearly lagging behind the development of insecure employment practices, as Silke Bothfeld and Sigrid Betzelt's chapter indicates, social protection policy is shoring up their expansion. In reconsidering the decommodifying effects of social policy in the contemporary work–welfare nexus, the authors' use of the concept of 'autonomy' provides an alternative means to establish the impact of changes in state–citizen relations located in the rise of 'activation' policies, and the primacy now accorded to full labour market participation. In a cross-national European comparison, their focus is the nature and form of activation policies and how these affect individual autonomy, measured by quality, status differentiation and user participation in the process of employment-related social security reform. In their overview of labour market deregulation, changes to active labour market policies and unemployment benefit schemes, the analysis demonstrates a general decline in both the quality and security afforded by employment; a trend that is accelerated by both the policy push for maximum participation and the demise of the 'core worker' as a referent of standards.

From outside the toxified 'work incentives' debate in the UK, Anders Freundt, Simon Grundt Straubinger and Jon Kvist tackle the question of fertility and unemployment traps within contemporary social security systems. Their analysis explores cross-national differences between seven Northern European countries in the relationship between social security arrangements and opportunities for employment and family-building. Using economic indicators, the chapter focuses on the comparison between the situations of lone parents and single people in order to examine the interface between economics and choices to work and have children. Lone parents are the focus because they are the fastest-rising family form and continue to represent the greatest challenge to the largely obsolete breadwinner model in many welfare states. The chapter shows a clear division between the social-democratic Nordic states and the others – Germany, the Netherlands and the UK. While this patterning may come as no surprise, the findings support the case for universalism rather than means-testing as the key to removing obstacles to employment and avoiding divisions between employed and unemployed people in family welfare.

In the final chapter in this section, the focus returns to the UK and the gender impact of the current recession. All the preceding chapters have drawn attention to gender divisions in both unemployment and employment disadvantage, and, in this chapter, using a range of national data sets, Susan Harkness examines the differential gender impact of the recession in the UK in detail. In the context of three decades of change in women's employment patterns, the chapter highlights characteristics of the current recession that have significant policy implications. In general, women's employment has not been affected to the same extent as that of men – the so-called 'silver lining' of gendered occupational segregation. However, the interpretation of greater numbers of women in low-paid, part-time, low-quality jobs as a good welfare outcome is dubious, especially given the changing importance of women's incomes within couple households. What this and all the chapters in this section show is that there continues to be a disconnect between social and labour market change and policies for work and welfare. As both Adrian Sinfield and Julia S. O'Connor observe, this distance between policy and reality can only be reduced when economic, employment and social policies are recognised as integral to one another.

Notes
[1.] See: www.ilo.org/global/research/global-reports/global-employment-trends/2013/WCMS_202323/lang--en/index.htm
[2.] See: http://ec.europa.eu/economy_finance/eu/forecasts/2011_autumn/dk_en.pdf

ELEVEN

'What unemployment means' three decades and two recessions later

Adrian Sinfield

Introduction

In 1979, the Conservative election poster, 'Labour isn't working', showed a long queue of people winding to the 'unemployment office'. The powerful image is still remembered and copied: 'austerity isn't working' was part of UK Uncut's campaigning before the 2012 Budget.[1] Little more than three years after the Conservative victory in 1979, unemployment had reached not only 2 million, but 3 million – over 13% by the measure then used.[2] I wrote *What unemployment means* (Sinfield, 1981) to challenge two dominant views: that we should learn to accept that much lower unemployment was a thing of the past, almost an accident of the 1950s and 1960s; and that unemployment was 'a price worth paying' with little care for those who had to pay that price. A generation on, with unemployment high again, the editors of *Social policy review* asked me to reflect on the significance of unemployment today and how it has changed from the recessions of the 1980s and 1990s.

In this chapter, current trends in unemployment are compared with the past before discussing some of the main similarities and changes in its impact. Emphasis is given to the continuing dismantling of social security and its effect on the link between unemployment and poverty, already long-established in the UK. The implications of the policy shift from a focus on unemployment to worklessness are discussed, with particular attention to the role played by leading politicians in shaping public perception of the 'deserving' and 'undeserving' to reinforce support for tougher and divisive policies.

By the winter of 2012–13, unemployment has been high for over three years – 7.8% by the Labour Force Survey measure that replaced the administrative count in 1997. Two and a half million people are out of work, 1 million part of the legacy of the credit crunch. The trends over time need to be spelt out to show the massive scale and harsh impact of the previous two recessions, after a long period of much lower post-war unemployment. The sudden peak of over one million on the administrative count in the early 1970s provoked the Heath government's 'U-turn' that quickly brought the numbers back below half a million. The oil-price crisis took it up to 1.5 million under Labour in 1976. After steadily falling until the 1979 election, unemployment more than doubled to over 3 million under the radical Conservative government. Dropping to 2 million in 1987, it rose back to 3 million in 1993. These recessions of the 1980s and 1990s brought great hardship and built up problems for the long term, with the concentrated impact of deindustrialisation still affecting many areas today.

From 1993, unemployment fell to its lowest level for a generation, around 5% from 2001 to 2008. By the second quarter of 2009, it had leapt to nearly 8% in less than a year, and there it has remained. Fears of 3 million or even 4 million unemployed have not been realised, although most forecasters predict at least small increases in 2013 and many predict a triple-dip recession. However, comparing official unemployment counts today with a generation ago is made more difficult by the many changes. In particular, it is estimated that there may be nearly another 1 million 'hidden unemployed' among those drawing Employment and Support Allowance (ESA) (Beatty et al, 2012).

One marked difference in the double-dip recession this time compared to the 1980s and 1990s is that Gross Domestic Product (GDP) dropped much more, by 6%, but employment fell very much less and recovered more quickly. The initial fall was well below 3% and levelled out after a year. There have been many closures, but not on the massive scale of the 1980s. Redundancies peaked in 2009 but have dropped well below half that level. In contrast to the earlier recessions, the UK rate of total unemployment has been well below the EU average, which is currently 10.7%, ranging from 4.3% in Austria to 26.2% in Spain, with Greece close behind.

This time, 'unemployment rose because of an old-fashioned collapse in demand following the bursting of a speculative financial sector bubble' (Gregg and Wadsworth, 2011, p 23). In contrast, the previous recessions were largely due to anti-inflationary policies. Employers have not been laying off workers with the same alacrity as in the early days of the

Thatcher regime, and some are deliberately retaining staff in hope of an improvement. Trade unions with much-reduced memberships have accepted shorter working weeks and less pay in real terms to retain jobs.

Despite the double dip in this recession, employment has increased and unemployment fallen. This is partly due to more part-time workers, with more of these, one in five, wanting full-time work. Whether the economy has started to grow sustainably is much debated. Past official predictions have proved very optimistic: output is still 3% below the pre-recession level and investment has yet to rebound. Living standards have been flat for eight years while inflation looks likely to increase with rising energy, transport and food costs. The continuation of government policies that give priority to cutting the deficit further restricts demand, with long-term consequences for unemployment and the wider society, especially as most public spending cuts have yet to come. In addition, there is little external demand to pull the UK economy up and Eurozone policies may help to keep it down.

The experience of unemployment today

The sharp rise in unemployment with the credit crunch in 2008 brought many predictions that this time would be different, with the greatest impact falling on the financial sector, supported by repeated portrayal of highly paid staff carrying their belongings out of Lehman Brothers at Canary Wharf. But, as demand fell and spending dropped, jobs were lost much more widely.

Four years on, prolonged high unemployment does not receive as much attention as might be expected. It may be due to the four-year flatness, its lower level compared to past recessions and the lack of major redundancies seen to devastate communities. In spite of some heavy losses in manufacturing, the most visible closures have been widely spread, particularly in wholesale and retail: the collapse of Woolworths and MFI, for example, brought many thousand job losses, but mainly in branches closing across the whole country without the concentrated local impact of a shipyard, mine or steelworks shutdown.

At present, the hardest-hit regions are among those that have long had higher unemployment – the North East, Yorkshire and Humberside, London and the West Midlands. The range of regional differences, from 5.8% to 9.8%, is reduced from a generation ago. Even the North East, now as in the past the hardest-hit mainland region, has remained closer to the average. Some of the worst affected in the past are much less so now: Northern Ireland, for many years well above the rest, has spent most of the last six years below the average. Scotland and Wales have also fallen below it for much of that time. However, the narrowing may be partly due to the higher proportion of 'hidden' unemployed diverted to ESA in the more depressed areas than elsewhere (Beatty et al, 2012).

The concentration of high unemployment by area is still remarkable. Over the last seven years, the three Birmingham constituencies of Ladywood, Sparkbrook and Hodge Hill have appeared among the worst half-dozen every month (with just two exceptions for Sparkbrook) and have been joined most frequently by Liverpool Walton, Birmingham Erdington, Tottenham, Middlesbrough, West Belfast and Wolverhampton SE, in that order. Again, the worst levels are not as far above the average as in the past, at present, only one reaching 11.8% against a national claimant rate of 4.8%, although some districts within these areas are much harder hit.

In comparison to the past, more women are out of work this time, although unemployment is still higher among men. The change reflects women's increased labour force participation, their greater concentration in retail and the public sectors where jobs are being cut back, and the pressures on mothers, particularly single mothers, to return to the labour market.

The jobless rate for younger workers is much further above the overall rate than in the 1990s recession, while that for workers aged 50 and over is much lower. This is partly a long-term trend, with those aged 16 and 17 particularly vulnerable (ONS, 2011, Table 3), but it is also due to many companies choosing to avoid layoffs. This has helped to protect older and established workers at the expense of young people entering the labour market. Those under 25 are some three times more at risk of being out of work than those older than them, and unemployment among new graduates has doubled.

Unemployment among black African and Caribbean groups is again much higher than the national average, while it is lower for Indian and Chinese groups. With the recession, unemployment among young black people has increased to more than double the average, passing 50% for first women, then men (Ball et al 2012 revealing that the Office for National Statistics [ONS] had stopped publishing these analyses).

As unemployment rose in the 1980s, redundancies tended to receive the most attention and research. These brought major hardships, but many of those laid off were better trained and experienced than those already out of work and often found work sooner. The lower paid and less skilled were much less secure, with greater chances of both prolonged and recurrent unemployment (Moylan et al, 1984), and they remain so today. In depressed areas, many still bearing the scars of earlier recessions, they may be even more at risk. Families can be much harder hit, with parents losing their jobs and children yet to find work after leaving school, which has an impact on the whole community as more shops close and public services and facilities are run down.

Unemployment can lead to a 'scarring effect', especially if it is prolonged (Gallie and Paugam, 2000, p 359). The proportion out of work over a year is the most frequently used measure of hardship in unemployment. In the August–October quarter of 2012, this reached 36% (904,000 – the highest number since 1996): half of these had been out of work for two years or longer. The scarring can become permanent, as subsequent wages are likely to be less. The more skilled were more likely than the less skilled to suffer from reduced wages after two years back in work (Gregory and Jukes, 2001), but it needs to be borne in mind that many, if not most, jobs for those with less skills do not last two years. Their greater vulnerability to repeated unemployment has long been a particular problem.

Repeated, in contrast to prolonged, unemployment continues to be neglected in official statistics and most research, with the important exception of the Joseph Rowntree Foundation's recurrent poverty programme (Goulden, 2010). Its work reveals that 'churning' (movement in and out of work) brings considerable insecurity, especially if the worker becomes locked into a demoralising low pay–no pay cycle (Shildrick et al, 2010, 2012b). The cycle is not a creation of recession although that makes it worse: it has persisted through higher employment years. In the early 1960s, I interviewed 92 men out of work in North Shields. While the average time unemployed at interview was just six weeks, (freakishly, the UK average at the time), the mean duration out of work over the previous five years was one and a quarter years (data from employment exchange records provided with the men's permission; see Sinfield, 1970). A larger follow-up in the mid-1970s recession found a substantial group moving in and out of work (North Tyneside CDP, 1978).

Churning is more widespread than is realised. A fuller understanding of labour market insecurity, its industrial and occupational patterns and variations, and their interaction with local labour markets is hampered by the lack of regular detailed statistics on movements in and out of work, as opposed to on and off benefits. Getting a job does improve the chances of escaping poverty, but fuller evidence is needed on that. A rare longitudinal analysis shows that entering full-time work only takes two thirds of households out of low income: that is more likely when a new full-time worker joins the family (Barton et al, 2010).

Hard work hidden lives, the report of the Commission on Vulnerable Employment (COVE, 2008), underlined the particular need for more detailed analysis of 'sub-prime' jobs and their many forms of insecurity and exploitation. But inequalities in terms of the quality and security of work, and its conditions and prospects, also require more attention across the whole labour force.

Poverty out of work and the dismantling of social security

'Loss of employment is the single most significant cause of entry to poverty' (Smith and Middleton, 2007, p13). The high risk of poverty during unemployment is even higher for the lower paid because their jobs are less secure and they are less able to protect themselves by building up savings. In *What unemployment means* (Sinfield, 1981, ch 2:4), I was concerned to spell out the continuing link between the experience of unemployment and poverty, with the rise in unemployment being the main driver for increasing poverty. Despite much research evidence that benefit levels were inadequate, media and political focus on the 'artful dodger on the Costa del Dole' resulted in little support. A generation on, the high risk of poverty in unemployment persists in the UK. While many dispute this, presuming generous benefits, others seem to accept it as inevitable. The sharp contrast to most of our EU partners shows that it is not. In 2007, 10 countries had poverty rates during unemployment more than 20 percentage points lower than the UK rate of 58% and only three had rates within 10 percentage points of the UK. Just one, Estonia, had a higher rate (Eurostat, 2010, Table 1).

The poverty of many out of work is deepening, with growing demands for food parcels from the increasing number of food banks, greater indebtedness and even the use of 'payday' loans, homelessness, and the return to bed and breakfast provision on a grand scale. The significance of poverty has been underlined by a large European panel study analysing labour market experience over time and across countries. It found:

> a vicious cycle of disadvantage, whereby people can be progressively marginalised from the employment structure. But the central factor underlying this process is poverty. Unemployment heightens the risk of people falling into poverty, and poverty in turn makes it more difficult for people to return to work. (Gallie et al, 2002, p 18)

The high risk of poverty when out of work makes the effective working of income-maintenance systems even more important in protecting individuals and families. Benefits during unemployment have always been more limited and circumscribed with conditions than other transfer payments. Despite greatly increased unemployment, the Thatcher governments 'turned the screw' on benefits out of work (Atkinson, 1989, ch 8). The extent of the tightening and the dismantlement of social insurance no longer seem to be remembered. Earnings-related supplements to short-term benefits, additions for dependants, support for short-time working and reduced benefits for an incomplete contribution record were all removed, while contribution conditions were made more demanding, particularly for those with earlier unemployment. The basic disqualification period was increased from up to six weeks, in force since the start in 1911, to 13 and then to 26 weeks, without any evidence for the change. The tightening continued under John Major, with the introduction of Jobseeker's Allowance (JSA) in 1996, cutting the maximum insurance duration from one year to six months.

In 1997, New Labour took over the core Conservative aim of strengthening incentives to work. Their policies did place more emphasis on some carrots to 'make work pay', but they did little to remove or lighten the sticks that their predecessors had introduced for those out of work. In 1999, tax credits and a national minimum wage helped those who were able to find work, but the benefits of most left out of work were not lifted, with the important exception of extra help for families – first, increases to means-tested additions for younger children; second, Child Tax Credits from 2003 available for all children, whether or not a parent was working. However, basic out-of-work benefits continued to fall behind, increasing the risk of poverty for those without children (Kenway, 2009).

Under successive governments, greater prolonged unemployment was seen less as a particular hardship warranting special help, and more as proof of a change in behaviour among those long out of work. They were described as 'resting on benefits' by one Conservative Minister for Employment in 1996, or 'languishing on benefits' by a Labour Prime Minister to an EU audience in 2004. But analysis of the labour market over half a century shows that the rate of long-term unemployment has remained closely linked to the overall rate of unemployment lagged by some months (Webster, 2005). There was no more reason to suspect that those long out of work were more likely to be avoiding work than in the past, but the belief has probably become even more pervasive, closing off arguments for stimulating demand. The stress on 'work-first' policies has not abated with increased unemployment. The imposition of sanctions has also tightened and increased with new sanctions (CAS, 2012). Since October 2012, a 'more robust' sanctions regime with increased penalties for repeated non-compliance has further tightened conditionality 'to ease the transition [to Universal Credit] for claimants and staff' (DWP, 2012, paras 4.2, 7.3).

In a few decades, the balance between the contributor and the National Insurance system has changed dramatically. Since the 1970s, the value of unemployment benefit has fallen by one half, from over one fifth of average pay to a tenth, even further down the European rankings. The employee's National Insurance contribution rate was then 6.5% of earnings, today it is 12%, nearly twice as much (Brendan Barber, quoted in TUC, 2012, p 4). Contributory-based benefits were then received by well over half of those drawing any benefits while unemployed, now the proportion is less than one fifth. The rejection of compensation out of work in return for contributions in work has been taken further by cutting insurance against sickness and disability to a maximum of one year.

The wider functions of social security have been neglected and, in particular, its value in maintaining demand and so preventing further loss of jobs by providing support when wages have stopped (Dolls et al, 2012). A good benefit system can be a social as well as an economic stabiliser, moderating unemployment effects, preserving cohesion and solidarity, and preventing greater social exclusion (ILO, 1984; Sinfield, 2001, 2012). Comparative studies have shown that:

> the higher the level of expenditure, the lower the level of poverty among those out of work, irrespective of a country's overall level of unemployment…. Rich, high employment countries where social spending is low end up with high poverty. This leads to the conclusion that, if it is possible to attain a low risk of poverty without substantial spending, it has not yet been demonstrated. (Cantillon, 2009, pp 232, 240; see also Brady 2009, p 143)

Present and coming reforms, particularly Universal Credit, with benefit caps and penalties for underoccupancy, seem very unlikely to improve the support, material and otherwise, for those who are out of work. It is not at all clear that 'making work pay' will be strengthened for those seeking full-time work or that the trumpeted removal of 'cliff edges' (where a job or increased pay can result in a sudden drop in total resources, such as free school meals and/or the loss of other benefits) will be achieved.

The shift to local and devolved Social Fund, passport and Council Tax benefits could lead to a multiplication of means-tested schemes. The continuing tightening of conditions, work requirements for benefits and sanctions will only increase pressure on out-of-work claimants, especially where there is no significant improvement in labour demand.

The policy shift from unemployment to worklessness

A generation ago, the response to persisting high unemployment was to reduce the numbers out of work and the size of the labour force with measures for early retirement, but in recent years, there has been 'an emergent trend towards a broadening of the category of unemployment' across many countries (Clasen and Clegg, 2011, p 337). In the UK, this has persisted, if not speeded up, despite the recession, continuing high unemployment and, it should be added, historically high employment rates. The term 'workless' used to be interchangeable with unemployed and jobless, but it has come to be extended to include the economically inactive – those who are sick and disabled and lone parents not working, who are being classified in terms of distance from employment, 'closer to' or 'further from' the labour market.

The breaking down of artificial barriers separating different administrative categories of people not in employment can clearly have advantages. Many who are not drawing benefits as unemployed still say that they want a job and, indeed, many move into employment straight from these other benefits: more could do so if they could get the help they need. Many lone parents cannot access decent and affordable childcare to take the jobs they want, and countries with more, better and cheaper childcare have fewer lone parents out of work.

The changes in the UK have been dominated by supply-side strategies that hold the individual responsible for their workless state and pay little attention to issues of labour demand, the regional and area dispersion of jobs, and the working conditions, pay and prospects of these jobs. Since the 1980s, successive governments have built on their predecessors' reforms to integrate benefit and employment services into a 'work-first' 'activation' regime for the wider group of 'the workless' (Finn, 2011), extending now to mandatory work requirements for some on ESA. The implications of applying 'a narrowly defined, hollowed out concept of employability' for those who become subject to it are harsh and bring false economies (Lindsay, 2010, p 123).

Public attitudes are often cited to justify tougher policies 'in fairness to the taxpayer'. In 2011, more than twice as many respondents as two decades ago, when unemployment was very similar, told the British Social Attitudes survey that unemployment benefits are 'too high and discourage work' (BSA, 2012, p 23, Table A-3). Since then, already inadequate benefits have fallen further behind wages; conditions and sanctions have been tightened and implemented more often and more vigorously; and the reclassification of many inactive as active has brought many more on to lower benefits – and unemployment is still high.

A generation ago, those drawing sickness and disability benefits were regarded much more sympathetically than the unemployed and lone parents. The hardening of attitudes against these groups too has, in my view, been much influenced by successive governments' overemphasis on benefit fraud (as opposed to tax 'non-compliance') and on getting other 'workless' off benefits and into jobs as well as those registered as unemployed (Baumberg et al, 2012). 'The workless tend to be viewed as worthless' (Marsden, 1982, p 2): a generation on, the stigma has been extended to a wider group.

Politicians' coaching of the media and manipulation of public attitudes have not received the attention they deserve.[3] Political attacks on benefits and their recipients have, of course, a long history in pre-democratic Poor Law thinking, but they were very rare when I first began research into the experience of unemployment in 1963. They were sharpened by the 'scroungerphobia' that was fanned by politicians in the 1970s (Deacon, 1981; Golding and Middleton, 1982), and from the 1980s on, senior ministers began to play a greater role in shaping public views. In 1987, John Moore marked his appointment as Secretary of State for Social Security by comparing the 'sullen apathy of dependence' created by the welfare state with the 'sheer delight of personal achievement' and then dismissed the concept of relative poverty as a socialist distraction from capitalist success (Moore, 1987, 1989). Peter Lilley was the first Secretary of State for Social Security to express his ambition to 'change the culture of social security'. What he meant was demonstrated by his 1992 Gilbert-and-Sullivan rendition, 'I've got a little list', linking benefit offenders and 'sponging socialists', to a standing ovation from the Conservative Party conference. The next year, he gained another for his xenophobic 'Crook's Tour', denouncing EU citizens coming to claim from 'La Societé de something for nothing'.

Subsequent Labour government moves to bring lone parents and many of those on Incapacity Benefit into the labour market tended to be accompanied by a punitive and often demeaning rhetoric, although ministers varied in their evocation of a benefit culture (Wright, 2011). Under the Coalition, the theme of growing dependency in an 'entitlement culture' has been picked up with more frequency and vigour, particularly by the Secretary of State for Work and Pensions, Iain Duncan Smith. In his March 2011 Keith Joseph Memorial Lecture, an event much publicised by the Conservatives, he referred to those who 'have seen their parents, their neighbours and their entire community sit on benefits for life'. The claim was repeated:

> The Universal Credit is about understanding that people who have been out of work all their lives ... and have never seen a family or even a community member in work ... have to see the financial benefits from taking up employment. (Duncan Smith, 2011)

Challenged later to name the 'entire community' where no one worked, the Secretary of State said that he had nowhere specific in mind and 'community' indicated 'circle' (letter to author). Repeated exposures of the lack of evidence for 'cultures of worklessness' have little effect (eg Shildrick et al, 2012a). Like Weebles, these myths wobble back up as soon as they are knocked down, in part at least because they serve powerful interests.

Summing up British labour market policies over the 20th century, William Walters concluded:

> Today social and employment policy is characterized by its avoidance of questions about the wider system, in favour of a focus on the 'margins', and its downplaying of the involuntary dimension of unemployment while opting for a very subjective and personalized approach to the problem. (Walters, 2000, p 9)

In the 21st century, this trend has accelerated with increased *Blaming the victim* (Ryan, 1971).

The dominant supply focus on reinforcing individual responsibility to work and winkling out fraud closes off discussion about the means of strengthening demand, the adequacy of benefits and take-up, and the quality of service provision. It was even proposed to stop official analyses of take-up. Separate worlds are created of 'shirkers' and 'workers', or 'skivers' and 'strivers'. 'Hard-working' taxpayers have to pay out to the takers, 'resting on benefits', as if taxpayers never face any of the social insurance risks and people receiving benefits never work and pay no taxes at all, even indirect ones. 'In such thinking, any idea that inequalities of wealth, income, power and life chances play a role in shaping people's lives is immediately relegated to a secondary position, if acknowledged at all' (Mooney and Wright, 2011, pp 140–1). The general pattern of *Regulating the poor* (Piven and Cloward, 1972) contrasts with the deregulation of the wealthier and more powerful that contributed to the financial crisis and to massive losses of tax revenue.

The further impact of high unemployment on the wider society

The individualist focus on worklessness has also meant, if not reinforced, continuing neglect of the impact of increased unemployment more widely. A society with unemployment remaining high for many years is likely to be qualitatively different to one that is able to provide adequate opportunities for all who want work. A recession affects many more people than those currently out of work, for there are many other ways in which the effects of unemployment impinge on the rest of society and its institutions (Sinfield, 1981, ch 5; forthcoming).

High unemployment affects the distribution of resources, power and opportunity among different groups and classes in society. The extent to which 'liability to unemployment or insecurity of tenure' is 'the distinguishing feature of the proletarian estate' (Briefs, 1937, quoted in Lockwood, 1958, p 55) can still reinforce and even widen class divisions and social and economic inequality. The shift in the balance of power between the employer and the worker is significant. Those with less bargaining power in the labour market, including minority ethnic and religious groups, become even more vulnerable to exclusion and deprivation. The risk of low pay and poor working conditions is increased and may have further impact on those on the margins or even outside the labour market (Bambra, 2011).

This is not to say that the maintenance of high employment is sufficient to avoid such problems, but for many it can be a necessary requirement. Many basic social policies such as equal opportunity to work depend upon unemployment being kept low for their success. Even if it is not the cause of a problem, it can impede measures to tackle it, which depend upon sufficient demand and fair access to employment opportunities (Reubens, 1970).

However, experience over time and across countries confirms that the impact of unemployment on wider society can be significantly modified (Cantillon, 2009). The ways that society, its institutions and its members respond to changes in unemployment may be critical (Therborn, 1986; White, 1911). This is why emphasis in this chapter has been placed on how governments frame economic and labour market problems in ways that shift responsibility away from them and on to those out of work, and on spelling out the implications of this for social division and exclusion.

Conclusion

While unemployment in the current recession may not have risen as much as in the last two recessions, it is still unnecessarily high, and the less skilled and lower paid continue to be more vulnerable, with young people particularly so this time. Those without work are even less well protected from poverty and more tightly policed than a generation ago. The erosion of contributory social insurance and the dismantlement of social security under successive governments is a significant shift in the continuing 'individualisation of the social' (Ferge, 1997).

In *The sociological imagination* (Mills, 1959), C. Wright Mills gave unemployment as his first illustration of the link between:

> the personal troubles of milieu [and] the public issues of social structure.... Both the correct statement of the problem and the range of possible solutions require us to consider the economic and political institutions of the society, and not merely the personal situation and character of a scatter of individuals. (Mills, 1959, p 9)

But in the UK, recognition of the wider problem of worklessness has come to be dominated by attacks on 'welfare dependency' that reinforce social exclusion for both those traditionally recognised as unemployed and others who are now also more likely to be treated as work-shy. A generation ago, I was challenging the treatment of most of the unemployed as second-class citizens. Now, others have been pushed down to join them in what increasingly looks like the restoration of a third class whose rights are even more tenuous and subject to challenge in the new poor laws.

What unemployment means today is shaped by a very different view of full employment from Beveridge's: 'decent jobs, fair wages, of such a kind and so located that the unemployed can reasonably be expected to take them' (Beveridge, 1944, p 18). A conventional liberal, Beveridge did not think that *any* job was the answer. Governments do not choose to help those they regard as undeserving (or at least not the poor ones). They are even less likely to change policies to help those people that they have actively worked to make sure most of us believe are undeserving. Coming reforms will increase conditionality and may well leave many more out of work and their families locked into poverty and insecurity by a safety net with more holes sagging further.

'Unemployment is divisive ... "the misery that generates hate"' (Deacon, 1981, p 86; with the Bronte quote from the title page of Beveridge's [1944] *Full employment in a free society*). Its impact is likely to be further exacerbated more widely by the scale of 'austerity' cuts in public services in a markedly more unequal society. The individualisation of unemployment as a social problem reinforcing images of two worlds – 'us the taxpayers' and 'them on benefits' – shifts attention from the structural foundations of inequality in society and in the labour market in particular. More attention needs to be paid to the political economy of the labour market and the distribution of 'decent jobs' and 'fair wages'. Unemployment and sub-employment are primarily characteristics of society and its workings, not of the individual in the labour market.

'Beveridge is in process of being abandoned. Whether he can be rescued is at present unclear' (Taylor-Gooby, 2012, p 229). In launching Universal Credit, Iain Duncan Smith described it as 'Beveridge for today, with a hint of Tebbit' (headline in the *Daily Telegraph*, 6 Nov 2010). He went out of his way to praise the Beveridge of *Voluntary action* (1948) over his more famous *Report on social insurance and allied services* (1942), but he failed to recognise Beveridge's stress on structural policies. Calling the last chapter 'First things first', Beveridge began:

> the Report of 1942 set out a practical programme for putting first things first. There was to be bread and health for all at all times before cake and circuses for anybody at any time, so far as this order of priority could be enforced by redistribution of money. (Beveridge, 1948, p 319)

Acknowledgements

I particularly want to thank Dorothy Sinfield for her continued, quiet support and patient comments on many drafts. I am also grateful to Daniel Clegg, Dan Heap, John Veit-Wilson and Sharon Wright for advice and guidance.

Notes

[1.] See: www.ukuncut.org.uk/blog/austerity-isnt-working

[2.] Today, we have more data on the numbers out of work than when we were dependent on the administrative count that relied on people registering as unemployed. This had many shortcomings, undercounting unemployment among married women, young people and others who might be less likely to register as they were not eligible for benefit. It became even more unreliable as an indicator of labour demand with the frequent restrictions to benefits under Thatcher. Particular changes, largely made to save money, limited the count from 1982 to claimants for benefit (including National Insurance credits), no longer requiring all unemployed people to register for work. This made the measure even less adequate for measuring labour supply, and from 1997, the main measure of unemployment has been obtained by household surveys, now the Labour Force Survey. Often referred to as the International Labour Office (ILO) count because it is based on the ILO and Organisation for Economic Co-operation and Development (OECD) agreed definition of unemployment, it includes anyone who has not worked for as much as one hour that week, has looked for work in the last four weeks or has a job waiting and could start work within two weeks. But, it might be noted, it excludes those required to work for benefit even though they are not being paid and the survey sample size limits detailed breakdown. Claimant numbers, based on the whole population of claimants, can be used for local and other detailed analyses, but their limitations need to be borne in mind. While earlier benefit changes reduced the numbers claiming, current ones bring many lone parents and past Employment and Support Allowance (ESA) recipients on to the claimant count (but see also Beatty et al, 2012). In this chapter, numbers (drawn from ONS [2012] and earlier issues) will refer to the ILO count unless otherwise specified: the administrative count is indicated by 'registered' before 1982 and 'claimant' since. Broader measures include, for example, 'discouraged workers' who have not looked for work in that period and/or people working part-time who say that they want full-time work.

[3.] Publication of an analysis of the representation and 'othering' of working-age people on benefits in Scotland was accompanied by the leaders of the main political parties signing an anti-stigma statement before the last Scottish election (Mooney and Wright, 2011; also follow the Poverty Alliance 'Stick Your Labels' campaign on Facebook).

References

Atkinson, A.B. (1989) *Poverty and social security*, New York, NY: Harvester Wheatsheaf.

Ball, J., Milmo, D. and Ferguson, B. (2012) 'Half of UK's young black males are unemployed', *The Guardian*, 9 March.

Bambra, C. (2011) *Work, worklessness, and the political economy of health*, Oxford: Oxford University Press.

Barton, A., Drummond, R. and Matajic, P. (2010) *Low-income dynamics 1991–2008 (Great Britain)*, London: Department for Work and Pensions.

Baumberg, B., Bell, K. and Gaffney, D. (2012) *Benefits stigma in Britain*, London: Turn2us.

Beatty, C., Fothergill, S. and Gore, T. (2012) *The real level of unemployment 2012*, Sheffield: Sheffield Hallam University.

Beveridge, W.H. (1942) *Report on social insurance and allied services*, London: HMSO.

Beveridge, W.H. (1944) *Full employment in a free society*, London: Allen and Unwin.

Beveridge, W.H. (1948) *Voluntary action*, London: Allen and Unwin.

Brady, D. (2009) *Rich democracies, poor societies: how politics explain poverty*, Oxford: Oxford University Press.

Briefs, G. A. (1937) *The proletariat*, London: McGraw-Hill.

BSA (British Social Attitudes) (2012) *British Social Attitudes 29*, London: NatCen.

Cantillon, B. (2009) 'The poverty effects of social protection in Europe: EU enlargement and its lessons for developing countries', in P. Townsend (ed) *Building decent societies: rethinking the role of social security in development*, Basingstoke: ILO and Palgrave Macmillan, pp 220–41.

CAS (Citizens Advice Scotland) (2012) *Voices from the front line: sanctions*, Edinburgh: CAS.

Clasen, J. and Clegg, D. (2011) 'The transformation of unemployment protection in Europe', in J. Clasen and D. Clegg (eds) *Regulating the risk of unemployment*, Oxford: Oxford University Press, pp 333–45.

COVE (Commission on Vulnerable Employment) (2008) *Hard work hidden lives*, London: Trades Union Congress.

Deacon, A. (1981) 'Unemployment and politics in Britain since 1945', in B. Showler and A. Sinfield (eds) *The workless state*, Oxford: Martin Robertson, pp 59–88.

Dolls, M., Fuest, C. and Peichl, A. (2012) 'Automatic stabilizers and economic crisis: US vs Europe', *Journal of Public Economics*, vol 96, pp 279–94.

Duncan Smith, I. (2011) 'Welfare reform: the wider context', Keith Joseph Memorial Lecture, Centre for Policy Studies, London.

DWP (Department for Work and Pensions) (2012) *Explanatory Memorandum to The Jobseeker's Allowance (Sanctions) (Amendment) Regulations 2012*, London: DWP.

Eurostat (2010) *In-work poverty in the EU*, Luxembourg: EC, http://epp.eurostat.ec.europa.eu/cache/ITY_OFFPUB/KS-RA-10-015/EN/KS-RA-10-015-EN.PDF

Ferge, Z. (1997) 'The changed welfare paradigm: the individualisation of the social', *Social Policy and Administration*, vol 31, no 1, pp 20–44.

Finn, D. (2011) 'Welfare to work after the recession: from the New Deals to the Work Programme', in I. Greener, C. Holden and M. Kilkey (eds) *Social Policy Review 23*, Bristol: Policy Press, pp 127–46.

Gallie, D. and Paugam, S. (2000) 'The social regulation of unemployment', in D. Gallie and S. Paugam (eds) *Welfare regimes and the experience of unemployment in Europe*, Oxford: Oxford University Press, pp 351–74.

Gallie, D., Paugam, S. and Jacobs, S. (2002) 'Unemployment, poverty and social isolation: is there a vicious circle of social exclusion?', *European Societies*, vol 5, no 1, pp 1–32.

Golding, P. and Middleton, S. (1982) *Images of welfare: press and public attitudes to poverty*, Oxford: Martin Robertson.

Goulden, C. (2010) 'Cycles of poverty, unemployment and low pay', *JRF Round-Up*, 9 February.

Gregg, P. and Wadsworth, J. (2011) 'Unemployment and inactivity', in P. Gregg and J. Wadsworth (eds) *The labour market in winter: the state of working Britain*, Oxford: Oxford University Press, pp 22–38.

Gregory, M. and Jukes, R. (2001) 'Unemployment and subsequent earnings: estimating scarring among British men 1984–94', *Economic Journal*, vol 111, no 475, pp 607–25.

ILO (International Labour Office) (1984) *Into the twenty-first century: the development of social security*, Geneva: International Labour Office.

Kenway, P. (2009) *Should adult benefits for unemployment now be raised?*, York: Joseph Rowntree Foundation.

Lindsay, C. (2010) 'Re-connecting with "what unemployment means": employability, the experience of unemployment and priorities for policy in an era of crisis', in C. Holden, M. Kilkey and G. Ramia (eds) *Social Policy Review 22*, Bristol: Policy Press, pp 121-148.

Lockwood, D. (1958) *The blackcoated worker*, London: Allen and Unwin.

Marsden, D. (1982) *Workless* (2nd edn), Beckenham: Croom Helm.

Mills, C.W. (1959) *The sociological imagination*, New York, NY: Oxford University Press.

Mooney, G. and Wright, S. (2011) 'Presenting and representing poverty', in J.H. McKendrick, G. Mooney, J. Dickie and P. Kelly (eds) *Poverty in Scotland 2011*, London: CPAG, pp 133–45.

Moore, J. (1987) *The future of the welfare state*, London: Conservative Party Office.

Moore, J. (1989) *The end of the line for poverty*, London: Conservative Party Office.

Moylan, S., Millar, J. and Davies, R. (1984) *For richer, for poorer? DHSS cohort study of unemployed men*, London: DHSS.

North Tyneside CDP (1978) *In and out of work*, North Tyneside: North Tyneside CDP.

ONS (Office for National Statistics) (2011) *Social trends*, London: ONS.

ONS (2012) *Labour market statistics December 2012*, Statistical Bulletin, London: ONS.

Piven, F.F. and Cloward, R. (1972) *Regulating the poor: the functions of public welfare*, London: Tavistock.

Reubens, B. (1970) *The hard-to-employ: European programs*, New York, NY: Columbia University Press.

Ryan, W. (1971) *Blaming the victim*, London: Orbach and Chambers.

Shildrick, T., MacDonald, R., Webster, C. and Garthwaite, K. (2010) *The low pay, no pay cycle: understanding recurrent poverty*, York: Joseph Rowntree Foundation.

Shildrick, T., Furlong, A., MacDonald, R., Roden, J. and Crow, R. (2012a) *Are 'cultures of worklessness' passed down the generations?*, York: Joseph Rowntree Foundation.

Shildrick, T., MacDonald, R., Webster, C. and Garthwaite, K. (2012b) *Poverty and insecurity: life in low-pay, no-pay Britain*, Bristol: Policy Press.

Sinfield, A. (1970) 'Poor and out of work in Shields', in P. Townsend (ed) *The concept of poverty*, London: Heinemann, pp 220–35.

Sinfield, A. (1981) *What unemployment means*, Oxford: Martin Robertson.

Sinfield, A. (2001) 'Benefits and research in the labour market', *European Journal of Social Security*, vol 3, no 3, pp 209–35.

Sinfield, A. (2012) 'Strengthening the prevention of social insecurity', *International Social Security Review*, vol 65, no 1, pp 89–106.

Sinfield, A. (forthcoming) 'The wider impact of unemployment', in U.-C. Kiehe and E.A.J. van Hooft (eds) *Handbook of job loss and job search*, Oxford: Oxford University Press.

Smith, N. and Middleton, S. (2007) *A review of poverty dynamics research in the UK*, York: Joseph Rowntree Foundation.

Taylor-Gooby, P. (2012) 'Beveridge overboard? How the UK government is using the crisis to permanently restructure the welfare state', *Intereconomics*, vol 47, no 4, pp 224–9.

Therborn, G. (1986) *Why some peoples are more unemployed than others*, London: Verso.

Trades Union Congress (TUC) (2012) *Making a contribution: social security for the future*, London: Touchstone.

Walters, W. (2000) *Unemployment and government: genealogies of the social*, Cambridge: Cambridge University Press.

Webster, D. (2005) 'Long-term unemployment, the invention of "hysteresis" and the misdiagnosis of structural unemployment in the UK', *Cambridge Journal of Economics*, vol 29, no 6, pp 975–95.

White, M. (1991) *Against unemployment*, London: Policy Studies Institute.

Wright, S. (2011) 'Relinquishing rights? The impact of activation on citizenship for lone parents in the UK', in S. Betzelt and S. Bothfeld (eds) *Activation and labour market reforms in Europe*, Basingstoke: Palgrave Macmillan, pp 59–78.

TWELVE

Precarious employment and EU employment regulation

Julia S. O'Connor

Introduction

Precarious employment is generally identified within the broader rubric of non-standard employment, which encompasses several forms of employment, including part-time work, fixed-term contracts, self-employment and agency work (European Industrial Relations Dictionary, 2011). These forms of non-standard employment are seen as integral to the strategy to increase labour market flexibility and participation in EU policy documents relating to the European Employment Strategy and the Europe 2020 framework, and have increased in several EU countries through explicit policies during the current crisis. This chapter makes a threefold argument. First, non-standard employment is not a homogeneous category in terms of employment characteristics and workers' rights and security. Second, the scope and coverage of EU employment regulation of non-standard employment, in particular, EU Directives, do not afford protection to individuals in the most precarious employment. This is because these workers are not likely to be in a position to vindicate the formal rights afforded by such regulation, and many are in forms of employment not explicitly targeted by EU employment regulation. Third, precarious employment is a significant potential, and unequally shared, risk of flexibility strategies, and a commitment to combine security with flexibility, that is, 'flexicurity', in EU labour market discourse does not obviate this risk.

The immediately following section situates precarious employment within the employment spectrum. This leads on to identification of the major forms of non-standard employment and the associated EU regulation. It then explores EU Directives on non-standard employment, focusing on the extent to which they afford protection to workers in precarious employment situations. This is followed by identification of forms of non-standard employment not targeted by specific Directives, where the magnitude of precariousness is even more difficult to specify, such as homeworking and undeclared/black and grey market work. The concluding section situates precarious employment in the broader employment, economic and social context.

Standard, non-standard and precarious employment

The standard employment contract is usually defined as full-time, regular, open-ended, secure employment with a single employer, which incorporates standard working hours guaranteeing a regular income. Via social security systems geared towards wage-earners, standard employment provides ill-health and unemployment protection and public pension cover, and often supplementary occupation-linked pension coverage or the potential to purchase this on the market. While this covers the elements of the historical definition of the standard employment contract, there is increasing variation in the character and quality of standard employment. Standard employment was never universal. The changed situation of households with caring responsibilities, whether single or dual breadwinner, and the broader labour market changes associated with intensified globalisation, bring the issue of non-standard employment and its consequences into sharp relief. Non-standard or atypical employment encompasses fixed-term contracts, part-time work, self-employment and agency work, independent or homework (European Industrial Relations Dictionary, 2011). It may also include on-call and zero-hour contracts, freelance contracts, and forced and bogus self-employment. Some of these employment situations are preferred choices, well-paid and secure, for example, some freelance contractors, independent professionals and self-employed trades people, whose employment and immediate and long-term economic and social security circumstances are very different from workers in precarious employment.

The terminology relating to 'precarious' employment is contested not only on theoretical and methodological grounds, but also on the grounds of linguistic and national policy history differences, which, it is argued, constrain the validity of cross-national comparison (Barbier, 2005). Nevertheless, precarious employment is part of the current policy discourse in the EU and elsewhere (see, eg, D'Amours, 2009; Evans and Gibb, 2009; Kalleberg, 2009; Vosko et al, 2009; ILO, 2011a; Countouris, 2011). Paugam (2002) and Kalleberg (2009) point to two dimensions of precariousness: 'employment precariousness', relating to contractual conditions – remuneration and security; and 'work precariousness', relating to poor working conditions and absent or low autonomy, motivation, self-fulfilment and opportunities to develop skills.[1] The ILO identifies 'precarious work' as '"atypical work" that is *involuntary* – the temporary worker without employment security, the part-time worker without any pro-rated benefits of a full-time job, etc.' (ILO, 2010, p 35, fn 34, emphasis added). Kalleberg captures other important dimensions: the absence of alternative employment opportunities and 'diminished opportunities to obtain and maintain particular skills' (Kalleberg, 2009, p 2, fn 2). He further points out that income precarity, unsafe working conditions and the unavailability of collective bargaining representation, identified by Rodgers (1989) and Standing (1999), are determinants or consequences of these characteristics.

In this chapter, 'precarious employment' refers to employment that is: lacking employment or job and income security and employment-linked social protection provision; characterised by poor work conditions and the absence of opportunities for skill development and self-fulfilment; involuntary in the context of the absence of alternative employment opportunities; and characterised by the absence of the opportunity for collective representation. The combination of these elements indicates that the problem of precariousness in employment is broader than insecure employment and cannot be unambiguously identified with any particular form of employment. Furthermore, a key characteristic is that it can have negative lifetime consequences, as reflected in absence of social protection.

Non-standard employment and EU employment regulation

Non-standard forms of employment are promoted at the EU level and by national governments as mechanisms to reduce unemployment and to increase the employment rate, particularly for groups such as women, young people and migrants, who are under-represented in the labour market. While these forms of employment undoubtedly enhance labour market flexibility, they also increase the risk of economic insecurity and the infringement of workers' rights and conditions. This is recognised in EU Directives on some forms of non-standard employment. Directives require the unanimous agreement of all member states and once passed, all member states must take action to transpose them into national law. They cover a broad range of areas such as anti-discrimination, equal treatment of men and women in the workplace, maternity rights, parental leave, social security and pension rights and the provision of information to, and consultation with, employees, including Directives on work councils and on collective redundancies. While all of these are relevant to workers in standard and non-standard employment, the concern here is with Directives that have been developed specifically to address non-standard employment, and the extent to which they afford protection to those in precarious employment. Part-time work, fixed-term contracts and temporary agency work are the forms of non-standard/atypical employment with the most clearly targeted EU Directives. These are also the largest categories of non-standard employment in the EU27 (see Table 12.1).

Part-time work increased from 16% to 19% as a share of the EU27 labour force between 2000 and 2010, and fixed-term contracts increased from 12% to 14%. The share of self-employment was 15% of the EU27 labour force, one percentage point lower than in 2000. There is some overlap between these figures, for example, in part-time fixed-term work and part-time self-employment, but the exact magnitude of this overlap is difficult to quantify. A further factor that is noteworthy about non-standard work is the cross-national variation within particular forms, for example: part-time work tends to be higher in the EU15 countries than in the EU12; fixed-term contracts are 15% or less in most EU27 countries but are far higher in Poland (27%), Spain (25%) and Portugal (23%); and self-employment is generally higher in the more recent EU member states, especially Romania and Bulgaria, where over a quarter of the labour force is self-employed – at 35%, Greece had the highest rate of self-employment in the EU in 2009. Exact figures on temporary agency work are not available, but it is estimated to account for about 2% of the EU27 labour force, varying from 2% or less in France, Belgium and the Netherlands to 5% in the UK (Arrowsmith, 2006).

EU Directives on non-standard employment and protection of precarious workers

This section outlines the key forms of protection mandated by the Directives on non-standard employment (see Table 12.2), with a particular focus on the extent to which they afford protection to those in precarious employment.

Table 12.1: Country-level data on part-time work, fixed-term contracts and self-employment, EU27, 2000 and 2010

	% total employment						
	Part-time work			Fixed-term contracts		Self-employed	
	2000	2010	% female employment	2000	2010	2000	2009
EU27[1]	16.2	19.2	31.9	12.3	14.0	16.6	15.5
EU15	16.6	21.5	35.3	13.7	13.7	14.4	14.0
Belgium	18.9	24.0	42.3	9.1	8.1	17.1	16.2
Germany	19.4	26.2	45.5	12.7	14.7	10.0	11.0
France	16.7	17.8	30.0	15.2	15.1	9.2	9.1
Italy	8.4	15.0	29.0	10.1	12.2	26.4	23.4
Luxembourg	10.4	17.9	36.0	5.3	7.1	7.3	5.9
Netherlands	41.5	48.9	76.5	13.7	18.5	13.9	13.4
Denmark	21.3	26.5	39.0	9.7	8.6	6.8	6.2
Ireland	16.4	22.4	34.7	5.9	9.3	18.6	17.8
UK	25.1	26.9	43.3	7.0	6.1	12.1	13.7
Greece	4.5	6.4	10.4	13.5	12.4	39.0	35.4
Spain	7.9	13.3	23.2	32.2	24.9	15.8	13.7
Portugal	10.9	11.6	15.5	19.9	23.0	16.9	13.2
Austria	16.3	25.2	43.8	8.0	9.3	13.9	14.2
Finland	12.3	14.6	19.6	16.3	15.5	12.2	12.1
Sweden	19.5	26.4	40.4	15.8	15.3	6.5	5.4
Cyprus	8.4	9.3	12.7	10.7	13.5	23.2	17.2
Malta	6.8	12.4	24.9	4.1	5.7	11.2	12.3
Estonia	8.1	11.0	14.5	3.0	3.7	9.0	8.2
Latvia	11.3	9.7	11.4	6.7	6.8	15.1	11.6
Lithuania	10.2	8.1	9.3	4.4	2.4	19.7	15.1
Hungary	3.5	5.8	8.0	7.1	9.7	19.1	11.0
Poland	10.5	8.2	11.5	5.8	27.3	27.4	22.8
Slovenia	6.5	11.4	14.7	13.7	17.3	18.4	17.3
Slovakia	2.1	3.9	5.4	4.8	5.8	8.3	15.4
Czech Republic	5.3	5.9	9.9	8.1	8.9	17.4	18.7
Bulgaria	3.2	2.4	2.6	6.3	4.5	28.2	26.9
Romania	15.9	11.0	11.4	2.8	1.1	45.4	28.8

Note: [1] Countries listed by date they became members from original six to the 2004 and 2007 member states.
Sources: http://epp.eurostat.ec.europa.eu/portal/page/portal/statistics/search_database and European Commission (2010a) statistical annex for self-employment.

Table 12.2: Non-standard employment and associated EU directives

Forms of non-standard employment	EU directives	Key provision
Part-time work	Directive on part-time work 97/81/EC (Framework Agreement signed by social partners in 1997)	The objective is to remove discrimination against part-time workers, improve the quality of part-time work and facilitate the flexible organisation of working time 'in a manner which takes into account the needs of employers and workers' (Clause 1)
Fixed-term contracts	Directive on fixed-term contracts 99/70/EC (Framework Agreement signed by social partners in 1999)	'[F]ixed term workers shall not be treated in a less favourable manner than comparable permanent workers solely because they have a fixed-term contract or relation unless different treatment is justified on objective grounds' (Clause 4.1)
Temporary agency work	Directive on temporary agency work 2008/104/EC	'The basic working and employment conditions of temporary agency workers shall be, for the duration of their assignment at a user undertaking, at least those that would apply if they had been recruited directly by that undertaking to occupy the same job' (Article 5.1)
Self-employment	Directive 2010/41/EU on the application of the principle of equal treatment between men and women engaged in a self-employed capacity. This directive repealed 86/613/EEC, which was inadequate in terms of the recognition and protection of spouses and life partners who work on an informal basis in the business	'Where a system of social protection for self-employed works exists in a Member State, that Member State shall take the necessary measure to ensure that spouses and life partners ... benefit from a social protection in accordance with national law' (Article 7) 'The Member States shall take the necessary measures to ensure that female self-employed workers and female spouses and life partners ... may, in accordance with national law, be granted a sufficient maternity allowance enabling interruptions in their occupation activity owing to pregnancy or motherhood for at least 14 weeks' (Article 8)

Part-time work Directive and very atypical working time

The 1997 EU Directive on part-time work implemented the Framework Agreement reached by the EU social partners in 1997. It identifies a part-time worker as:

an employee whose normal hours of work, calculated on a weekly basis or on average over a period of employment up to one year, are less than the normal hours of work of a comparable full-time worker ... in the same establishment, having the same type of employment contract or relationship, who is engaged in the same or similar work/occupation. (Council Directive 97/81/EC of 15 December 1997)

The employment conditions of part-time workers cannot be less favourable 'than comparable full-time workers solely because they work part-time unless different treatment is justified on objective grounds' (Clause 4). Several European Court of Justice (ECJ) rulings have dealt with infringement of the provisions of the Directive on part-time work in relation to hours worked, salary thresholds for employment protection legislation coverage, bonus and severance payments, and inclusion in occupational pension schemes (Bell, 2011). This ECJ route to vindication of rights is dependent not only on knowledge of rights and remedies, but also on individual and/or collective resources, in particular, trade union membership. ILO research has pointed to lower levels of collective representation among part-time workers (ILO, 2004) as does a more recent Organisation for Economic Co-operation and Development (OECD) position paper (OECD, 2010).

The definition of part-time work varies cross-nationally but is generally taken as less than 30 hours per week.[2] The majority of part-time employees in EU15 countries work substantial part-time, that is, 20–34 hours per week. Short part-time work, fewer than 10 to 15 hours a week depending on the country definition, is an area of concern in several countries and is characterised by the European Working Conditions Observatory (EWCO) as a 'very atypical' form of work. This ranges from less than 1% of the workforce in Central and Eastern European countries, to 2% in Southern European/Mediterranean countries, 3% in Belgium, 4% in Austria and the Netherlands, and 8% in the UK (EWCO, 2010). Short part-time is predominantly female and is found mostly in the food industry, personal care and cleaning, and the domestic services sector. It is difficult to assess the implementation of employment regulation in these areas because of the privacy of the employment locations and the 'invisibility' of the workers involved.

Recent OECD research demonstrates that the benefits of work–life flexibility associated with part-time work are outweighed by lost earning potential and job insecurity, access to training and promotion, and union membership (OECD, 2010). This echoes the European Trade Union

Institute's identification of low part-time hours as 'problematic not only because of lower monthly incomes but also because in some countries marginal employment of this kind grants no or only restricted access to social security benefits' (ETUI-REHS, 2007, p 34).

Directive on fixed-term contracts and very atypical contracts

The EU Council Directive on fixed-term contracts identifies a fixed-term worker as:

> a person having a contract of employment or relationship entered into directly between an employer and a worker, where the end of the employment contract or relationship is determined by objective conditions such as reaching a specific date, completing a specific task, or the occurrence of a specific event. (EU Council Directive 1999/70/EC Clause 3 (1))

It obliges member states to put measures in place to prevent the abuse of fixed-term workers, by specifying the grounds for the justification of the renewal of fixed contracts, and the maximum duration and/or number of successive contracts (Clause 5). Member states have been obliged by the ECJ to adhere to the provisions of this Directive and to pay compensation for failure to implement it properly (Zappala, 2006; European Foundation for the Improvement of Living and Working Conditions, 2008a).

All EU countries have transposed the fixed-term workers Directive and this has led to significant changes in employment law, increasing protection in some countries, such as the UK and Ireland, and a broadening of the categories of workers who could be hired on fixed-term contract in others, such as France. There is a substantial body of case law and practice relating to the interpretation of two aspects of the Directive, namely, the scope of equal treatment – particularly relating to pay – and the nature of the objective reasons that may allow for unequal treatment. The ECJ has ruled that the scope is broad and the objective reasons for exclusion must be transparent in the specific context in which it occurs (Lorber, 2011). For example, while pay is not a matter for EU legislation, the ECJ has ruled that 'employment conditions' cover aspects of pay such as length of service allowances (European Commission Legal Service, 2007). In relation to reasons for exclusion from equal treatment, the ECJ has ruled that Clause 4(1) (see Table 12.2) is unconditional and sufficiently precise to underpin a challenge against a member state in a national court in relation to payment of a length of service increment to a temporary public servant starting from the date the Directive should have been transposed and not the date it was transposed and even though a national provision relating to public servants had no reference to the Directive (ECJ, 2010).

In assessing the experience of fixed-term employment, the European Labour Force Survey found that almost half of fixed-term contracts were involuntary in 2004 – 48% compared to 37% in 2001. A study covering the period 1995–2005 focusing on job quality, as measured by relative wage and skill intensity in the EU15, concluded that there was little change in the prevalence of fixed-term contracts overall but that 'they remain relatively concentrated in the lower paid jobs in the EU as a whole' (Stehrer et al, 2009, p ii). In *Employment in Europe 2010*, the European Commission (2010a, p 117) points to a large increase in temporary employment in some member states from 2008 to 2009 resulting from government policy, specifically, the reform of employment protection legislation to increase flexibility '"at the margin" i.e. substantially deregulating the use of temporary contracts while maintaining stringent firing rules on permanent contracts'. While contributing to increased employment, the increased use of temporary contracts has also contributed to the emergence of dual or segmented labour markets with well-protected 'insiders' while the 'outsiders' are 'living in a precarious situation and at risk of frequent spells of unemployment with poor prospects of career advancement' (European Commission, 2010a, p 117). These outsiders are predominantly young and low skilled, and are particularly vulnerable during economic downturns. They are in a precarious situation not only because of the absence of employment security, 'but also in terms of income security, because of the limited access of temporary workers to social security benefits in general, and unemployment insurance in particular' (European Commission, 2010a, p 117). Changed economic conditions may exacerbate such vulnerability, as demonstrated by the decline in temporary employment during the current recession in some countries, most dramatically in Spain, where this form of employment had increased significantly since the early 2000s (European Commission, 2010a, p 41). In the context of the absence of alternative employment opportunities, this illustrates well the analytical and policy value of recognising the pervasive impact of precarious employment and, in particular, the absence of employment-related social protection on individual life chances.

The EWCO identifies a 'temporary contract of six months or less' as a 'very atypical contractual arrangement' (European Foundation for the Improvement of Living and Working Conditions, 2010a). Because of data quality, the exact magnitude of these arrangements is impossible to ascertain, as are cross-national trends. However, some broad patterns can be identified. First, workers involved in very short fixed contracts vary from very low-skilled workers to highly skilled professionals. Second, the nature and pattern of usage varies cross-nationally: in some countries, there is extensive use of a probationary period of six months or less, which may lead to indefinite employment or job termination; in others, casual and seasonal work in the agricultural and tourism sectors is a regular pattern and particularly difficult to quantify. Attempts to regulate such work are being made in several EU countries, largely through measures to combat undeclared work (European Foundation for the Improvement of Living and Working Conditions, 2008b, 2009). Finally, the collective organisation of fixed term-workers in general, and short-term fixed contract workers in particular, is extremely difficult. While trade unions in several EU countries are developing strategies to recruit members from under-unionised groups, including atypical workers, this is within the context of declining union density, particularly in the private sector (European Foundation for the Improvement of Living and Working Conditions, 2010b).

Directive on temporary agency work

The protection of agency workers was the subject of a Council Resolution in 1974 but the Directive on temporary agency work (2008/104/EC) was not agreed until 2008. The preamble to the Directive identifies temporary agency work as an important contribution to the enhancement of flexibility for employers and work–life balance for employees, in the context of the December 2007 European Council endorsement of the common principles of flexicurity, which, the Directive states, 'strike a balance between flexibility and security in the labour market and help both workers and employers to seize the opportunities offered by globalisation'. The key objective of the Directive on temporary agency work (2008/104/EC) is to ensure that the 'basic working and employment conditions of temporary agency workers shall be ... at least those that would apply if they had been recruited directly by that undertaking to occupy the same job' (Article 5.1).

There is considerable scope for derogation from this provision if the agreement of social partners is obtained; this includes the qualifying period for equal treatment (Article 5.4). The protection afforded by this directive is weak relative to the Directives on fixed-term contracts and on part-time workers. In contrast to the limit on the number and length of successive fixed-term contracts, it does not provide for the standardisation of successive temporary agency contracts. It explicitly allows for derogation from the equal treatment provision, provided that the social partners agree, 'where temporary agency workers who have a permanent contract of employment with a temporary-work agency continue to be paid in the time between assignments' (Article 5.2). This is a significant limitation in view of the increased emphasis on outsourcing of particular functions within the manufacturing and services sectors. Furthermore, despite its reference to work–life balance, it takes a minimalist approach to the equal treatment principle and 'fails to secure for agency workers the ability to take advantage of the few entitlements offered by the current EC and national packages of family friendly rights, and in particular parental leave' (Countouris and Horton, 2009, p 338).

Agency work is still used as it was traditionally, as a source of temporary employment between full-term standard employment positions and to meet short-term heavy demand or as a cover for periods of absence by permanent employees. While it is still estimated at about 2% of the workforce in the EU15, which is much lower than other forms of non-standard employment, there are significant variations across the EU15 member states. It expanded rapidly in almost all EU15 countries in the mid- to late 1990s and was the most rapidly growing form of atypical employment in the EU during the 1990s (European Foundation for the Improvement of Living and Working Conditions, 2007). A significant proportion of temporary agency work appears to be lower-skilled service sector, manufacturing and clerical/administrative work. It is used in several EU countries to engage seasonal, often migrant, workers in the agricultural sector. However, temporary agency work is used in some countries, including the UK, France, Germany and Italy, to provide skilled technical and engineering professionals (Arrowsmith, 2006, Table 2). In the UK and Ireland, temporary agency work is used extensively to provide health professionals, especially nurses and care assistants. Because the transposition deadline of the Directive on temporary agency work was 5 December 2011, evidence on its effectiveness is scarce. However, there is already evidence of employers paying compensation from the transposition date to agency workers who were paid less than directly employed staff in the health care sector in Ireland. This was agreed once the Directive was transposed in May 2012 (Walsh, 2012). Health care is a strongly unionised sector, which is likely to have assisted in ensuring conformity with the associated legislation.

Falling between the cracks

The discussion so far has focused on single forms of non-standard employment, but such forms of employment often overlap, for example, part-time and temporary work, sometimes incorporating an 'on-call' dimension; likewise, agency work is often part-time and/or may also incorporate an 'on-call' and/or zero-hours contract dimension. These overlapping forms of employment are a regular feature of the service sector, particularly in catering and retail, where jobs are often taken by students, migrant workers, those – usually women – caring for dependent people and by others who may be constrained in terms of availability for less precarious work. The composition of the workforce and the ease of employee replacement make this kind of employment particularly difficult in terms of mobilisation to vindicate rights mandated in Directives. This exacerbates the difficulty of enforcement of employment regulation, particularly in the context of an abundance of potential employees with few alternative opportunities. The next section focuses on forms of employment not covered by targeted Directives. These encompass some highly rewarded employment situations, but also some of the most precarious employment situations in terms of the criteria outlined in the definition of precariousness underpinning this analysis.

Non-standard employment in the absence of targeted Directives

Self-employed/freelance/economically dependent workers

There is no targeted Directive on self-employment, although there is a Council Recommendation calling on member states to improve health and safety for self-employed workers (Europa, 2003). Directive 86/613/EEC on the equal treatment of men and women in self-employment, which applied from 1986, was repealed and replaced in 2010 by Directive 2010/41/EU, which gives recognition and protection to spouses/life partners who work on an informal basis in self-employed businesses (see Table 12.2). EUbusiness (2010) estimates that 11% of self-employed workers rely on spouses and partners working on an informal basis.

In 2010, 30% of the self-employed in the EU employed other workers (European Commission, 2010b, p11). The remaining 70% covers a wide range, from independent professionals and craft-workers, who may be in highly secure economic positions that allow them to compensate for contractual insecurity, to people in highly insecure and often low-income employment or 'forced' and/or 'false' self-employed workers and economically dependent workers, which are often overlapping categories. The latter refers to workers who are nominally self-employed but have a service contract with one employer on whom they are dependent for all or most of their income. A recent study concludes that 'the "service" they sell individually to employers falls outside the traditional scope of "professional services", which means that the tasks are simple, do not require specific skills and no professional knowledge or competence is needed' (European Foundation for the Improvement of Living and Working Conditions, 2010c, p 27). This supports an earlier study based on analysis of British Labour Force data from 2002, which concludes that economically dependent workers are distinct from employees and self-employed individuals, have lower labour market skills, attachment and autonomy, and are used by firms to increase labour flexibility (Böheim and Muehlberger, 2006).

Abuses of self-employment include the use of false and/or forced self-employment to avoid paying minimum wage rates and social protection contributions. The European Employment Observatory review cites evidence of concerns relating to the quality of 'self-employment', including: low income, with 18% of self-employed people classified as poor compared to 6% of employees; long-working hours, that is, over 48 hours per week; poor health associated with working conditions; and fewer opportunities for training than employees (European Commission, 2010b, pp 26–9). Some of these issues could be addressed by general Directives, including the health and safety Directives and the working time Directive 2003/88/EC, which addresses maximum weekly working hours, breaks, weekly rest period, night work, shift work and patterns of work. The related Directive 2002/15/EC on the organisation of the working time of persons performing mobile and road transport activities 'temporarily' excluded self-employed drivers from its scope (up to 23 March 2009) as a concession to the European Council, which strongly opposed their inclusion. Spain and Finland sought to have the Directive annulled, but their legal challenges were rejected by the ECJ (Rodgers, 2009). The Commission's report favouring exclusion of self-employed drivers was rejected by the Economic and Social Committee and the European Parliament. Self-employed drivers are now formally covered by the Directive, but the European Commission is still committed to its position and will not bring infringement proceedings against member states who do not enforce it. Lisa Rodgers (2009, p 342) concludes that: 'Given the Commission's clear admission of the economic advantages for the self-employed of avoiding the application of working time legislation, it seems that the risk to workers of being forced into a position of false self-employment remains high'.

In addition to employment quality, social security is a key issue for self-employed workers. This is an area where there is very marked cross-national variation in terms of formal provision. The European Foundation for the Improvement of Living and Working Conditions review points out that social protection reforms 'have tended to include self-employed workers and increase protections (as well as contributions)' (European Foundation for the Improvement of Living and Working Conditions, 2010b, p 21). Despite this, self-employed workers are still excluded from mandatory employee schemes in some countries, for example, in the UK and Ireland, and are not entitled to unemployment, disability and invalidity benefits. The 2010 amendment of the equal treatment Directive as it applies to self-employment has the potential to improve the situation in relation to maternity rights (see Table 12.2). The European Foundation for the Improvement of Living and Working Conditions review paints a particularly stark picture in relation to Eastern European member states where 'no formal employment relationships exist which can be linked to economically dependent work' and the latter generally refers to bogus or false self-employment, and, 'in some countries, such as Estonia and Hungary, national correspondents define bogus self-employment as a quite common practice also present in the public administration' (European Foundation for the Improvement of Living and Working Conditions, 2010b, p 31).

A fundamental problem for self-employed workers is the issue of collective representation and the vindication of rights to which they are entitled. Those in more secure areas of self-employment are likely to be effectively represented by professional organisations and/or trade associations and/or can afford to purchase private health and pensions coverage. The problem of non-representation is an issue for those in the least secure and most precarious forms of self-employment.

Undeclared/black/grey market labour

In October 2007, an EU Commission paper recommended that member states should reduce taxes on labour, increase control of cross-border firms and remove labour market barriers to immigrants in order to reduce black market work, that is, employment undeclared for tax purposes (European Commission, 2007). The Commission argued that black market labour absorbs up to 20% of some countries' Gross Domestic Product (GDP), particularly Italy, Spain and Portugal. It identified the growing demand for household and care services related to the EU's ageing population and the increase in jobs on more flexible pay and contract terms as contributory factors to the increase in undeclared employment. A Commission survey showed that apart from household services, which are the key area for undeclared employment across the EU, it is also evident in seasonal activities and the construction sector, where part of wages are often paid in cash, and among students, the self-employed and unemployed people. Some of this undeclared activity may involve involuntary participation by people with no other employment option, and is unlikely to be covered by social protection. The European Commission's (2007) proposals on undeclared work centre on the reduction of taxes on labour and red tape. More recent communications on this issue within the Europe 2020 rubric have focused on the potential for quality jobs in the personal and household services area.[3]

Domestic employment is estimated by the ILO to account for 1–2.5% of the labour force in economically developed countries. There is considerable cross-national variation in the extent of domestic work, which is overwhelmingly female and much of which involves migrant labour. The ETUC identifies it as one of the fastest-growing economic sectors in Europe (ETUC, 2012). It is also one of the most invisible. While there is no targeted EU Directive relating to domestic work, the ILO adopted a Convention and Recommendation on decent work for domestic workers in 2011 (ILO, 2011). It is noteworthy that the UK and the Czech Republic were the only EU countries among the eight who abstained.[4] The UK pointed to its existing legislation to protect domestic workers and the Czech Republic favoured a non-binding Recommendation. Progress on the rights and conditions of domestic workers will depend on individual countries ratifying the Convention and the effective implementation of measures preventing infringement.

While the degree of visibility of the employment location is not a universal indicator of the level of protection of workers' rights in non-standard employment, relative invisibility tends to be characteristic of the 'very atypical' variants of those forms of non-standard employment in which protection of workers' rights is weakest and/or most easily infringed. This includes other forms of contracts than those highlighted in this chapter, specifically outsourcing and subcontracting, which often harbour very atypical non-standard employment contracts (O'Connor, 2009).

EU employment regulation: hitting and missing the target

Non-standard forms of employment are an important dimension of the EU commitment to achieving full employment, including the target of 75% employment of 20- to 64-year-old men and women by 2020. Despite data limitations, the evidence relating to very atypical and involuntary part-time and fixed-term employment, lower-skilled service and manufacturing agency work, and dependent worker self-employment, often forced or false self-employment, points to the existence of precarious employment enclaves within several forms of non-standard employment. The exact dimensions of precarious employment in the EU27 cannot be specified due to serious data deficiencies and the overlap of some forms of non-standard employment, such as part-time and fixed contract employment and part-time and self-employment. Data deficiencies are undoubtedly related to the 'invisible' nature of the work and locations of much precarious employment. Yet, it is also worth considering if the deficiencies reflect the low priority of the issues raised and recognition of the difficulties of addressing them in the context of overarching policy commitments to increasing flexibility and labour market participation of under-represented groups. There is considerable evidence of over-representation of women, young people and migrant workers in particular forms of non-standard employment in general, and in precarious employment in particular. The exception is self-employment, but there is growing evidence that young people and migrant workers are disproportionately represented in forced self-employment.

The EU Directives on part-time work and fixed-term/temporary contracts are effective for those in the more typical ranges of non-standard employment who have the personal and/or collective resources to vindicate their rights. Because of its recent transposition, the effectiveness of the temporary agency Directive cannot be established, but it is noteworthy that its provisions are weaker than the other Directives. Workers in precarious employment enclaves are least likely to be in a position to vindicate their rights under these Directives, not only because of the insecurity of their employment, but also because information on the protections afforded by Directives is not likely to be disseminated in these employment situations. This is exacerbated by the non-availability of, or difficult access to, collective bargaining. In the history of workers' struggles, precarious employment is a relatively recent term but what it denotes is not a new phenomenon. It bears a stark similarity to the focus of trade union struggle during the first half of the 20th century in Europe and elsewhere: absence of security in relation to employment tenure and of social protection in the event of unemployment, ill-health and ageing as well as poor conditions within work. These are precisely the conditions that characterise workers in precarious and poor-quality employment in the current period and reflect their high level of commodification. These problems are magnified for migrant workers, especially migrant seasonal workers, and exacerbated by language differences. Furthermore, there are no targeted EU Directives to regulate some forms of non-standard employment, including involuntary self-employment, where there is growing evidence of precariousness.

The danger of a two-tier labour market divided between securely employed 'insiders' with good conditions and 'outsiders' in precarious employment has been recognised in EU policy documents, including those on flexicurity since the early 2000s. Despite acknowledging that 'vulnerable groups', specifically 'young, temporary workers and migrants', have been hit hardest by the crisis, recent Commission documents still argue that flexicurity policies 'helped to weather the crisis'. The solution proposed is a more effective and consistent approach by member states adopting all the components of flexicurity (European Commission, 2010c). This is surprising in the context of the Commission's recognition of structural changes in the labour market that indicate a polarisation, reflecting a hollowing out of the labour market that disproportionately affects jobs in the middle of the wage distribution (European Foundation for the Improvement of Living and Working Conditions, 2010d; European Commission, 2011, p 39).[5] The same conflict can be identified at EU and member state level. On the one hand, there are pressures for flexibility to facilitate capital accumulation and labour market conditions associated with the intensification of economic and financial globalisation, and the associated competitiveness pressures. On the other hand, there are attempts to balance these with effective labour regulation and social protection. One has to ask if the present regulatory framework at EU and member state level is adequate to meet the needs of those in the most vulnerable employment situations, and if labour market programmes and the social protection systems in individual member states are attuned to their needs.

Conclusions

In conclusion, precarious employment is characterised by the absence not only of employment security, but also of income security, employment-linked social protection, opportunities for skill development and self-fulfilment, and the opportunity for collective representation; it is involuntary in the context of the absence of alternative employment opportunities. This means that it is not merely an immediate experience, but has long-term consequences for the individual concerned and her/his dependants. Furthermore, depending on social location and demographic characteristics, labour market and social protection policy can prevent precariousness or, alternatively, transform short-term employment insecurity into long-term precariousness. The implication of this for policy analysis and practice is that it is necessary to think in terms of economic, employment and social policies and their mutual interaction. It has to be recognised that the strategic goals set by Europe 2020, and, in particular, the objective of inclusive growth, will be realised only if it is based on a more balanced interaction of social, employment and economic policies than is evident to date. This is unlikely unless it becomes a policy objective and focus of political discourse, involving all the relevant stakeholders at the member state level, and if this is reflected in the policy commitments and agreed targets.

Acknowledgements

I am grateful to the editors and to Goretti Horgan for their helpful comments.

Notes

[1] Proponents of flexicurity make a distinction between employment and job security.

[2] In the Netherlands, the cut-off is 35 hours per week and this is the definition used by Eurostat and in Table 12.1.

[3] See *Towards a job rich recovery* (European Commission, 2012) Working document on exploiting the employment potential of the personal and household services, http://eur-lex.europa.eu/LexUriServ/LexUriServ. do?uri=COM:2012:0173:FIN:EN:PDF

[4] The other abstainers were Thailand, Singapore, Malaysia, Sudan, El Salvador and Panama. The Trades Union Congress strongly opposed the British abstention and are supporting a civil society initiative for ratification (see: www.tuc.org.uk/international/tuc-19975-f0.cfm).

[5] It is noteworthy that Arne Kalleberg (2011), who has identified the increase of polarisation and precariousness in the US labour market from the 1970s to 2000s, advocates a new social contract adapted to the US built on the Dutch and Danish flexicurity principles.

References

Arrowsmith, J. (2006) *Temporary agency work in an enlarged European Union*, Dublin: European Foundation for the Improvement of Living and Working Conditions, www.eurofound.europa.eu/publications/ htmlfiles/ef05139.htm

Barbier, J.C. (2005) 'La précarité, une catégorie française à l'épreuve de la comparaison internationale', *Revue française de sociologie*, vol 46, pp 352–71.

Bell, M. (2011) 'Strengthening the protection of precarious workers: part-time workers', Resource for Course: Decent Work for Precarious Workers, ITC ILO, Turin, June, http://actrav-courses.itcilo.org/en/ a4-04288/a4-04288-resources/itc-ilo

Böheim, R. and Muehlberger, U. (2006) 'Dependent forms of self-employment in the UK: identifying workers on the border between employment and self-employment', IZA Discussion Paper No 1963.

Countouris, N. (2011) 'Strengthening the protection of precarious workers: the concept of precarious work', Resource for Course: Decent Work for Precarious Workers, ITC ILO, Turin, June, http:// actrav-courses.itcilo.org/en/a4-04288/a4-04288-resources/itc-ilo

Countouris, N. and Horton, R. (2009) 'The temporary agency work Directive: another broken promise?', *Industrial Law Journal*, vol 38, no 3, pp 329–38.

D'Amours, M. (2009) 'Non-standard employment after age 50: how precarious is it?', *Relations Industrielles/Industrial Relations*, vol 64, no 2, pp 209–29.

ECJ (European Court of Justice) (2010) 'C-444/09 – Gavieiro Gavieiro and Iglesias Torres (C-456-09), judgement of the Court (Second Chamber) of 22 December', http://curia.europa.eu/juris/liste. jsf?language=en&jur=C,T,F&num=C-444/09&td=ALL

ETUC (European Trade Union Confederation) (2012) '5th annual ETUC 8 March survey 2012', www.etuc.org/r/1347

ETUI-REHS (European Trade Union Institute) (2007) *Benchmarking Working Europe 2007*, Brussels: ETUI-REHS www.etui.org/ Publications2/Books/Benchmarking-Working-Europe-2007

EUbusiness (2010) 'Self-employed – equal treatment', www. eubusiness.com/topics/employment/self-employed-equal-treatment/?searchterm=spouses%20and%20maternity%20leave

Europa (2003) 'Council Recommendation 2003/134/EC of 18 February 2003 concerning the improvement of the protection of the health and safety at work of self-employed workers', http:// europa.eu/legislation_summaries/employment_and_social_policy/ health_hygiene_safety_at_work/c10310_en.htm

European Commission (2007) 'Communication from the Commission to the Council, the European Parliament, the European Economic and Social Committee and the Committee of the Regions stepping up the fight against undeclared work', Com (2007) 628 final, Brussels.

European Commission (2010a) *Employment in Europe 2010*, Luxembourg: Office of the Official Publications of the European Communities.

European Commission (2010b) *European Employment Observatory review – self employment in Europe 2010*, Luxembourg: Office of the Official Publications of the European Communities.

European Commission (2010c) 'Communication from the Commission to the European Parliament, the Council, the European Economic and Social Committee and the Committee of the Regions an agenda for new skills and jobs: a European contribution towards full employment', Com (2010) 682 final, Strasbourg.

European Commission (2011) *Employment and social development in Europe 2011*, Luxembourg: Office of the Official Publications of the European Communities.

Europena Commission (2012) Communication from the Commission *Towards a Job Rich Recovery* COM(2012) 173 final. http://eur-lex.europa. eu/LexUriServ/LexUriServ.do?uri=COM:2012:0173:FI:EN:PDF

European Commission Legal Service (2007) 'C-307 / 05 Del Cerro Alonso, judgement of 13 September 2007, social policy – non-discrimination against workers on fixed-term contracts', http:// ec.europa.eu/dgs/legal_service/arrets/listechrono_en.htm

European Foundation for the Improvement of Living and Working Conditions (2007) 'Temporary agency work in the European Union', www.eurofound.europa.eu/ewco/reports/TN0408TR01/ TN0408TR01.pdf

European Foundation for the Improvement of Living and Working Conditions (2008a) 'European Court ruling upholds applicability of EU law on fixed-term workers at national level', www.eurofound. europa.eu/eiro/2008/05/articles/eu0805019i.htm

European Foundation for the Improvement of Living and Working Conditions (2008b) 'Tackling undeclared work in the European Union', www.eurofound.europa.eu/publications/htmlfiles/ef0813. htm

European Foundation for the Improvement of Living and Working Conditions (2009) 'Measures to tackle undeclared work in the European Union', www.eurofound.europa.eu

European Foundation for the Improvement of Living and Working Conditions (2010a) *Very atypical work exploratory analysis of fourth European Working Conditions survey background paper*, Luxembourg: Publications Office of the EU.

European Foundation for the Improvement of Living and Working Conditions (2010b) 'Trade union strategies to recruit new groups of workers', www.eurofound.europa.eu

European Foundation for the Improvement of Living and Working Conditions (2010c) *Self-employed workers: industrial relations and working conditions*, Luxembourg: Publications Office of the EU.

European Foundation for the Improvement of Living and Working Conditions (2010d) *Shifts in the job structure in Europe during the Great Recession*, Luxembourg: Publications Office of the EU.

European Industrial Relations Dictionary (2011) 'Atypical work', www.eurofound.europa.eu/areas/industrialrelations/dictionary/definitions/atypicalwork.htm

Evans, J and Gibb, E. (2009) *Moving from precarious employment to decent work*, Geneva: ILO, www.gurn.info/en/discussion-papers/no13-dec09-moving-from-precarious-employment-to-decent-work

EWCO (European Working Conditions Observatory) (2010) 'Flexible forms of work: "very atypical" contractual arrangements', www.eurofound.europa.eu/ewco/studies/tn0812019s/tn0812019s.htm

ILO (2004) *Organising for social justice. Global report under the follow-up to the ILO Declaration on Fundamental Principles and Rights at Work*, International Labour Conference 92nd session 2004, report I(B), Geneva: ILO, www.ilo.org/declaration

ILO (2010) *Employment policies for social justice and a fair globalization*, International Labour Conference, 99th Session, 2010 Report VI, Geneva: International Labour Office. www.ilo.org/wcmsp5/groups/public/@ed_norm/@relconf/documents/meetingdocument/wcms_126682.pdf

ILO (2011a) *From precarious work to decent work. Policies and regulations to combat precarious employment*, Geneva: International Labour Organisation. www.ilo.org/wcmsp5/groups/public/---ed_dialogue/---actrav/documents/meetingdocument/wcms_164286.pdf

ILO (2011b) 'Decent work for domestic workers Convention 189 and Recommendation 201', www.ilo.org/wcmsp5/groups/public/---ed_protect/---protrav/---travail/documents/publication/wcms_170438.pdf

Kalleberg, A.L. (2009) 'Precarious work, insecure workers: employment relations in transition', *American Sociological Review*, vol 74, no 1, pp 1–22.

Kalleberg, A.L. (2011) *Good jobs, bad jobs: the rise of the polarized and precarious employment systems in the United States, 1970s to 2000s*, New York, NY: Russell Sage.

Lorber, P. (2011) 'Strengthening the protection of precarious workers: fixed term workers', Resource for Course: Decent Work for Precarious Workers, ITC ILO, Turin, June, http://actrav-courses.itcilo.org/en/a4-04288/a4-04288-resources/itc-ilo

O'Connor, J.S. (2009) 'Ireland: precarious employment in the context of the European Employment Strategy', in L.F. Vosko, M. MacDonald and I. Campbell (eds) *Gender and the contours of precarious employment*, Abingdon, Oxon: Routledge, pp 92–107.

OECD (Organisation for Economic Co-operation and Development) (2010) 'How good is part-time work?', position paper, www.oecd.org/dataoecd/15/16/45602882.pdf

Paugam, S. (2002) 'Pour une definition sociologique de la précarité professionnelle', *Politiques Sociales*, vol 61, nos 3/4, pp 15–27.

Rodgers, G. (1989) 'Precarious work in Western Europe: the state of the debate', in G. Rodgers and J. Rodgers (eds) *Precarious jobs in labour market regulation: the growth of atypical employment in Western Europe*, Geneva: International Institute of Labour Studies.

Rodgers, L. (2009) 'The self-employed and the Directive on working time for mobile transport workers', *Industrial Law Journal*, vol 38 (September), pp 339–42.

Standing, G. (1999) *Global labour flexibility: seeking distributive justice*, New York, NY: St. Martin's Press.

Stehrer, R., Ward, T. and Macias, E.F. (2009) 'Changes in the structure of employment in the EU and their implication for job quality', Research Reports 354, The Vienna Institute for International Economic Studies, http://ideas.repec.org/p/wii/rpaper/rr354.html

Vosko, L.F., MacDonald M. and Campbell I. (eds) (2009) *Gender and the contours of precarious employment*, Abingdon, Oxon: Routledge.

Walsh, A. (2012) 'Agency staff to get €2.5m in backpay from HSE', www.independent.ie/national-news/agency-staff-to-get-25m-in-backpay-from-hse-3117668.html

Zappala, L. (2006) 'Abuse of fixed-term employment contracts and sanctions in the recent ECJ's jurisprudence', *Industrial Law Journal*, vol 35, no 4, pp 439–44.

THIRTEEN

How do activation policies affect social citizenship? The issue of autonomy

Silke Bothfeld and Sigrid Betzelt

Introduction

Although paid employment has always remained the main route to social security, social rights represent a necessary precondition for citizens' social and political participation in Western democracies. By curtailing the detrimental effects of capitalist market processes, the public systems of social protection have – in the golden age of the Western welfare state – become the backbone of various social dynamics. However, since the 1980s, the continuous expansion of the welfare state has decelerated due to increasing economic and fiscal constraints that challenge its functioning.

Most prominently, the paradigm of 'social investment', including the idea of 'activating' social policy programmes, has reinforced the emphasis on paid employment as the main mechanism of social integration for all adult citizens. This paradigm shift from 'passive' to 'activating' social security provision reflects a change in the norms and objectives of social security provision, as well as a changing work ethic (Dean, 2007). The targets of social policy have changed accordingly, with a shifting focus from poverty protection and status security to the primary goal of labour market participation. In fact, the activation turn in labour market policy implies an incremental but continued reduction of social rights, such as increasing flexibility in terms of working time and wages, decreasing social benefits, and a restructuring of the profile of active labour market policies (ALMPs). At the same time, activation often entails an expansion of certain social services that facilitate the labour market participation of all adults, like public childcare or job placement services.

So, how can the fundamental change in the welfare state of the past two decades be adequately assessed and analysed? In the first section of this chapter, it is argued that a comprehensive concept of the citizen's individual autonomy can exemplify the scope and depth of this change. This subsequently calls for a precise definition of the *citizen's autonomy* and its interrelatedness with public action, which is developed in the first section. Autonomy, it is argued, offers a more complex and comprehensive concept for assessing social policy outcomes than many other normative notions such as 'well-being' or poverty protection as it refers to the individual's identity, her/his role in society, as well as her/his interaction with the public sphere and the state. But how does public action impact on individual autonomy within the dimension of the individual, the social and the political sphere? Based on findings from a cross-national study of European countries, the second section illustrates how programmes and instruments of activating labour market policies impact on the individual citizen by considering the quality of policy programmes, the conditions of access to social security schemes and status acquisition, and the mechanisms regulating the citizens' participation in social policy decisions.[1] The findings indicate the ambivalence of activation policies, encouraging labour market participation and, hence, increasing the economic independence of citizens on the one hand, but constraining citizens through an abundance of regulations and mechanisms on the other. The conclusions are rather sceptical, but a focus on autonomy demonstrates *why* social policymakers and scholars have to be concerned about ongoing change. The concept of autonomy allows, however, the search for an alternative social policy design, even in times of tight budgets in the wake of the economic and financial crisis.

Individual autonomy as a normative reference for assessing social policy reforms

Activation reforms have fundamentally changed the citizens' and the state's respective roles and the political recognition of social needs (Van Berkel and Hornemann Moeller, 2002; Serrano Pascual, 2007; Bothfeld and Betzelt, 2011a). Assessing the impact of these reforms on the individual citizen's life with reference to autonomy as a guiding principle allows us to integrate the concerns of the population as a whole – the poor as well as the middle classes – which each offer different but equally relevant perspectives on social policy reforms.

Moreover, individual autonomy constitutes a philosophical core concept, so we can for our purpose rely on many arguments from philosophical research:[2] (for an earlier discussion of the concept see

Bothfeld and Betzelt, 2011b) (for example, in Kantian moral philosophy, autonomy is defined as the citizen's fundamental capacity for self-determination; several authors deliberate autonomy within the relationship between citizens – including the tension between the individual and the common welfare; and in democratic theory, autonomy addresses the procedural and political dimension of the state–citizen relationship. Provided a broad perspective is adopted, autonomy offers an excellent analytical concept for assessing welfare provision and welfare-state change. In this section, we explain in what terms labour market reforms – more precisely, changes to the regulation of labour markets, ALMPs or income maintenance schemes for the unemployed – affect the citizen's autonomy. In order to grasp more adequately the impact of policies on the citizen's life situation, it is suggested to distinguish analytically its individual, social and political dimension, which will be discussed separately in the following sections.

The individual dimension: self-determination and the capacity to pursue individual aims and projects

The provision of social rights can be considered to support or even increase the individual autonomy of citizens, endowing them with material resources and social status; but an increase of individual autonomy does not result from generous benefits or strict employment protection rules alone. If autonomy is defined as the capacity for self-determination according to 'deeper' or authentic wants and reflections (Rössler, 2002; Friedman, 2003, p 8; Christman, 2009), there are two important implications.

First, autonomy is not necessarily incompatible with (economic) dependence, nor does it exclude the idea that people respond to external requirements that are not borne from their immediate needs or wishes. For example, social security provision mostly presupposes a certain contribution by citizens, such as working or paying taxes (Marshall, 1963). Both the activation paradigm and the notion of social investment have reinforced the social expectation that all adult citizens should work – irrespective of their personal circumstances (eg care obligations). Third-way theorists and economists consider this as unproblematic as they use autonomy synonymously with economic independence (see, eg, Esping-Andersen et al, 2002). But this narrow interpretation neglects some more complex aspects of social integration and dependence. Philosophical and sociological reasoning provides further consideration of individuals in terms of their individual identity with contingent biographic and historical experiences. The main criterion for autonomous decision-making, philosophers claim, is that individuals are capable of pursuing aims and projects, reflecting on their own preferences and refraining from their immediate needs, feelings and spontaneous ideas (Rössler, 2002; see also Darwall, 2006). It is the capacity of individuals to reflect on who they want to be and what they like to do, their capacity to figure out the '*authentic*' motives for their decisions, which is the major condition for autonomy (Rössler, 2002). In other words, self-determination is not necessarily equal to 'self-authorship of our lives' but denominates our capability to 'read and write' our lives, 'a constant search for coherence balanced against a realism borne out of efforts to understand ourselves and others better', as Pamela Sue Anderson (2003, p 158) underlines. This means that autonomy may be compatible with (economic) dependence[3] and even the enforcement of duties (eg work obligations). The precondition is that citizens can understand, share and accept the rules according to which duties are imposed (Forst, 1996). The second implication is that people are neither fully autonomous nor heteronomous. Rather, autonomy is a relational concept which implies that people are *more or less* autonomous in relation to their social environment. All individuals are principally vulnerable; but the degree of vulnerability differs between social groups according to individual characteristics, psychological strengths and weaknesses, the present life situation, or the exposure to particular social risks (Anderson, 2003, p 153ff).

The policy implications are that public intervention, even if standardised, can have very different effects on different social groups (eg men and women) or individuals. Consequently, a particular measure (eg a training course) may be empowering for some unemployed persons while others may perceive it as constraining. Addressing predefined needs, social policy intervention is never neutral or 'impartial' (Young, 1990) but privileges some specific needs at the expense of others, and thereby decreases or increases individual autonomy. As a criterion to assess how constraining or enabling social policies are, analysis of the *quality* of implemented policies is suggested: favourable policies in terms of autonomy would increase the leeway for the individual, not prescribing any specific behaviour but recognising diverse needs and expectations. Consequently, autonomy-fostering policies would loosen rather than strengthen the tie between labour market participation and social provision.

The societal dimension: mutual relationships and the concept of status

Welfare states are mechanisms of redistribution as well as of recognition of different social needs (Nullmeier, 2000). By redistributing wealth through taxes and social security schemes, and by allocating social benefits to certain statuses (eg socially insured workers, married couples), welfare states impact on the social structure of society in a specific way (Esping-Andersen, 1990). At the same time, social policies establish a culturally anchored and symbolic order by attributing unequal normative values (and material compensation) to different activities. For example, obligations towards job-search activities reflect a normative assessment of the duties of unemployed people. Such institutionalised expectations not only impact on the unemployed alone, but also shape social values as well as the expectations between co-citizens, the employed and the unemployed. Mutual recognition is conditioned by citizens' capacity to mutually recognise different needs as equally legitimate, which again is influenced by policies and institutions (Nullmeier, 2000). At the very least, recognition represents a precondition for the institutionalisation of specific needs and expectations. The matter of recognition has two important consequences for the assessment of the individual autonomy of citizens.

First, 'equal recognition' is not the same as social equality; rather, individual autonomy and social inequality between citizens can coexist – if the differences in social statuses are perceived as legitimate. Although citizens are formally equally endowed with the same rights – entitlements, benefits and services – these rights do *not* eliminate all social differences but allow access to, or maintain, a certain socio-economic status. Social statuses determine the allocation of material goods and level of social recognition, resulting in a hierarchical social order. But social statuses – representing a bundle of rules, rights and norms (Offe, 2003) – also provide a social role within a given society. A decent social status, therefore, may represent a kind of 'protected area' or 'corridor of action' for an individual's autonomous life, establishing a certain level of expected social security. Ideally, having a decent (though not necessarily high) reliable social status represents a source of security and identity for people in modern industrial societies. In employment-centred regimes, labour market policies (as well as education and training) are therefore crucial as they shape the conditions for upward mobility and the protection of a once-attained social status against the pitfalls of life.

Related to this argument is, second, the idea that mutual recognition and the definition and attribution of status along specific criteria comes along with mechanisms of inclusion and exclusion (Lister, 2007). An inclusive version of citizenship would be based on values like justice, recognition, self-determination and solidarity. Arguing against a merely economic view of citizenship, Lister emphasises recognition and identity as essential elements, embracing the right to be 'different' as well as cultural respect. Referring to the issue of women's unpaid caring work and the gendered division of domestic labour, feminist contributions strongly underline the need for recognising diversity, claiming 'an ethos of pluralisation' (Young, 1990). As gender inequality challenges the universalist idea of citizenship, Lister proposed the idea of a 'differentiated universalism in which the achievement of the universal is contingent upon attention to difference' (Lister, 2007, p 52). Of course, the lines of social division are also drawn along other social characteristics and an individual's feeling of affiliation is not solely determined by formally regulated rules of membership, but also by the symbolic order. Both are inherent in many institutions that shape our everyday lives and foster our respective roles within the social sphere.

Concerning citizens' autonomy, the recognition of diversity and upward mobility, which allow all members of society to achieve a decent and recognised status, are crucial policy issues. Thus, autonomy requires sensitivity to diversity, which may be realised by a high degree of permeability of boundaries between different statuses, and support for upward mobility, equal opportunity policies or affirmative action. In the domain of labour market policy, the rules of access to benefits and services would be widened rather than restricted, and social statuses would be protected against downward mobility.

The political dimension: realising participation and commitment

The necessity of protecting the autonomy of citizens is arguably most obvious within the political sphere, as autonomy is often understood as 'self-government', representing the precondition for democracy and political freedom (Forst, 1996; Christman, 2009). Political freedom and individual autonomy are closely interconnected, as the maintenance and development of individual autonomy is a prerequisite of political freedom (Forst, 1996, p 215). It is helpful to distinguish political from moral, ethical, social and legal perspectives on individual autonomy, as

Forst (1996) suggests, in order to complement T.H. Marshall's (1963) belief that the guarantee of social rights would complete the set of preconditions for citizens to participate in political life. Of course, the interrelationship between public intervention and citizens is highly relevant for individual autonomy, and policymakers and representatives of public authorities tread a fine line when formulating, deciding upon or implementing public social policies. Preserving respect for citizens' (ethical and moral) autonomy has the consequence that citizens have to be vested with rights and entitlements that allow them to interact with public authorities on equal terms.

From the autonomy perspective, social protection means not only helping people to make ends meet, but also protecting and supporting their capacity for self-determination and – in the sense of legal and ethical autonomy – conceding them the right to understand, co-determine, object to or accept public interventions. Political autonomy, understood as the right to equal participation and the 'right to justification', helps to redefine the responsibility issue: activation policies have typically caused a shift of responsibility and a redefinition of reciprocity (Bothfeld and Betzelt, 2011a). This is not problematic per se, as long as the individual's capacity to be self-responsible is respected. However, new requirements may conflict with the consensually shared concept of reciprocity if they unilaterally impose constraints and obligations on the unemployed. Individual (political and social) autonomy would be damaged if the individual's commitment to commonly shared obligations and duties were disrespected. As long as gainful employment remains the primary mechanism for social integration, the provision of benefits will be conditional upon certain behaviours of the beneficiaries, and always implies an aspect of social control (Ben-Ishai, 2012). But tensions may arise when the formal or implicit agreement between the state and its citizens is changed. The rise of legal claims against administrative decisions would indicate an incompatibility of existing and new legal norms.

New demands on citizens, if excessively increased, could overstrain the individual's agency. Although this is not an explicit policy aim but an outcome of the current liberal argument that benefits are necessarily a disincentive to active participation, increasing the pressure on individuals to shape their lives appears detrimental to the individual's commitment rather than supporting it. On the one hand, an own-earned income represents a source of self-esteem, self-reliance and social recognition and constitutes a major source of social identity for citizens in an industrial society; on the other hand, people may feel morally committed to their duty to contribute to society by working. Relying on benefits has undoubtedly a decommodifying effect but this does not respond to the individual's need to feel recognised and to contribute actively to the common objectives of a society.

Collective and individual needs are compatible only for as long as individuals feel committed to the collectively shared norms and values. Accordingly, political protests, strikes and demonstrations, individual attitudes of refusal, and defection indicate that people perceive implicit normative agreements to be undermined. Hence, autonomy-fostering social policies would be shaped in a way that citizens are encouraged and supported – and not forced – to achieve their potential. Policymaking processes would provide time and space for the citizens to understand, co-determine and accept new policies.

Considering all three spheres together: a concept of social citizenship that would grasp ongoing political change as well as social policy adjustments to social transformation processes, such as demographic change or new gender roles, needs to include more than social rights as they have been traditionally understood. A revised concept would rather draw attention to the question of how social policies help develop and protect citizens' capacity for autonomy (Ben-Ishai, 2012). And it would not be restricted to the individual sphere, but take account of the societal and the political spheres as well. All these dimensions of individual autonomy translate into three policy criteria, which will be used in the following empirical section as an analytical grid. It is argued, first, that whether social policies encroach upon or enhance individual autonomy depends on the *quality* of social provision and whether policies take account of the individual's specific needs and allow leeway for individuality (individual dimension). Second, considering how status and membership are constructed, it is important to see how the access to benefits or services is regulated, what lines are drawn between different *statuses*, and whether status protection is guaranteed and upward mobility is supported (social dimension). Third, the question is how citizens are encouraged to *participate* in decisions that are relevant to their everyday lives, and whether there are sufficient individual entitlements and procedures implemented for co-determination (political dimension). These three concepts – quality, status and participation – represent the analytical thread for our analysis of activation policies, more precisely, labour market regulation, active labour market policy and unemployment security schemes, which we present in the following section.

How do activation policies affect individual autonomy? An empirical illustration

Of course, citizens' individual autonomy is influenced by a multitude of legal regulations as well as explicit and implicit norms and values, of which social policy and, more precisely, activation policies represent just a small fraction. Nonetheless, over the past two decades, labour market policy reforms represent a crucial domain of change. As argued earlier, the individual, social and political dimensions of individual autonomy translate into three policy criteria: quality, status and participation. This section will give an overview of the general trends and governance instruments of activating labour market policy reforms and concentrate on the three major policy fields: labour market regulation, ALMPs (labour promotion) and income maintenance systems for the unemployed and economically 'inactive' population. The three policy criteria will help to assess the findings and to draw conclusions about the impact of activation on individual autonomy. We draw on evidence from European country case studies detailed in Betzelt and Bothfeld (2011a).

Labour market (de)regulation

A core idea of the EU employment strategy, launched at the Lisbon Conference in 1998, was to make labour markets more flexible in order to reduce long-term unemployment (Weishaupt and Lack, 2011). In Germany, the expansion of the low-wage sector was justified as a stepping-stone into regular employment. In many countries, governments supported the expansion of atypical employment such as fixed-term work (especially Spain; see Pérez and Laparra, 2011), marginal work exempted from social security contributions (especially Germany; see Betzelt and Bothfeld, 2011b) or temporary and temporary agency work (especially Italy and Spain; see, respectively, Graziano, 2011; Pérez and Laparra, 2011). In contrast to Spain, protection against dismissal has not been an issue in other countries.

Employment conditions are also indirectly affected by the standards for 'acceptable' employment or behavioural requirements placed on the unemployed. In most countries, unemployed people – after a certain period of time – have to accept working conditions below the previously attained level of pay, educational attainment or commuting times (Hasselpflug, 2005), and occupational protection – permitting benefit recipients to refuse a job if it required much lower skills – has often been abolished, even in the originally status-preserving 'conservative' states like Germany and France. In terms of job quality, one very obvious outcome of deregulation is, of course, the levelling of employment standards for atypical workers in terms of low pay and low employment security and stability. In most countries, we see increasing shares of working poor among this group (see Table 13.1; see also Goerne, 2011), and cumulated risks, such as discontinuous employment, limited career prospects and diminished access to social security coverage, as well as an increase of subjective economic insecurity (Burgoon and Dekker, 2010). The levelling of job quality standards for atypical workers implies, of course, an inferior employment status and, as transitions into 'regular' employment are rare (for Germany, see Giesecke, 2009), the chance to attain a higher social status is very limited.

Table 13.1: Activation in the field of labour market regulation and impact on autonomy along policy criteria

Labour market regulation General trends	QUALITY	STATUS	PARTICIPATION
Deregulation of labour markets: Incentives for atypical employment forms Easing dismissals Redefinition of 'acceptable' jobs for the unemployed	Unstable working careers In-work poverty Pressure on general working conditions	Erosion of core worker status (especially Germany, France) Diversification of employment statuses Deteriorating labour market status of weaker groups and dualisation of labour markets and social security provision (especially Italy, Spain)	Decreasing share of unionised workers and weakening of trade unions' power Political conflict between trade unions and government

Source: Betzelt and Bothfeld (2011a)

Obviously, this deregulation strategy has a detrimental effect on the quality of working conditions in terms of pay and employment protection, so that working careers become increasingly unstable (see left-hand column of Table 13.1). A particularly serious impact of labour market deregulation on the social status order is observed in Italy and Spain, which have experienced a 'dualisation'[4] of their employment regimes (see middle column of Table 13.1). In these countries, a growing gap is observed between certain well-protected core groups (male core workers, pensioners) and groups that are included neither in welfare provisions nor in regular and sustainable employment (women, young people, migrants). The deregulation strategy in Italy and Spain only affected the weaker groups, whereas the still strongly protected core worker status has remained untouched.

However, the direct and indirect deregulation of labour markets may also increase the pressure on regular employment, either by disciplining the workforce of core workers or by substituting regular jobs with atypical ones. In Germany, for instance, this strategy has contributed to declining wage levels and growing insecurity for the core workforce, so that the core worker status itself is exposed to erosion. On the individual level, this may cause a downward spiral and an irreversible loss of professional and social status attainment. The fear of unemployment is not solely due to an eventual loss of income, but is associated with the threat of losing a once-attained social status. The (real or suspected) loss of status evidently encroaches upon the citizen's autonomy. Concerning collective rights, it becomes increasingly difficult for workers and their representatives to defend a decent level of pay and protection, at least in periods of high unemployment (see right-hand column of Table 13.1). The flexibilisation strategy has clearly contributed towards further decreasing the share of unionised workers and has raised political conflict between governments and trade unions, for instance, in Spain, where a general strike in 2002 opposed this political strategy (Pérez and Laparra, 2011, p 157).

Active labour market policies

The main objective of activation policies, to enhance individual responsibility, creates a tension between the need to standardise the 'treatment' of a growing number of people to be activated, and the necessity to meet individual needs according to the citizens' personal circumstances (Van Berkel and Valkenburg, 2007). To find well-balanced (institutional) solutions to this tension is even more difficult under the condition of restricted public resources.

Overall, three main trends in ALMPs are observable. First, the replacement of 'human investment'-oriented long-term vocational training with measures of direct employment assistance (Bonoli, 2010), like short-term job-search training or employment subsidies (in France, see Béraud and Eydoux, 2011), indicates a shift in the profile of ALMPs to a more supply-side-oriented strategy. Second, a typical trend is the targeting of new groups of unemployed or 'inactive' persons, indicated by the abrogation of former exemptions from working obligations such as for certain social groups. Third, New Public Management (NPM) instruments became dominant, installing the cost–benefit ratio as a major allocation mechanism for activation measures and dismissing the logic of social compensation, with the aim of attaining a behavioural change among benefit recipients. Resources are now spent according to cost-saving client-segmentation procedures and on standardised terms, while front-line members of staff often have considerable discretion to decide upon individual cases. Moreover, implementation of activation policies has often been decentralised, including a delegation of budget authority to the local level, as, for example, in the Netherlands (Van Berkel, 2011).

Table 13.2: Activation in the field of active labour market policies (active labour promotion) and impact on autonomy along policy criteria

ALMPs General trends	QUALITY	STATUS	PARTICIPATION
Primacy of cost-efficiency principles (NPM) and shift in profile of ALMPs: Trend towards short-term training instead of upskilling Employment subsidies Extended working obligations Targeting; contractualisation Standardisation, client segmentation Decentralisation	Hard-to-place clients are disadvantaged Individual needs and wishes not sufficiently considered Lack of 'enabling' support Low quality of subsidised jobs	Blurred status between unemployed and inactive groups Definition of new target groups ambiguous: recognition of need for support but delegitimised status of inactive persons, partly stigmatising Deepening of social cleavages due to client-segmentation practices and reinforced labour market segmentation	Cost-efficiency logic of client segmentation neglects needs for ALMPs Lack of transparency and comprehensibility of rules and entitlements Conditions of individual rights and duties incalculable due to regional differences Lack of co-determination for citizens in activation process Contractual relationships with unclear effects on true participation

Source: Betzelt and Bothfeld (2011a)

Although these new governance modes of ALMPs might harbour some potential for better addressing the individual needs of the diverse groups of unemployed and 'inactive' people, our findings instead indicate unfavourable effects on citizen autonomy. First, the hidden agenda of cost containment behind many activation reforms[5] results in a decrease of the *quality* of ALMPs (see left-hand column of Table 13.2): the shift in profile in ALMPs is particularly disadvantageous for groups categorised as 'hard to place' in the labour market (as is the case in Germany, the Netherlands and France), who need tailor-made further training programmes or sufficient and affordable childcare infrastructure to pursue their life plans and to achieve their own potential. Employment subsidies may indeed promote labour market integration, but they often foster low standards of pay and high instability.

The definition of new distinctive target groups for activation – like young unemployed (in France, Germany or the Netherlands), immigrant women (in the Danish case) or long-term social assistance recipients or incapacitated persons (in Norway) – is ambiguous concerning the criterion of *status* (see middle column of Table 13.2). Targeted measures of active labour promotion may be supportive for unemployed/ inactive people, but they often include much stricter sanctioning rules. The abrogation of previously legitimate statuses by expanding work obligations – such as for inactive lone mothers or spouses in the UK (Wright, 2011), inactive or part-time working spouses in Germany (Betzelt and Bothfeld, 2011b), or migrant women in Denmark (Breidahl, 2011) – constrains the room for individual choice and disrespects the diversity of life circumstances. For example, in the UK, there is little support for affordable childcare, and the 'activated' women are pushed into low-wage jobs. Targeting programmes might even have counter-intentional effects of withdrawal from the labour market where they collide with socio-cultural norms, as in the case of migrants in Denmark.[6]

With regard to the third criterion of *participation* (see right-hand column of Table 13.2), the question is how unemployed people can choose and co-determine their contribution to becoming re-employed. Support is usually organised by 'reintegration contracts' (Kildal and Nilssen, 2011) or the monitoring of job search (Van Berkel et al, 2011), but, in many cases, the relevant rules regarding the individual's rights and duties are not sufficiently transparent or comprehensible – a crucial precondition for cooperation. The decentralisation of activation policies implies locally varying concrete conditions of activation and benefit receipt, resulting in a low degree of certainty and reliability; citizens do not know what to expect from the agencies (see especially the Dutch case; Van Berkel, 2011). The findings indicate that even in Norway, the citizen's wishes and preferences are not necessarily met due to the standardisation of programmes on offer, the latent threat of losing benefits and structural asymmetric power relations (Kildal and Nilssen, 2011).

Unemployment benefit schemes

Concerning the present level of protection secured by income maintenance schemes for the unemployed and inactive, there is a uniform tendency in all the countries studied. While the level of benefits provided by insurance schemes has remained stable, eligibility for benefit receipt has been narrowed and the payment duration shortened so that larger portions of the unemployed have to rely on the lower benefits of means-tested tax-financed schemes. This accompanies an enhancement of the principle of subsidiarity realised by stricter means tests, strengthened family maintenance obligations (eg in Germany) or household-related employment subsidies (in the case of France). In many cases, group-specific allowances have been abolished. This means that formerly distinct categories of citizens/beneficiaries (lone parents, older and incapacitated unemployed people) now all belong to the same uniform category of the (long-term) 'unemployed'. The shift to 'homogenising' means-tested schemes for various groups of unemployed (Clasen and Clegg, 2011) could have inclusive effects, as it overcomes the status segmentation of contribution-based schemes that traditionally exclude women and (other) groups with discontinuous work histories. However, financial compensation of (economic) inactivity may be justified for different reasons, but the standardised workfare requirement applied to any state of inactivity and enforced by severe sanctions indicates a deeply paternalistic approach to inactive people of working age.

In terms of *quality* and *status* (see left-hand and middle column of Table 13.3), activation reforms often increase poverty risks and financial hardship for those who lose access to status-preserving insurance benefits. This has severe status-deteriorating effects: the once-attained income and occupational status often cannot be regained by workers having discontinuous work histories, which mostly do not allow for upward mobility (Betzelt and Bothfeld, 2011b). The welfare states of Italy and Spain still lack any kind of sufficient public security provision, and are thus classified as sub-protective (Graziano, 2011; Pérez and Laparra, 2011): those unemployed without insurance entitlements, in particular, young people, have no source of social security provision except their family (Pérez and Laparra, 2011), meaning that social cleavages further increase.

The findings show that the potentially inclusive effects of a 'homogenisation' of means-tested schemes are often not realised. In

Table 13.3: Activation in the field of unemployment benefits and impact on autonomy along policy criteria

Unemployment benefit system General trends	QUALITY	STATUS	PARTICIPATION
Levelling of social security: Shift from insurance to means-tested schemes Cuts of benefit levels (tax-financed) Access restrictions to insurance schemes Withdrawal of group-specific benefits	Financial hardship, increased poverty risk Increasing portion of workforce without social security In-work poverty Pressure on groups who lost benefits	Accelerated loss of once-attained status when long-term unemployed In means-tested schemes: loss of individual entitlements and increased maintenance obligations (gendered effects) Growing social cleavages	Low participation in social life due to low standard of living for beneficiaries Lack of transparency, reliability and comprehensibility of rules Low benefit levels not tailored to needs produce resistance and aggression among recipients

Source: Betzelt and Bothfeld (2011a)

Germany, for instance, the stricter means tests in the new unemployment benefit scheme result in stronger economic family dependency as women cohabiting with a wage-earning spouse now lose their benefit entitlements even sooner than before. The new means tests entail expanded maintenance obligations to step-children and unmarried spouses, thus overstretching mutual responsibilities within a household. Moreover, the new rules for means-tested benefits in Germany mean that all adults in a household are now obliged to accept full-time employment if any household member is a benefit recipient (Betzelt and Bothfeld, 2011b). The lack of transparency and comprehensibility of rules also applies to the changed rules for income maintenance schemes, indicating that the criterion of *participation* is damaged in this domain as well (see right-hand column of Table 13.3). First of all, sanctioning has become a more widely used instrument in many countries (Immervoll, 2010), with particularly high sanctioning rates for certain groups like young people due to much stricter requirements (eg in Germany). Second, at least in Germany, benefit levels are regarded by many welfare experts and welfare associations as being too low to make ends meet (eg to cover housing and energy costs in the cities) and too complicated to understand and administer. This has led to legal as well as political conflicts. The large numbers of law suits against job centres, the increasing aggression against front-line staff (eg in Germany) and also political protests, particularly the protest movements of young people in Spain and the UK, indicate a lack of participation in collective as well as individual terms.

Concluding remarks

Analysing the impact of activation policies with regard to the three criteria of quality, status and participation reveals three major tendencies:

- *Re-commodification:* Labour market deregulation, changing profiles of ALMPs and overall reductions of social provision to unemployed people have contributed to the destabilisation of employment careers, deteriorated working conditions, abrogated opportunities to retrain and increased poverty risks. Altogether, these changes can be read as a decrease in the quality of labour market programmes, or as a tendency to re-commodification.
- *Erosion of core worker status:* Reshaping social security systems by incrementally replacing insurance with means-tested schemes, increasing the share of atypical workers, and reshaping ALMPs to speed up re-employment rather than enhance skills can be read as a process of deepening status segmentation contributing to processes of downward rather than upward mobility; in some countries, bringing about a 'dualisation' between core groups and weaker groups (Palier and Thelen, 2010). However, the reforms do not solely change the relative structure of social statuses, but also undermine the core worker status as such, which has been the reference for public intervention with the aim of protecting the middle classes. Abandoning the middle-class status as a reference for redistributive processes will, in the long run, lead to a general downgrading of social security provision and reinstall a high degree of market dependence.
- *Counter-participatory policies:* Top-down implementation of NPM principles in the absence of providing for sufficient individual rights to co-determination, a lack of transparency, reliability of rules and the standardisation of procedures that do not recognise the diversity of needs violate the citizen's capacities to participate and generate conflict and opposition or resignation. Individual refusal or increasing perception of insecurity as well as political protest and the occurrence of strikes show that the redefinition of responsibility and the new rules are not compatible with the expectations and needs of many citizens. The changes may indicate that the paternalistic

aspect of social provision has been reinforced, in contrast to a more empowering and emancipatory strategy.

What alternative policy approaches can be identified that aim for more social inclusion and higher labour market participation without encroaching upon the citizen's autonomy? A purely supply-side strategy of shifting the responsibility for economic sustainability onto the individual without acknowledging structural labour market problems and the fundamental power imbalances between labour and capital has proved a problematic and ineffective strategy. Reform debates and projects should rather clarify the state's responsibility for establishing or maintaining strong institutionalised guards against market forces (Marshall, 1963). Overall, the decommodification effect of social security is still crucial as social benefits and services are not solely necessary to protect against old and new social risks, but more generally to allow for opting-out opportunities for caring, education, recreating health or other 'good' reasons. The protection of a middle-class status (the 'core worker') necessitates that occupational and skills levels are secured in periods of unemployment, and employment standards like minimum wages and dismissal protection ensure decent working conditions. Only within such an institutionalised framework can individual citizens develop their autonomy. 'Activation' is not in principle incompatible with the concept of autonomy if it is spelled out within a framework that encourages the citizen's capacity to self-determination, initiates economically and socially valuable activities, and remains actively committed to the commonly shared values within a society.

Finally, does the present economic and fiscal crisis impede or even defeat social policies that protect individual autonomy? Of course, activation policies do not directly result from economic pressure but from a *normative* change, strongly connected to the neo-liberal paradigm and widely supported in the public discourse. But the crisis gives tailwind to further cuts in the social domain and hampers any supplementary social investment. For sure, the provision of generous benefits becomes a particular problem in times of public budget constraints, as does the provision of tailor-made programmes and costly services. But the crisis also shows how important social policy and the enhancement of individual autonomy is, and what happens if large segments of the population are suddenly exposed to existential risk. Instead of further austerity policies and cuts in public services and the social security net, an alternative strategy of sound macroeconomic and fiscal policies is called for, including demand-oriented wage policies (Dullien et al, 2011). The neo-liberal paradigm – including activation policies – has produced many detrimental effects and not responded appropriately to obvious market failure. What is needed, therefore, is a fundamental reorientation so that the promise of more individualised labour market policies is based on a sufficient (economic) basis, thereby taking the individual's preferences and capacities into account. Taking the issue of the citizen's autonomy seriously would provide policymakers and scholars with an alternative and optimistic perspective on democratic social policymaking.

Acknowledgements

This text has benefited a lot by the many comments and suggestions that colleagues have made to earlier versions of this chapter. We are indebted to all contributors to our collective volume and also to Jane Jenson, Björn Hvinden and Jean-Claude Barbier for their perspicacious questions and criticisms at the final conference of the EU network of excellence Reconciling Work and Welfare in Europe (Recwowe). Former comments by Christina Bergqvist (at the RC 19 meeting in Stockholm) and Amparo Serrano Pascual (at the Espanet conference in Budapest) have helped us to clarify the ambivalence of the concept of autonomy. And finally, the editors of this edited volume have done excellent work in drawing our attention to the remaining loose ends of our argument.

Notes

[1.] This chapter draws on the results of our collective volume *Activation and labour market reforms in Europe. Challenges to social citizenship* (Betzelt and Bothfeld, 2011a), comprising textracts from eight country case studies (D, F, UK, NL, DK, N, IT, ES) following the same analytical perspective.

[2.] Individual autonomy has been the subject of many philosophical debates. Feminists in particular have used the concept in order to make gender inequality in the public sphere more visible (Anderson, 2003; Friedman, 2003; with reference to social provision, see also Ben-Ishai, 2012). An early and most prominent account of different approaches to the concept of autonomy is *The inner citadel* by John Christman (1989). It is not possible to address all of the concepts and issues that are subject of contemporary philosophical debate around individual autonomy, but significant findings are referred to in order to clarify concepts and implications where necessary.

[3.] The economic and emotional dependence of women (within a marriage or traditional societal contexts) and their ways of coping with this is one of the main subjects of feminist reasoning in this domain (Anderson, 2003).

[4.] An increasing dualisation of welfare provision between 'insiders' and 'outsiders' has been posited by some scholars (Palier and Thelen, 2010) explicitly for Bismarckian welfare states such as France and Germany. In these countries, however, we observed more an erosion of the core worker status rather than simple dualisation (see also Barbier and Knuth, 2010), while in the sub-protective welfare states such as Italy and Spain, the dualisation hypothesis seems more convincing, although we would rather not refer to the neoclassical 'insider/outsider' terminology.

[5.] Bonoli (2010, p 23) found budget cuts of ALMPs in the period from the mid-1990s to 2008 in the six Western European countries examined and concluded that in this period of the 'activation turn', 'countries preferred the less costly alternatives' of ALMP measures instead of more costly upskilling training schemes.

[6.] As a measure especially targeting migrant women, the rules for married social assistance recipients in Denmark require 450 hours of regular employment within two years (Breidahl, 2011). The effects were ambiguous: many women withdrew from the labour market. At the same time, others, particularly those supported by local activation services, actually took jobs.

References

Anderson, P.S. (2003) 'Autonomy, vulnerability and gender', *Feminist Theory*, vol 4, no 2, pp 149–64.

Barbier, J.-C. and Knuth, M. (2010) 'Of similarities and divergences: why there is no Continental ideal-type of "activation reforms"', CES Working Papers no 75, Université Paris, http://centredeconomiesorbonne.univ-paris1.fr/bandeau-haut/documents-de-travail

Ben-Ishai, E. (2012) *Fostering autonomy. A theory of citizenship, the state, and social service delivery*, University Park, Pennsylvania State University Press.

Béraud, M. and Eydoux, A. (2011) 'Redefining unemployment and employment statuses: the impact of activation on social citizenship in France', in S. Betzelt and S. Bothfeld (eds) *Activation and labour market reforms in Europe. Challenges to social citizenship*, Work and Welfare Series, Houndmills: Palgrave Macmillan, pp 125–46.

Betzelt, S. and Bothfeld, S. (eds) (2011a) *Activation and labour market reforms in Europe. Challenges to social citizenship*, Work and Welfare Series, Houndmills: Palgrave Macmillan.

Betzelt, S. and Bothfeld, S. (2011b) 'The erosion of social status: the case of Germany', in S. Betzelt and S. Bothfeld (eds) *Activation and labour market reforms in Europe. Challenges to social citizenship*, Work and Welfare Series, Houndmills: Palgrave Macmillan, pp 103–124.

Bonoli, G. (2010) 'The political economy of active labour market policy', REC-WP 01/2010 Working Papers on the Reconciliation of Work and Welfare in Europe RECWOWE Publication, Dissemination and Dialogue Centre, Edinburgh, www.socialpolicy.ed.ac.uk/recwowepudiac

Bothfeld, S. and Betzelt, S. (2011a) 'Activation and labour market reforms in Europe: challenges to social citizenship. Introduction', in S. Betzelt and S. Bothfeld (eds) *Activation and labour market reforms in Europe. Challenges to social citizenship*, Work and Welfare Series, Houndmills: Palgrave Macmillan, pp 3–14.

Bothfeld, S. and Betzelt, S. (2011b) 'How do activation policies affect social citizenship? The issue of autonomy', in S. Betzelt and S. Bothfeld (eds) *Activation and labour market reforms in Europe. Challenges to social citizenship*, Work and Welfare Series, Houndmills: Palgrave Macmillan, pp 15–34.

Breidahl, K.W. (2011) 'Social security provision targeted at immigrants – a forerunner for the general change of Scandinavian equal citizenship? A Danish case study', in S. Betzelt and S. Bothfeld (eds) *Activation and labour market reforms in Europe. Challenges to social citizenship*, Work and Welfare Series, Houndmills: Palgrave Macmillan, pp 37–58.

Burgoon, B. and Dekker, F. (2010) 'Flexible employment, economic insecurity and social policy preferences in Europe', *Journal of European Social Policy*, vol 20, no 2, pp 126–41.

Clasen, J. and Clegg, D. (2011) *Regulating the risk of unemployment. National adaptations to post-industrial labour markets in Europe*, Oxford: Oxford University Press.

Christman, J. (eds) (1989) *The inner citadel: essays on individual autonomy*, Oxford: Oxford University Press.

Christman, J. (2009) *The politics of persons: individual autonomy and socio-historical selves*, Cambridge: Cambridge University Press.

Darwall, S. (2006) 'The value of autonomy and autonomy of the will', *Ethics*, vol 116, pp 263–84.

Dean, H. (2007) 'The ethics of welfare-to-work', *Policy & Politics*, vol 35, no 4, pp 573–89.

Dullien, S., Herr, H. and Kellermann, C. (2011) *Decent capitalism. A blueprint for reforming our economies*, Houndmills: Palgrave Macmillan.

Esping-Andersen, G. (1990) *The three worlds of welfare capitalism*, Cambridge: Polity Press.

Esping-Andersen, G., Gallie, D., Hemerrijk, A. and Myles, J. (eds) (2002) *Why we need a new welfare state*, Oxford: OUP.

Forst, R. (1996) 'Politische Freiheit', *Deutsche Zeitschrift für Philosophie*, vol 44, pp 211–27.

Friedman, M. (2003) *Autonomy, gender, politics*, Oxford: OUP.

Giesecke, J. (2009) 'Socio-economic risks of atypical employment relationships: evidence from the German labour market', *European Sociological Review*, vol 25, no 6, pp 629–46.

Goerne, A. (2011) 'A comparative analysis of in-work poverty in the European Union', in N. Fraser, R. Gutiérrez and R. Peña-Casas (eds) *Working poverty in Europe. A comparative approach. Work and welfare in Europe series*, Houndmills: Palgrave Macmillan, pp 15–45.

Graziano, P. (2011) 'Activation and the limited social citizenship status of young and female workers: the Italian case', in S. Betzelt and S. Bothfeld (eds) *Activation and labour market reforms in Europe. Challenges to social citizenship*, Work and Welfare Series, Houndmills: Palgrave Macmillan, pp 173–92.

Hasselpflug, S. (2005) 'Availability criteria in 25 countries', Working Paper 12/2005, Finansministeriet, Copenhagen, www.fm.dk/Publikationer/Arbejdspapirer/2005/~/media/Files/Arbejdspapirer/arbpap1205.ashx

Immervoll, H. (2010) 'Minimum income benefits in OECD countries: policy design, effectiveness and challenges', OECD Social, Employment and Migration Working Papers, no 100, OECD Publishing, Paris, http://dx.doi.org/10.1787/218402763872

Kildal, N. and Nilssen, E. (2011) 'Norwegian welfare reforms: social contracts and activation policies', in S. Betzelt and S. Bothfeld (eds) *Activation and labour market reforms in Europe. Challenges to social citizenship*, Work and Welfare Series, Houndmills: Palgrave Macmillan, pp 218–39.

Lister, R. (2007) 'Inclusive citizenship: realizing the potential', *Citizenship Studies*, vol 11, no 1, pp 49–61.

Marshall, T.H. (1963) 'Citizenship and social class', in T.H. Marshall (eds) *Sociology at the crossroads and other essays*, London: Heinemann.

Nullmeier, F. (2000) *Politische Theorie des Sozialstaats*, Frankfurt/Main and New York, NY: Campus.

Palier, B. and Thelen, K. (2010) 'Institutionalizing dualism: complementarities and change in France and Germany', *Politics & Society*, vol 38, no 1, pp 119–48.

Pérez, B. and Laparra, M. (2011) 'Chances and pitfalls of flexible labour markets: the case of the Spanish strategy of labour market flexibility', in S. Betzelt and S. Bothfeld (eds) *Activation and labour market reforms in Europe. Challenges to social citizenship*, Work and Welfare Series, Houndmills: Palgrave Macmillan, pp 147–72.

Rössler, B. (2002) 'Problems with autonomy', *Hypatia*, vol 17, no 4, pp 143–62.

Serrano Pascual, A. (2007) 'Activations regimes in Europe: a clustering exercise', in A. Serrano and L. Magnusson (eds) *Reshaping welfare states and activation regimes in Europe*, Brüssel: Lang, Peter, pp 275–317.

Van Berkel, R. (2011) 'The local and street-level production of social citizenship: the case of Dutch social assistance', in S. Betzelt and S. Bothfeld (eds) *Activation and labour market reforms in Europe. Challenges to social citizenship*, Work and Welfare Series, Houndmills: Palgrave Macmillan, pp 195–217.

Van Berkel, R. and Hornemann Moeller, I. (2002) 'The concept of activation', in R. van Berkel and I. Hornemann Moeller (eds) *Active social policies in the EU. Inclusion through participation?*, Bristol: Policy Press, pp 45–71.

Van Berkel, R. and Valkenburg, B. (eds) (2007) *Making it personal: individualising activation services in the EU*, Bristol: Policy Press.

Van Berkel, R., Sirovátka, T. and De Graaf, W. (eds) (2011) *The governance of active welfare states in Europe*, London: Palgrave Macmillan.

Weishaupt, J.T. and Lack, K. (2011) 'The European Employment Strategy: assessing the status quo', *German Policy Studies*, vol 7, no 1, pp 9–44.

Wright, S. (2011) 'Relinquishing rights? The impact of activation on citizenship for lone parents in the UK', in S. Betzelt and S. Bothfeld (eds) *Activation and labour market reforms in Europe. Challenges to social citizenship*, Work and Welfare Series, Houndmills: Palgrave Macmillan, pp 59–78.

Young, I.M. (1990) *Justice and the politics of difference*, Princeton, NJ: Princeton University Press.

FOURTEEN

Modernising social security for lone parents: avoiding fertility and unemployment traps when reforming social policy in Northern Europe

Anders Freundt, Simon Grundt Straubinger and Jon Kvist

Introduction

European family structures and labour markets have changed markedly over the last 40 years but social security reforms have lagged behind in responding to these changes in many countries. The share of lone-parent households in Organisation for Economic Co-operation and Development (OECD) countries rose from 5.5% in the mid-1980s to 8.1% in the mid-2000s (OECD, 2011, p 215). The extent of lone-parent households is even greater in Northern Europe. In the Netherlands, for example, one in four households with children are a lone-parent household. This amounts to half a million lone-parent households in 2011, up from 361,000 in 1995 (CBS, 2013). There is a general rise in the numbers of lone parents working, but the extent varies across Europe (OECD, 2011, p 215). In some countries, the number of lone parents working is minimal and only prevalent in the more privileged socio-economic groups, whereas in other countries, the number is much larger and more even across socio-economic groups. Mainly in Nordic countries, lone parents work to the same extent as other single persons, other parents or both.

In the context of ageing populations and pressures on public budgets, all countries want to raise employment, and thus also among lone parents. For this purpose, governments look to ways of modernising social security that are both employment- and family-friendly. For governments, learning from other countries is an obvious strategy in view of the large cross-national differences in the scope and distribution of lone-parent employment. Indeed, many cross-national differences in lone-parent employment may, in part, be explained by policy differences. For example, child family allowances intend to compensate for the costs of raising children, and even act as an incentive to increase fertility rates in some countries. Special allowances for lone parents may aim to secure a minimum income. Working family tax credits and care schemes may serve to motivate or assist parents to work. Housing benefits may serve to provide a minimum standard in housing and motivate higher fertility (McDonald, 2002, p 437) or perhaps target lone-parent households. In total, the various tax and benefit schemes make up complex tax–benefit packages that impact on lone parents differently even within a country, depending on what income they have.

The complexity of tax–benefit packages and difference across countries and socio-economic groups of social security for lone working parents may not come as a surprise when considering that they touch upon a number of issues of considerable social, political and economic significance. These include values about families, children's well-being, income distribution, gender equality, insurance against market risks, labour supply and population questions. This complexity and diversity is not taken into account in many studies and reports that either compare single policy schemes for different families, different packages of schemes for one group of families, or, simply, single policy schemes for a single family type or proxy (like an average of different family types).

Several studies have relied on single-case indicators, where one typical case is compared to the situation of a similar typical case not facing the given social contingency. The wage of the average production worker (APW) (now the average worker [AW]) is the single-case indicator that is used in the two perhaps most important databases: the Social Citizenship Indicator Program (SCIP) and the Comparative Welfare Entitlements Dataset (CWED). The main problem potentially associated with the single-case indicators is that important policy nuances about social security and economic incentive structures for different income groups are lost. Something also acknowledged by the creator of CWED (Scruggs, 2006, p 363).

Individual schemes may be studied and designed in isolation by policymakers depending on whether the goal of the scheme is to compensate expenses, secure minimum standards, boost labour supply or increase fertility rates. In reality, however, various schemes interact and it is their combined effect that may be expected to impact on people's lives, incentives and behaviour. This may help explain why policy reforms often have unintended effects. There are different types of unintended effects, and here two sets of unintended effects that tend to keep people in unfortunate situations are examined. The focus is on benefits that through their meagre size or design may contribute to preventing people from having children and preventing people from entering employment. Such situations are called, respectively, the fertility trap and the unemployment trap.

The two traps are defined in the following way:

1. Fertility trap: When social security does not reward or compensate part of the cost of parenthood.
2. Unemployment trap: When social security provides economic disincentives to work or when public schemes work against the transition into work.

The question addressed in this chapter asks how social security can be modernised to boost employment among lone parents without creating fertility traps. Women in some countries (Germany, the Netherlands and the UK) tend to leave their job at the birth of their first child and come back part time, whereas in other countries (the Nordic), women's participation in the labour market resembles that of men throughout life (Cousins, 1999, p 75). Second, there is large variation in the general labour market participation of lone parents in Northern Europe. The Nordic countries, in particular, have high levels of employment and low levels of poverty compared to other countries. The OECD ascribes some of this difference to the extensive childcare systems in the Nordic countries (OECD, 2011, p 216).

To investigate the fertility trap, this chapter compares the economic situation of the lone parent with that of a single person. The economic difference between the situation of the single person and the lone parent can be seen as the 'price' or 'reward' of becoming a parent (assuming that most parents did not anticipate being a lone parent prior to conception). To investigate the unemployment trap, the economic difference in disposable income of the lone parent in employment and in unemployment is compared. In the investigation, the situations across income levels, countries and labour market participation are also compared. The data used for the analysis is the OECD Tax–Benefit Model augmented by further data collection undertaken by the authors for validation.

The chapter is set out as follows. First, the social schemes related to lone parents are outlined. The second section describes how institutional tax–benefit data for seven countries have been validated and computed. Third, social security for lone parents in relation to the unemployment and fertility traps is analysed and compared. Finally, the chapter concludes by discussing the policy implications of the analysis.

Social security for lone parents

From previous studies, it is known that social schemes have important implications for the scope and distribution of fertility and employment (McDonald, 2002; OECD, 2011). Population ageing and its major cause, persisting very low fertility, is a concern for most OECD countries because of the long-term consequences for economic growth and the sustainability of the welfare state. The fertility rate in almost every OECD country has fallen below the level – approximately 2.07 children per woman – required for population replacement. There are many reasons why individuals choose to postpone childbearing or restrict family size, including economic, social and biological obstacles. Policies may aim at mitigating the effect of some of these obstacles, or it could be that their outcomes are reinforcing such obstacles. To the extent that family decisions concerning fertility are influenced by economic decisions, various cash benefits, ranging from birth bonuses and tax breaks for children, to more generous allowances for higher-parity births, may impact fertility. It is not suggested that family decisions are based on economics alone, but the economic influence on decisions is the focus in this chapter. According to traditional economic theory, children are considered a normal good (Becker, 1981), and the economic factors determining the demand for children in a family are the result of income and substitution effects. In other words, the number of children being born depends positively on the family's income but negatively on the cost of having children. The cost of children is traditionally divided into *direct* and *indirect cost*. Whereas the former refers to the actual expenditure related to the child, the latter refers to alternative cost, such as losses of income due to time spent on the child instead of work. The indirect cost, in particular, is seen to affect the choice of having the first child. Both the indirect and direct cost decrease as society organises in a way that allows for the balance of work and family (McDonald, 2002, pp 424–5). In regimes without family-friendly policies, such as childcare subsidies and family benefit, a trade-off between women's labour supply and fertility should be expected, because the costs of having children increase with the earnings potential of mothers. Family-friendly policies like childcare subsidies, however, loosen this trade-off (Esping-Andersen, 2009). Although the literature is not unanimous on this topic regarding single policy measures (Gauthier and Philipov, 2008, p 7), a study conducted by Bradshaw and Finch (2006) reveals that whole packages of financial support for families can have the effect of increasing fertility levels.

According to Castles (2003), there is a strong positive relationship between fertility and formal childcare provision. Unlike most other OECD countries, especially the Southern European countries, the Nordic countries stand out with relatively high publicly subsidised childcare coverage. This may explain the dramatic change in the cross-national incidence of fertility in advanced societies in the past two decades. Previously, the fertility rate was high in countries with low female labour market participation, but now the fertility rate is higher in countries with high female labour market participation, as is the case in the Nordic countries (Castles, 2003, p 211).

There is a gap between the complexity and cross-national diversity of social security for lone parents in employment on the one hand, and the simplicity inherent in most of the existing studies based on the SCIP and CWED databases mentioned earlier on the other. One notable exception to this practice among scholars has been the work of Jonathan Bradshaw et al. Through many years, they have advanced the comparative study of tax–benefit packages for different stylised family types, addressing in particular important questions related to the adequacy of benefits and poverty among families (eg Bradshaw and Richardson, 2009; Bradshaw, 2010). The analysis provided here follows the same tradition of comparing tax–benefit packages for different family types by building on the OECD Tax–Benefit Model (for more technical details, see 'Data and method' section). Hence, we study the combined package of unemployment benefits, housing benefits, family benefit and tax credits, taxation and the expenses related to childcare and accommodation.

Data and method

Comparative studies of social security face at least two challenges regarding measurement: first, that the data reflect the relevant schemes of social security; and, second, that the data are comparable across time and place, thereby accounting for functional equivalence (Adcock and Collier, 2001). Social issues may not be dealt with in the same way across countries since welfare architectures and welfare mixes differ.

Some countries provide cash benefits, while other countries rely more on tax credits (Straubinger et al, 2011; Freundt et al, 2012). Often, claimants receive more than a single public benefit at one time. Finally, it is necessary not only to look at benefits, but to consider all expenses related to the life of a family, such as childcare payments and housing costs, and to take into account tax-related issues, such as tax credits and different tax brackets.

To meet these challenges, the OECD Tax–Benefit Model microsimulation is used to '*profile*' and '*stack*' the public benefits related to lone parents in seven European countries.[1] The '*profiling*' refers to examining several income levels at the same time. '*Stacking*' analysis is a term for analysis that includes multiple taxes/benefits at the same time. The countries are all Northern European – Denmark, Sweden, Norway, Finland, Germany, the Netherlands and the UK – countries that may learn from each other through systematic comparisons. There are three main reasons why these seven countries have been chosen. First, the countries face many of the same systemic problems and therefore have the potential to learn from each other. Second, all of the three welfare regimes put forward by Esping-Andersen (1990, 1999) are represented by one or several countries. Third, as mentioned earlier, the Nordic countries are those with the highest fertility rates, and thus it is important to include them all in the analysis to assist policy learning.

Summary of country differences in provision

All seven countries provide a standard family benefit either as a fixed amount, an amount reduced by increasing income or as tax credits. All Nordic countries provide a standard family benefit as a fixed amount and lone parents have a right to receive advance maintenance payments. In Denmark, Norway and Finland, lone parents receive an additional fixed amount, which is not the case in Sweden. There is an income-dependent lone-parent benefit in Norway, which suggests that the family support schemes are more generous towards low-income and unemployed families.

The UK, the Netherlands and Germany also provide the standard family benefit as a fixed amount. Germany also provides a supplement for lone parents and advance child payments as fixed amounts. The UK, Germany and the Netherlands differentiate from the Nordic countries by also granting family benefit as tax credits. Although all of the family benefits in the UK are provided as tax credits, both the unemployed and employed are eligible. The benefits are, instead, tapered with income.

Table 14.1: Social security for lone parents and single persons

Schemes	Description	General schemes for single persons	Additional schemes and special rules for lone parents
Unemployment benefit	Unemployment benefit is the main income of the unemployed. It is displayed with the basic allowance if such is available and after tax if the unemployment benefit is taxable	Both universal and means-tested benefit: SW (arbetslöshetsförsäkring), FIN (grunddagpenning), UK (Jobseeker's Allowance [JSA]) Only income-related benefit: DK (dagpenge), NW (arbeidsledighetstrygd), NL (werkloosheidsuitkering), GE (Arbeitslosengeld)	Additional unemployment benefit: NW, FIN, NL, GE
Housing benefit	Housing benefit where the rent is assumed to be 20% of the gross income of the employed. The unemployed are not assumed to move	Means-tested benefit: DK (boligsikring), SW (bostadsbidrag), FIN (bostadsbidrag), NL (huurtoeslag), GE (Wohngeld), UK (housing benefit)	Housing benefit, means-tested: NW (bostøtte) Additional housing benefit: DK, SW, UK
Family benefit	Family benefit contains all sorts of family- and lone parent-related benefits. This includes lone-parent benefits, standard child benefits, advance maintenance payments, child tax credits and so forth		Standard child benefit, universal: DK (barnefamilieydelse), SW (barnbidrag), NW (barnetrygd), FN (barnbidrag), NL (kinderbijslag), GE (Kindergeld), UK (child benefit) Lone-parent benefit, universal: DK, NW, FN, GE Lone-parent benefit, means-tested: NW, NL Advance maintenance payments: DK (barnebidrag), SW (underhållsstöd), NW (barnebidrag), FN (underhållsstöd), GE (Unterhaltvorschuss) Tax credits, both for people in and out of work: tapered with income: UK (child tax credit) increased with income: GE (Kinderfreibetrag) Tax credit, only for people in work, tapered with income: NL

Schemes	Description	General schemes for single persons	Additional schemes and special rules for lone parents
Net expense for childcare	The expense for a three-year-old child in kindergarten minus the subsidy provided either as a tax credit, a benefit or a reduction in the fee		Subsidy or reduction in fee, means-tested: DK, SW, NW, FN, GE Tax credits, only for people in work: GE, NL, UK *(childcare element)*
Tax credit	Any tax credit which is not related to either family benefit or childcare. Most often a working tax credit besides the basic allowance	Working tax credits: DK, SW, NW, FIN, GE, NL, UK	Additional working tax credits: UK *(lone-parent element)*

Note: DK – Denmark; SW – Sweden; NW – Norway; FN – Finland; NL – the Netherlands; GE – Germany; UK – United Kingdom

Germany and the Netherlands, on the other hand, provide the standard child benefit for all lone parents but also extra tax credits for employed lone parents. Germany and the UK provide very generous child benefits for the unemployed. In fact, the UK offers the highest child benefit of all the seven countries throughout the income spectra of the unemployed. The subsidisation of childcare in all seven countries is of substantial significance for lone parents, since the impact on disposable income is high.

Social security in seven countries

The following analysis attempts to draw out answers to the questions raised by the earlier discussion of fertility and unemployment traps: 'Does social security ensure a standard of living for lone parents that is not lower than that of a single person, thereby increasing fertility potential?'; 'Does the welfare state ensure sustainable disposable income regardless of employment status?'; 'Does the welfare state provide affordable childcare options for lone parents so that paid work can be undertaken?'; and 'Does the welfare state provide social benefits that do not create economic disincentives to work?'

The analysis of the fertility and the unemployment traps uses the following indicators: disposable incomes that are the same or lower for lone parents compared to single people are seen as an indicator of the fertility trap; the first indicator of the unemployment trap is when childcare is not affordable, provided and subsidised in a manner that ensures that childcare can be obtained regardless of employment status; and benefits that are tapered with income, dependent on employment status, are taken as a second indicator of the unemployment trap. The analysis is organised into two parts: first, the disposable income of lone parents and single persons is compared in order to analyse the potential of the fertility trap; and, second, the unemployment trap is surveyed through the childcare and economic work incentive indicator.

The fertility trap: when lone parenthood is not rewarded or compensated

By fertility traps, a situation where disposable income is decreased as a result of becoming a lone parent is implied. The trap is avoided or mitigated when the loss in income is diminished by the presence of the social security system. In Tables 14.2 and 14.3, negative figures imply the existence of a fertility trap. Table 14.2 shows the difference in disposable income and the single benefits between unemployed lone parents and unemployed single persons. All of the amounts are measured using Purchasing Power Parities (PPPs) in US dollars. Negative figures indicate that single persons have a higher disposable income than lone parents, and positive figures the opposite.

The AW measure was introduced by the OECD as a replacement of the APW. Whereas the APW was the average wage in the manufacturing industry, the AW is close to the average wage in the country. Due to the decreasing numbers of workers in the manufacturing industry, a new measure was requested. The variation between the AW (0.5 AW–2.0 AW) used here, is the percentage variation in income. That means the 0.5 AW is 50% of 1 AW and so forth. The idea is to show the income span from relatively low income to relatively high income. These comments are valid for Table 14.3 as well.

When examining the fertility trap, it is apparent that the compensation of parenthood can be implemented in several ways. The Netherlands, Norway, Finland and Germany use unemployment benefit as a means to counter the extra expenses related to being a parent. They do so by increasing the unemployment benefits for lone parents compared with single person. In contrast, Denmark, Sweden and the UK increase housing benefits for lone parents compared to single persons, thereby mitigating the expenses related to being a parent. The four Nordic countries curb the fertility trap by providing both very generous childcare subsidies and family benefits, whereas Germany, the Netherlands and the UK all present less generous schemes in these two respects.

All seven countries provide unemployment benefit for lone parents. However, Norway, Germany, the Netherlands and Finland increase unemployment benefit for lone parents compared to single persons, whereas Denmark, Sweden and the UK do not. For people on lower incomes, two of the four Nordic countries (Finland and Norway) succeed in countering the fertility trap through unemployment benefit to a greater extent than is the case for the Continental European countries. At 1 AW, the differences between the two Nordic countries and the conservative countries are less pronounced. For higher incomes (1.5–2 AW), it is noticeable that Finland bears a resemblance to the dictum of Saint Matthew – 'to those who have, shall more be given' – in that it maintains a progressive difference in unemployment benefits in favour of lone parents (Korpi and Palme, 2004; Straubinger et al, 2011; Freundt et al, 2012).

Table 14.2: The difference in amounts between unemployed lone parents and unemployed single persons, Purchasing Power Parities in US dollars, 2008

AW level	DK	FN	NW	SW	GE	NL	UK
0.5 AW							
Unemployment benefit	0	4,566	9,381	0	1,118	1,687	0
Housing benefit	1,193	421	–	1,3301	532	0	0
Family benefit	4,058	3,309	4,111	3,091	3,892	2,045	5,296
Net expense for childcare	–146	–337	–320	–469	–600	–5,133	–8,506
Tax credit	–	–	–	–	–	–	–
Disposable income	5,105	4,349	13,171	3,953	4,943	–242	–3,210
1 AW							
Unemployment benefit	0	4,946	5,545	0	1,922	1,687	0
Housing benefit	2,592	2,777	–	2,129	0	0	1,764
Family benefit	4,058	3,309	3,689	3,091	3,892	1,774	5,296
Net expense for childcare	–359	–997	–664	–588	–935	–5,942	–8,506
Tax credit	–	–	–	–	–	–	–
Disposable income	6,291	5,943	8,571	4,633	4,879	–929	–1,446
1.5 AW							
Unemployment benefit	0	5,919	5,545	0	2,585	1,687	0
Housing benefit	2,575	0	–	2,129	0	0	2,202
Family benefit	4,058	3,309	3,689	3,091	3,892	1,564	5,296
Net expense for childcare	–359	–1,390	–664	–588	–1,883	–6,124	–8,506
Tax credit	–	–	–	–	–	–	–
Disposable income	6,274	2,691	8,571	4,633	4,594	–1,616	–1,008
2 AW							
Unemployment benefit	0	7,159	5,545	0	2,647	1,687	0
Housing benefit	2,575	0	–	2,129	0	0	2,202
Family benefit	4,058	3,309	3,689	3,091	3,892	1,564	5,296
Net expense for childcare	–359	–1,784	664	–588	–1,883	–6,124	–8,506
Tax credit	–	–	–	–	–	–	–
Disposable income	6,274	2,254	8,571	2,109	4,656	–2,382	–1,008

Note: AW – Average Worker (wage); DK – Denmark; FN – Finland; NW – Norway; SW – Sweden; GE – Germany; NL – the Netherlands; UK – United Kingdom

Table 14.3 shows the difference in disposable income and the single benefits between the employed lone parent and the employed single person.

Table 14.3: The difference in amounts between the employed lone parent and the employed single person, Purchasing Power Parities in US dollars, 2008

AW level	DK	FN	NW	SW	GE	NL	UK
0.5 AW							
Housing benefit	1,043	0	0	532	0	1,210	1,490
Family benefit	4,058	3,309	10,401	3,091	3,892	2,045	5,296
Net expense for childcare	−246	−1059	−664	−586	−1507	−823	−1,701
Tax credit	−	−	−	−	−	−	375
Disposable income	4,855	2,250	9,639	3,037	3,045	6,231	5,459
1 AW							
Housing benefit	356	0	0	0	0	0	817
Family benefit	4,058	3,309	2,424	3,091	3,965	1,093	2,855
Net expense for childcare	−1,312	−2,393	−2,669	−1,173	−5,524	−1,925	−8,506
Tax credit	−	−	−	−	−	−	0
Disposable income	3,101	916	2,533	1,919	−453	3,534	−4,834
1.5 AW							
Housing benefit	0	0	0	0	0	0	0
Family benefit	4,058	3,309	2,424	3,091	4,557	896	2,195
Net expense for childcare	−1,955	−2,393	−2,669	−1,677	−5,524	−3,641	−8,506
Tax credit	−	−	−	−	−	−	0
Disposable income	2,103	916	2,580	1,415	360	1,621	−6,311
2 AW							
Housing benefit	0	0	0	0	0	0	0
Family benefit	4,058	3,309	2,424	3,091	4,580	896	1,435
Net expense for childcare	−1,955	−2,393	−2,669	−1,677	−5,524	−5,273	−8,506
Tax credit	−	−	−	−	−	−	0
Disposable income	2,103	916	3,197	1,415	385	−11	−7,071

Note: AW − Average Worker (wage); DK − Denmark; FN − Finland; NW − Norway; SW − Sweden; GE − Germany; NL − the Netherlands; UK − United Kingdom

Although all of the countries do support lone parenthood, some succeed to a greater extent than others. This is apparent when paying attention to the disposable income in both Tables 14.2 and 14.3. For all income levels, regardless of employment status, except at the lowest income (0.5 AW), the UK fails to create a situation where parenthood is not related to a lower disposable income. In contrast, Denmark, Finland, Norway, Sweden and Germany enable a higher disposable income for lone parents compared to single persons regardless of income level and employment situation (although Germany diverges from this at 1 AW in employment). The Netherlands resembles the UK in the situation of unemployment. In the situation of employment, the Netherlands resembles its Nordic peers. Therefore, all of the Nordic countries, and to some extent Germany, can be said to curb the fertility trap, whereas this is the case to a lesser extent for the UK and the Netherlands.

As can be seen in Table 14.3, neither Norway, Germany nor Finland provide an extended housing benefit for lone parents in work at the lowest income level (0.5 AW) of concern. At the 1 AW income level, only the UK and Denmark grant eligibility to extra housing benefit for working lone parents compared to single person. In both Sweden and Norway, parenthood is a prerequisite for housing benefit, and in Norway, eligibility is granted for income levels lower than the ones considered here. Along with Norway, the Netherlands does not stress housing benefit in relation to parenthood. The Dutch system offers no more generous benefits for lone parents than for single persons at any income level. Three countries emphasise housing benefit as a means to counter the fertility trap. These countries are Denmark, Sweden and the UK, who all provide greater housing benefits for the unemployed lone parent compared to the unemployed single person throughout 2 AW. In comparison, Norway, Germany and the Netherlands grant no more generous housing benefits for unemployed lone parents above the 1 AW level. Finland positions itself somewhere in the middle between those who prioritise housing benefit and those who do not. The entitlements to housing benefit in the UK are fairly generous in general, but particularly so for lone parents. Compared to the rather meagre unemployment benefits, housing policy is of significance. Denmark and the UK are the two countries where housing benefits partly counter the fertility trap (Straubinger et al, 2011; Freundt et al, 2012).

Unemployment traps: when social security provides economic disincentives to work or when public schemes work against the transition into work

Through the unemployment trap, it is attempted to capture the economic incentives to take up paid work and the role of affordable childcare. The analysis here also explores whether public schemes create obstacles associated with the transition to work. Figure 14.1 shows disposable income for employed lone parents. The way benefits are provided can be detected in the shape of the curves.

Figure 14.1: The disposable income of employed lone parents, 2008

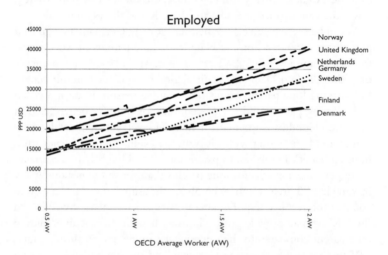

Note: The order of the countries is ranked by the disposable income in purchasing power parities (PPP) for previous income at the level of twice the average worker. Therefore, the order of the countries is not the same for Figures 14.1–14.3. When the disposable income goes below zero, it implies that the expenses related to rent and childcare exceed income. Remember the assumptions: lone parents do not move to cheaper accommodation due to unemployment and keep the child in day care regardless of employment status. The figure contains all relevant benefits and expenses.

Although the Nordic countries are similar in their approach to creating economic job incentives and in- and out-of-work mobility, some differences remain. Denmark, Sweden and Finland all gradually decrease childcare subsidies with income, while Norway displays three different income ceilings, which implies substantial marginal effects on the childcare subsidy as income exceeds the different ceilings (see Figures 14.1 and 14.2).

Regarding both affordable childcare and unambiguous economic work incentives, three of the four Nordic countries (Finland, Denmark and Sweden) succeed in reconciling work and welfare in that they provide very generous childcare subsidies and family benefits for lone parents that do not interfere with the economic incentive to take up paid work, since the benefits are not limited to those participating in the labour market. Norway resembles its Nordic peers with regard to childcare, but not in relation to economic work incentives. As noted earlier, in Norway, due to the income ceilings, the transition into work and climbing the income ladder is not economically rewarded. In relation to childcare, Germany and the UK all perform poorly on both the childcare and economic incentives indicators compared to their Nordic counterparts. Germany and the UK do not provide very generous support for childcare expenses and the support is granted through tax credits, and is strongly tapered with income. The Netherlands provides generous tax credits for the employed, but the tax credit is less generous for the unemployed looking for work. Moreover, the tax credits are tapered gradually with income. The system of means-tested tax credits, which presuppose labour market attachment, is considered a forceful promoter of the unemployment trap. Figure 14.2 shows the disposable income for unemployed lone parents and their economic

Figure 14.2: The disposable income of unemployed lone parents between 0.5 and 2 AW, Purchasing Power Parities in US dollars, 2008

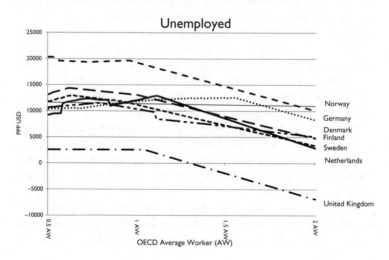

situation, assuming that their child is in childcare and that they are thus available for employment.

The systems of family benefits in Germany, the Netherlands and the UK show large variations. The UK de facto operates as Norway. Germany grants both generous universal benefits that prevent material deprivation, and increases tax credits with income instead of tapering them, thereby providing strong economic incentives to undertake paid employment, but also to climb the income ladder. In terms of the unemployment trap, increasing tax credits are considered less obstructive compared to tax credits tapered with income. The Netherlands performs poorly on both the childcare and economic work incentives indicators since the universal benefit is very low, and the tax credits are means-tested.

In Germany and the UK, the prevailing system of subsidies for childcare that are granted through the use of tax credits has two inverse related effects compared to the universal access found in the Nordic countries. Since labour market attachment is a prerequisite for receiving tax credits, unemployed people are not eligible for childcare subsidies. On the one hand, this means that the economic incentive for parents to be employed is rather substantial, given that otherwise one will have to pay the entire fee, which can amount to a high percentage of disposable income – the transition into the labour market not only increases one's income, it also lowers the price of childcare. On the other hand, though, if lone parents should happen to be out of work at the time of birth or if unemployment strikes them, economic incentives are mitigated or even eroded. As discussed earlier, the price of childcare has a strong impact on the availability for employment. If lone parents have limited funds, they may not be able to afford childcare and therefore opt out of this care altogether, which will impact on future availability for employment. The point is that lone parents need employment to be eligible for childcare subsidies, but also need childcare to be able to take a job. When subsidies are granted as tax credits, some lone parents risk being kept out of the labour market because of ill-suited scheme structures. This can be a direct cause of the unemployment trap.

The main implication of universal family support schemes is that every lone parent receives the same amount regardless of income and employment situation, and thus the marginal effects do not obstruct the transition from unemployment to employment, nor the climbing of the income ladder.

Norway further differs from Denmark, Sweden and Finland with regard to the additional means-tested family benefit. This implies that family support schemes are more generous towards low-income and unemployed families. The income of the employed at the 1 AW level is above the income threshold, suggesting a substantial marginal effect on disposable income. On the one hand, higher benefits for lower incomes work as barriers against material deprivation, but, on the other hand, targeting benefits at those with very low incomes has the potential of obscuring the economic incentive for the transition from 'out of work' to 'in work', and of progression in the income spectrum. More directly, compared to the three other Nordic countries, provisions in Norway disservice the children of lone parents by jeopardising the economic incentive to take up a job and thereby the possibility of superior material well-being.

Figure 14.3: The net replacement rates (NRRs) for lone parents between 0.5 and 2.AW

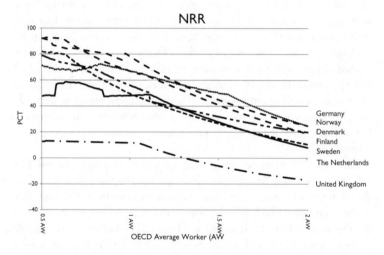

Figure 14.3 shows the net replacement rates (NRRs) for lone parents. The graph is a very simple measure of the difference in income between employment and unemployment. In terms of economic incentives, it appears at first glance as if the biggest difference in income, and thereby where most can be gained through employment, is the UK. This is true, but as put forward earlier, the structures of the tax credits mask the reality. The economic 'wall' of childcare payments risks keeping lone parents out of the labour market. The childcare system in the UK is clearly not promoting the 'into work' transition for lone parents.

In contrast, even though Germany also provides most benefits on the basis of tax credits, some are not. Germany increases the family tax credit with income and thereby performs well on the childcare indicator. The Netherlands is an interesting mix between the UK and the Nordic countries in that childcare tax credits are provided for both the employed and the unemployed seeking work. But the tax credits are more generous for employed people and they are means-tested for both the employed and unemployed. In Norway, most benefits are very generous but are mostly income-dependent. Moreover, the tapering of benefits is not gradual and therefore has substantial marginal effects. Economic work incentives for lone parents in Norway are mostly negative since for every penny earned, another is withdrawn from the subsidies (Straubinger et al, 2011; Freundt et al, 2012).

Denmark and Sweden mostly provide universal non-income-dependent benefits, which work against the unemployment trap. Since benefits are very generous in general, not much is actually gained through employment, and this is especially the case for lower earners in Denmark. Finland is a mixed case and provides both income- and non-income-related benefits. The social security of very low-income workers (0.5 AW) in Denmark and Norway shows a difference in income between employment and unemployment of only eight percentage points. On the one hand, strong protection works against economic marginalisation, but, on the other hand, it does not provide an economic incentive to take up paid work.

All of the countries deliver housing benefit on the basis of need. The UK, Denmark and Sweden, however, do use the benefit in a slightly different manner than the remaining countries and ensure the eligibility of those employed on lower incomes. This promotes employment since the tapering of housing benefit has a less marginal effect on disposable income when this is increasing, thereby mitigating the negative effects on the economic work incentives indicator.

Concluding remarks

In this chapter, two of the potential traps when modernising social security have been analysed – the fertility trap and the unemployment trap – and important cross-national differences between seven Northern European countries have been detected. Each of the Nordic countries avoids the fertility trap by providing sufficient financial support to compensate for the expenses related to parenthood. At the same time, work–family reconciliation is possible due to affordable childcare.

Combined, these policies are likely to have a positive effect on fertility rates in the Nordic countries and help explain why Nordic fertility rates are among the highest in the OECD countries. The Nordic countries mitigate the unemployment trap to some degree through provision of affordable childcare and concomitant high childcare coverage. However, economic incentives suffer, especially in Norway for low-income groups, because some of the benefits are tapered in such a way that lone parents lose in benefits what is earned by working.

The UK, and to some extent Germany, may enjoy a double effect of changing the basis for subsidising childcare. At the moment, middle- and high-income lone parents do have positive economic incentives to work because the childcare tax credits are wastable (ie premised on income from employment) and because of the existence of means-tested benefits. Moving away from means-tested child family benefits and from indirect support through the tax system to directly subsidised childcare, as in the Nordic countries, may contribute to higher fertility rates and labour market participation, especially for middle- and high-income groups. Finally, both the UK and the Netherlands may consider rewarding parenthood in a manner where it is not associated with lower disposable income.

For other countries, some more general lessons may be learned. In fact, the analysis suggests that three reform elements are important for countries in need of modernising their social protection systems to avoid fertility traps and unemployment traps. First, policy needs to make sure that parenthood is rewarded through public subsidies. Second, affordable childcare is required to counter the unemployment trap. Finally, when using tax credits, these should be non-wastable.

That said, the analysis also indicates that countries may use different tax–benefit packages to boost employment and fertility. Although the Nordic countries are said to have a common social-democratic welfare regime and, indeed, do resemble one another in terms of fertility rates, there is certainly variation between the Nordic social security systems. Denmark and Sweden are rather similar and come close to the social-democratic welfare regime. However, Norway and Finland also bear characteristics of the Nordic model, but share elements also of the conservative model, and in the Norwegian case, also with the liberal model. Hence, countries modernising their social protection system may not need to adopt a Nordic welfare regime or a copy of a specific tax–benefit package. This gives a certain solace to the future as countries where the need to modernise social security is biggest in

Europe may also be the countries that are also most adversely affected by the current debt crisis.

Note

[1.] Our point of departure is the Tax–Benefit Model, created and updated yearly by the OECD based on national tax and benefits. First, we validated the calculations from the OECD Tax–Benefit Model by collecting the information on the tax and social policies at stake from independent sources, such as ministries or national agencies. Alterations were made to either correct factual errors or to make a more realistic scenario. Factual errors, mainly incorrect amounts, thresholds and percentages, about Danish, Swedish, Norwegian, Finnish, Dutch, German and British welfare schemes were discovered and corrected in the model. The calculation of rent was altered in the model from 20% of one average worker to 20% of gross income. The alteration was made because people on low incomes usually live in cheaper accommodation and pay less rent than those on higher incomes. Second, we calculated the net expense for childcare and the disposable income for the single person and the sole parent in and out of work. Third, we deducted the disposable income for the single person from that of the sole parent to investigate the fertility traps for sole parents. Fourth, we calculated the difference between employment and unemployment of single parents to investigate the unemployment trap for sole parents (for further details on the schemes and calculations, see Straubinger et al, 2011; Freundt et al, 2012).

References

Adcock, R. and Collier, D. (2001) 'Measurement validity: a shared standard for qualitative and quantitative research', *The American Political Science Review*, vol 95, no 3, pp 529–46.

Becker, G. (1981) *Treatise on the family*, Cambridge, MA: Harvard University Press.

Bradshaw, J. (2010) 'An international perspective on child benefit packages', in S.P. Kamerman and A. Ben-Arieh (eds) *From child welfare to child well-being: an international perspective on knowledge in the service of policy making*, Dordrecht: Springer, pp 293–307.

Bradshaw, J. and Finch, N. (2006) 'Can policy influence fertility?', in H. Emanuel (ed) *Ageing and the labour market: issues and solutions, international studies in social security*, Antwerp: Intersentia, pp 151–68.

Bradshaw, J. and Richardson, D. (2009) 'An index of child well-being in Europe', *Child Indicators Research*, vol 2, pp 319–51.

Castles, F.G. (2003) 'The world turned upside down: below replacement fertility, changing preferences and family-friendly public policy in 21 OECD countries', *Journal of European Social Policy*, vol 13, no 3, pp 209–27.

CBS (2013) *Size and composition household*, Available at: statsline.cbs.nl (assessed 21 March 2013).

Cousins, C. (1999) *Society, work and welfare in Europe*, London: Palgrave Macmillan.

Esping-Andersen, G. (1990) *The three worlds of welfare capitalism*, New Jersey, NJ: Princeton University Press.

Esping-Andersen, G. (1999) *Social foundations of post-industrial economies*, Oxford: Oxford University Press.

Esping-Andersen, G. (2009) *The incomplete revolution*, Princeton, NJ: Polity Press.

Freundt, A., Straubinger, S. and Hansen, H. (2012) 'Documentation for unemployment insurance benefits and other public schemes in seven European countries', Working Paper, Center for Welfare state Research, University of Southern Denmark.

Gauthier, A.H. and Philipov, D. (2008) 'Can policies enhance fertility in Europe?', *Vienna Yearbook of Population Research 2008*, vol 6, pp 1–16.

Korpi, W. and Palme, J. (2004) 'Robin Hood, St Matthew, or simple egalitarianism? Strategies of equality in welfare states', in P. Kennett (ed) *A handbook of comparative social policy*, Cheltenham: Edward Elgar, pp 153–79.

McDonald, P. (2002) 'Sustaining fertility through public policy: the range of options', *Population*, vol 57, no 3, pp 417–46.

OECD (organisation for Economic Co-operation and Development) (2011) *Doing better for families*, Paris: OECD.

Scruggs, L. (2006) 'The generosity of social insurance, 1971– 2002', *Oxford review of economic policy*, vol 22, no 3, pp 349–64.

Straubinger, S., Freundt, A. and Hansen, H. (2011) 'Profiling and stacking public benefits for the single parent in and out of work in 2008', Working Paper, Center for Welfare state Research, University of Southern Denmark.

FIFTEEN

Women, families and the 'Great Recession' in the UK

Susan Harkness

Introduction

Since the onset of recession in 2008, little attention has been paid to the question of whether men's and women's experience of the downturn in the UK jobs market has differed, or to the implications of these gender differences for families. This chapter is an initial attempt to examine these issues for the UK. It assesses how, over the four years since the onset of the 'Great Recession' at the end of 2008, and a period of prolonged labour market weakness, male and female employment and unemployment rates, hours of work, wages and family incomes have changed. Analysing this wide range of indicators allows us to build a rich picture of how recession has affected men's and women's labour market position and their families' incomes.

The year 2008 marked the end of a long period of economic growth. Under New Labour, low- to middle-income families had seen substantial improvements in their incomes, employment rates had grown and the incidence of poverty had fallen. While these gains were partly a result of favourable economic conditions, policy changes were also of considerable importance (Hills and Stewart, 2005). But in the third quarter of 2008, the British economy entered recession for the first time in 15 years and compared to the last recession in 1990–93, the role of women in the workforce (and consequently at home) had changed considerably. Between 1992 and 2008, employment grew by five percentage points (ppt) to 67%, while the gender pay gap fell by almost 10 ppt to just over 20% in 2008.[1] At the same time, women's employment and earnings are of increasing importance in helping families avoid poverty: first, because a growing number of families are headed by a single female; and, second, as within couples, not having a second earner is increasingly associated with a high risk of poverty (Harkness, 2010). Women's work is therefore of much greater importance to families' economic well-being today than in earlier recessions, and the question of whether the current recession has had a different effect on male and female employment is therefore one of considerable policy significance. To date, there has been little research in this area and it is this gap in the literature that this chapter aims to fill.

The chapter has two primary interests: first, to analyse the implications of the economic downturn for gender inequalities in the labour market; and, second, to assess how this has influenced both the level and composition of family income, in particular, asking how this has influenced women's role as 'breadwinners'. It finds that in terms of employment levels, women have fared better than men in a difficult labour market since 2008 and, as a result, their employment and earnings have played an increasingly critical role in maintaining family incomes. Had the contribution of women's earnings to the family budget not increased since 2008, the fall in family income would have been larger. The changes in women's employment and earnings that have taken place over the course of the economic downturn have both reinforced and accelerated trends that have been happening over the last 30 years, with women's role in the labour force and as family breadwinners becoming increasingly important since the onset of the economic crisis.

Background and methods

In the third quarter of 2008, the UK economy entered recession for the first time in 15 years. Gross Domestic product (GDP) contracted by 7% between 2008 and 2010. While modest growth subsequently returned, the economy contracted again in the final quarter of 2011 and in 2012 output remained 5% lower than it had been at its 2008 peak. The National Institute of Economic and Social Research (NIESR) has described this period as one of economic depression. While in the UK, recession has often been described as a period where the economy experiences at least two consecutive quarters of negative economic growth, there is no single definition of recession. Recession in the US, for example, is defined by the National Bureau for Economic Research (NBER) Business Cycle Dating Committee, and considers a wide range of measures of economic activity, including employment rates, data on hours of work and personal incomes.[2] A wide definition of recession would include one where the economy is described as such when it is operating at a level of reduced economic activity. It is in this wide sense that this chapter uses the term.

In past recessions, when output has fallen, so too has employment. The current recession in the UK has been unusual in that while there has been a substantial decline in output, the effect on employment has been much more muted. A number of studies show that unemployment and joblessness saw only a surprisingly modest rise (eg Elsby and Smith, 2010), with most of the negative employment effects being concentrated among the young (Bell and Blanchflower, 2010). On the basis of the numbers in employment, Chris Giles of the *Financial Times* argues that the 2008 recession would be described as 'short and shallow' (*Financial Times*, 2012). Nonetheless, other commentators have noted that the labour market has experienced a phase of prolonged weakness (Philpott, 2012), and in spite of the evidence which suggests that the number of people in work has not changed much, the number of people seeking and unable to find work has grown, with unemployment reaching an 18-year high in January 2012, at 2.68 million, and forecast to remain at around 8% until 2016 (NIESR, 2012; ONS, 2012a). Part of the reason for this divergence may reflect an increase in job search among those previously out of the labour market (the 'inactive') as a result of reductions in working hours and falling real wages leading to a squeeze on families' real incomes (Whittaker, 2012).

Evidence from past recessions has shown that women's employment has often been sheltered from its worst effects (Rubery, 1988). Yet, a number of reports since 2008 have expressed fears that the recession might hit women disproportionately hard (eg TUC, 2009; Fawcett Society, 2012). To date, the evidence on how women have been affected has been lacking, with most reports focusing on changes over single quarters, or single years, since the recession's onset. This study examines the cumulative and longer-term effects on women's employment and earnings since the onset of the economic downturn.

This chapter uses a number of recently available micro-data sources to examine these trends. First, aggregate data on employment and occupation from the Annual Population Survey, available from NOMIS, is used to assess overall trends in employment by gender. This is supplemented by Quarterly Labour Force Survey (QLFS) data on employment and hours of work. This data source has the advantage of allowing the analysis to be broken down further by family type. Results are reported for data from the first quarter, January to March, of the years 2007 and 2012. The QLFS data do not however provide information on household incomes. They are therefore supplemented by data from the Households Below Average Income (HBAI) series, which is used to examine changes in the level and composition of family income between 2007 and 2011.

The rest of this chapter is structured as follows. The following sections review how male and female employment, hours of work and earnings have changed, and look at how this has varied by gender, since the onset of the recession. It examines some possible reasons for these differences before going on to examine how these trends have varied across family types. Finally, the implications of these changes for family income are assessed before concluding.

Gender differences in employment and the recession

Aggregate employment data show that the total number of jobs in the economy fell by fewer than 2% over the course of the recession, and that by 2012, the number of people in work had recovered to its 2008 peak (see *Financial Times*, 2012). But data from the Annual Population Survey (APS) show that this overall trend in employment disguises significant variations by gender and, notably, age. Table 15.1 and Figure 15.1 show how male and female employment and unemployment rates have shifted since the onset of recession in late 2008. Restricting the sample to those aged between 16 and 64, Table 15.1 shows that since its peak in 2007/08, the employment rate declined by 2.4 ppt to 2011/12. Most of this decline occurred by 2009/10, with no subsequent recovery in the two years to 2011/12. The fall in employment was however much more marked for men than for women: men's employment fell by 3.6 ppt to 75.1% between 2007/08 and 2009/10, with little subsequent change by 2011/12. Women, on the other hand, saw a much smaller drop in employment, with a decline of just 1.1 ppt by 2009/10, although it declined by a further 0.3 ppt in the two years to 2011/12. The employment data therefore indicates that women have fared better than men over the course of the current recession and, as a result, the 'employment gap' between men and women has closed: at the start of the recession, men were 12.3 ppt more likely to be in employment than women; by 2011/12, this gap had closed to 10.2 ppt.

An alternative measure of economic well-being is the unemployment rate. This is one of the most widely recognised indicators of recession (Bureau of Labor Statistics, 2012). For women, however, trends in employment and unemployment have frequently diverged, with falling levels of employment not always being matched by a rise in the unemployment rate, as women who lose their jobs withdraw from the

Table 15.1: Employment by gender and age

	2007/08	2009/10	2011/12	Change
All age 16–64				
Employment rate	72.5	70.2	70.1	−2.4
Unemployment rate	5.2	8.0	8.2	3.0
Males age 16–64				
Employment rate	78.7	75.1	75.2	−3.5
Unemployment rate	5.5	9.1	8.9	3.4
Females age 16–64				
Employment rate	66.4	65.3	65.0	−1.4
Unemployment rate	4.9	6.8	7.4	2.5

Source: NOMIS data from the Annual Population Survey

labour market (Smith, 2009). But how have trends in unemployment compared with those of employment under the current recession? Figure 15.1 shows female unemployment to have grown by 2.3 ppt to 7.4% in 2012, and while it remained below the male unemployment rate of 8.9%, this suggests that the recession has had a larger effect on women than the employment statistics suggest. The rise in the unemployment rate, in the absence of similarly large falls in employment, indicates a rise in economic activity rates, with previously inactive women increasing their job search in response to growing male unemployment and the growing pressure on real earnings levels. But policy changes have also been important – from the end of 2008, lone parents whose youngest child was aged over 12 were no longer eligible to claim Income Support (IS) on the basis of their parental status. Most were transferred over to Jobseeker's Allowance (JSA), which carries with it the condition that claimants must be available for and seeking work. Since then, lone parents have only been allowed to claim IS if they have young children; the age of the youngest child that allows a claim for IS has been increasingly reduced. In May 2012, only those with a youngest child under 5 years old could claim IS and, as a result, the number of lone parents on JSA grew from 8,305 in September 2008 to 78,145 in September 2010 and 143,645 in September 2012 (ONS, 2012b). Receipt of JSA requires claimants to be available for, and searching for, work, which therefore means that those who were previously defined as 'inactive' are now classed as unemployed. This policy change makes it difficult to interpret changes to the female unemployment rate over time (male unemployment has however been much less affected). Nonetheless, the overall trend does suggest that in spite of relatively stable female employment rates, other factors, including pressure on male employment and declining real wages, as well as policy changes, have placed increased pressure on women to work and that a growing number of these women (7.4% of all those in the labour force in 2012) were unable to find work.

Figure 15.1: Changes in male and female employment and unemployment rates (age 16–64)

a. Change in employment rate

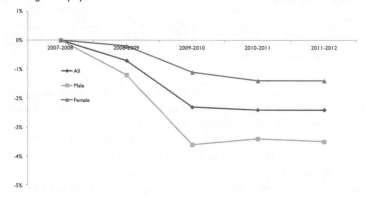

b. Change in unemployment rate

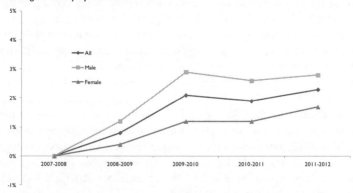

Source: NOMIS data from the Annual Population Surveys.

Why have women fared better than men?

Why has women's employment fared better than men's over the course of the current recession? One explanation may be that gender segregation in the labour market has continued to protect women from the worst employment effects of an economic downturn. Rubery (1988) noted that job segregation by gender, which has led to women being concentrated in service sector occupations, has shaped the course of earlier recessions. They describe this as the 'silver lining' of labour market segmentation, as those occupations in which women are concentrated have in the past been sheltered from the worst employment effects of recession. A number of studies show that the manufacturing and construction industries have borne the brunt of job loss during the current economic downturn (see, eg, Smith, 2009), with these industries, which tend to be dominated by men, exhibiting greater cyclical fluctuation than others – so, for example, jobs in construction and manufacturing are likely to see a sharper downturn in employment during recession than, for example, government or services. The former sectors tend to be dominated by men, who tend therefore not only to suffer greater job losses during recession, but also, on the upside, tend to see more rapid employment growth once economic recovery takes hold (Hoynes et al, 2012).

To illustrate the importance of occupation to gender differences in employment trends over the course of the current recession, Figure 15.2 plots the percentage change in the number of people employed in 81 different occupational groupings between 2008 and 2010 (the employment peak and trough) against the share of men in each occupational category (measured in 2008). Occupations are classified on the basis of the SOC 2000 three-digit occupational codes.[3] The points on the scatter plot are scaled by the overall job size of each occupational grouping. The line of best fit is also fitted (with each point weighted in the regression by size). The figure shows that those occupations that have seen the largest job losses are those in male-dominated occupations. Fitting a regression line to this data confirms the observed relationship and shows a statistically significant negative relationship between job growth over the recession and the pattern. The fitted line tells us that in jobs: where men make up just 10% of employees, employment is predicted to grow by close to 2%; where men make up half of all employees, employment is expected to fall by 0.8%; and where men comprise 90% of employees, employment is predicted to fall by 3%. Analysis of the data also shows that men and women lost jobs at a similar rate across occupations, and so it is the difference in occupations in which men and women work that explains gender differences in overall changes in employment.

Figure 15.2: Percentage change in employment between 2007 and 2010 plotted and the share of jobs that were male in 2007 by occupation

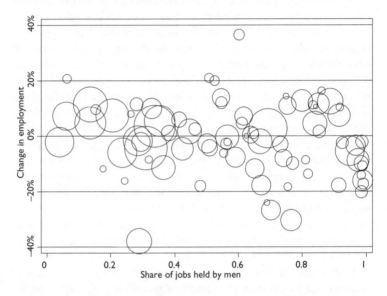

Note: NOMIS data from the Annual Population Survey. The regression line of best fit is Y=0.026-0.068X. The coefficient on X has a standard error of .002.

A detailed look at the occupations that have seen the biggest job losses between 2007 and 2010 shows that these are almost all heavily dominated by male workers. Those occupations with the largest job losses were: process operatives; elementary plant process operatives; assemblers and routine operatives; plant and machine operatives; elementary construction occupations; and textile and garment trades. In each of these occupations, the number of jobs fell by between 18% and 30% and women accounted for between just 2% and one third of the workforce. The only exceptions were 'administrative occupations in government and related sectors', where 71% of the workforce was female and where employment fell by 38%, and sales occupations, where women made up about half the workforce but for whom employment shrank by 18%. Overall, however, women accounted for less than one third of workers in the most rapidly declining occupational groupings and this has therefore helped to protect them from the worst employment effects of the economic downturn.

Job changes and job quality

Recessions have long been argued to accelerate the pace of industrial change, with job losses in occupations and industries that have been in long-term decline accelerating (see, eg, Stiglitz, 1993). The current recession is unlikely to be an exception and the previous section has shown that there have been significant job losses concentrated in male-dominated manufacturing occupations. Analysis of the NOMIS data shows that most of these job losses have been focused on low- to middle-earning occupations – those in the third to fifth earnings deciles. These trends in job losses reinforce those observed since the late 1970s by Goos and Manning (2007), who have shown that since the 1970s, job growth has been strongest in what they term 'good' (high-paid) and 'bad' (low-paid) jobs. This, they argue, has led to the increasing polarisation of work into 'lovely' and 'lousy' jobs. For women, jobs remain disproportionately concentrated at the bottom end of the wage distribution, particularly for those working part-time, and this is an area where job growth has been strongest (Harkness, 1996).

An important question, then, is whether the current recession has reinforced trends in job polarisation and what this means for women. Goos and Manning's (2007) highly influential and widely cited study defines 10 job-quality deciles, each decile being defined by the median wage within each occupational category. The 'worst' jobs are those with the lowest wages, the 'best' those with the highest. Using the same methodology here, job-quality deciles are defined using median wages for occupations based on two-digit SOC 2000 occupational codes.[4] Figure 15.3 (top panel) plots the percentage changes in employment across these deciles. A clear picture emerges – those occupations in the two bottom and three top job-quality deciles have seen a small increase in the numbers employed since 2008, while occupations in the third to sixth deciles have seen employment drop, with particularly large falls in employment in the fourth and fifth deciles. The second panel of Figure 15.3 shows how these changes relate to gender and shows that women are heavily over-represented in the bottom two deciles, where jobs have grown, and under-represented in the middle deciles, where there has been the largest decline in employment. However, while women are doing well, in terms of employment levels, from the growth in low-quality (or 'lousy') jobs, they have seen much smaller gains in high-quality (or 'lovely') jobs, where they remain under-represented. Further analysis of this data also shows that within these low-paid occupations, the gender earnings ratio also tends to be higher – so, among those in poor-quality jobs, it is women who are relatively well paid compared

Figure 15.3: Changes in employment and female employment shares by job-'quality' decile

a. % change in employment between 2007 and 2010 by job-quality decile

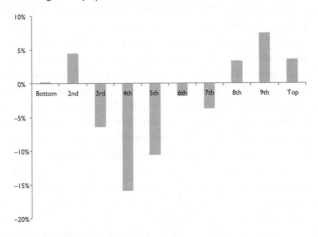

b. Female over- and under-representation by job-quality decile

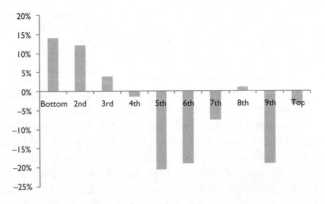

Note: All data from NOMIS. Job-quality deciles are defined on the basis of the median wage in 2007. In (a) the graph shows the excess (deficit) of women in each decile. It assumes that in each decile, there should be a 0.5 share of women in employment if jobs were equally distributed. In the bottom decile, therefore, the over-representation of women is 0.14, implying that 64% of jobs in this decile were held by women in 2007.

to their male equivalents. But the same is not true for those in higher-paid occupations – not only have women gained less from job growth in these high-paid areas, but where they do work in these better-paid occupations, the relative pay of women tends to be lower.[5]

Overall, the emerging picture suggests that the occupations that have been most strongly hit by the recession are in the middle of the job-quality distribution, while the numbers employed in poor-quality ('lousy') jobs has shown a small rise, to the advantage of women, who are strongly over-represented in these areas. At the top of the wage distribution, the number of jobs has continued to rise in numbers but women have gained much less from this change as they remain under-represented in these areas. The number of jobs in middle-ranking occupations, on the other hand, has seen a sharp fall, and it is in these jobs that men are over-represented.

The data presented here suggest that the current recession has therefore continued the long-run trend, observed since the 1970s, where jobs in the middle of the earnings distribution have disappeared while those both at the very top and bottom of the wage distribution have continued to grow. Women's under-representation in the middle of the job-quality distribution has, to date, protected their employment rates over the course of the recession. However, the less-good news is that although women's employment has remained stable, the trends in job quality suggest that women are becoming increasingly concentrated in low-paying occupations at the bottom of the wage distribution.

Family status and changes in employment, hours and earnings during the recession

For women, family status is an important predictor of employment status and hours worked. Mothers, in particular, tend to be concentrated in lower-paying and part-time jobs, and given the trends observed in the previous section, we might therefore expect the recession to have had different effects on the employment of women with and without children. Table 15.1 and Figure 15.6 illustrate how employment rates have changed over the course of the current recession for both men and women according to their family status. Single childless men have seen the sharpest fall in employment, of 4.8 ppt between 2008 and 2012, and the age composition of this group is likely to explain much of this change, as employment losses have been focused on the young. For married or cohabiting men, employment changes have been much smaller, with a fall of around 1 ppt, and with employment levels remaining at 90%. Single women without dependent children have also seen employment fall by just over 2 ppt. Women with partners (with or without children), who have lower employment rates on average than men or single childless women, have seen no change in their employment rate, while for lone mothers, the employment rate has grown by 2 ppt.

The data on employment changes suggest that women, particularly mothers, have been relatively sheltered from the worst employment effects of the recession. But while employment may have shown only a modest change over the course of the recession, they may have been affected in other ways, for example, as a result of changes in their working hours or earnings. Analysis of data on usual working hours (including overtime) using data from the QLFS does indeed suggest that there has been little change in hours of work over the course of the recession for men, childless women or for mothers with partners. But for lone mothers, the pattern of working hours has shown a marked shift, with a substantial fall in the numbers working full-time and an increased concentration in the numbers working just over 16 hours a week (the hours threshold to qualify for in-work tax credits, which are intended to incentivise work and provide a significant boost to earnings).

Recent reports have suggested that the current recession has seen a rapid rise in the number of 'underemployed' workers (ONS, 2012c). The OECD defines 'underemployed' as those working part-time because they have been unable to find full-time work. While the earlier data do suggest that there has been little change in hours worked other than among lone parents over the course of the recession, it also shows that more people that are working part-time would like to work full-time. Among men, the proportion in part-time work who would like to work full-time doubled between 2008 and 2012, with 28% working part-time because they were unable to find a full-time job in 2012. For women, underemployment has also grown: 9% of mothers in couples who work part-time want full-time work, up from 5% in 2008; while 15% of lone mothers in part-time work wanted to work full-time, twice as many as in 2008. So, underemployment is indeed growing, but other than for lone mothers, this does not reflect changes to working hours – on the contrary, for all but lone mothers, hours of work have shown little change since 2008.

So why do people want to work more? One explanation for this may be that increased hours are desired because individuals want to work more as the real value of wages falls. Data from the Labour Force Survey also show that the median real wage fell by 3% between 2007 and 2012, a figure confirmed by Office for National Statistics (ONS) estimates (ONS, 2012d). For both men and women with partners, wages saw similar falls between 2008 and 2012, with these reductions taking place across the wage distribution. But again, lone mothers stand out as facing a different experience to other workers, with an increased concentration of mothers working at low wages.

The decline in real wages over the period was therefore most dramatic for lone mothers, whose wages in 2008 were already low. This, combined with declining hours of work, means that lone mothers appear, in spite of employment gains, to have suffered the largest blows to earnings and hours over the course of the recession.

Couples' and families' employment patterns and income sources

Of course, the influence of recession on well-being might be felt not just through its impact on individual employment, but also through its influence on the employment opportunities of other family members. If a man loses his job, for example, a female partner may face greater pressure to search for work or increase her working hours (for early analysis of the effects of recession, see Harkness and Evans, 2011). How the recession has influenced families' employment and earnings, rather than just that of individuals, therefore matters for those living in couples. Data from NOMIS show how the combined economic status of households has changed for those aged 16–64 between 2007 and 2011. It is striking that during the current recession, and unlike previous recessions, the growth in 'workless' households has been relatively small – there were just 1 ppt more workless households in 2011 than in 2007. But the number of 'working' households, where all adults in the household unit are employed, has fallen by 4 ppt, and the share of 'mixed households', where some but not all adults work, has grown by 3.1 ppt. The remaining discussion focuses on the effects of the recession on families with dependent children, first looking at what has happened to employment and earnings patterns among two-parent families, and then assessing how incomes have changed for both lone- and two-parent families. Income and earnings data come from the HBAI micro-data sets from 2007 to 2011 and is not directly comparable to the QLFS data reported earlier.

Family employment patterns for couples with children are shown in Figure 15.4. Between 2007 and 2012, there was no increase in the number who were workless among these families; the number of single-earner male and female 'breadwinner' families grew; and the share of dual-earner families fell. Among this latter group, a notable change is the declining share of families with both a male full-time and female part-time worker, the share of which has dropped by 2 ppt. On the other hand, there has been a small rise in the share of families with children where both work full-time.

Figure 15.4: Changes in family employment patterns among couples with dependent children, 2007 and 2012

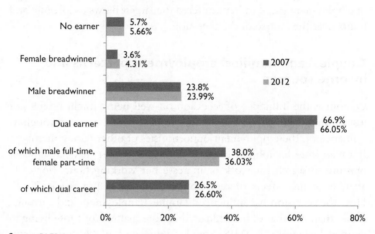

Source: QLFS data

What implications do these changes have for the composition of family income? Here, we focus on how incomes have changed among families with children. Using data from the HBAI series, we can see how income and its components have changed between 2008 and 2011. Figure 15.5 reports gross income (excluding tax credits), gross total earnings, gross male and female earnings, benefit income and tax credits, and finally net income for couples with children. All figures are reported in constant prices. Of particular interest here is: first, how total earnings, and earnings of male and female partners, have changed over the course of the recession; and, second, how these changes have been reflected in changes to net family income. Among couples with children, gross weekly earnings fell on average by 3.6%. But this change in total earnings disguises important gender differences: average gross male earnings falling by 7.7%, while average gross female earnings increased by 6.6%. Increased receipt of tax credits and benefit income, alongside changes in taxation, further tempered falling gross incomes, with net income falling just 1% over the three years.

Figure 15.5: Income sources and levels for families with children, 2008 and 2011

a. Couples with dependent children

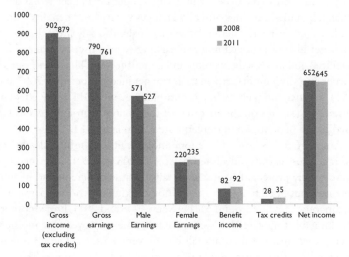

b. Lone mothers

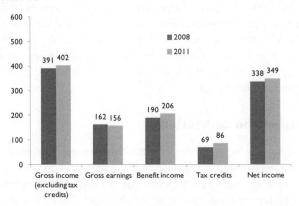

Note: Gross income is the sum of gross earnings, benefit income and other income (not shown on the graph).

Source: HBAI data

Of course, these changes disguise variations across family type. Further analysis of the data shows that there are some variations by employment status. Net incomes, for example, fell most for families with one full-time and one part-time worker. These families faced a real fall in net incomes of 4%, with this decline mainly driven by declining male earnings. On the other hand, for those with two full-time workers, net income grew by 1.7%, with increased female earnings offsetting losses in male pay, and the small fall in total earnings offset by changes in taxes and benefits. Those with a single earner, whether male or female, also saw little change to their net incomes as declining real earnings were offset by reduced tax liabilities and increased tax credit and benefit receipt. Those without an earner also saw a modest rise in their real net incomes between 2007 and 2011, an effect unlikely to have continued beyond 2011 as the effect of austerity measures on the incomes of the poorest (through cuts to tax credits and benefits) were implemented from late 2012.

Among families headed by a lone mother, although the real value of average gross earnings declined between 2008 and 2011, net incomes were largely protected against such falls because tax credit and benefit income continued to rise. For those not working or working part-time, net income grew by around 5% between 2008 and 2011. Lone mothers working full-time fared less well, with full-time employed lone mothers seeing their real net incomes fall by an average of 2%. These findings fit closely with reports from the Institute for Fiscal Studies (IFS) on incomes over the course of the recession. They also show large falls in gross incomes and earnings across households, but that these falls were largely moderated by the tax and benefit system (Cribb et al, 2012), a trend that is unlikely to continue in the future as austerity measures, which are set to reduce the generosity of tax credits and benefits in future years, are brought in.

Discussion and conclusions

This chapter has explored the effects of the economic downturn in the labour market on men, women and families, and explored gender differences in the ways in which men and women have been affected. These differences have significant implications for family life. The analysis of data has shown that, in contrast to what might be expected, the recession has had little impact on the employment levels of women: employment rates in 2012 were roughly the same as they had been in 2008. Early fears that women would be disproportionately affected by job loss have not therefore been borne out (see, eg, Rake, 2009; TUC,

2009). Instead, this analysis has shown that women's employment levels have held up better than those of men since the start of the economic downturn in 2008. Women have been protected from job losses largely because those occupations that have seen the largest falls in labour demand, with the exception of public sector administration, have been largely dominated by men. Analysis of earlier recessions in the UK (Rubery, 1988) and of the current recession in the US (Hoynes et al, 2012) have similarly shown men to have borne the brunt of job losses, largely because those industries that are most subject to cyclical variations in demand (ie manufacturing and construction) are also those that are most male-dominated. In the US, the current recession has been widely labelled a 'man-cession' (Hoynes et al, 2012). However, while the evidence on changes in female employment is encouraging, trends in recent years may not indicate a permanent move towards closing the gender employment gap. In the US, where recovery has made further headway, it has been shown that although women faced fewer job losses during the downturn, they also saw fewer job gains during the recovery (Kochhar, 2011).

While gender segregation may have protected women from job losses in recent years, there are other consequences of these changes. The analysis of Goos and Manning (2007) suggests that there has been a long-term hollowing out of jobs in the middle of the income distribution and an increase in labour demand for those doing 'lovely' and 'lousy' jobs. Women tend to be concentrated in the latter category, and it is the growth of 'lousy' jobs that appears to have protected female employment levels over the course of the current recession. This continuing trend, while helpful in the short term in terms of reducing the male–female employment gap, also means that women have become increasingly concentrated in jobs at the bottom of the labour market.

While there has been little change in the female employment rate over the last four years, there is clear evidence that women are facing greater pressure to work. Since 2008, the female unemployment rate grew by 2.5 ppt to reach 7.4% in 2012. At the same time, among women working part-time, there has been a significant growth in the numbers that are doing so involuntarily because they have been unable to find full-time work. This rise in underemployment does not reflect changes in working hours – other than for lone parents, hours of work have shown little change over the course of the recession. Rising unemployment and underemployment, in the absence of falling employment rates or hours of work, suggest a growing pressure on women to work and this is likely to have been a consequence of both policy changes that have increased job-search requirements for those claiming benefits and also increased financial pressure on women to work as male employment rates and men's and women's real wages have fallen.

A further major effect of the current recession has been to put pressure on the incomes of those in work as their real wages have become increasingly squeezed (Whittaker, 2012). While earnings are known to have shown a considerable fall (Cribb et al, 2012), what has not been widely reported on before is the distinct difference in the experience of men and women. The results reported here for couples with children show that while male weekly real earnings dropped considerably (by 7%), the contribution of female earnings to the family budget has been increasing, and because of this, total family real earnings fell by a smaller amount (just under 4%). Without the increased contribution of women's earnings to the family budget, the fall in family income that has occurred since 2008 would have been much greater.

The changes in women's status in the labour market and as breadwinners at home that has been taking place over the last 30 years appears to have been accelerated over the course of the 2008 economic downturn. Yet, while women's earnings have become increasingly important to family income, and while there has been a corresponding decline in the male breadwinner, women's labour market position remains relatively weak, with many women concentrated in low-paying sections of the labour market. Thus, while there have been recent reports of improvements in the gender pay gap (ONS, 2012e), this may well reflect falling male wages rather than any improvement in women's economic position. As such, gains that have been seen in women's labour market standing over the course of the downturn may struggle to be sustained during economic recovery. In parallel with this, women who have taken on the role of breadwinner are often not those that are most economically advantaged. Lone parents, for example, while seeing employment gains over the course of the current recession, remain one of the most vulnerable and low-income economic groups even when in work, and unlike other women, they have seen a reduction in their working hours and weekly earnings over the course of the recession. Among those in couples with children, if the woman works, she is much more likely to be the main breadwinner (defined as earning more than her partner) if she is in the lowest income decile than if she is in the top (see Figure 15.6).

Figure 15.6: Share of employed women with greater weekly earnings than their partner (couples with children), by family income quintile

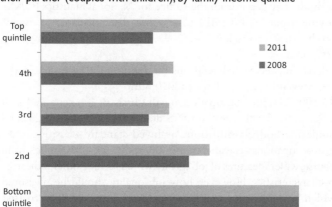

Source: HBAI data

The recession has hit the employment and earnings prospects of families. At the same time, the government have implemented a series of public sector spending cuts. While the effect of some of the cuts in public sector employment have already been felt, the effects of further changes to the tax and benefit system are yet to be seen (the discussion here has considered how tax and benefit changes influenced overall family income only up to 2011, the latest period for which data are available). These data suggest that up to early 2011, changes in tax and benefits helped to protect families from the effect of falling real wage levels. The effect of further changes to the tax and benefit system, which took place in late 2011, have yet to be observed. These changes have substantially reduced income transfers to low- and middle-income families, with those with children facing a disproportionately large effect. Between 2011 and 2014, couples with children are expected to see a 6% fall in income and lone parents are expected to fare as poorly (Family and Parenting Institute, 2012). If these changes are to be compensated for, female earnings will be of even greater importance and any threat to 'expensive' policies that promote female employment, such as family-friendly working, maternity leave or childcare provision, which may result from austerity measures, will further set back the position of women and their families (Rake, 2009).

Notes

[1.] Data on the pay gap is from the Office for National Statistics (ONS). Employment data is NOMIS time-series data, available at: www. nomisweb.co.uk/reports/lmp/gor/2092957698/subreports/nrhi_time_ series/report.aspx?

[2.] For details on recent deliberations on defining the recession in the US, see: www.nber.org/cycles/sept2010.html

[3.] SOC 2000 classifies occupation on the basis of job type and skill levels. For more details, see the ONS definition at: www.ons.gov.uk/ons/guide-method/classifications/archived-standard-classifications/standard-occupational-classification-2000/about-soc-2000/index.html

[4.] Of course, wider measures of job quality would include other indicators of job characteristics. However, how job quality should be measured and which characteristics should be included is widely debated (see, eg, Green, 2006). In addition, such data is not widely available and no consistent annual series of job quality exists.

[5.] Authors own analysis of NOMIS data. Further details available from the author upon request.

References

Bell, D.N.F. and Blanchflower, D.G. (2010) 'Youth Unemployment: Déjà Vu?', IZA Discussion Paper No 4705.

Bureau of Labor Statistics (2012) 'BLS spotlight on statistics: the recession of 2007–2009', US Bureau of Labor Statistics, www.bls.gov/spotlight/2012/recession/pdf/recession_bls_spotlight.pdf

Cribb, J., Joyce, R. and Phillip, D. (2012) 'Living standards, poverty and inequality in the UK', IFS Commentary C124, Institute for Fiscal Studies, London.

Elsby, M.W.L. and Smith, J.C. (2010) 'The great recession in the UK labour market: a transatlantic perspective', *National Institute Economic Review*, vol 214, no 1, pp R26–R37.

Family and Parenting Institute (2012) 'Families in an age of austerity: the impact of austerity measures on households with children', Family and Parenting Institute, http://www.familyandparenting.org/NR/rdonlyres/30F86FFB-8911-4E40-BEF3-D7B071C9C6F8/0/FPI_IFS_Austerity_Jan_2012.pdf

Financial Times (2012) *The UK's short and shallow recession*, http://blogs.ft.com/money-supply/2012/09/07/the-uks-short-and-shallow-recession/#axzz26Mh9NE00

Goos, M. and Manning, A. (2007) 'Lousy and lovely jobs: the rising polarization of work in Britain', *The Review of Economics and Statistics*, vol 89, no 1, pp 118–33.

Green, F. (2006) *Demanding work: the paradox of job quality in the affluent economy*, Princeton, NJ: Princeton University Press.

Harkness, S. (1996) 'The gender earnings gap', *Fiscal Studies*, vol 17, no 2, pp 1–36.

Harkness, S. (2010) 'The contribution of women's employment and earnings to household income inequality: a cross-country analysis', working paper, Luxembourg Income Survey Working Paper Series, Luxembourg.

Harkness, S. and Evans, M. (2011) 'The employment effects of recession on couples in the UK: women's and household employment prospects and partners' job loss', *Journal of Social Policy*, vol 40, no 4, pp 675–93.

Hills, J. and Stewart, K. (eds) (2005) *A more equal society? New Labour, poverty, inequality and exclusion*, Bristol: Policy Press.

Hoynes, H.W., Miller, D.L. and Schaller, J. (2012) 'Who suffers during recessions?', No w17951, National Bureau of Economic Research.

Kocchar, R. (2011) 'Two years of economic recovery: women lose jobs, men find them', Pew Research Centre, Washington, DC.

NIESR (National Institute of Economic and Social Research) (2012) 'NIESR monthly estimates of GDP', 7 December, National Institute of Economic and Social Research, London.

ONS (Office for National Statistics) (2012a) 'Labour market statistics, January 2012', Office for National Statistics, Newport.

ONS (2012b) 'Labour market statistics, November 2012', Office for National Statistics, Newport.

ONS (2012c) 'Underemployed workers in the UK', November, Office for National Statistics, Newport.

ONS (2012d) 'Earnings in the UK over the past 25 years, 2012', November, Office for National Statistics, Newport.

ONS (2012e) 'Annual survey of hours and earnings, 2012 provisional results', November, Office for National Statistics.

Philpott, J. (2012) 'Age, gender and the jobs recession', Work Audit, April, CIPD, London.

Rake, K. (2009) 'Are women bearing the burden of the recession?', Fawcett Society, March, London.

Rubery, J. (1988) *Women and recession*, London: Routledge.

Smith, M. (2009) 'Analysis note: gender equality and recession', Grenoble Ecole de Management, Grenoble.

Stiglitz, J.E. (1993) 'Endogenous growth and cycles', No w4286, National Bureau of Economic Research.

TUC (Trade Union Congress) (2009) 'Women and recession', Trade Union Congress, London.

Whittaker, M. (2012) 'Squeezed Britain', Resolution Foundation, London.

Index

Page references for notes are followed by n

L

M

N